THE CAMBRIDGE COMPA
ENGLISH SHORT

This *Companion* provides an accessible overvie
England, Scotland, Ireland, Wales and other international sites. A collection of international experts examines the development of the short story in a variety of contexts from the early nineteenth century to the present. The experts consider how dramatic changes in the publishing landscape during this period – such as the rise of the fiction magazine and the emergence of new opportunities in online and electronic publishing – influenced the form, covering subgenres from detective fiction to flash fiction. Drawing on a wealth of critical scholarship to place the short story in the English literary tradition, this volume will be an invaluable guide for students of the short story in English.

Ann-Marie Einhaus is Senior Lecturer in Modern and Contemporary Literature at Northumbria University in Newcastle-upon-Tyne, England. She is the author of *The Short Story and the First World War* (Cambridge University Press) and co-editor, with Barbara Korte, of *The Penguin Book of First World War Stories*.

A complete list of books in the series is at the back of this book.

THE CAMBRIDGE
COMPANION TO
THE ENGLISH SHORT STORY

THE CAMBRIDGE COMPANION TO
THE ENGLISH SHORT STORY

ANN-MARIE EINHAUS
Northumbria University

CAMBRIDGE
UNIVERSITY PRESS

CAMBRIDGE UNIVERSITY PRESS

Shaftesbury Road, Cambridge CB2 8EA, United Kingdom

One Liberty Plaza, 20th Floor, New York, NY 10006, USA

477 Williamstown Road, Port Melbourne, VIC 3207, Australia

314–321, 3rd Floor, Plot 3, Splendor Forum, Jasola District Centre, New Delhi – 110025, India

103 Penang Road, #05–06/07, Visioncrest Commercial, Singapore 238467

Cambridge University Press is part of Cambridge University Press & Assessment, a department of the University of Cambridge.

We share the University's mission to contribute to society through the pursuit of education, learning and research at the highest international levels of excellence.

www.cambridge.org
Information on this title: www.cambridge.org/9781107446014

© Cambridge University Press & Assessment 2016

This publication is in copyright. Subject to statutory exception and to the provisions of relevant collective licensing agreements, no reproduction of any part may take place without the written permission of Cambridge University Press & Assessment.

First published 2016

A catalogue record for this publication is available from the British Library

Library of Congress Cataloging-in-Publication data
Names: Einhaus, Ann-Marie, editor.
Title: The Cambridge companion to the English short story / edited by Ann-Marie Einhaus.
Description: New York, NY: Cambridge University Press, 2016. |
Series: Cambridge companions to literature |
Includes bibliographical references and index.
Identifiers: LCCN 2015039556 | ISBN 9781107084179 (hardback)
Subjects: LCSH: Short stories, English – History and criticism. | English fiction – 19th century – History and criticism. | English fiction – 20th century – History and criticism. | English fiction – 21st century – History and criticism.
Classification: LCC PR 829. C 18 2016 | DDC 823/.0109–dc23
LC record available at http://lccn.loc.gov/2015039556

ISBN 978-1-107-08417-9 Hardback
ISBN 978-1-107-44601-4 Paperback

Cambridge University Press & Assessment has no responsibility for the persistence or accuracy of URLs for external or third-party internet websites referred to in this publication and does not guarantee that any content on such websites is, or will remain, accurate or appropriate.

CONTENTS

Notes on contributors		*page* ix
Acknowledgements		xiii
Chronology		xv
Introduction ANN-MARIE EINHAUS		1

PART I CONTEXTS

1	Writing and publishing the short story PAUL MARCH-RUSSELL	15
2	Social realism in the short story ANTHONY PATTERSON	28
3	The short story and the anxieties of empire BARBARA KORTE	42
4	The short story, identity, space and place DAVID MALCOLM	56

PART II PERIODS

5	Romantic short fiction DAVID STEWART	73
6	Victorian short stories JOHN PLOTZ	87
7	The short story in the early twentieth century ANN-MARIE EINHAUS	101

CONTENTS

8 Mid-twentieth-century stories   115
   VICTORIA STEWART

9 The short story from postmodernism to the digital age   128
   MAEBH LONG

PART III   GENRES

10 Comic short fiction and its variety   145
   KATE MACDONALD

11 The detective short story   159
   MARTIN PRIESTMAN

12 The gothic in short fiction   173
   LUKE THURSTON

13 The British science fiction short story   187
   ANDREW M. BUTLER

14 Microfiction   201
   MARC BOTHA

Guide to further reading   221
Index   225

NOTES ON CONTRIBUTORS

MARC BOTHA completed his PhD in literary theory and modernism in the Department of English Studies at Durham University in 2012. His forthcoming monograph, *A Theory of Minimalism* (2016), formulates a comprehensive, interdisciplinary and transhistorical theory of minimalist aesthetics grounded in contemporary philosophical discourse. He is a Lecturer in English Studies (20th and 21st Century Literature and Theory) at Durham University, UK, and an Honorary Research Fellow in English at the University of Witwatersrand, South Africa. His research is focused in three specific areas – minimalism, cosmopoetics and fragility – and is situated at the intersection of cultural theory and contemporary aesthetic practice, often spanning literature, music, visual and intermedia arts. He continues to investigate all types of minimalism, from canonical figures such as Beckett, Carver and Robison, to the experiments of Concrete Poetry and a new generation of minimalist writers of electronic literature and flash fiction.

ANDREW M. BUTLER is based at Canterbury Christ Church University and is the author of *Eternal Sunshine of the Spotless Mind* (2014) and *Solar Flares: Science Fiction in the 1970s* (2012), as well as the editor of *Christopher Priest: The Interaction* (2005) and *An Unofficial Companion to the Novels of Terry Pratchett* (2007) and co-editor of *Terry Pratchett: Guilty of Literature* (2000; 2004), *The True Knowledge of Ken MacLeod* (2003), *A Celebration of British Science Fiction* (2005), *The Routledge Companion to Science Fiction* (2009) and *Fifty Key Figures in Science Fiction* (2010). In addition, he has written books on Philip K. Dick, cyberpunk, postmodernism, Terry Pratchett and film studies. He is non-voting Chair of Judges for the Arthur C. Clarke Award. His research blog is https://andrewmbutler.wordpress.com/.

ANN-MARIE EINHAUS is a senior lecturer in modern and contemporary literature in the Department of Humanities at Northumbria University, Newcastle-upon-Tyne. Her monograph *The Short Story and the First World War* was published by Cambridge University Press in 2013, and she has published a range of journal articles and book chapters on other aspects of early-twentieth-century and First

NOTES ON CONTRIBUTORS

World War writing. Her research interests comprise First World War writing, the short story, early-twentieth-century fiction, memory studies and the interrelation between literature and history/historiography more generally.

BARBARA KORTE is a professor of English literature at the University of Freiburg (Germany), with special interest in British literature and culture from the nineteenth century to the present. Her publications include *English Travel Writing: From Pilgrimages to Postcolonial Explorations* (2000), *The Penguin Book of First World War Stories* (2007) and *Poverty in Literature* (2014).

MAEBH LONG is a senior lecturer in literature in the School of Language, Arts and Media at the University of the South Pacific. She is the author of *Assembling Flann O'Brien* (2014), a monograph of theoretical engagements with Flann O'Brien/Myles na gCopaleen/Brian O'Nolan. In addition to work on Irish and British modernist and contemporary literature, her research contains a strong focus on literary theory and philosophy, particularly the texts of Jacques Derrida.

KATE MACDONALD taught English literature and British cultural history in several European universities after a career in academic publishing and is currently a visiting fellow in the Department of English Literature at the University of Reading. She has published widely on John Buchan, periodicals, book history and publishing culture, and her most recent monograph is *Novelists Against Social Change: Conservative Popular Fiction 1920–1960* (2015). Her current research is on depictions of bodily impairment in the popular print culture of the First World War.

DAVID MALCOLM is a professor of English Literature at the University of Gdańsk. He is the author and co-author of books on Jean Rhys, Ian McEwan, Graham Swift, John McGahern and the British and Irish short story. He translates from Polish and German and writes reviews for the *Times Literary Supplement*. He is one of the organizers of the between.pomiędzy festival/conference held annually in Sopot, Poland.

PAUL MARCH-RUSSELL teaches comparative literature and liberal arts at the University of Kent. His previous publications include *The Short Story: An Introduction* (2009) and, co-edited with Maggie Awadalla, *The Postcolonial Short Story: Contemporary Essays* (2012). He is an editorial advisor to the journal *Short Fiction in Theory and Practice*, and a member of the European Network for Research in Short Fiction. He is also part of an international research project, based at the University of Santiago de Compostela, exploring contemporary short fiction by British female writers. Forthcoming publications include chapters for *The Cambridge History of the English Short Story*, *The Edinburgh Companion to the Short Story in English* and, on the short story cycle, *American Literature in Transition: 1990–2000*. When not working on the short story, he is editor of

NOTES ON CONTRIBUTORS

Foundation: The International Review of Science Fiction, commissioning editor for *SF Storyworlds* and the author of *Modernism and Science Fiction* (2015).

ANTHONY PATTERSON is an assistant professor of English literature at Celal Bayar University in Manisa, Turkey. He has published on a number of writers of the late Victorian and Edwardian periods including George Gissing, H. G. Wells, George Egerton and Arnold Bennett. His monograph *Mrs Grundy's Enemies: Censorship, Realist Fiction and the Politics of Sexual Representation* was published in 2013. He is also the co-editor of two recent volumes: *Vile Women: Challenging Representations of Female Evil in Fact, Fiction and Mythology*, edited with Marilena Zacheos, was published in 2014; *We Speak a Different Tongue: Maverick Voices and Modernity, 1890–1939*, edited with Yoonjoung Choi, was published by Cambridge Scholars Press in 2015. He is currently working on a monograph exploring the British social realist short story.

JOHN PLOTZ, a professor of English at Brandeis University, is the author of two academic books about Victorian literature, *The Crowd* (2000) and *Portable Property* (2008), as well as a young-adult novel, *Time and the Tapestry: A William Morris Adventure* (2014). He is currently completing 'Semi-Detached: The Aesthetics of Partial Absorption' (2016), which includes chapters on John Galt, Millais and the Pre-Raphaelites, George Eliot, Henry James and Willa Cather. He has also begun work on a project about American and British literary Naturalism and its relationship to Darwin and nineteenth-century environmental thinking: authors studied include Richard Jefferies, George Marsh and Thomas Hardy. Honours include a Guggenheim and residential fellowships from the National Humanities Center and the Radcliffe Institute for Advanced Study.

MARTIN PRIESTMAN is a professor of English Literature at the University of Roehampton. His research, teaching and publishing activities are divided between the Romantic period and crime fiction. He is the editor of *The Cambridge Companion to Crime Fiction* (2003); other publications on the genre include *Crime Fiction from Poe to the Present* (2nd ed., 2013) and *Detective Fiction and Literature* (1990). On the Romantic period his books include *The Poetry of Erasmus Darwin: Enlightened Spaces, Romantic Times* (2013) and *Romantic Atheism: Poetry and Freethought, 1780–1830* (1999).

DAVID STEWART is Senior Lecturer in Romanticism at Northumbria University, Newcastle-upon-Tyne. He has published widely on Romantic-period writing, especially periodicals, poetry and print culture. His book *Romantic Magazines and Metropolitan Literary Culture* was published in 2011, and his articles have appeared in *Studies in English Literature*, *Essays in Criticism*, *Romanticism*, *Review of English Studies* and elsewhere.

VICTORIA STEWART is a reader in modern and contemporary literature in the School of English, University of Leicester. She is the author of *Women's*

Autobiography: War and Trauma (2003), *Narratives of Memory: British Writing of the 1940s* (2006) and *The Second World War in Contemporary Fiction: Secret Histories* (2011). She is currently writing a monograph provisionally titled *Crime Writing in Interwar Britain: Fact and Fiction in the Golden Age*.

LUKE THURSTON is a senior lecturer in modern literature and the director of the David Jones Centre at Aberystwyth University. His publications include *Literary Ghosts from the Victorians to Modernism: The Haunting Interval* (2012) and *James Joyce and the Problem of Psychoanalysis* (2004), as well as many articles, chapters and translations in the field of modernist literature and psychoanalysis. He is currently working on a study of war, testimony and artistic experiment in May Sinclair, Wyndham Lewis and David Jones.

ACKNOWLEDGEMENTS

Throughout my own career as a student, doctoral researcher and academic, I have found Cambridge *Companions* to be invaluable aids to learning, to teaching and to familiarizing myself with new areas, ideas and authors. It has been a privilege to edit my own *Companion*, and I would first and foremost like to thank Ray Ryan at Cambridge University Press for giving me this opportunity and for suggesting and supporting this publication on the short story. My sincere thanks also go to Caitlin Gallagher, Alexandra Poreda, Nishanthini Vetrivel, S. Rajagopal and the rest of the teams at Cambridge University Press and Newgen for their dedicated and professional support throughout this project. The process of writing my own contributions and editing the *Companion* has taught me just how much work goes into these useful volumes, and I am immensely grateful for the advice and feedback I received from a number of colleagues at Northumbria University, particularly Katherine Baxter, Victoria Bazin, Laura Fish and Paul Frazer, who gave up their valuable time to read and comment on various parts of this book. My contributors have been a joy to work with, and special thanks are due to Maebh Long, who stepped in and shared her expertise on postmodern literature at the eleventh hour. Needless to say, any remaining errors or incongruities are on my head only, and I apologize wholeheartedly to my colleagues, friends and particularly my partner, Ben Lowing, for my complaints about indexing.

CHRONOLOGY

1603	Death of Queen Elizabeth I; James I succeeds to the throne
1614	Thomas Overbury, *Characters*
1625	Death of King James I; Charles I succeeds to the throne
1635	Francis Quarles, *Emblems*
1642	Start of the English Civil War
1649	Charles I executed
1653	Oliver Cromwell installed as Lord Protector
1658	Death of Oliver Cromwell
1660	Restoration: Charles II succeeds to the throne
1685	Death of King Charles II; James II succeeds to the throne
1688	Glorious Revolution: King James II ousted in favour of the Protestant William of Orange
1702	Death of King William III; Anne I succeeds to the throne
1711	The *Spectator* begins publication in its first incarnation
1714	Death of Queen Anne; George I succeeds to the throne
1727	Death of King George I; George II succeeds to the throne
1731	The *Gentleman's Magazine* begins publication
1732	The *London Magazine* begins publication
1760	Death of King George II; George III succeeds to the throne
1773	The *Newgate Calendar* first appears

CHRONOLOGY

1785	The *London Magazine* discontinued
1811	Regency period begins
1815	Napoleon defeated at the Battle of Waterloo
1817	*Blackwood's Edinburgh Magazine* begins publication
1820	Death of King George III; George IV succeeds to the throne; Regency period ends Washington Irving, *The Sketch-Book of Geoffrey Crayon* The *London Magazine* is revived
1821	The *New Monthly Magazine and Literary Journal* begins publication
1824	Mary Russell Mitford, *Our Village: Sketches of Rural Character and Scenery*
1829	The new *London Magazine* discontinued
1830	Death of King George III; William IV succeeds to the throne
1832	Harriet Martineau, *Illustrations of Political Economy*
1833	John Galt, *Stories of the Study*
1836	*Bentley's Miscellany* begins publication Charles Dickens, *Sketches by Boz*
1837	Death of King William IV; Victoria succeeds to the throne Samuel Morse patents his electric telegraph in the United States Charles Dickens, *Pickwick Papers*
1842	Edgar Allan Poe, Review of Nathaniel Hawthorne's *Twice-Told Tales*
1850	*Household Words* begins publication
1859	*Household Words* discontinued; *All the Year Round* begins publication
1860	The *Cornhill Magazine* begins publication
1868	William Gladstone becomes prime minister for the first time
1870	Education Act
1876	Alexander Graham Bell patents his telephone
1868	*Bentley's Miscellany* discontinued

CHRONOLOGY

1882	Robert Louis Stevenson, *New Arabian Nights*
1888	*Collier's Once a Week* begins publication Rudyard Kipling, *Plain Tales from the Hills* and *The Phantom 'Rickshaw and Other Eerie Tales*
1890	Vernon Lee, *Hauntings*
1891	The *Strand Magazine* begins publication
1893	Hubert Crackanthorpe, *Wreckage* George Egerton, *Keynotes*
1894	The *Yellow Book* begins publication Arthur Morrison, *Tales of Mean Streets*
1895	*All the Year Round* discontinued *Collier's Once a Week* renamed *Collier's Weekly* (later *Collier's*) The *Windsor Magazine* begins publication
1896	Guglielmo Marconi makes first public transmission of wireless signals The *Savoy* begins and ceases publication
1897	The *Yellow Book* discontinued H. G. Wells, *Thirty Strange Stories*
1898	Joseph Conrad, *Tales of Unrest* Henry James, *The Turn of the Screw*
1901	Death of Queen Victoria; Edward VII succeeds to the throne Brander Matthews, *The Philosophy of the Short-Story*
1903	Emmeline Pankhurst founds Women's Social and Political Union
1904	Rudyard Kipling, *Traffics and Discoveries*
1905	*Blackwood's Magazine* relocates from Edinburgh to London
1907	Rudyard Kipling wins Nobel Prize for Literature The *Gentleman's Magazine* in its final incarnation discontinued
1908	The *English Review* begins publication
1910	Death of King Edward VII; George V succeeds to the throne
1911	*Rhythm* begins publication Katherine Mansfield, *In a German Pension*

1913	*Rhythm* is discontinued
1914	Start of the First World War James Joyce, *Dubliners* Gertrude Stein, *Tender Buttons* Publication of *Blast* vol. 1
1915	'War number' of *Blast* published
1917	Bolshevik revolution in Russia Stacy Aumonier, *The Friends, and Other Stories*
1918	End of the First World War Assassination of Tsar Nicholas II and his family Representation of the People Act: universal male suffrage and suffrage for women over thirty
1919	Paris Peace Conference Amritsar massacre P. G. Wodehouse, *My Man Jeeves*
1920	Government of Ireland Act and the creation of Northern Ireland
1921	Irish Free State created by Parliament
1922	Irish Civil War Mussolini marches on Rome The *Criterion* begins publication The *Happy Magazine* begins publication Katherine Mansfield, *The Garden Party and Other Stories* Elizabeth Bibesco, *Balloons*
1923	Failed Nazi coup in Munich
1924	First Labour government; Ramsay Macdonald becomes prime minister A. C. Ward, *Aspects of the Modern Short Story*
1925	Treaty of Locarno The *New Yorker* begins publication
1926	General Strike BBC chartered US-based *Amazing Stories* begins publication
1928	Representation of the People Act: suffrage extended to all women over twenty-one

CHRONOLOGY

1929	New York stock market collapses
1930	Death of D. H. Lawrence *Astounding* begins publication
1931	Statute of Westminster grants legislative independence to the self-governing Dominions
1933	Hitler becomes the German chancellor; Germany leaves the League of Nations Roosevelt announces 'New Deal' *'Blackwood' Tales from the Outposts* anthology published
1934	Nazis purge internal opposition (labelled 'Röhm-Putsch' by the Nazis) Japanese invasion of Manchuria
1936	Start of the Spanish Civil War Berlin Olympics Death of King George V; Edward VIII succeeds to the throne Edward VIII abdicates; George VI succeeds to the throne *New Writing* (later *Penguin New Writing*) begins publication *Novae Terrae* begins publication as science fiction fanzine
1937	Neville Chamberlain becomes prime minister The *English Review* discontinued / merged with the *National Review*
1938	Germany annexes Austria November pogroms (labelled 'Reichskristallnacht' by the Nazis)
1939	Start of the Second World War The *Criterion* and the *Windsor Magazine* discontinued The *Cornhill Magazine* suspended *Novae Terrae* renamed into *New Worlds*
1940	Start of the Battle of Britain; London Blitz *Horizon* begins publication Ban on new journals in Britain from May The *Happy Magazine* discontinued
1941	US-based *Ellery Queen's Mystery Magazine* begins publication
1943	Cleanth Brooks and Robert Penn Warren, *Understanding Fiction* Alun Lewis, *The Last Inspection*

1944	D-Day landings Julian Maclaren-Ross, *The Stuff to Give the Troops* William Sansom, *Fireman Flower and Other Stories*
1945	End of the Second World War Liberation of Auschwitz US atomic bombing of Hiroshima and Nagasaki Nuremberg Trials The *Cornhill Magazine* revived as a quarterly publication Elizabeth Bowen, *The Demon Lover and Other Stories*
1946	National Health Service Act George Orwell, 'The Decline of the English Murder' Sid Chaplin, *The Leaping Lad and Other Stories*
1947	Indian independence; India partitioned into India and Pakistan A. L. Barker, *Innocents: Variations on a Theme*
1948	Arrival of the *Empire Windrush*
1949	NATO founded Germany partitioned *Horizon* discontinued US-based *Magazine of Fantasy and Science Fiction* begins publication
1950	The *Strand Magazine* discontinued *Penguin New Writing* discontinued
1952	Death of George VI; Elizabeth II succeeds to the throne Nadine Gordimer, *The Soft Voice of the Serpent and Other Stories*
1953	Death of Stalin
1955	Warsaw Pact
1956	Suez crisis Hungarian uprising crushed by Soviet troops
1957	*Collier's* discontinued Samuel Selvon, *Ways of Sunlight* Lawrence Durrell, *Esprit de Corps: Sketches from Diplomatic Life*
1958	Norman Friedman, 'What Makes a Short Story Short?'

CHRONOLOGY

1959	*Best Detective Stories* anthology published (ed. Edmund Crispin) Alan Sillitoe, *The Loneliness of the Long-Distance Runner*
1960	Cyprus and Nigeria gain independence
1961	South Africa removed from the Commonwealth
1962	Frank O'Connor, *The Lonely Voice: A Study of the Short Story*
1963	Nell Dunn, *Up the Junction*
1965	Race Relations Act addresses racial discrimination in the United Kingdom for the first time
1967	Legalization of abortion and homosexual acts between consenting adults
1968	*England Swings SF* anthology published (ed. Judith Merril)
1969	Samuel Beckett wins Nobel Prize for Literature *Winter's Crimes* anthologies begin publication
1970	J. G. Ballard, *The Atrocity Exhibition*
1973	Britain joins the European Economic Community Bridport Prize launched
1974	Gabriel Josipovici, *Mobius the Stripper: Stories and Short Plays* *Science Fiction Monthly* begins publication
1975	The *Cornhill Magazine* discontinued
1976	Charles E. May, *Short Story Theories* *Science Fiction Monthly* discontinued Jean Rhys, *Sleep It Off, Lady* Ian McEwan, *First Love, Last Rites* Raymond Carver, *Will You Please Be Quiet, Please?*
1978	Scottish and Welsh Devolution Acts
1979	Margaret Thatcher becomes prime minister John Berger, *Pig Earth* Angela Carter, *The Bloody Chamber and Other Stories*
1980	*Blackwood's Magazine* discontinued
1982	Falklands War *Interzone* begins publication

CHRONOLOGY

	Short Shorts anthology published (eds. Irving and Ilana Wiener Howe) Pat Barker, *Union Street*
1984	*The Penguin Classic Crime Omnibus* anthology published (ed. Julian Symons)
1986	First *Sudden Fiction* anthology published (eds. Robert Shapard and James Thomas) Final *Winter's Crimes* anthology published; series discontinued *The Oxford Book of English Ghost Stories* anthology published (eds. Michael Cox and R. A. Gilbert)
1987	Patrick White, *Three Uneasy Pieces*
1988	*The Penguin Book of Modern British Short Stories* anthology published (ed. Malcolm Bradbury)
1989	Fall of the Berlin Wall Miriam Tlali, *Soweto Stories*
1991	The Gulf War Collapse of the Soviet Union *The Penguin Book of Modern Women's Short Stories* anthology published (ed. Susan Hill)
1992	*Flash Fiction* anthology published (eds. Denise and James Thomas and Tom Hazuka)
1993	Anglo-Irish Peace Declaration in Northern Ireland Irvine Welsh, *Trainspotting* Michael Moorcock, *Earl Aubec, and Other Stories*
1994	End of apartheid in South Africa IRA declares truce in Northern Ireland Salman Rushdie, *East, West* Bernard MacLaverty, *Walking the Dog, and Other Stories*
1996	Publication of *Micro Fiction* anthology (ed. Jerome Stern)
1997	Tony Blair becomes prime minister Hanif Kureishi, *Love in a Blue Time* Manzu Islam, *The Mapmakers of Spitalfields*
1998	Scottish Parliament re-established; National Assembly for Wales created US-based *McSweeney's* begins publication

CHRONOLOGY

1999	Euro introduced; Britain declines participation
2001	Terrorist attack on the World Trade Center, New York War on Terror begins
2002	Save Our Short Story campaign launched Jackie Kay, *Why Don't You Stop Talking*
2003	War in Iraq
2004	*Walking a Tightrope* anthology published (ed. Rehana Ahmed) Launch of the Small Wonder short story festival
2005	Terrorist attacks on London public transport BBC National Short Story Award launched The US-based *Atlantic Monthly* stops publishing monthly fiction China Miéville, *Looking for Jake, and Other Stories*
2006	Short Story Radio founded
2007	Edge Hill Prize launched
2008	*Flash: The International Short-Short Story Magazine* begins publication *The Mammoth Book of Best British Mysteries* anthology published (ed. Maxim Jakubowski)
2009	*Sunday Times* EFG Short Story Award launched Kazuo Ishiguro, *Nocturnes: Five Stories of Music and Nightfall*
2010	David Cameron becomes prime minister Bridport Prize category for flash fiction launched Michèle Roberts, *Mud: Stories of Sex and Love*
2011	LitNav short story app launched by Comma Press
2012	Costa Short Story Award launched First UK National Flash-Fiction Day William Nelles, 'What Makes a Very Short Story Very Short?' Keith Ridgway, *Hawthorn & Child*
2013	Death of Margaret Thatcher Teju Cole, *Seven Short Stories about Drones*
2014	*OxCrimes* anthology published (intro. Ian Rankin) Hilary Mantel, *The Assassination of Margaret Thatcher*

ANN-MARIE EINHAUS

Introduction

What is the English short story? Where does it figure in the larger literary field? And who can lay claim to its invention as a modern literary form? Twentieth- and twenty-first-century critics of short fiction have spent the best part of a century debating these and other questions about the short story genre, with few (if any) unanimously agreed answers to offer – but with broad agreement on two counts: the short story in its modern sense is notoriously elusive, and it is perpetually struggling to assert itself in the face of a host of practical, critical and aesthetic challenges. Any new volume attempting an account of the English short story needs to offer some answers of its own as to defining and placing the short story, and this volume is fortunate in being able to draw on a long tradition of short story criticism.

A transatlantic discrepancy in approaches to defining the short story in English can be traced back to the boom in short story criticism during the 1980s, represented on either side of the Atlantic by Clare Hanson and Susan Lohafer, two critics who sought to explore and define the short story in new ways. Hanson's *Short Stories and Short Fiction, 1880–1980* (1985) approached the modern short story historically by identifying two major strands of short prose, the short story as a plot-based narrative, associated largely with popular magazine culture, as opposed to plotless short fiction, including symbolist, modernist and postmodern narratives such as the prose poem, psychological sketch, Bowen's 'free story' and postmodern experimental fiction. Lohafer's *Coming to Terms with the Short Story* (1983), by contrast, adopted a theoretical approach in exploring the short story in terms of its story-ness and reader reception, specifically readers' progression through the story. While both critics deal with remarkably similar time frames and acknowledge similar influences on their work, their methods of working towards a framework for the analysis and appreciation of short fiction thus differ markedly, and in many ways exemplify the divide between theory-driven genre criticism in North America compared to the dominance of historical and thematic enquiries in British approaches to the short story.[1]

Despite their different approaches and divergent national contexts, and despite the fact that Hanson primarily scrutinizes British and Irish writers where Lohafer looks almost exclusively at American authors, Lohafer and Hanson are in broad agreement that the origins of the modern short story lay with Edgar Allan Poe and American magazine culture. Indeed, criticism of the short story in the English language for many decades centred primarily on American short fiction: while the United States was seen as the birthplace of the modern short story proper, Britain was regarded as the latecomer to the game and its nineteenth-century periodical culture considered in thrall to serialized three-decker novels rather than the short tales printed in American magazines. In 1941, H. E. Bates – himself an English writer of short fiction – readily identified Gogol and Poe as the true originators of the modern short story, revealing the strong orientation even among British writers towards the work of their American and continental counterparts.[2] Charles E. May is but one later critic who traces back the 'modern' short story in English exclusively to American authors such as Irving, Hawthorne and Poe,[3] while Barbara Korte has explained this perception of American origins in part by Poe's pre-eminence as a 'genre *Übervater*'.[4] Korte and others have contested this bias, observing that short stories were written and published in Britain as early as in America, even though they did not achieve the same importance as in the United States and other (former) British colonies, where they were valued as 'a form of literary expression comparatively independent from the literary market of the "mother country"' because they could be published and distributed 'in a medium – magazines and newspapers – producible within the respective regions themselves'.[5]

The strong American slant in English-language short story criticism does mean that the best-known writers of the genre during the nineteenth century are mostly American: critical works on the short story up to the 1990s feature first and foremost American masters of the genre such as Poe, Stephen Crane and Ambrose Bierce, besides short story writers in other languages such as Anton Chekhov and Guy de Maupassant. In recent years, however, British and European critical opinion in particular has shifted towards a greater appreciation of earlier examples of the British and Irish short story, as well as other English-language short fiction distinct from the North American tradition of short story writing. In the past couple of decades alone, several scholars' work on British (and Irish) short fiction has redressed the previous imbalance, not least Korte's *The Short Story in Britain* (2003), David and Cheryl Alexander Malcolm's *Companion to the British and Irish Short Story* (2008), and Emma Liggins's, Andrew Maunder's and Ruth Robbins's

Introduction

The British Short Story (2011). More period-specific works include Harold Orel's *The Victorian Short Story* (1986) or, as a more recent example, Tim Killick's *British Short Fiction in the Early Nineteenth Century* (2008), which details early developments of the short form in Britain by looking at pre-Victorian short fiction, particularly of the Romantic era. Dean Baldwin's *Art and Commerce in the British Short Story 1880–1950* (2013) moreover stresses the intimate links between publication, creation and reception of short fiction in Britain, serving as a useful counterpoint to Andrew Levy's *The Culture and Commerce of the American Short Story* (1993) published two decades earlier, which despite its similar title had focused less on commercially motivated writing and more on an attempt to define the short story as an American national art form. Other recent volumes – most notably Paul March-Russell's *The Short Story: An Introduction* (2009) and March-Russell and Maggie Awadalla's *The Postcolonial Short Story* (2012) as well as numerous other volumes on contemporary and/or postcolonial short fiction – adopt an international approach and consider the short story more broadly along thematic lines, combining various theoretical angles (such as postmodernism and postcolonialism) with attention to particular subgenres.

Looking at short story criticism today, we seem to have come full circle from historical enquiry by author and what Lohafer has called 'practical poetics',[6] through an intense phase of theorization and into a second wave of historical, thematic and practical enquiry. From the late 1970s (marked by the publication of Charles E. May's *Short Story Theories* in 1976) to the late 1990s, theoretical short story criticism experienced a heyday, largely but not exclusively based in the United States. Critics such as May, Lohafer and Mary Rohrberger strove to move towards a more unified theoretical approach to the short story genre, despite numerous acknowledgements of the 'protean nature of the literary short story',[7] and with an implicit exclusion of the non-literary, non-artistic (i.e. popular and/or genre fiction). Their enquiries utilized a wide variety of fashionable theoretical approaches and ranged from endeavours at categorization and definition of the short story, to investigations of the relationship of the short story to the literary canon, and cognitive and reader-response-based approaches to short fiction. March-Russell suggests that the cognitive approach to short fiction in particular should be seen as located within 'the context of universities seeking to legitimate their relevancy to contemporary society' by adopting the methods and terminology of the social sciences and psychology.[8] Cognitive approaches to short fiction continue to be topical today,[9] and the trend in the cognitive analysis of short fiction is part of larger endeavours to grasp our understanding and processing of a text or story. This method of analysis generally runs parallel to a move away from attempts at formulating universal theories of the short story in favour of more specialized, subgenre-, theme- or period-specific research as well as a revival in practical criticism in the shape of writers' manuals and numerous volumes on short story writing and teaching.[10] This move away from more broadly conceived definitions and towards a more practical or pragmatic approach, however, does not mean that the vexed question of how to define the short story has gone away.

Attempts to define the short story in specific formal or aesthetic terms – starting with Poe's 'unity of effect'[11] – have all come up against the fundamental problem that one size simply does not fit all. Any definition based on content, function, formal or aesthetic features is likely to capture only a subsection of short fiction, leading to a neglect of historical development and/or variety. The joint problem faced by attempts to define the short story in formal or aesthetic terms is that they tend to exclude short stories that have variously been labelled as popular, commercial, written for entertainment, plot-based, traditional or mimetic.[12] In March-Russell's words, '[c]ritical attempts to gloss the short story as a "well-made" structure omit […] the irreducible complexity of the short story form', not least with reference to its popular subgenres.[13] Indeed, the more popular forms of the short story, particularly its perceived magazine variety, have repeatedly been branded as detrimental to the prestige of the genre as a whole, as in Thomas A. Gullason's argument that the commercially successful formulae imposed by fiction magazines had

> further damaged the short story and made it seem a standardized and mechanized product. *The New Yorker, The Saturday Evening Post, Mademoiselle,* the old *Collier's* and others – all have set up, whether consciously or unconsciously, certain taboos and formulas to impose further controls on the short story. As if this were not enough, the magazines further created controls by the simple expedient of word count. This has helped to create another unhealthy image for the short story: art as a filler. And the filler suggests the newspaper world, something of short duration, a thing of the moment. Moreover, the fact that the short story is continually linked with popular magazines makes it seem a cheap potboiler.[14]

An exclusion of the popular and the commercial from an understanding of the short story 'proper' is not perhaps entirely accidental. The influence of modernist, and in particular New Critical ideas of what constitutes a 'literary' short story pervades twentieth-century short story criticism, both implicitly in terms of the selection of authors whom critics included in their work, and explicitly in statements such as Lohafer's claim that 'Poe's theories and

Introduction

practice were co-opted by the hacks of later decades when the short story was too often seen as a formula-driven genre for slick magazines': in her eyes a debasement of the form that led to a loss of prestige for the short story in the hierarchy of genres.[15] While it is certainly true that, as Ailsa Cox notes, '[s]hort fiction was at the heart of the modernist experiment', it is important to remember with Cox that 'the short story has also been integral to the development of popular genres, including science fiction, tales of the supernatural, crime fiction and horror'[16] – and, one might add, that the form owes as much to the mass-market magazine as the literary periodical.

The aim of this collection is not to offer an exhaustive overview of the many different subgenres and contexts of the short story, but to trace the development of some of its varying forms and concerns over time. Rather than pin definitions of the short story to particular aesthetic characteristics such as fragmentariness, a capacity to capture the moment, a lack of historicity, the ability to speak of and for marginalized experiences or groups, or similar – all of which tend to apply only to specific kinds of short stories at specific points in time – it seems helpful to conceive of the short story genre as open and, in Joyce Carol Oates's words, sufficiently 'democratic' to contain within it the greatest possible degree of variety and idiosyncrasy.[17] Norman Friedman's proposal of distinguishing between what he calls 'genre traits' (in the case of the short story, its relative shortness) and 'period traits' (such as a modernist, non-narrative reliance on symbols and images in many early-twentieth-century stories) serves this purpose of accommodating the largest possible base of texts, and helps pre-empt any unnecessary confusion of genre characteristics as opposed to fashions in literary writing that apply to all prose genres.[18] Friedman's distinction serves excellently to counter the argument that the short story is not inherently different from the novel or novella, and can be linked to a practical definition of the short story as a piece of prose fiction that is too short to ordinarily be published on its own, as proposed by Helmut Bonheim.[19] Whatever commercial or aesthetic principles short stories follow, they are ultimately circumscribed by this essential if variable brevity. As Cox has pointed out, 'it has become increasingly obvious that the search for a closed definition must be self-defeating' and fortunately the realization that 'we no longer need to preface every argument with a declaration of specificity' has taken a wide critical hold.[20]

Just as short story critics have struggled with matters of definition, they also tend to deplore the genre's perceived lack of canonicity. 'Canon' and 'canonization' remain contentious terms in the early twenty-first century, and we find ourselves faced with radically divergent conceptions of canonicity even within the field of literary studies: a 'practical' canon of classroom texts; an ideological canon furthering the political interests of the ruling classes; an aesthetic canon whose choice is based on particular literary merit and amounts to a list of texts of timeless aesthetic value; or a canon of availability, of texts preserved as opposed to texts lost and forgotten in archives and libraries.[21] Looking at canonization from a more practical angle, a literary text may be of supreme aesthetic value, but as long as it fails to be printed and made accessible to the right kind of audience, it has no hope of entering any canon at all. Publishing and marketing concerns; the matter of who reads a text and for which reasons; these practical factors have a significant impact on canonization. This is where the particular predicament of the short story lies: whereas a novel will usually be published (potentially following serialization) in one autonomous piece, and re-published as long as it sells, a short story is usually first published in a newspaper or magazine, and depends for its re-publication on the choices made by anthology editors. The exception are short stories by successful authors, which may be reprinted in a collection of short stories by that author and will usually lag far behind that author's novels in sales; an independent publication, while possible, usually happens on the costly initiative of the author or – these days – online. While the findings of a 2003 survey of short story reading habits and publication, carried out by the British Council, confirm that publishers and readers alike prefer short story collections by already established authors,[22] the new possibilities for more flexible publication offered by the Internet may well serve to further an ever-increasing democratization of the short story form. Although this is in many ways a positive development as it potentially makes short fiction more accessible, it brings with it problems of its own, not least the problem of a new kind of obscurity in the vast and hard to navigate landscape of online publication.

As a number of chapters in this *Companion* explore, most short fiction over the past two centuries was produced for gift books, magazines and periodicals. It was frequently written to order, often highly formulaic, and closely bound to particular subgenres such as the detective story or the supernatural tale. Consequently, short stories belong to a highly transient genre, and many of them have never received any critical attention because they disappeared from view almost as soon as they were published. In most cases, scholars and critics devote their attention to stories written by well-known authors, seen as supplementing their longer prose, or stories that serve to exemplify particular literary fashions or movements. The result is a skewed critical awareness of British and Irish short fiction in particular, which tends to focus on very specific, primarily experimental forms of the short story in Great Britain and Ireland. At present, the short story is a frequently state-sponsored and popular form in Britain as well as North America, not least thanks to the spread of creative writing programmes,

Introduction

short story competitions and the use of short stories in teaching, discussed in greater depth in March-Russell's chapter. New Critics Cleanth Brooks and Robert Penn Warren based their influential textbook, *Understanding Fiction* (1943), on a selection of short stories they considered superior examples of narrative fiction, and even today, Cox explains the popularity of short fiction in teaching by its capacity to be a useful vehicle for close reading practice.[23]

Given the short story's firm place in the curriculum, whether taught as the subject of critical analysis or as creative expression, it seems short story critics can afford to be generous, and, as Oates suggests, 'democratic' in their definition and understanding of the short story as an old genre flourishing today in a diversity of old and new forms. What sets this *Companion* apart from other accounts of the short story in English is its awareness of the changing publishing environments for short fiction, and its consideration of the diversity of authors and influences in each period and subgenre covered. Without laying claim to completeness, the chapters in this volume endeavour to capture the complexity of the short story's evolution from the early nineteenth to the twenty-first century by tracing the effects of perpetually changing modes of publication, the wide variety of audiences for short fiction, and the diversity of commercial and aesthetic influences across a range of periods, themes and subgenres.

This volume sits alongside a separate *Cambridge Companion to the American Short Story* and consequently provides an introduction to and overview of short stories written in the English language outside of North America. Its focus is not only on authors native to England, Scotland, Ireland and Wales, but also on writers from Commonwealth countries and former British colonies writing in English (other than the United States). The short story in English can naturally not be seen as divorced from the American short story altogether, and influences on the English short story exerted by North American writers as well as authors in other languages are repeatedly addressed as part of a chapter structure focused on socio-historical contexts, historical development and a number of important subgenres. Similarly, rather than devote chapters or sections to writers of a particular gender, sexual orientation, ethnic background or nationality, individual chapters treat the fullest possible range of writers and short stories alongside each other wherever possible. In adopting this approach, this volume hopes to avoid pigeonholing particular groups of writers in favour of a more inclusive and comparative approach to different kinds of short fiction. This means that the short story's engagement with issues related to gender, race/racism, sexuality, feminism or identity (national or otherwise) is scrutinized across a range of different chapters. Barbara Korte's chapter on the short story and anxieties of Empire, for instance, looks at writers on both sides of the colonizer/colonized divide; David Malcolm's discussion of space and place in short fiction includes explorations of gendered and racially defined space(s); Maebh Long's account of late-twentieth- and early-twenty-first-century short fiction engages with the gender politics underlying postmodern fictions and Marc Botha's contribution investigates the potential of microfiction to give poignant expression to homosexual and postcolonial experience among others.

This *Companion* adopts the view that 'it was a print medium, the periodical press, which helped the short story shape itself into a genre in its own right'.[24] Rather than begin with early modern prose tales or – as is more common – with mid- to late-nineteenth-century tales, the starting point of this *Companion* are the prose sketches and stories published in literary magazines and story collections of the early nineteenth century. This choice of a point of departure is motivated by a focus on the short story's close relationship with its principal media of publication, the magazine or periodical on one hand, and the story collection or anthology, on the other. While collections of short tales or novellas predate the Romantic period, and while the influence of these earlier forms is acknowledged in individual chapters, the literary magazine and its impact on the short prose form came into its own in the late eighteenth and early nineteenth centuries. Research such as Tim Killick's and David Stewart's has shown the centrality of the Romantic magazine market to the development of the short form, particularly with the establishment of major literary magazines such as the *London Magazine* (revived in 1820) and *Blackwood's Edinburgh Magazine* (1817 onwards).[25]

Part I (Contexts) scrutinizes a number of key social, historical and political factors that constitute significant backdrops for or influences on the short story genre. The chapters in this initial section range from investigating processes of writing and publishing short stories to ways the short story addresses broader social concerns and issues of race, gender and identity. Paul March-Russell's opening discussion of the contexts in which short stories are written and published goes a long way towards disproving Frank Cottrell Boyce's recent claim that one 'can't read a short story online', and complicates if not entirely refutes Boyce's observation that '[p]ublishers – with heroic exceptions such as Comma in Manchester and McSweeney's in San Francisco – hate publishing [short stories]'.[26] Anthony Patterson's chapter on social realism in the short story explores the genre's enduring capacity for revealing 'how social class forms and affects the individual', pitching the short story against the dominance of the social novel in this field. Korte's chapter extends this enquiry to look at the ways short fiction

Introduction

in particular can reveal the fissures and anxieties of colonialism and postcolonial identities in Britain and beyond, while Malcolm addresses the issue of space. His chapter reflects on not only the limited space of the short story itself – its essential brevity – but also its engagement with different kinds of space: space as place, and the marginalized, mimetic, non-mimetic and fantastic spaces opened up by short fiction.

In Part II (Periods), the broad approach of this volume means that each period covered will not simply be equated with one particular school or movement of short story writing. Moving from the Romantic period to the present, chapters will take into account a variety of different writers and publishing contexts for each period, from the literary to the popular. David Stewart's chapter on Romantic short fiction clearly identifies annuals and magazines as the 'home' of short fiction, and traces the development of Romantic-era short stories and tales alongside other kinds of texts published in early-nineteenth-century periodicals, as writers and readers alike were trying to determine what constituted a short story proper. In the same spirit, John Plotz's chapter offers an alternative interpretation of the relationship between the long Victorian novel, the British short story and the magazine market by locating short fiction not simply alongside but indeed *within* the three-decker novel. The emphasis on means of publication, on magazines, collections and anthologies, is continued in chapters by Einhaus and Victoria Stewart. Einhaus's chapter focuses on the early twentieth century as the heyday of both magazine stories and modernist short fiction, concluding that the boundaries between these seemingly distinct categories are fluid and subject to similar vagaries of the publishing market. Victoria Stewart traces the development of the short story further into the twentieth century, capturing the impact of wartime experience and changes to the publishing industry on the genre. Maebh Long's chapter on short fiction from postmodernism to the digital age takes this section into the present, stretching from the heyday of postmodern experimental short fiction in the late 1960s and 1970s to the effect of digital and online publication with the advent of the Internet.

To supplement the overview of different contexts and periods, the third and final part (Genre) engages with a selection of the most significant subgenres that have fuelled the short story throughout its development as a modern literary form. Kate Macdonald's chapter on comic short fiction redresses a long-standing tendency on the part of literary scholars to ignore or belittle the humorous in fiction, and offers the first-ever investigation of comedy in short stories as 'the salt that enhances taste, and crosses the boundaries of form and genre'. In his chapter on short detective fiction,

Martin Priestman explores the origins of this perennially popular form of modern entertainment in short stories rather than novels. Similarly, Luke Thurston's contribution scrutinizes the manifestation in short fiction of a literary mode – the gothic – commonly associated with longer novels. Andrew M. Butler's chapter on short science fiction links the development of sf closely to developments in the magazine market, arguing that '[t]he contours of the field of SF have been shaped by editors and economics, as well as the emergence of particular writers'. Last but not least, Marc Botha's account of short fiction – or microfiction – closes this volume with an in-depth and wide-ranging discussion of the shortest in short fiction, which adopts a particularly broad temporal approach from antiquity to the present, and takes into account not only problems of definition and scope, but publication and particularly the new possibilities opened up by online publication and social media tools. While the list of subgenres covered here can by no means be exhaustive, the forms chosen for this final section – comic, detective, gothic and science fiction stories as well as the particularly prolific subgenre of what Botha terms microfiction – best reflect the short story's close relationship with its various means of publication, from the magazine to the Internet.

NOTES

1. One should note, however, that by the time both critics followed up their book-length studies on the short story with edited volumes of short story criticism – Hanson's *Re-reading the Short Story* (1989) and Lohafer's *Short Story Theory at a Crossroads* (1989, with Jo Ellyn Clarey) – Hanson was also beginning to move in the direction of a cognitive and reader-centred enquiry in her own essay on the poetics of short fiction. See Clare Hanson, '"Things Out of Words": Towards a Poetics of Short Fiction', *Re-reading the Short Story*, ed. Clare Hanson (Basingstoke: Macmillan, 1989), pp. 22–33.
2. H. E. Bates, *The Modern Short Story: A Critical Survey* (1941; Boston, MA: The Writer, 1965), p. 26.
3. Charles E. May, *The Short Story: The Reality of Artifice* (1995; London; New York: Routledge, 2002), pp. 6–7. See also Susan Lohafer's claim that 'the first theorist of the short story was Edgar Allan Poe', in Barbara Lounsberry, Susan Lohafer, Mary Rohrberger, Stephen Pett and R. C. Feddersen (eds.), *The Tales We Tell: Perspectives on the Short Story* (Westport, CO: Greenwood, 1998), p. ix.
4. Barbara Korte, *The Short Story in Britain: A Historical Sketch and Anthology* (Tübingen: Francke, 2003), p. 7.
5. Korte, *Short Story in Britain*, pp. 7–8.
6. Susan Lohafer, *Coming to Terms with the Short Story* (Baton Rouge: Louisiana State University Press, 1983), p. 5. Prominent practitioner-critics include Poe, of course, but also British, Irish and other English-language writers

Introduction

 such as H. E. Bates, Frank O'Connor, Seán Ó Faoláin, Elizabeth Bowen or Nadine Gordimer, to name but a few.

7 Lohafer, *Coming to Terms*, p. 7.
8 Paul March-Russell, *The Short Story: An Introduction* (Edinburgh: Edinburgh University Press, 2009), p. 85.
9 See, for example, Ailsa Cox, 'Postgraduate Research', *Teaching the Short Story*, ed. Ailsa Cox (Basingstoke: Palgrave Macmillan, 2011), pp. 161–73 (p. 163).
10 See, for example, Tom Bailey (ed.), *On Writing Short Stories* (Oxford: Oxford University Press, 2000); Ailsa Cox, *Writing Short Stories: A Routledge Writer's Guide* (London; New York: Routledge, 2005); Cox, *Teaching the Short Story*; Carolyn Lewis (ed.), *The Short Story: A Guide to Writing Short Stories* (Bristol: SilverWood, 2012).
11 Edgar Allan Poe, 'Review of *Twice-Told Tales*', *Short Story Theories*, ed. Charles E. May (Athens: Ohio University Press, 1976), pp. 45–51 (p. 46).
12 Eileen Baldeshwiler, for instance, distinguishes between lyric and mimetic (or epical) short stories in 'The Lyric Short Story: The Sketch of a History', *Short Story Theories*, ed. May, while Mary Rohrberger works with a binary distinction between lyric stories and 'simple narratives' in 'Between Shadow and Act: Where Do We Go From Here?', *Short Story Theory at a Crossroads*, eds. Susan Lohafer and Jo Ellyn Clarey (1989; Baton Rouge: Louisiana State University Press, 1998), pp. 32–45, and Clare Hanson divides short prose into the plot-based short story and plotless short fiction in *Short Stories and Short Fiction, 1880–1980* (Basingstoke: Macmillan, 1985).
13 March-Russell, *Short Story*, p. viii.
14 Thomas A. Gullason, 'The Short Story: An Underrated Art', *Short Story Theories*, ed. May, pp. 13–31 (p. 21).
15 Susan Lohafer, 'Introduction', *The Tales We Tell*, eds. Lounsberry et al., p. xi.
16 Ailsa Cox, 'Introduction', *Teaching the Short Story*, p. 1.
17 Joyce Carol Oates, 'The Origins and Art of the Short Story', *The Tales We Tell*, eds. Lounsberry et al., pp. 47–52 (p. 47).
18 Norman Friedman, 'Recent Short Story Theories: Problems in Definition', *Short Story Theory at a Crossroads*, eds. Lohafer and Clarey, pp. 13–31 (pp. 20–1).
19 See Helmut Bonheim, *The Narrative Modes: Techniques of the Short Story* (Cambridge, MA: Brewer, 1992), pp. 165–6.
20 Cox, 'Introduction', p. 6.
21 For some representative approaches to the idea of a literary canon, see, for example, Jan Gorak, *The Making of the Modern Canon: Genesis and Crisis of a Literary Idea* (London: Athlone, 1990); John Guillory, *Cultural Capital: The Problem of Literary Canon Formation* (Chicago: University of Chicago Press, 1993), and Harold Bloom, *The Western Canon: The Books and School of the Ages* (New York: Harcourt Brace, 1994). See also Frank Kermode's seminal essay 'Canons', *Dutch Quarterly Review of Anglo-American Letters*, 18 (1988/1), pp. 258–70.
22 For a summary of the report, see March-Russell, *Short Story*, pp. 49–51.
23 Cox, 'Introduction', p. 1.
24 Korte, *Short Story in Britain*, p. x.

25 See Tim Killick, *British Short Fiction in the Early Nineteenth Century: The Rise of the Tale* (Farnham: Ashgate, 2008), and David Stewart, *Romantic Magazines and Metropolitan Literary Culture* (Basingstoke: Palgrave Macmillan, 2011).
26 Frank Cottrell Boyce, 'Distraction techniques: Neil Gaiman's new book proves you can't read a short story online', *New Statesman*, 24 February 2015, www.newstatesman.com/culture/2015/02/distraction-techniques-neil-gaiman-s-new-book-proves-you-can-t-read-short-story [Accessed 27 February 2015].

PART I

Contexts

1

PAUL MARCH-RUSSELL

Writing and publishing the short story

To write and to publish are both transitive verbs, implying a direct object, yet there is little directly objective about the 'short story'. The origin of the term is shrouded in mystery although it seems to have acquired its modern usage in the United States during the late 1870s. Several critics have, however, pointed to the belatedness with which the idea of the short story caught on in British literary circles. In 1883, for example, when Anthony Trollope used the term it was to refer to one of his works as 'a short story, about one volume in length',[1] while in 1901, Brander Matthews' popularization of Edgar Allan Poe's critical writings as an aesthetic theory of the short story was reviewed derisively by the *Academy*.[2] For Dean Baldwin, Poe's ideas were of most benefit for magazine editors who, in the proliferating marketplace of the 1880s and 1890s, viewed the self-sufficient short story – as opposed to the open-ended serial – as a ready means of filling space.[3] The economics of magazine publication thus underwrite the history of the British short story and not solely in terms of commercial development. For short-lived little magazines such as the *Yellow Book* (1894–7), the *Savoy* (1896) and, into the modernist period, *Rhythm* (1911–13) and *Blast* (1914), the brevity of the short story typified not only the exquisite pleasure of transitory experience but also the sharpness and clarity of the significant detail. According to Tim Armstrong, this 'contradictory position' was not inherent only in Poe's theories of short fiction, but also in the emerging modernist ethos that 'emphasizes the detachment of close reading and borrows from mass culture a stress on the embodied, on the shock effect.'[4]

Yet what this ambiguity also implies is that definition of the short story as a thing in itself is displaced onto the activity of writing and publishing; the short story is not to be approached as a textual product, but as a contextual process. Or as Katherine Mansfield frames the dilemma:

> Suppose we put it in the form of a riddle: 'I am neither a short story, nor a sketch, nor an impression, nor a tale. I am written in prose. I am a great deal

shorter than a novel; I may be only one page long, but, on the other hand, there is no reason why I should not be thirty. I have a special quality – a something, a something which is immediately, perfectly recognizable. It belongs to me; it is of my essence. In fact I am often given away in the first sentence. I seem almost to stand or fall by it. It is to me what the first phrase of the song is to the singer. [...] What am I?'[5]

Despite the aesthetic overtone upon the 'untranslatable charm' of the work of art,[6] Mansfield emphasizes the performative role of artistry such that it defies generic categorization. In the ensuing discussion, I want to keep this distinction in the foreground: that the short story is not something which *is*, but which is *done*. This delineation is not time-bound to Mansfield's modernist moment, but underscores the varied modes of contemporary short story production as well as the hopes and anxieties for the form's renaissance or survival.

Now, ostensibly, seems to be a good time for the short story in the United Kingdom. According to Nielsen BookScan – the most reliable indicator for sales and trends in the United Kingdom – the combined sales for short story collections and short fiction anthologies have risen from £2.8 million in 2012 to £4.1 million in 2014. Nevertheless, this rise still represents a decline from the peak of 2010, in which recorded sales were £6.5 million; this despite the publication of Hilary Mantel's *The Assassination of Margaret Thatcher* (2014) as well as collections by other well-known and popular novelists such as Joanne Harris and Kate Mosse. In total, ten collections in 2014 sold five thousand or more copies, as opposed to seven in 2013, but whether these sales necessarily advanced the short story as an art form or encouraged readers to experiment with the work of lesser-known writers in addition to the tried and tested, known to them from the more high-profile world of the novel, is hard to say. Although since 2001 total recorded sales for short fiction have amounted to £67.2 million, in combining short story collections with anthologies as a single publishing category, Nielsen BookScan obscures the figures for the single-author collection as opposed to the themed, and often more commercially driven, anthology. The data analysis that services such as Nielsen BookScan provide, although invaluable from the point of view of statistics, cannot by itself be translated into a qualitative account of the short story. Furthermore, despite the gradual rise in sales since 2012, it is impossible to read into any one year a prediction for what is likely to occur in the near future. As the overall decline from 2010 indicates, the short story market is – as has always been historically the case – a precarious one, liable to contraction as well as occasional bursts of inflation.

The economic reality of the short story undermines the optimism of reviewers who, reading the tea leaves of isolated incidents, attempt to predict an impending revival for the short story. Such revivalism, according to the writer and critic Chris Power, has warped critical understanding of the short story:

> Any form that includes agonising about its unpopularity as one of its basic features is going to encounter difficulties. [...] By constantly rehearsing the same positions critics and commentators reinforce the perception that short stories not only are, but deserve to be, a minority interest.[7]

Sam Baker's article in the *Telegraph*, following the triple victories of the North American writers Lydia Davis (winner of the Man Booker International Prize in 2013), Alice Munro (winner of the Nobel Prize, also in 2013) and George Saunders (winner of the inaugural Folio Prize in 2014), is a case in point.[8] From these coincidental successes, Baker detects a pattern: 'the renaissance of the short story' which, along with Saunders, 'was catapulted into public view and on to the bestseller lists'. Baker indulges in familiar revivalist rhetoric – 'it's been a while since the short story, long the poor relation of the novel, experienced such consistent and growing adulation' – which he supports by referring to new short story prizes, collections by big literary names and statistics – a 35 per cent sales increase in 2013 according to the *Bookseller* – although his use of data is historically decontextualized. The major pre-determinant for change, though, Baker argues, is technology; he quotes Elizabeth Day, co-founder of the short story salon Pindrop:

> Many people struggle to find the time to engage with a full-length novel when they're dealing with emails every second of every day or having to meet deadlines or rush home to put the kids to bed. A short story offers the perfect antidote – it's the equivalent of listening to a single track of music instead of the whole album.

Day, however, is not an impartial witness and several problems underline her observation. First, her claim about declining attention spans due to the acceleration of modern life is hardly a new one – it features in Poe's 1842 review of Nathaniel Hawthorne's *Twice-Told Tales*; the defining document of short story criticism – while, second, it fails to explain the continuing popularity of the novel; any increases in sales for short fiction are far outweighed by the dominance of the longer form. Third, in comparing the short story with the audio download, Day dwells solely on the single short story – she does not address the short story collection as an integrated work – and suggests that it is a more lightweight, ephemeral form than the novel. Baker's conclusion that 'we don't want to lose ourselves – we no longer have time to be lost' not only plays up to the alleged lack of moral depth in the short story, but also actively presents the form as a passive or culturally disaffected medium (again, unlike the physical and artistic presence of the novel).

By contrast, Power asserts that 'most short stories must be dense if they are to have any effect at all', whereas 'one of the great pleasures of the novel' is 'to occasionally wander and drift'.[9]

As Power argues, the rhetoric of revivalism results in generalized discussions of the short story form – as opposed to analysis of actual short stories and collections – often in a self-defeating comparison with the novel. The latter, too, is generalized in these accounts so that the alleged panacea of technology is associated with furthering the short story rather than what new technological formats and platforms are doing to the form, content and composition of the novel. Regarding both novel and short story as subject to a volatile and transforming literary marketplace would be one way of circumventing the implicit hierarchical distinctions within these discussions. In that sense, critical analysis of contemporary fiction would be catching up with the shape and construction of such episodic novels as David Mitchell's *Cloud Atlas* (2005) and Ali Smith's *Hotel World* (2001). The porous generic boundaries between novel and short story collection, as registered in these texts, may also be an acknowledgement of the changing demography for literary consumption. It has often been claimed that the emergence of the short story, as part of the developing magazine culture of the nineteenth century, provided literature for the time-poor: office workers and shop-girls on their way to and from work, mothers and housewives caring for large or extended families, quick literary fixes at lunchtime, or a short read before bedtime. By contrast, with the growth of the twenty-first-century precariat, where time-poverty is a common complaint across the traditional class divides, novel-reading tends in practice towards shorter bursts rather than more sustained attention. In this situation, the writers of episodic novels may now be drawing more on the short story form in order to accumulate longer narratives for time-pressurized readers. However, far from constituting absorption of the short story into the novel form, this development also indicates a positive dynamic between the two prose genres. As the novelist and award-winning short story writer Sarah Hall has acknowledged: 'short stories have made me a better writer [...] The things that have to be done in a short-story structure [have made] me step up my game'.[10]

Instead of focusing on the short story form, or making misleading comparisons with the novel, as a means of assessing its health, it might be more useful to look at the recent history of the Edge Hill Prize, the only UK award that honours the short story collection. It was first given in 2007 and has grown in size and scope; in 2014, forty-four books were longlisted, an indication not only of more works being submitted by publishers for consideration, but also, perhaps, of more short story collections being published. The prize has also acted as a barometer for trends within the short story – trends that are more detectable over a period of time rather than the snapshot approach favoured by literary reviewers. Its first two winners, Colm Tóibín and Claire Keegan, are representative of the enduring popularity of the short story in Ireland: their successes re-emphasize the special case of Irish short fiction as opposed to the history of the form on the UK mainland.[11] In 2013, a third Irish writer, Kevin Barry, collected the prize, but his collection, *Dark Lies the Island* (2012), displays a relish for the strange and the fantastical to be found in two previous winners: Chris Beckett's science fiction collection *The Turing Test* (2008), and Jeremy Dyson's macabre *The Cranes that Build the Cranes* (2009). Whereas other more established, more novel-oriented prizes, such as the Man Booker, have come under criticism for either not representing genre fiction or for subsuming its tropes within another more respectable genre, 'litfic',[12] the Edge Hill Prize has openly acknowledged the origins of the short story within mass as well as minority culture. Literariness, in this sense, becomes not a cultural marker between genres but, as in the Russian Formalist usage of *ostranenie* (defamiliarization), as an effect that occurs within and across genres, often as the result of a writer pushing the limits of generic convention and expression.[13] In 2014, the longlist included books by the science fiction writer Adam Roberts, the fantasy author Tom Lloyd, the crime writer Peter James, and the weird fiction authors Nina Allan and Peter Crowther.

At the same time as pulling in one direction to represent the work of popular subgenres, the Edge Hill Prize has also followed another, equally characteristic trajectory of the short story: the condensation of detail that marks the blurred boundary line between short prose fiction and poetry. In 2011 and 2014, respectively, the poets Graham Mort and John Burnside won the prize for short story collections while other writers who have worked between prose and poetry, such as Ken Edwards, Jackie Kay and Michèle Roberts, have been nominated for the award. In 2012, the prize featured an all-woman's shortlist, a sign perhaps of not only the strong association between the short story form and women's writing,[14] but also of dissent at the sexist criticism levelled in the novel-reading world at what was then the Orange Prize for Fiction (now the Baileys Women's Prize for Fiction). Yet, as one of the shortlisted authors, Zoe Lambert, has maintained:

> But it's still difficult if you are a debut or unknown short story writer who brings out a collection. You're just not in the same game as novelists. [...] Mainstream publishers and agents aren't interested in you unless you write 'something longer' or can turn it into a novel.[15]

Lambert's preference for working outside the mainstream as both a writer and freelance teacher has deeper implications for the cultural framework of the short story, some of which are embodied by the Edge Hill Prize. As an academically instituted award, it lacks the higher profile of commercially funded prizes, such as the BBC National Short Story Award, the Costa Short Story Award or the *Sunday Times* EFG Short Story Award. It belongs, in that sense, with a host of less well-known prizes, but unlike the awards associated with literary organizations such as the Asham Trust, the Bridport Arts Centre and the Royal Society for Literature, the Edge Hill – by dint of its falling within the academic sector – has a more archival relationship to the short story. This is not to suggest that nomination for the Edge Hill cannot be a boost to a young writer's career – a recent example would be that of Carys Bray – just as the award of the Bridport in 1990 gave a boost to Kate Atkinson. However, there remains the sense that the Edge Hill has a more nurturing, curatorial approach to the short story by awarding innovations that feed from and back into the tradition of the genre. Canonization – both the curse and the highest tribute to be paid to any literary work by the academy – persists as the critical framework in which the Edge Hill operates and, in that sense, the work that it does on behalf of the short story complements similar tendencies in the academy on behalf of other outsider forms, such as linguistically innovative poetry.

Despite its relatively low profile, the Edge Hill Prize remains the enduring public face of what was the Northwest Short Story Network, a loose affiliation of universities that also included Chester, Liverpool John Moores and Manchester Metropolitan. The first continues to publish *Flash: The International Short-Short Story Magazine* (2008 onwards), an initiative complemented in the south of the country by the University of Chichester's online short story forum, *Thresholds*, edited by Vicki Heath and Alison MacLeod. These universities not only work with local enterprises, such as small presses and literary festivals (e.g. Small Wonder in East Sussex, part-funded by the Asham Trust), but also promote the culture of reading and writing short stories through their creative writing programmes. Although their respective publicity officers will give most attention to the published authors produced by these programmes, their cultural work is their most important achievement. If the short story provides these universities with a niche to market, this institutional compromise is arguably outweighed by the benefit of nurturing a short story culture, something which the United Kingdom has lacked as opposed to the United States.

Yet too often elsewhere, this benefit is forsaken where a deep appreciation of the short story is not already embedded within the make-up of the creative writing department. The hope that creativity as a form of critique through imaginative play would transform creative writing into a dissident subject area with implications for the rest of literary studies has, I fear, been lost.[16] Although this discussion lies outside the purview of this chapter, it is worth noting that too often, it seems, creative writing has turned into an instrumental teaching practice where the focus is on the immediate needs of the consumer (formerly known as the student) and not on the creation of a wider literary culture that would actually do more to benefit the aspirations of the student-consumer. The effect of this myopia is not only damaging to the idea of the humanities more generally, but also to the short story in particular, where the brevity of the form is used not as the basis for aesthetic understanding, beyond the terms already established by Poe, but as the means for providing bite-size chunks of literature that fit the design parameters of an over-regulated, over-specified undergraduate module.

In the United States, the preponderance of such courses resulted, first, in a glut of imitations based on the minimalist model of writers such as Raymond Carver, and second, the rearguard action of Dave Eggers in founding his publishing company, McSweeney's, in 1998, so as to promote the work of contemporaries such as George Saunders and David Foster Wallace. It is worth considering whether a similar situation might be developing here in the United Kingdom. With fewer public outlets for short stories outside of the women's magazine market, young writers may be tempted either to take a consensual approach and to reproduce the models that they have been taught at university or, alternatively, to deliberately conflict with the mainstream and create their own initiatives. Yet even here, an artistic risk is involved since in constructing himself or herself as an outlier, the author is implicitly marking a reaction-formation towards a projected mainstream literary culture, a nebulous distinction that effaces the fractured state of current fiction publishing. In the United States, McSweeney's is no longer an outlier – in many respects, it represents the new orthodoxy just as the minimalists had done before: a transition made all the easier by McSweeney's posing as the reaction to an otherwise indistinct mainstream fiction.

The United Kingdom, with its less developed short story culture, may not have yet reached such a situation, but tensions are discernible. Although there has been a boom in short story prizes, a familiarity about the nominees is also apparent. For example, although the BBC National Short Story Award can claim an advantage over the Edge Hill Prize by having had three all-women shortlists in 2009, 2013 and 2014, several writers have appeared more than once, most notably the 2014 winner, Lionel Shriver, with three nominations. In addition, despite the proliferation in prizes, several writers such as Sarah Hall, Tessa Hadley, Jon McGregor and Jane Rogers have appeared on more than one shortlist at a time – not necessarily a surprise if their writing is indeed among the best of its year. But, since its inception in 2006, the BBC Award has featured few postcolonial writers and, of those, authors such as Helen Oyeyemi and Zadie Smith are among the most celebrated novelists of their generation. The influence, in particular, of *Granta* can also be felt with a number of their past and current Best Young Novelists, including Hall, Oyeyemi, Smith, Naomi Alderman and Rose Tremain, making the shortlists. Although *Granta* has long promoted the short story, the magazine has tended to advocate for literary realism, beginning with its support of Carver and his contemporaries, and to regard the short story as an apprenticeship for the novel.[17] The relative lack of fantasy, with the notable exceptions of Hall's award-winning 'Mrs Fox' (2013) and Sarah Maitland's 2009 runner-up, 'Moss Witch', is conspicuous. In addition, despite the continuing absence of a UK equivalent to the *New Yorker*, the influence of the stereotypical *New Yorker* story – well-made, building to a moment of crisis – is apparent in such award-winning pieces as Shriver's 'Kilifi Creek', D. W. Wilson's 'The Dead Roads' (2011) and James Lasdun's 'An Anxious Man' (2006).[18]

These problems are magnified by the *Sunday Times* EFG Short Story Award which, although the world's richest prize for a single short story, is open to any writer published in the United Kingdom; in 2014, it was won by the Pulitzer Prize – winning novelist Adam Johnson. The Costa Award's solution to this dichotomy, by being a non-jury prize, has led to some intriguing winners, for example 2014's victor, Zoe Gilbert, a PhD candidate at the University of Chichester, but the prize remains separate from Costa's main book awards. Each of these high-profile, commercially funded prizes persists in presenting the short story as a self-contained item which not only places impediments between the writing and the potential audience by casting it as an auratic art[19] – a bizarre contradiction when the short story's mass cultural origins are taken into account – but also fails to connect the genre with the most significant innovations in short fiction publishing. In this respect, the Edge Hill Prize has the advantage with its 2014 longlist being dominated by small-press and independent publishers; not only the established small presses such as Comma and Salt or genre presses such as PS Publishing, but also imprints in Ireland and Wales such as Arlen House, New Island Books, Parthian and Seren. To what extent these non-metropolitan developments are relatable to the short story as an art form that works on the periphery of the cultural centres, as for example in Frank O'Connor's influential formulation of 'submerged population groups',[20] or to the revivified politics of regionalism and economic decentralization is, at this short distance, too hard to say. They do, however, point to the emergence of distinct, local voices that are not being represented by the slew of high-profile prizes that, for their own financial self-interest, tend to take a hierarchical, top-down approach to short fiction. The extent to which this non-representation is also connected to the reduction of short fiction content on BBC Radio, once the nation's most important forum for new and classic short stories, is moot since in March 2015 the planned cuts to radio broadcasting remain only half-finished.[21]

Comma has also been at the forefront of pioneering short story apps to be downloaded to the reader's smartphone or tablet. LitNav, launched in 2011, builds on Comma's series of city-themed anthologies by presenting international fiction from across five continents, each story located within a particular city. The app is personalized to the consumer's needs according to the length of journey, preferred genre, location and mode of transport. The story can either be read in a conventional e-book format or listened to while the narrative unfolds in real time with an on-screen map and key sites of interest highlighted. In that sense, the app draws also on the travelogues associated with the popular *Lonely Planet* series of guides which, despite the claim that these are stories to be consumed during the daily commute, seem also to be targeting a particular type of consumer – a would-be cosmopolitan type, possibly socially aspirational, with interests that range beyond the parochial. The app comes with standard features such as bookmarks, downloads and sharing facilities so that, in theory at least, the stories may not only be personalized to individual interests but to communal ones disseminated across the virtual space of social media. Although the influence and popularity of apps such as LitNav and Ellipsis may be too soon to judge, in contrast with Kindle Singles, financed and promoted by a huge international player in the form of the online retail outlet Amazon, it is most likely that their potential users will already be readers of short fiction and, in the case of much of the output of Kindle Singles, narrative non-fiction. To what extent apps are taking short stories to a new readership, or building on a pre-existing audience just as the app format itself seems to develop the traditional consumption pattern of a short story published in a mass-market magazine, is hard to discern.

Although such technological innovations are to be welcomed, it has to be acknowledged that these are initiatives spearheaded by publishers who are seeking to consolidate their place and status within an increasingly confused and fractured market due to the effects of economic recession, the rise of e-publishing and changing demographics with a concomitant rise in niche or specialized readerships and publications. Presses such as Comma, Route and Salt may be independents, but within the narrow confines of the UK short story market, they carry considerable prestige which they are understandably loathe to lose. While promoting the short story via new media, the press is also seeking to legitimate its position within an uncertain publishing landscape. By contrast, a greater potential for artistic expression, free from the compromises of working with a publisher, is to be seen in the personal initiatives of writers such as Jeff Noon that began with his 'Microspores', flash fictions in the form of 140-character-long tweets, for example: 'For sale: one pair of wax and feather wings, suitable for adult human. Used for one flight only. Slightly sun-damaged.'[22] In characteristic fashion, Noon asked his readers to illustrate, adapt or contribute their own Microspores (now to be found on his website). Following these experiments, Noon developed 'echovirus12', an unfolding and possibly never-ending Twitter strand in which readers are asked to supply their own microfiction, echoing the previous tweet supplied by another reader, but creating a fresh tangent to the narrative that can in turn be echoed by a further reader, and so on. The interactive, rhizomatic structure of echovirus12 far outweighs the social media – sharing facilities of apps such as LitNav, which are not only circumscribed by the design of the app itself, but also by the organization of social media sites. Instead, in echovirus12, questions of authorship, readership and re-writing are explicitly foregrounded within the otherwise limited structure of the 140-character tweet, the arbitrary imposition echoing the compositional rules of avant-garde composers such as John Cage or literary movements such as OuLiPo. It is no coincidence that not only has the short story become a medium for such experiments, but also that these innovations have overlapped with the counter-cultural affinities of science fiction and the Internet. For instance, the first UK literary prize to honour digital short fiction was the speculative fiction award, the Kitschies (in March 2015).

In addition to traditional print outlets such as *Ambit* and *Stand*, and more recent university-based magazines such as the *Warwick Review* (2007 onwards), the Internet has been seen as a boon, with online magazines such as *3:AM*, launched in Paris in 2000, but published in English with a strong commitment to Anglocentric poetry and short fiction; *Paraxis* which, due to its co-editors Carys Bray, Andy Hedgecock and Claire Massey, traverses the intersections between mainstream literary and popular genre fiction; and the self-declared *Short FICTION*, published by the University of Plymouth. Other titles such as *Structo*, launched in 2008, appear in both print and electronic form.[23] These titles not only extend the tradition of the little magazine, but also, as in the case of *3:AM*, the counter-cultural or punk fanzine. They achieve this result, though, within the orbit of the university sector; as such, they are subject to the institutional pressures as outlined previously, but they are also distinguished by a high and varied level of content not simply confined to the work of established authors. Their distinctiveness, however, is in contrast to the many websites that have proliferated where short stories can be published with little editorial control on the part of the site owner. Although, on one hand, the Internet has enabled greater publication of short fiction beyond the traditional – and limited – outlets for short stories in the United Kingdom, on the other hand, without the editorial content of these outlets, the Internet has not markedly improved the quality of short fiction. Instead, within a slew of self-published work, real gems may be lost or tainted by association while the apprenticeship of the novice short story writer has not necessarily been aided by these electronic publishing opportunities.[24] In some respects, the Internet may be regarded as the recapitulation of nineteenth- or twentieth-century mass-market publishing with electronic publishing, shading also into the phenomenon of fan or 'slash' fiction, the twenty-first-century equivalent to the interminable serials published in penny dreadfuls and shilling shockers. Such associations do not necessarily improve the quality or public image of the short story, but they do re-emphasize the ambiguous identification of the short story as both rarefied object and commodified artefact. The split identity of the short story in the twenty-first century not only re-invokes the divided cultural origins of the genre in the nineteenth century, but also indicates the masses – for better, for worse – of short story production that are not being registered by high-profile literary prizes.

The basis for some of these problems, for which the Internet is at best only a partial solution, was recorded in the survey conducted by Jenny Brown Associates and Book Marketing Limited on behalf of the Save Our Short Story campaign, and published in March 2004.[25] Of its recommendations, an annual anthology devoted to British short fiction began publication only in 2011, edited on behalf of Salt by the author and creative writing tutor at Manchester Metropolitan University, Nicholas Royle. Although Royle is a committed advocate not only for the short story, but for little magazines and small presses alike, his choices – despite being occasionally eclectic – nevertheless represent his own preferences in short fiction. An annual change in editor, as with the *Best American Short Stories* series, might in the long term be a more innovative move. On the other hand, the BBC's annual publication of its award nominees, although to be appreciated, serves also to legitimate the institutional kudos; it is not necessarily an adequate substitute for the series of anthologies published by former BBC editor Di Spiers. Equally, the recommendation for a high-profile prize awarded to the best short story collection has not been fulfilled – the Edge Hill, although excellent, lacks public recognition. Lastly, with the dissolution of the short story campaign, continuing research, education and financial support at a grass-roots level remain patchy. Despite the growth in academic interest, writing and publishing the short story remains an indistinct process.

Acknowledgements

The author would like to thank Ailsa Cox, John Lewis, Alison MacLeod and Courttia Newland for their advice in writing this chapter.

NOTES

1. Anthony Trollope, *An Autobiography* (London: Oxford University Press, 1950), p. 160.
2. Anon, 'Review of Matthews' *The Philosophy of the Short-Story*', *What Is the Short Story?* eds. Eugene Current-García and Walton R. Patrick, 2nd edn (Glenview, IL: Scott, Foresman, 1974), pp. 48–50.
3. Dean Baldwin, 'The Tardy Evolution of the British Short Story', *Studies in Short Fiction*, 30.1 (1993), 31–2. See also Baldwin's more recent *Art and Commerce in the British Short Story, 1880–1950* (London: Pickering & Chatto, 2013).
4. Tim Armstrong, *Modernism: A Cultural History* (Cambridge: Polity Press, 2005), pp. 51–2.
5. Katherine Mansfield, 'Wanted, a New Word' (1920), *The Poetry and Critical Writings of Katherine Mansfield*, eds. Gerri Kimber and Angela Smith (Edinburgh: Edinburgh University Press, 2014), pp. 620–1.
6. Walter Pater, *Studies in the History of the Renaissance*, ed. Matthew Beaumont, 2nd edn (Oxford: Oxford World's Classics, 2010), p. 124.
7. Chris Power, 'The Short Story Is Dead! Long Live the Short Story!' (2014), p. 7, http://blogs.chi.ac.uk/shortstoryforum/wp-content/uploads/2014/04/THE_SHORT_STORY_IS_DEAD_Chris_Power.pdf [Accessed 17 March 2015].
8. Sam Baker, 'The Irresistible Rise of the Short Story', *Telegraph* (18 May 2014), www.telegraph.co.uk/culture/books/10831961/The-irresistible-rise-of-the-short-story.html [Accessed 17 March 2015].
9. Power, 'The Short Story Is Dead!', p. 11.
10. Quoted in Baker, 'The Irresistible Rise of the Short Story'.
11. On the Irish short story, see Elke D'Hoker and Stephanie Eggermont (eds.), *The Irish Short Story: Traditions and Trends* (Bern: Peter Lang, 2015); and Heather Ingram, *A History of the Irish Short Story* (Cambridge: Cambridge University Press, 2009).
12. See, for example, China Miéville, 'A Life in Writing', *Guardian* (14 May 2011), www.theguardian.com/books/2011/may/14/china-mieville-life-writing-genre [Accessed 19 March 2015]; and Kim Stanley Robinson, 'Science Fiction: The Stories of Now', *New Scientist*, 2726 (19 September 2009), 46–9.
13. In this regard, see also Jacques Derrida, 'The Law of Genre', *Acts of Literature*, ed. Derek Attridge (London: Routledge, 1992), pp. 221–52.
14. See Mary Eagleton's suggestive essay, 'Genre and Gender', *Re-Reading the Short Story*, ed. Clare Hanson (Basingstoke: Macmillan, 1989), pp. 56–68.
15. Quoted in Kerry Ryan, 'The Purpose of All Wars', *3:AM Magazine*, www.3ammagazine.com/3am/the-purpose-of-all-wars/ [Accessed 20 March 2015].
16. This was a hope that I had formerly expressed in *The Short Story: An Introduction* (Edinburgh: Edinburgh University Press, 2009), pp. 86–7. See also chapter 11, 'Creative Writing', *An Introduction to Literature*,

Writing and publishing the short story

Criticism and Theory, eds. Andrew Bennett and Nicholas Royle, 4th edn (Abingdon: Routledge, 2014), pp. 88–95; and Rob Pope, *Creativity: Theory, History, Practice* (London: Routledge, 2005). The economic and institutional forces to which creative-critical writing has been subject have been examined by, among others, Stefan Collini, *What Are Universities For?* (London: Penguin, 2012); Thomas Docherty, *For the University: Democracy and the Future of the Institution* (London: Bloomsbury, 2011); and Joanna Williams, *Consuming Higher Education: Why Learning Can't be Bought* (London: Bloomsbury, 2013). Marina Warner has recorded the pressures upon her as a creative writing tutor at the University of Essex in 'Learning My Lesson', *London Review of Books*, 37.6 (19 March 2015), 8–14.
17 See, for example, Ian Jack, 'Introduction', *Granta*, 81 (2003), 11.
18 As Ben Yagoda suggests in *About Town: The New Yorker and the World It Made* (London: Duckworth, 2000), the content of the *New Yorker* was historically more varied in its short story content. The stereotype of the well-made story was largely the construction of (often hostile) reviewers; its persistence in contemporary short fiction can be read as a detriment to formal innovation.
19 On the myth of the aura in art, see Walter Benjamin, 'The Work of Art in the Age of Mechanical Reproduction' (*1936*), *Illuminations*, ed. Hannah Arendt, trans. Harry Zohn, 2nd edn (London: Fontana, 1992), pp. 214–16. In his essay 'The Storyteller' from the same year, Benjamin accords an auratic power to the oral tale; the short story by contrast is a fallen art form. The contradictions between Benjamin's positions on minority, mass and folk-cultures echo Theodor Adorno's insistence on '*more* dialectics' in his correspondence with Benjamin. See *The Complete Correspondence, 1928–1940*, ed. Henri Lonitz, trans. Nicholas Walker (Cambridge: Polity, 1999), p. 131.
20 Frank O'Connor, *The Lonely Voice: A Study of the Short Story* (1963; Hoboken, NJ: Melville House, 2004), p. 17.
21 See also Paul March-Russell, 'Whose Culture? Whose Anarchy? The Short Story and the Bonfire of the Humanities', *Thresholds* (2011), http://blogs.chi.ac.uk/shortstoryforum/whose-culture-whose-anarchy/ [Accessed 23 March 2015].
22 Jeff Noon, 'Microspores #40', http://microspores.tumblr.com/post/162974 51732/40 [Accessed 25 March 2015].
23 A current list of print and electronic magazines can be found at Tania Hershman's website, *ShortStops*, http://shortstops.info/literary-magazines-that-publish-short-stories/ [Accessed 25 March 2015].
24 In 'The Art and Business of Short Fiction', as part of *Strange Horizons*' online symposium on 'The State of British SF and Fantasy' (28 July 2014), Nina Allan makes similar observations within the context of the science fiction story. www.strangehorizons.com/2014/20140728/1britsf-a.shtml#allan [Accessed 25 March 2015].
25 In lieu of the Save Our Short Story website, which is now defunct, an account of this survey can be found in chapter 5 of March-Russell, *The Short Story: An Introduction*. It is significant that this survey remains the only comprehensive overview of short story publishing – a successor is sorely needed. It is also significant that the group behind the short story campaign has since re-organized itself as the Book Trust, a primarily educational project with a broader remit than short fiction alone.

2

ANTHONY PATTERSON

Social realism in the short story

There has been a resurgence of interest in the formal complexities of social realism since its marginalization by many critics in the 1980s and 1990s, when realism was often viewed 'as the simple straw man whose role is only to show up the authentic and original literary or critical action occurring elsewhere'.[1] The collection of essays in which this comment by Rachel Bowlby appears, *Adventures in Realism* (2007), and other recent works such as Fredric Jameson's *Antinomies of Realism* (2013), challenge such critical attitudes, the former showing realism to be a complex negotiation between social reality and literary form, the latter exploring the equally complex relationship between narrative and affect.[2] A more nuanced and inclusive understanding of realism is pertinent here because if realism is dismissed merely as an impoverished interlude between the rich experimentations of romanticism and modernism then any survey of social realism in the short story would barely extend beyond the writing of Arthur Morrison. Happily this is not the case. Social realism endures, has been, and indeed is, more innovative and experimental than has often been considered. It is not, moreover, reducible to one sole purpose, ideology or style. As will be shown in this brief survey, there are many ways of 'doing' social realism.

Defining social realism, however, can be as difficult as defining the short story. Arthur Morrison's complaint in March 1897 that the term *realism* was used 'with no unanimity of intent' still resonates.[3] For the purpose of this chapter, social realism – as distinct from other types of realism such as psychological, magical or socialist – will broadly relate to fiction that specifically registers how social class forms and affects the individual. As a historical practice, social realism extended the subject matter of literature, invariably moving to its centre lower-class characters who had hitherto been moralized, sentimentalized or ignored by other genres of fiction. By the late nineteenth century, and partly through the influence of French naturalism, English social realism was often synonymous with depiction of social problems, slum fiction and slice-of-life documentary writing. While social realism need not necessarily be equated with stark depictions of working-class life, and while many other genres of fiction such as gothic, horror and romance may include elements of social realism, it would be fair to say that what sets apart social realism is its concentration on exploring quotidian life in ways that plausibly correlate to the lived experience of the lower-middle and working classes although, of course, such plausibility relies on adhering to a number of literary conventions that produce, to appropriate Roland Barthes, their reality effects.[4]

However dynamic and innovative social realism might be, the short story has not always been viewed as its most appropriate vehicle, the very brevity of its form often understood as an impediment to the exploration of complex social realities. For Georg Lukács, the short story cannot embody historical change and thus reveal the inner contradictions of social formations. Its very incompleteness 'is indicative of a pessimism that denies the revolutionary potential of art'.[5] The expansion of the short story in the 1890s, moreover, has been related to the demise of the three-decker novel, and thus its very development has been seen to come at the expense of the supposed greater mimetic certainties of the realist novel, or, in Fredric Jameson's vein, more in tune with the dominance of scene over narrative, which characterizes much modernist writing. Furthermore, the short story has its origins in magazine fiction, a commercial fiction arguably at odds with the kind of graphically disturbing depictions often associated with the genre.[6] As I will argue, however, social realism and the short story form have propitiously proved more compatible than many critics and commentators believed. For all of its supposed ontological and epistemological limitations, the genre of the social realist short story has proved impressively robust and adaptive.

The moral tale

The precise origins of the social realist short story are difficult to pin down, but the moral tales of improvement of the late eighteenth and the early nineteenth centuries offer a valuable starting point, if mainly one of departure. Whereas, for example, many later social realist stories depict working-class life for a predominantly middle-class readership, the moral tales of this earlier period, although read by all sections of society, were ostensibly addressed to the lower orders in an attempt to counteract the moral danger of the cheap novels and romances that were believed to have a pernicious effect on them. If social realism can never quite be severed from some form of didacticism, the short story as moral training for the lower classes, which would prevail into the nineteenth century in the form of temperance tracts, is not recognizably one of its traits.

The greatest exponent of these tales was arguably Hannah More, a friend of Edmund Burke and a member of the Bluestocking Circle. Possibly the most famous of More's tales is 'The Shepherd of Salisbury Plain', which appeared in one of More's *Cheap Repository Tracts*, an incredibly popular series that More claimed sold two million copies.[7] 'The Shepherd of Salisbury Plain' is a first person narrative told from the perspective of Mr Johnson, 'a very worthy and charitable man'.[8] He encounters the titular hero whose immersion in the Bible has taught him that it is better to be poor and exposed to heat and cold than it is to be rich and exposed to sin and temptation. Even so, through Mr Johnson's generosity, the shepherd is removed from his hovel and set up as a Sunday School teacher, so that through his 'pious councils' and 'prudent instructions' he can enable parishioners to understand and 'delight in the public worship of God'.[9] While depicting the living conditions of the lower orders, in its espousal of the enduring Christian values of humility and piety, the story is more akin to pastoral than social realism.

Dickens and Gaskell

To a degree, such moral training can also be found in the short stories of Charles Dickens. As if to prove Lukács right, Dickens's shorter fiction can lack the more vivid realism of his novels. However, *Sketches by Boz* (1836), a miscellany of sketches and tales, contains, as Dickens's biographer John Forster recognized, 'unusually truthful sketches of a sort of life between the middle class and the low, which […] was quite unhackneyed ground'.[10]

'A Drunkard's Death', for example, is a cautionary tale that charts a drunk's decline, culminating in his suicide. While recognizing that some are impelled to drink because of 'misery or misfortune' the narrator claims that '[b]y far the greater part have wilfully, and with open eyes, plunged into the gulf from which the man who once enters it never rises more'.[11] In contrast, in a sketch of a gin shop, Dickens argues that temperance societies could more effectively close gin shops through suggesting an 'antidote against hunger, filth, and foul air', rather than preaching against the evil consequences of drink.[12] The sketch contrasts the 'light and brilliancy' of the gin palace with the 'wretched houses' of those who frequent them, detailing the overcrowded and filthy conditions in which they live to underline that poverty rather than deficient morality is the cause of insobriety.[13] Arguably the most impressive piece in the miscellany is 'A Visit to Newgate'. Although again the piece is not a story, Dickens deploys narrative to convince his readers of the terrible mental anguish of the condemned man as he 'wakes cold and wretched' from 'his dream of escape' to face the sober reality of his cell, in which '[e]very object [...] is too frightfully real to admit of doubt or mistake'.[14] The passage is relayed with startling immediacy; the felon's feelings on waking to his grim circumstances are all narrated with the kind of evocative detail that would become one of the trademarks of later social realist fiction.

Like Dickens, Elizabeth Gaskell wrote a variety of short fiction, but comes closest to social realism with stories such as 'Libbie Marsh's Three Eras'. The story charts the developing relationship between a seamstress and a crippled boy and his mother, a washerwoman. As Shirley Foster has noted, 'Libbie Marsh's Three Eras' is about moral transformation and self-sacrifice.[15] The former can be seen in the changed behaviour of Margaret Hall, the boy's mother, who becomes 'a different woman to the scold of the neighbourhood [...] touched and softened by the two purifying angels, Sorrow and Love', the latter in the sacrifices of the titular heroine who saves up her money to buy the boy a canary for Saint Valentine's Day.[16] If moralist traits persist, the story also contrasts the harsh realities of 'ugly, smoky Manchester' with the rural idyll of Dunham, a 'complete sylvan repose' which laps 'the soul in green images of the country'.[17] Another Gaskell story, 'Lizzie Leigh', treats a favourite subject of social realists, the fallen woman, although realistic detail is again bridled by Christian morality as its eponymous protagonist repents her 'wickedness'. Lizzie's fall, caused by her ill treatment in city life, is couched in Victorian melodrama. The story becomes a Christian parable as the prodigal daughter returns home, praying 'always and ever for forgiveness'.[18] The story emphasizes Lizzie's sinful ways rather than the environmental conditions that lead her to prostitution. While these examples of Gaskell's short fiction reflect on the social and economic conditions of the lower classes, Christian values and consequently moral agency still predominate and thus the stories tend to offer less nuanced representations of class than can be found in Gaskell's novels such as *Mary Barton* (1848) and *North and South* (1855).

Arthur Morrison and New Realism

A less sentimental and moralistic fiction can be found in the work of later nineteenth-century writers such as Arthur Morrison and George Gissing. Gissing's 'The Day of Silence', for example, makes an interesting comparison with Dickens's 'A Drunkard's Death'. Gissing's story also narrates how imbibing alcohol may precipitate a watery demise, but this is not a cautionary tale even though the tipsy Jem Pollock accidentally causes the death of a father and son. 'The Day of Silence' depicts the loving relationships of an impoverished family. Mrs Burden is proud of her son and although husband and wife argue, they do so partly because '[d]omestic calm as understood by the people who have a whole house to themselves is impossible in a Southwark garret'; they wrangle 'without bitterness, without vile abuse'.[19] Unlike More's exemplary shepherd, Dickens's wretched drunk or Gaskell's redeemed prostitute, the Burden family are seen, to a much greater degree, from the inside; their tale is not one of exemplary virtue, degenerate vice or moral redemption, but of quotidian tragedy.

Published three years before 'The Day of Silence', Rudyard Kipling's 'The Record of Badalia Herodsfoot' prefigures the slum short story made popular by Arthur Morrison. The story narrates Badalia Herodsfoot's death at the hands of her drunkard husband as she attempts to protect the charitable funds that have been placed in her keeping. The story can be seen as a transitional text in that it still strikes a sentimental note as Badalia refuses to denounce her husband, and surely echoes the theme of Christian sacrifice when Badalia exclaims, 'Gawd forgive you Tom for what you …' as her husband beats her to death; however, Kipling's attempts to represent working-class life by replicating dialect and graphically describing the ills of poverty, drunkenness and violence with minimal authorial intrusion would be followed by many later realist writers.[20]

It is moot to argue over the extent to which what came to be denominated 'new realism' was influenced by the naturalism of Emile Zola, but Morrison's *Tales of Mean Streets* (1894) arguably comes closest to Zola's sense of clinical observation. The sense of detachment is certainly strong in the first and perhaps finest story in the volume, 'Lizerunt', which narrates the major adult events in the life of Elizabeth Hunt, including her courtship, the births of her children and, as with Badalia Herodsfoot, her brutal treatment at the hands of her husband, Billy Chope. The story ends with Chope throwing Lizerunt out onto the street so that she can prostitute herself for him. Although Morrison utilizes cockney dialogue and clearly evokes scenes and events with which he had some familiarity, 'Lizerunt' also contains passages such as the following:

> Of course there were quarrels very soon; for the new Mrs. Chope, less submissive at first than her mother-in-law, took a little breaking in, and a liberal renewal of the manual treatment once applied in her courting days. But the quarrels between the women were comforting to Billy; a diversion and a source of better service.[21]

It has been argued that Morrison was writing against the grain of the assumptions of the philanthropic middle classes who tended to both oversimplify and over-sentimentalize the slum dwellers of the East End.[22] In this way, Morrison's fiction disturbs a middle-class narrative of working-class suffering and offsets the fetishization of the poor evident in the attitudes of those who went slumming in the East End. However, a tension can exist in Morrison's narratives between the adoption of an affectless prose – which might succeed in rescuing working-class otherness from the philanthropic view of a monolithic poor – and the detached narratorial voice (an example which has been quoted previously) through which the poor are rendered. Morrison the observer can, on occasions, appear as loftily removed from the culture he describes as the philanthropic middle classes with whom he takes issue.

Such distance is also evident in the short fiction of Hubert Crackanthorpe, who is credited with bringing much of French naturalism to the English short story. The first story of the collection *Wreckage* (1893), 'Profiles', features a typical naturalist decline plot in which a young woman begins by deceiving her fiancé and eventually succumbs to prostitution, disappearing into the world of London vice, last glimpsed in 'a little public-house at the back of Regent Street'.[23] Perhaps the most naturalistic story in tone is 'A Struggle for Life', in which a mother goes to beg money for her child from its presumed father as he carouses with prostitutes only to end by prostituting herself. The first person narrative is told with some Olympian disdain for what the narrator describes as 'these dregs of the population':

> It was a Saturday night, so the place was quite full – bargemen with grimy furrows across their bronzed face[s]; plenty of typical river casuals sucking stumpy clay-pipes; in a corner a group of pasty-faced youths quarrelling over their greasy cards; and scattered about the room some riverside prostitutes, their cheap finery all bedraggled with mud.[24]

Alan Sillitoe's claim that Arthur Morrison's fiction could treat the working class as if 'they lived in a zoo' is even more applicable to Crackanthorpe.[25]

Crackanthorpe, like Gissing and Morrison, extended what could be written about in the short story and challenged both the aesthetics and perceived function of the form by introducing characters and milieus ignored by many mainstream writers. At their best, such as Gissing's 'The Day of Silence', these slum stories offer subtle narratives that undermine accepted social understandings of the lower classes, yet at their worst, as in Crackanthorpe's 'A Struggle for Life', the attempt at objective narration can often give a sense of the lower classes as a very distant other and the reader engaged in a vicarious act of late-Victorian slumming. The point, though, is less to criticize Crackanthorpe than to register that central to the development of social realism has been the difficult struggle to authentically represent social realities, however shocking, in ways that were accessible, and to a degree amenable, to a largely middle-class readership.

ANTHONY PATTERSON

Social realism in the early twentieth century

In the early twentieth century the slum fiction of the 1890s gave way to more varied representations of the lower classes. The Edwardians whom Virginia Woolf lambasted as representative of an outmoded material realism, H. G. Wells, Arnold Bennett and John Galsworthy, all produced a substantial number of short stories, although Wells's stories do not stray much beyond scientific romance.[26] The characters in Bennett's and Galsworthy's short fiction often focus on the middle or lower-middle classes. When lower-class characters are depicted in Galsworthy, such as Megan in 'The Apple Tree' and the unnamed prostitute in 'Virtue', they are often viewed through the gaze and concerns of those who belong to classes above them.[27] Bennett's 'Death of Simon Fuge' concerns the cultural differences between metropolitan refinement and provincial sincerity.[28] His Five Towns characters are educated art and music enthusiasts, but also down-to-earth pragmatists who care as much about council rates and the local football team as they do about the recently deceased and artistically acclaimed local painter Simon Fuge. Here Bennett, whose own background was lower class and provincial, examines a cultural and regional divide through the voice of a refined narrator exploring, if ironically, the heart of potteries' darkness. Such divides would be increasingly thematized by a number of lower-middle- and working-class writers of the twentieth century whose sense of social and cultural dislocation would increasingly complicate the kind of hermetic view of the lower classes as witnessed by some earlier writers of social realist fiction.

More obscure than Woolf's Edwardians are short story writers such as A. E. Coppard and Neil Lyons. While Coppard is perhaps more famous for his supernatural tales, some of his short fiction falls within the social realist tradition even if the setting tends to be rural rather than urban. Indeed, in 'Weep Not My Wanton' a poeticized rural setting is contrasted with the violent actions of a drunken father who strikes his young son believing he has lost a sixpence. The story's denouement reveals the son has taken his punishment to safeguard the money for his mother.[29] Neil Lyons's 'Chummie, An Interlude' also involves a sixpence and alcohol as it narrates an encounter between a drunk begging for money and a pompous narrator. While in Coppard's story the space between educated narrator and lower-class character is narrowed by the sympathetic depiction of the boy and his mother, in 'Chummie', Lyons deploys irony to show the contempt the narrator, a man of 'principles', shows for the drunk he describes as 'a debased and bestial brother, young, but indescribably soiled with sin and dirt'.[30] Thus the undeserving poor drunk is viewed through the condescending lens of a self-righteous middle-class narrator. If Morrison depicts the working class in an attempt to displace a limiting bourgeois sentimentalism, Lyons attacks a bourgeois conceit of social superiority that moralizes poverty. However, the narrator's disdain in 'Chummie' for a dreg of the population also has parodic resonance with Hubert Crackanthorpe's detached narrator in 'A Struggle for Life'.

One cannot leave the first half of the twentieth century without some consideration of modernism, which has dominated British literary studies of this period. A firm line has often been drawn between realist and modernist fiction, the short story viewed as a vehicle for the more experimental fiction of modernism with its elliptic, fragmentary nature and its concentration on what Henri Bergson called *durée*. However, James Joyce's *Dubliners* (1914), for example, a seminal modernist text, clearly depicts the stultifying social environment of contemporary Dublin. A story such as 'Eveline' emphasizes the limitations of the social and patriarchal structures that cast their paralysis over Joyce's Dublin characters. The case could also be made with reference to the short fiction of D. H. Lawrence. 'Odour of Chrysanthemums' might focus on the epiphanic sense of otherness a wife experiences for her husband after his body is returned home after a mining accident, but the narrative also vividly depicts working-class life. Liggins, Maunder and Robbins note that the story's 'detailism is what is found in realist writing' even if it 'is overlaid with other forms of significance, among which the symbol of the flower is key'.[31] Lawrence's use of symbolism is unquestionable, but Liggins makes the further claim that Lawrence's short fiction is modernist short fiction because it 'evokes rather than describes'.[32] Perhaps rather than emphasizing a divide between realist and modernist practice, one might see Lawrence's working-class short stories as extending the range of social realist expression. Lawrence is clearly not a social realist in the sense that Arthur Morrison is, but his short fiction, at least at the time of writing 'Odour of Chrysanthemums', is not shorn of interest in the effects of the social environment on individuals whose own ideas are often at variance with social understandings, values and mores. Indeed, this struggle, if in a radically different context, between the individual's sense of lived experience and the demands of social expectation is, as we shall see, central to the short fiction of many working-class writers after the Second World War.

The fifties

The post-war period witnessed a renewed interest in social realist narratives in a variety of media, including the short story. Writers such as Alan Sillitoe, Stan Barstow and Nell Dunn produced new and often controversial representations of working-class life. An influential forerunner of these writers was Sid Chaplin, whose most famous story, 'The Leaping Lad', Stan Barstow acknowledged, had 'shown us all that it was possible to write without meretriciousness from the inside of working class life'.[33] Chaplin captures as much as any short story writer of the period the authentic voice and concerns of the working class, in Chaplin's case of the Durham pit community in which he was born, in which he was schooled and in which he worked. The narratorial detachment previously noted is breached by Chaplin's intimate knowledge of chapel, pub and pit and his nuanced awareness of the rhythms of local speech. In 'Hands', a young miner is rebuked by his father for his previous night's drunken behaviour. Both work in the same pit and the story narrates an accident in which the father dies; the final image is of his severed hands, a sight witnessed by the surviving son. The harsh working conditions of the miners are contrasted with the tender bonds of father and son as nature above the ground, 'the bursting joy of spring', is juxtaposed with the locked gates of the cage that drops them into the dark world below, 'a spider web of galleries', to become part of 'the vast machine driving through the strata barrier for black spoil'.[34]

If Chaplin's stories revolve around the tightknit mining communities of Durham, where generational bonds still hold firm, Chaplin's admirer, Stan Barstow, writes of working-class societies in which community has already begun to fracture and the young are set against the traditional values and norms of their parents. In 'The Human Element', Harry West is a loner, a fitter by trade, as he announces himself, who claims he prefers motorbikes to girls, but in a fit of desire becomes engaged to his landlord's daughter. The story is comic in tone as West's prepossession and misogynistic disdain are undermined by his mounting desire for Thelma Baynes, who, although West describes her as 'simple', clearly outwits him.[35] However, beneath the humour, Barstow depicts a society of dull convention to which West's response is to take pride in material possessions such as his motorbike and his new shoes. In 'The Desperadoes', Vince Elspey, the leader of a small Teddy-boy gang, stabs to death a bouncer who has humiliated him. Through exploring Vince's interior world in which a violent destructiveness vies with feelings of tenderness for a young girl, the story demonstrates a new interest in youth culture and especially delinquency. Chaplin's world of working-class solidarity in the face of exploitative working conditions is replaced by one in which a new emerging youth culture resists social conformity, one in which having a 'bit of fun' and 'breaking out now and again' is a response to a ubiquitous 'they' who 'want everything their way' and 'ordinary decent people' are 'the stupid ones, the ones everybody puts on'.[36]

Similar sentiments can be found in Alan Sillitoe's 'The Loneliness of the Long-Distance Runner', a narrative about Smith, a borstal boy and a promising long-distance runner who is entered to compete in the Borstal Blue Ribbon Prize Cup. Although clearly the fastest runner, Smith stops before the end of the race to prevent the borstal and especially its governor from basking in the glory his run would bring and because, as Smith says, winning means 'running right into their white-gloved wall-barred hands and grinning mugs and staying there for the rest of my natural long life'.[37] The story is told from Smith's viewpoint and addresses the reader directly as an 'In-law bloke' as opposed to an outlaw such as Smith.[38] As with 'The Desperadoes', 'The Loneliness of the Long-Distance Runner' reflects a growing antinomianism among the young working class opposed to the state which regulates working-class life and perpetuates the class system, but also at odds with the traditional working-class values as those represented by Smith's father, who has worked all his life in a mill for meagre reward.

Although Nell Dunn's *Up the Junction* (1963) is not short of male delinquents, this series of stories concentrates more on the hedonistic response of women to the drudgery of work. The stories are vignettes of London life set in illegal abortion clinics, prisons, streets, pubs and clip joints. The stories depict less rebelliousness against the establishment than the escape the women seek from the tedium of their factory jobs in sexual escapades, fashion, pop music and workmate solidarity. The stories are plotless first person accounts, which intersperse snatches of pop songs among keen observations and dialogue. 'The Gold Blouse' is set in a sweet factory and narrates the various conversations of the women who work there. The story culminates in one of the girls, Sheila, who is hunchbacked and pregnant, revealing a gold blouse under her tatty clothes. The girls in the factory modernize the blouse, cutting off the arms and making a V in its back. The story ends with an image of the gold sleeves: 'On the brown lino, amid discarded sweet papers and cigarette ends, the gold sleeves lay gleaming in the raw electric light.'[39] Dunn's work is both clearly social realist in its focus on vividly portraying the world of working-class women, but also experimental in its abandonment of the kind of external detailing and plot structures associated with earlier forms of social realism. The stories often work, as does 'The Gold Blouse', by poignant and comic juxtapositions that reveal both the vibrant humour of her characters and the often fraught circumstances of their lives. As much as Barstow and Sillitoe, Dunn reflects a changing social and cultural landscape in which youth culture, hedonism and materialism conflict with more traditional class values.

Contemporary social realism

In *Union Street* (1982), a series of linked stories about the often desperate lives of women, Pat Barker clearly follows in the tradition of social realist writers such as Nell Dunn. John Brannigan claims that Barker interacts with the genre 'with a number of literary techniques and styles less familiar to social realism', although again an argument could be made that Barker, by doing so, and like previous writers such as Lawrence and Dunn, further extends the range of social realist writing.[40] The title of the 'novel' is ironic: union either in terms of family or workers' solidarity seems to belong to a distant past; the street is no longer the centre of community, but the location of atomized and often hopeless lives. The first story, 'Kelly Brown', marks the passage of a young girl into adulthood through the trauma of rape. Barker adopts what Brannigan calls an omnipresent rather than omnipotent third person narrative which moves 'between characters without moving beyond what they know and how they think'.[41] Although dysfunctional families are not necessarily the preserve of post-industrial fiction, as the stories of Morrison and Gissing amply demonstrate, a sense of post-industrial malaise broods over the lives of Kelly's family. Neither Kelly's family home nor its environs offer shelter or protection, the streets are derelict outside, the houses unkempt inside, the sky is described as lifeless, a mist hangs around the chemical works; light is described as orange and greasy on the night that Kelly is raped outside a disused factory. On Kelly's nocturnal wanderings she comes across tramps, teenagers having sex, sexual predators and abandoned babies. If Barstow and Sillitoe show conscious youthful rebellion against working-class traditions and values, and Nell Dunn's *Up the Junction* celebrates the lives of working-class women even as it depicts their troubles, Barker's *Union Street* shows working-class traditions and values disintegrating in the wake of socio-economic and cultural change, leaving working-class women with little at all to celebrate.

A writer who also incorporates modernist techniques into the social realist tradition is James Kelman. Kelman's stories about the marginalized working classes are characterized by a concentration on scene rather than plot, by narrative irresolution, minimalist concrete prose, and a concern with exploring subjective experience. However, unlike most modernist fiction, Kelman's stories are told through the demotic language of his largely dispossessed working-class characters. Thus Kelman marshals modernist strategies for political effects; his fractured, elliptic, plotless stories reflect a fractured reality for the marginalized sections of the working class he depicts that seeks to counteract the manufactured realism of contemporary capitalist society. In 'Greyhound for Breakfast' Ronnie casually contemplates suicide as he walks a greyhound he has bought for eighty pounds, frightened to go home to his wife to confess what he has done. The story is told from Ronnie's perspective, often in stream of consciousness, the style appropriate for the circularity of Ronnie's walks and his seemingly aimless life. Indeed, for Ronnie all life consists of 'is running round and round trying to fucking catch it, a crock of gold, and did they catch it, did they fuck'.[42] Contrary to Lukács's critique of the limitations of the short story, Kelman's fiction demonstrates the effectiveness of the form to reflect the psychological interiority of the broken lives of his Glaswegian characters.

The idea that the short story might be the most effective form for social realism is also reinforced by the work of another Scottish writer, Irvine Welsh. Although his most famous work, *Trainspotting* (1993), is often classified as a novel, its episodic nature has also been recognized as 'a ragged accretion of short stories' by Michael Brockington and 'a series of unrelated stories' by Sarah Hemming.[43] Interestingly, *Trainspotting* has also been viewed as a critique of social realism as a bourgeois literature often written about but not by those it portrays and one that is based on a limiting category of class, a category perhaps inappropriate for Welsh's Leith characters.[44] The point has also been made that Welsh was writing in a post-Thatcherite era in which the very idea of society itself was questioned, and when alternatives to capitalism often appeared less tenable.[45] However, a counterargument could be made that much social realism from Arthur Morrison to James Kelman has emerged from within working-class cultures, however fractured or diverse, and has been produced by writers who are fully aware of the complex difficulties of representation in what remains a predominantly bourgeois form. Indeed, Welsh might very well be seen to be part of such a tradition. Moreover, Welsh, like other writers discussed in this chapter, shows the extent to which social realism is not historically specific, but historically contingent in terms of its aesthetics and its politics. It is protean and inherently receptive to social change if also reflective of a persistent need to explore the lives of those who have been and still often are excluded from mainstream society. It is for these reasons as much as any others that social realism merits more scholarly attention than it currently receives.

NOTES

1 Rachel Bowlby, 'Foreword', *Adventures in Realism*, ed. Matthew Beaumont (Oxford: Blackwell, 2007), p. vii.
2 Fredric Jameson, *Antinomies of Realism* (London: Verso, 2013).
3 Arthur Morrison, 'What Is a Realist', *New Review* (March 1897), quoted in Lillian R. Furst and Peter N. Scrine, *Naturalism* (Fakenham: Methuen, 1971), p. 7.

4 See Roland Barthes, 'The Reality Effect', *The Rustle of Language*, trans. Richard Howard (Oxford: Blackwell, 1986), pp. 141–8.
5 Paul March-Russell, *The Short Story: An Introduction* (Edinburgh: Edinburgh University Press), p. 121.
6 See Emma Liggins, Andrew Maunder and Ruth Robbins, *The British Short Story* (Basingstoke: Palgrave Macmillan, 2010).
7 Anne Stott, *Hannah More* (Cambridge: Cambridge University Press, 2003), p. 143.
8 Hannah More, 'The Shepherd of Salisbury Plain', *The Works of Hannah More* (1794; New York: Harper, 1843), pp. 190–200 (p. 190).
9 More, *Works*, p. 200.
10 John Forster, *Forster's Life of Dickens*, ed. George Gissing (London: Chapman, 1903), p. 42.
11 Charles Dickens, 'The Drunkard's Death', *Sketches by Boz* (1836; London: Chapman, 1854), pp. 287–304 (p. 287).
12 Dickens, 'Gin Shops', *Sketches by Boz*, pp. 111–13 (p. 113).
13 Dickens, 'Gin Shops', pp. 111–13 (p. 113).
14 Dickens, 'Visit to Newgate', *Sketches by Boz*, pp. 122–30 (p. 130).
15 Shirley Foster, 'Elizabeth Gaskell's Shorter Pieces', *The Cambridge Companion to Elizabeth Gaskell*, ed. Jill Matus (Cambridge: Cambridge University Press, 2007), pp. 108–30.
16 Elizabeth Gaskell, 'Libbie Marsh's Three Eras', *Lizzie Leigh and Other Tales* (Leipzig: Tauchnitz, 1855), pp. 318–46 (p. 346).
17 Gaskell, 'Libbie Marsh's Three Eras', p. 332.
18 Gaskell, 'Lizzie Leigh', *Lizzie Leigh,* pp. 1–34 (p. 34).
19 George Gissing, 'The Day of Silence', *Human Odds and Ends* (London: Lawrence and Bullen, 1898), pp. 92–110 (p. 97).
20 Rudyard Kipling, 'Record of Badalia Herodsfoot', *Many Inventions* (1893; New York: Double Day, 1931), pp. 326–60 (p. 352).
21 Arthur Morrison, 'Lizerunt', *Tales of Mean Streets* (London: Methuen, 1894), pp. 31–64 (p. 43).
22 See Adrian Hunter, 'Arthur Morrison and the Tyranny of Sentimental Charity', *English Literature in Transition*, 56.3 (2013), 292–312.
23 Hubert Crackanthorpe, 'Profiles', *Wreckage* (London: Heinemann, 1893), pp. 1–55 (p. 53).
24 Hubert Crackanthorpe, 'A Struggle for Life', *Wreckage*, pp. 107–24 (p. 107).
25 Quoted in Hunter, 'Arthur Morrison', p. 292.
26 See Virginia Woolf, *Mr Bennett and Mrs Brown* (London: Hogarth, 1924).
27 See John Galsworthy, *The Apple Tree and Other Stories* (London: Penguin, 1988).
28 Arnold Bennett, 'The Death of Simon Fuge', *The Grim Smile of the Five Towns* (1907; Maryland: Serenity, 2009), pp. 113–59.
29 A. E. Coppard, 'Weep Not My Wanton', *Adam & Eve & Pinch Me* (New York: Knopf, 1922), pp. 45–52.
30 Neil Lyon, 'Chummie, An Interlude', *Stories of Today and Yesterday* (London: Harrap, 1929), pp. 120–3 (p. 120).
31 Liggins et al., *British Short Story,* p. 62.

32 Liggins et al., *British Short Story*, p. 63. Indeed, Lawrence's short story was seen as a response to Ford Madox Ford's call as the editor of the *English Review* for 'a new realism that reflected the lives of the working class and the poor'. See Janet Hubbard Harris, *The Short Fiction of D. H. Lawrence* (New Brunswick, NJ: Rutgers, 1984), p. 26.
33 Stan Barstow, Foreword to Sid Chaplin, *In Blackberry Time*, eds. Michael and Rene Chaplain (Newcastle: Blood Axe Books, 1987), pp. 11–13 (p. 12).
34 Sid Chaplin, 'Hands', *The Leaping Lad and Other Stories* (1946; Harlow: Longman, 1970), pp. 30–5 (pp. 31–2).
35 Stan Barstow, 'The Human Element', *The Desperadoes and Other Stories* (1961; London: Corgi, 1973), pp. 9–18.
36 Stan Barstow, 'The Desperadoes', *Desperadoes*, pp. 154–87.
37 Alan Sillitoe, 'The Loneliness of the Long-Distance Runner', *The Loneliness of the Long-Distance Runner* (1959; London: Allen, 1988), pp. 7–54 (p. 40).
38 Alan Sillitoe, 'The Loneliness of the Long-Distance Runner', p. 45.
39 Nell Dunn, 'The Gold Blouse', *Up the Junction* (1963; London: Virago, 2013), pp. 19–26 (p. 26).
40 John Brannigan, *Pat Barker* (Manchester: Manchester University Press, 2005) p. 15.
41 Brannigan, *Pat Barker*, p. 15.
42 James Kelman, 'Greyhound for Breakfast', *Greyhound for Breakfast* (1987; London: Mirnerva, 1996), pp. 206–30 (p. 226).
43 Quoted in Matt McGuire, 'Welsh's Novels', *The Edinburgh Companion to Irvine Welsh*, ed. Berthold Schoene (Edinburgh: Edinburgh University Press, 2010), pp. 19–30 (p. 19).
44 See Schoene, 'Introduction', *Edinburgh Companion to Irvine Welsh*, pp. 1–9.
45 Schoene, 'Introduction', p. 7.

3

BARBARA KORTE

The short story and the anxieties of empire

Short stories, colonialism and postcolonialism

The British Empire's mechanisms of domination and its ideology of white racial superiority eventually gave rise to new societies and identities, including an ethnically and culturally diverse United Kingdom. The short story appears to be 'disproportionately represented in the literatures of colonial and postcolonial cultures'.[1] This is partly explained by the lack of a book market in many colonial and postcolonial contexts, which gives periodicals a special importance for the dissemination of literature, and with it a preference for short over long forms of fiction. More essentially, as a form that has been perceived as 'fragmented and restless',[2] inclined to dissidence,[3] and 'particularly suited to the representation of liminal or problematized identities', the short story seems to speak 'directly to and about those whose sense of self, region, state or nation is insecure'.[4] It is an ideal literary space for articulating the moments of translation and hybridity in which new identities come into being,[5] and it has recently been discussed in the framework of 'minor' literature that 'occurs in a language which is "deterritorialized" [...] and thus predisposed "for strange and minor uses"'.[6] Whether the short story is 'uniquely adaptable or amenable to the colonial or postcolonial context as a whole' is hard to determine, but its use 'by particular writers in particular situations' reveals its special contribution to 'the literature of colonial disturbance'.[7] A focus on the particular also suits the heterogeneity of the colonial context, which comprised white self-governing colonies, crown colonies ruled from London, protectorates as well as chartered territories,[8] and which later gave rise to a great variety of 'new' English literatures. This chapter will first look at stories about colonial India and Africa, and then turn to stories that respond to one specific constellation of postcoloniality: the situation generated by migration from the (former) colonial periphery to the (former) colonial centre. For both contexts, the modern short story's defining features – such as allusiveness, significant omission or open-endedness – have been employed to reflect the tensions and anxieties produced by the British colonial project and its aftermath.

Colonial short stories

During the era of high empire (c 1870 to 1918), British writers used the short story to map the empire, its ideology and its practices. How popular such stories were is suggested by the fact that a twelve-volume selection, *'Blackwood' Tales from the Outposts*, could be extracted from just a single magazine.[9] Many colonial stories were written with strong imperialistic conviction, such as G. A. Henty's tales for young and adult readers that show the same spirit as his novels,[10] but others inspect the imperial project more critically. It is in 'the precariousness of this shadowy picture of the empire' that the short story came into its own and disrupted 'the ostensible ideological self-positioning of colonial adventure tales'.[11] However, even critical stories satisfied their readers' fascination with the otherness of the colonial world. In Somerset Maugham's definition, the 'exotic story' is a type of story whose scene 'is set in some country little known to the majority of readers, and which deals with the reactions upon the white man of his sojourn in an alien land and the effect which contact with peoples of another race has upon him'.[12] The phrasing of this definition reveals that Maugham's notion of the exotic was 'inseparable from considerations of British colonialism in all of its political and racial, philosophical and psychological, complexity',[13] and this is illustrated by his own stories. In 'The Force of Circumstance' (1924), for instance, an Englishwoman cannot understand that her new husband, who was born in Malaya, lived with a 'native' wife at his outstation before their marriage and has three children with her. To him, this is the 'regular thing' because the 'circumstances out here are peculiar',[14] but she leaves him after a few months and the man permits the Malay woman to return because he cannot bear the loneliness of his remote post. Maugham traced the origin of the exotic story to Rudyard Kipling, who coined the notorious phrase 'The White Man's Burden' in his poem of 1899. It was above all through the short story, however, that Kipling captured the Anglo-Indian experience during the final decades of the nineteenth century. These stories illustrate that the empire was 'at its most anxious' when it was 'at its most triumphal',[15] and that its attempts to 'set up distinct categories and impose racial divisions' were precarious because colonial territories always remained 'contact zones criss-crossed by other cultural perceptions, multiple different histories and stories'.[16]

Born in Bombay and familiar with India's cultures and people, Kipling became the canonical writer on Anglo-India. He was not the only voice of the raj, and not the only author to turn to the short story; in particular, two women writers, Flora Annie Steel and Alice Perrin, have been rediscovered as writers who presented the raj with other themes and from other perspectives than Kipling.[17] But Kipling's Indian stories are themselves more complex and ambivalent than some earlier critics assumed who saw Kipling merely as an apologist of imperial rule. Kipling's stories do not simply indulge in a picturesque exoticism or present the adventure of Empire with the aplomb of a Henty story. Believing in responsible imperialism, Kipling portrayed above all the efforts and human cost with which the empire was maintained, and he also showed some sympathy for Indians and their culturally different points of view.[18]

Most of Kipling's Indian stories were first published in India and for the Anglo-Indian community who served the raj. Kipling returned to this community in 1882, after finishing his education in England, and worked as a journalist for the *Civil and Military Gazette* (founded 1872) and later the *Pioneer* (founded 1865). He rose to popularity when he published his first collection, *Plain Tales from the Hills* (1888), in Calcutta and two years later in London. His stories about Anglo-India appealed to readers in the metropolis not only because they depicted a foreign world, but also because their style and use of the form was, as Walter Allen notes, fresh, 'based on the vernacular, on speed and directness of narration, on an unerring eye and economy of means'.[19] Kipling's stories have strong narrative voices, but their narration is only superficially self-assured, being marked by irony, contradictions and disconcerting omissions. His Anglo-Indian characters are likewise ambivalent: they are imbued with a basic belief in white supremacy and the necessity to rule people who supposedly cannot rule themselves, but they also, in John McClure's words, 'perceive themselves as existing at the very limits of exposure and anxiety',[20] and quite a few are precariously attracted by India's otherness. Such frictions within the Anglo-Indian experience emerge most poignantly in stories that address interracial love relationships. These relationships and with them the perceived risk of miscegenation were not infrequent, but they were considered a severe transgression of the borders through which the Anglo-Indian community tried to shield itself from the Indian 'other'. The taboo of mixing is proclaimed authoritatively at the beginning of 'Beyond the Pale' (1888): 'A man should, whatever happens, keep to his own caste, race and breed.' This apodictic statement by the narrator seems to be illustrated by the ensuing narrative in which wilful transgression of the 'safe limits of decent everyday society' leads to disaster. Christopher Trejago, an imperial official with 'too deep an interest in native life',[21] falls in love with a widowed Indian girl 'who prayed the Gods, day and night, to send her a lover; for she did not approve of

The short story and the anxieties of empire

living alone'.[22] When the secret relationship is revealed to the girl's family, who see their own taboos violated, the girl's hands are cut off at the wrists, and Trejago is haunted by the event for the rest of his life.

Helen Bauer notes that Kipling often places his male Anglo-Indians 'at the axis of where physical and psychic survival intersect with allegiance to socially approved values', thus demonstrating 'both the precariousness of those values and, simultaneously, man's dependence on them' as a safeguard against psychological disintegration in an alien and exhausting environment.[23] 'At the End of the Passage' (1888) introduces four characters with a high risk of disintegration because their service turns them into 'lonely folk who understood the dread meaning of loneliness'.[24] One of them, the engineer Hummil, is about to break under the stress of his Indian colonial experience. He is so overworked that he cannot sleep any more, develops hallucinations of a blind face that chases him down a passage, and eventually dies of fear. The community and care of his friends no longer provide a defence against the strains which 'responsible' imperialism brings with it.

'The Man Who Would Be King' (1888) takes another approach. Almost a parable of imperial adventure, the story dissects what happens when imperialist desire is pursued without a sense of duty and responsibility. Daniel Dravot and his companion Peachey Carnehan are uneducated men whose imperialist ambitions are driven by selfish concerns. They have decided that India is too small for them and proceed to unexplored Kafiristan, where they manage to bring some parts of the country under their control. Dravot is crowned as king and worshipped as a god, with Carnehan as his co-ruler. At first the men even manage to improve the administration and agriculture of their realm. Then, however, Dravot's imperial aspirations become unrestrained ('we shall be Emperors – Emperors of the Earth!'),[25] and when he also desires a woman as his queen, the indigenous priests begin to suspect his godlike status and instigate a rebellion against him – an event which Carnehan compares to one of the British Empire's greatest shocks, the so-called Indian Mutiny of 1857. Just as the British had not expected their Indian soldiers and subjects to rise against them, Dravot has misjudged his situation and arrogantly endangered the belief in superiority on which his rule depended. Dravot is killed, but Carnehan survives the crucifixion to which he is subjected and is sent back to India, with Dravot's severed but still crowned head in his luggage. A broken man, he tells his story to the frame narrator, a journalist who leaves it to the readers to judge Carnehan's narrative about selfish rule.

With its morally questionable protagonists, 'The Man Who Would Be King' has been compared to Joseph Conrad's 'An Outpost of Progress' (1897).[26] This story is set at the time of the so-called Scramble for Africa

45

when many European powers attempted to get a share of the 'Dark Continent'. Conrad was born in Russian-ruled Poland, the son of a patriot who resisted the czar's imperialism. With this experience as a subject of colonial power, and what he later observed in the wider world as a merchant seaman, Conrad judges colonialism more harshly than Kipling. Like the longer 'Heart of Darkness' (1899/1902), 'An Outpost of Progress' is set in the Belgian Congo, which was infamous for its reckless exploitation of people and resources. The story contrasts the limited perception of its characters with that of the external narrator whose scathing irony marks the story's tone. Its title 'exploits one of the most familiar phrases in imperialist rhetoric' and its main characters embody two institutions of imperial rule:[27] Kayerts is an administrator, and his assistant Carlier a former soldier. However, from the outset they are characterized as 'perfectly insignificant and incapable' opportunists whose failure is predictable when they are put in charge of an isolated station of the Great Trading Company. Finding themselves in a disconcerting, strange 'wilderness' and in contact with 'pure unmitigated savagery, with primitive nature and primitive man',[28] they feel uplifted by the rhetoric of an article about 'Our Colonial Expansion' that speaks of 'the rights and duties of civilization, of the sacredness of the civilizing work' and praises the men who bring 'light, and faith and commerce to the dark places of the earth'.[29] Kayerts and Carlier fail this high-flown rhetoric in all three respects. While Kipling's servants of Empire perform their duties with stoic endurance, Conrad's two characters gradually lose control while they eagerly await the arrival of the steamer that will take them back to the civilized world. They are unable even to resist their African employee Makola, who sells their station hands to slave dealers because they require the ivory he gets in exchange. After tolerating this inhumanity, the two Europeans succumb to moral and physical decay. Their crisis culminates when the steamer is late and they run out of provisions. In the end, as they struggle over the last sugar for their coffee, Kayerts shoots Carlier and then commits suicide just as, ironically, the steamer is finally approaching. He is found hanged on the cross of his predecessor's grave by the 'Managing Director of the Great Civilizing Company (since we know that civilization follows trade)',[30] as the narrator states cynically. Kayerts's swollen tongue is stretched out as if in bitter mockery of the imperial mission, which the story portrays as in the process of destroying itself.

Stories of diversity

A form itself 'in flux', the short story has been noted for its capacity to provide 'glimpses of societies in the process of transformation' and to record 'shifts in linguistic practice, social theory and critical expectation' that are typical in decolonizing and postcolonial contexts.[31] Not only has it become an important form in the new literatures that developed in Britain's former possessions, but also for representing and reflecting the consequences of migration from these former possessions to Britain. Migration has had a lasting impact on British culture after the Second World War, and it is now commonly associated with the iconic *Empire Windrush*, a ship which brought West Indian migrants to Britain in 1948. Migration from the Caribbean was followed by an influx from the Indian subcontinent. Although these migration patterns are not the only ones to have contributed to the ethnic diversity of the contemporary United Kingdom, they have had the greatest literary impact to date and form the backdrop of many short stories. A celebratory approach to migration emphasizes how it reconfigured notions of English- and Britishness and helped to create a new, polyphonic British literature. However, the experience of post-war migration is also one of continued racism and the necessity to resist discrimination. White British story writers have rarely engaged with these issues, but there is a remarkable early story by Muriel Spark that satirizes Britain's denial of the fact that its history of slavery, colonization and global trade led to racial mixing also in the 'mother country'. With poignant use of the short story's capacity for surprising twists, 'The Black Madonna' (1958) exposes the hypocrisy of a white couple who live near Liverpool, one of Britain's major ports for the Atlantic trade, and take pride in their friendship with two Jamaicans, but whose marriage breaks apart when their first child is born black – not as a result of infidelity but because of African ancestry in the mother's family history.[32]

Early stories by writers of West Indian descent respond to the anxieties that a new life and hostile environment created for the first arrivals. The stories of the Trinidadian writer Sam Selvon, who came to Britain in 1950, were collected in *Ways of Sunlight* (1957). The volume's division into stories set in Trinidad and London respectively reflects the migrant's cultural inbetweenness. Several of the stories are told in the first person and in Creole, thus feeding a tradition of Caribbean oral storytelling into metropolitan literature. The London stories articulate the estrangement, poverty and prejudice with which West Indians were confronted in 1950s Britain, but their humour also points to a spirit of survival and resistance. 'Obeah in the Grove' is a trickster story in which migrants who have been evicted from their accommodation practise a magic rite to revenge themselves on their white landlords. The landlords had accepted black tenants only in order to scare unprofitable white ones away, but now the obeah drives them out of their own house, and the migrant community can enjoy a gratifying moment of empowerment.[33]

The late 1980s and early 1990s saw a notable 'surge in texts re-examining Britain's colonial past and its continuing legacy'.[34] It comprises stories by writers of a wide range of different ethnic backgrounds and beliefs of different generations, from first- to third-generation immigrants. 'Mammie's Form at the Post Office' is a story by E. A. Markham, who was born in Montserrat. The story presents the dilemma of an elderly first-generation migrant at a post office where she tries to send a hundred dollars back home to the West Indies for repairs of the family grave. She argues with the 'boy behind the counter'[35] over what might be 'home' and 'abroad' and leaves the office outraged when she is asked to pay far more than she had expected because, as it later occurs to her, she did not specify that she wanted to send West Indian dollars, and the 'boy' could only think of US-American dollars. In contact with a 'postcolonial' British man, the woman who came from the colonies runs up against problems of communication and cultural ignorance.

Markham's Mammie would today be referred to as a member of the 'Windrush generation'. The experience of this generation also engages younger black writers in the United Kingdom such as Jackie Kay. In 'Out of Hand', a story from her first collection, *Why Don't You Stop Talking* (2002), another elderly black woman examines her once beautiful hands, remembers how she arrived on the *Windrush*, and wonders why she stayed in Britain despite the rejection to which she was exposed: 'How come she thought England was her country? How did that happen? How was it that she thought when she got on that *Windrush* that she was coming home?'[36] At the end of the story, she refers to the *Windrush* as 'that huge fiction of a ship',[37] and the phrase makes the reader wonder about the word 'fiction' in relation to a ship whose historical reality was widely acknowledged when the story was published. It could refer to the migrants' illusive hopes, but also the *Windrush*'s status as a historical myth for a country that was beginning to reconstruct its identity as a culturally diverse society with a multi-ethnic legacy. With its suggestive openness, the ending illustrates Kay's belief that

> [a] short story is a small moment of belief. Hard, uncompromising, often bleak, the story does not make things easy for the reader. It is a tough form for tough times. [...] A story asks the reader to continue it after it has finished or to begin it before it began.[38]

The title story of *Why Don't You Stop Talking*, which is set in the present, has a similarly haunting ending. It consists of the first person narration of a mixed-race and overweight woman who lives alone in a council flat. Her distress and aggression find vent in unrestrained and abusive talking, for instance when she visits a supermarket and feels provoked by the stare of

The short story and the anxieties of empire

a slim white woman. The narrator's self-loathing eventually makes her cut off – and so punish – the tongue that always gets her into trouble. This self-mutilation ends the story with a shock, especially because the narration continues through the very act that robs the woman of her capacity to speak: 'I pick up the razor and I cut my tongue. [...] The blood is generous and very red and it pours down my face. I wish they could all see me now.'[39] The character is obviously a marginalized person, but her race seems to be only one factor responsible for her isolation and resulting disturbance. The story thus employs the form's capacity for unexpected twists to disrupt simple equations between race and social marginalization.

A similarly disruptive approach is taken in a story by Courttia Newland, 'Flight of Freedom'. The world which this London-born writer frequently depicts in his fiction is that of council estates and their underprivileged inhabitants. As editor of an important anthology of texts by writers of African descent in Britain, Newland chose the title *IC3*, which is explained in the introduction as 'the police identity code for black' and 'the only collective term that relates to our situation here as residents'.[40] While such statements signal Newland's concern with ongoing racial discrimination in the United Kingdom, the short story form offers him alternatives to the social realism to which such concern is often inclined. Newland is an active promoter of the short story through the independent 'Tell Tales' collective, which he co-founded in 2003. 'Flight of Freedom', which was published in a *Tell Tales* anthology, develops a situation that might lead to the suicide of its protagonist, a petty drug dealer living on an estate, but then turns this situation into a fantasy whose strangeness challenges preconceptions which readers might have about the story's milieu. The strangeness is established in the very first sentence when the first person narrator notices that he is growing wings: 'His first inkling that something strange was happening came when he noticed an annoying itch on both shoulder blades.'[41] The story ends when he decides to hurl himself from the window of his flat on the fourteenth floor of Trelick Towers, the tallest council block in Europe: 'Marcus opened his eye to see the city – *his city* – new, fresh, and alive in a way it had never quite been. [...] The thought brought an effortless smile to his lips.'[42] This ending literally stops the narrative in the air and leaves it to the reader to decide whether the character will fly out of his old life or jump into a real death.

The 1990s saw the publication of two important story collections by writers of South Asian descent whose approaches to issues of migration and cultural hybridity are very different: Salman Rushdie's *East, West* (1994) and Hanif Kureishi's *Love in a Blue Time* (1997). Rushdie, a victim of conflicting cultures who was still hiding from the *fatwa* imposed on him in 1989,

49

presents himself as a writer with a cosmopolitan outlook and a wide range of narrative styles at his disposal, from fabulation to realism. The arrangement of *East, West* into three sections – 'East', 'West' and finally 'East, West' – creates a trajectory for the collection that 'seems pointed towards reconciliation and yet the single comma – the pause of hesitancy – remains tantalisingly poised between the two regions'.[43] The 'East' part begins with 'Good Advice Is Rarer than Rubies', a story that contests the idea that everyone in the subcontinent desires to emigrate to the United Kingdom. A beautiful woman uses the advice of an expert precisely to avoid a union with her fiancé because she prefers her independence as an *ayah* in Lahore to an arranged marriage in London.[44] In the collection's final story, 'The Courter' from the 'East, West' part, another *ayah* returns to India because she can no longer bear to be torn between East and West. At the same time, the younger self of the first person narrator is applying for a British passport because it will provide him with mobility and a way to escape his father's influence. These decisions are embedded in a love story that unfolds between the old *ayah*, Mary, and a migrant from Eastern Europe whom the narrator calls Mixed-Up. The harmony of their ethnically mixed relationship is disturbed by a racist incident typical of the early 1960s during which the story is set. No permanent bodily harm is caused, but the event aggravates Mary's heartache and longing for home: 'London was killing her, by not being Bombay.'[45] The narrator, who has stayed in Britain, remains poised between worlds, being pulled 'this way and that, East and West, the nooses tightening, commanding, *choose, choose*'.[46] Between these initial and final stories, *East, West* explores other facets of Eastern and Western life, and the various ways the two can be entwined, including different traditions of storytelling.

While *East, West* presents itself as a programmatically hybrid collection with a global perspective, Kureishi is more narrowly concerned with Britain, in a manner that has been characterized as 'post-ethnic' and concerned with 'a transnational and translational community'.[47] In most of the stories in *Love in a Blue Time*, the characters' ethnicity is unspecified or presented as partly a matter of choice. However, the volume includes two stories in which the tensions and anxieties in societies shaped by migration are still a major theme. 'My Son the Fanatic' (first published in 1995) explores the conflict that breaks out within a Punjabi family in London when Ali, the British-born son of the taxi driver Parvez, becomes a devout Muslim in protest against the rejection he feels in British society, and rejects his father's being 'too implicated in Western civilisation' in turn.[48] The story ends with an unresolved clash between Ali and Parvez, whose dream of doing well in England, also through his son, has been destroyed. 'We're Not Jews' is set a few decades further in the past, presumably the late 1960s or 1970s because the story's two main adult characters have been in the same air-raid shelter during the Second World War. At the core of the story is the discrimination suffered by a white Englishwoman who has married an Asian, and her mixed-race son, Azhar. They are abused by a father and son, Big Billy and Little Billy, when they are returning from Azhar's school where they have complained about Little Billy's bullying. Big Billy is a primitive thug, but he has power enough to provoke Azhar's mother to protest, 'We're Not Jews.' This remark, about which her son is not 'sure what she meant',[49] gives the story complexity. It suggests a wider historical context of racial persecution: the Holocaust, the Jewish diaspora, but also the discrimination Jewish people experienced in Britain during the war. Azhar's mother obviously feels that, as a white Briton, she does not deserve to be treated like a Jew, and she is unwilling to leave her country to escape persecution, as her husband proposes. As the ending suggests, this would not be a solution for her son, who follows his father's conversation in Urdu or Punjabi 'in incomprehension', posed between one culture he does not understand and another one that rejects him.[50]

Kureishi's 'ethnic' stories form only a fraction of *Love in a Blue Time*, just as Jackie Kay treats race only in a few stories of *Why Don't You Stop Talking*, and only as one factor among others that determine contemporary urban identities. A more implicit and inclusive treatment of race and ethnicity also characterizes a story collection by Manzu Islam, who came to Britain from Bangladesh in 1975 and worked in East London as a racial harassment officer at the height of right-wing 'Paki-bashing'. One half of the stories in *The Mapmakers of Spitalfields* (1997) is set in Bangladesh, the other in East London, thus suggesting the cultural division of migrant life in a manner similar to Selvon's *Ways of Sunlight* or Rushdie's *East, West*. The London stories present the area around Brick Lane as a space that has been transformed and remapped by migrants, but is still haunted by instances of 'everyday' racism. In 'The Tower of the Orient', a young couple, Munir and Soraya, move into a London tower block, their hope for a new life symbolized by the lilac bushes and daffodils they see around their new home. The blossoms have no fragrance, however, and intertextual references to T. S. Eliot's *The Waste Land* forebode the nightmare with which the story ends for the young woman. Traumatized by an event in her youth when she fell – or was pushed – into a well, the young woman develops a fear of the lift, which is aggravated by racist graffiti and an encounter with an aggressive bulldog. The woman's distress becomes so intense that she fears the worst when her husband returns home and she hears the lift coming up. What has begun as a migrant's dream of a new life ends disconcertingly like a thriller: 'Soraya pushes the button, the cable starts to pull once more, the cage is humming the whisper and the growl, *God, what's next!* and the scarlet drips are dripping on the dead land, where they have mown down the flowers with savage swipes of sickles.'[51]

The stories and collections mentioned in this section present the United Kingdom as a country that has become ethnically and culturally diverse, while also registering ongoing discrimination. However, the stories refrain from generalization. They depict particular experiences of particular characters and so suggest that *the* migrant experience does not exist, and that the experiences of migrant life are as multifaceted as those of other Britons. This is also a point behind Rehana Ahmed's anthology for young readers, *Walking a Tightrope* (2004), that is meant to capture 'the diversity of Britain's South Asian population for a contemporary multicultural readership' and to resist 'any fixed idea of what it is to be Asian in Britain'.[52] The fluidity of the short story form is suited to capturing this unfixedness, which is also a result of the dynamics between the United Kingdom's different migrant groups. In Andrea Levy's 'Loose Change' (2005), the narrator, a black teacher who defines herself as a Londoner, is confronted with a girl who has just arrived as a refugee from Uzbekistan and who helps her with some loose change for a vending machine. She feels pity for the girl who has to sleep in the street, but would not like to have her in her own comfortable flat, even though her own grandmother once received an act of kindness from a stranger when she arrived from the Caribbean. The story ends with the narrator walking abruptly away from the girl, as if to insure herself against the anxieties of migration that are part of her own family background.[53] The black Londoner in Levy's story tries to shield her identity as clearly from a new migrant group as Kipling's and Conrad's colonials attempted to border their identities off from Indian and African otherness. The short story negotiated the anxieties inherent in the British imperial project, and it has remained an important genre for exploring and questioning the legacy of the empire in Britain itself. Writers with a wide range of migrant backgrounds are now part of British literature, and they take a natural place in anthologies of the twenty-first-century British short story. Nevertheless, while the short story now frequently registers cultural hybridity, cosmopolitanism and even post-ethnicity, it continues to capture moments in which the legacy of empire gives occasion for anxiousness.

NOTES

1 That is, the short story is overrepresented in (former) colonies: Adrian Hunter, *The Cambridge Introduction to the Short Story in English* (Cambridge: Cambridge University Press, 2007), p. 138.
2 Nadine Gordimer, 'The Flash of Fireflies', *Short Story Theories*, ed. Charles E. May (Athens: Ohio University Press, 1976), pp. 178–81 (p. 180).

3. Maggie Awadalla and Paul March-Russell, 'Introduction: The Short Story and the Postcolonial', *The Postcolonial Short Story: Contemporary Essays*, eds. Maggie Awadalla and Paul March-Russell (Basingstoke: Palgrave Macmillan, 2013), pp. 1–14 (p. 4).
4. Hunter, *Cambridge Introduction*, p. 138.
5. Catherine Ramsdell, 'Homi K. Bhabha and the Postcolonial Short Story', *Postmodern Approaches to the Short Story*, ed. Farhat Iftekharrudin et al. (Westport: Praeger, 2003), pp. 97–106 (p. 97).
6. For this application of Deleuze and Guattari see Hunter, *Cambridge Introduction*, p. 139.
7. Hunter, *Cambridge Introduction*, p. 139.
8. Elleke Boehmer, 'Introduction', *Empire Writing: An Anthology of Colonial Literature 1870–1918* (1998; Oxford University Press, 2009), pp. xv–xxxvi (p. xv).
9. *'Blackwood' Tales from the Outposts* (Edinburgh: Blackwell, 1933), including such volumes as *Frontiers of Empire* (I), *Small Wars of the Empire* (II), *Pioneering* (IV), *Soldiers' Tales* (VII), or *Tales of Africa* (IX).
10. See, for instance, *Tales of Heroines and Heroes: Rare Short Stories by G. A. Henty*, ed. Dennis Butts (The Henty Society, 2003).
11. Mariadele Boccardi, 'The Story of Colonial Adventure', *A Companion to the British and Irish Short Story*, eds. Cheryl Alexander Malcolm and David Malcolm (Oxford: Wiley-Blackwell, 2008), pp. 19–34 (p. 30).
12. W. Somerset Maugham, 'Introduction', *Tellers of Tales*, ed. W. S. Maugham (New York: Doubleday, 1939), pp. xiii–xxxix (p. xxxiii).
13. Robert Gish, 'The Exotic Short Story: Kipling and Others', *The English Short Story 1880–1945: A Critical History*, ed. Joseph M. Flora (Boston, MA: Twayne, 1985), pp. 1–37 (p. 3).
14. W. Somerset Maugham, 'The Force of Circumstance', *The Complete Short Stories of W. Somerset Maugham* (London: Heinemann 1951), vol. 1, pp. 481–505 (p. 495).
15. Boehmer, 'Introduction', p. xx.
16. Boehmer, 'Introduction', p. xxiii.
17. See Saros Cowasjee (ed.), *The Oxford Anthology of Raj Stories* (Oxford University Press, 1998).
18. Harold Orel, *The Victorian Short Story: Development and Triumph of a Literary Genre* (Cambridge: Cambridge University Press, 1986), p. 145. See also Elliot L. Gilbert, *The Good Kipling: Studies in the Short Story* (Manchester: Manchester University Press, 1972).
19. Walter Allen, *The Short Story in English* (Oxford: Clarendon Press, 1981), p. 64.
20. John A. McClure, *Kipling and Conrad: The Colonial Fiction* (Cambridge, MA: Harvard University Press, 1981), p. 4.
21. Rudyard Kipling, 'Beyond the Pale', *Plain Tales from the Hills* (1888; New York: Scribner's, 1911), pp. 189–98 (p. 189).
22. Kipling, 'Beyond the Pale', p. 190.
23. Helen Pike Bauer, *Rudyard Kipling: A Study of the Short Fiction* (New York: Twayne, 1994), p. xiii.
24. Rudyard Kipling, 'At the End of the Passage', *The Phantom 'Rickshaw and Other Stories* (1888; New York: Scribner's, 1911), pp. 328–61 (p. 330).

25 Rudyard Kipling, 'The Man Who Would Be King', *The Phantom 'Rickshaw and Other Stories*, pp. 39–97 (p. 81).
26 Gish, 'Exotic Short Story', p. 15.
27 Gail Fraser, 'The Short Fiction', *The Cambridge Companion to Joseph Conrad*, ed. J. H. Stape (Cambridge: Cambridge University Press, 1996), pp. 25–44 (p. 36).
28 Joseph Conrad, 'An Outpost of Progress', *The Complete Short Fiction of Joseph Conrad*, vol. 1 (London: Pickering & Chatto, 1992), pp. 38–61 (p. 40).
29 Conrad, 'An Outpost of Progress', p. 44.
30 Conrad, 'An Outpost of Progress', p. 60.
31 W. H. New, 'Short Fiction (Overview)', *Encyclopaedia of Post-colonial Literatures in English*, vol. 3, eds. Eugene Benson and L. W. Conolly (London: Routledge, 1994), pp. 1439–43 (p. 1443). New's overview introduces a section on the development of the short story in different parts of the former British Empire. See also Jacqueline Bardolph and Viola André (eds.), *Telling Stories: Postcolonial Short Fiction in English* (Amsterdam: Rodopi, 2001); Awadalla and March-Russell (eds.), *The Postcolonial Short Story*.
32 Muriel Spark, 'The Black Madonna', *The Complete Short Stories* (London: Viking, 2001), pp. 371–89.
33 Sam Selvon, 'Obeah in the Grove', *Ways of Sunlight* (1958; Harlow: Longman, 1979), pp. 167–74.
34 Michael Parker, 'Hybrid Voices and Visions: The Short Stories of E. A. Markham, Ben Okri, Salman Rushdie, Hanif Kureishi, Patricia Duncker, and Jackie Kay', *A Companion to the British and Irish Short Story*, pp. 308–29 (p. 308).
35 E. A. Markham, 'Mammie's Form at the Post Office', *Something Unusual* (London: Ambit Books, 1986), pp. 44–7 (p. 44).
36 Jackie Kay, 'Out of Hand', *Why Don't You Stop Talking* (2002; London: Picador, 2003), pp. 157–69 (p. 168).
37 Kay, 'Out of Hand', p. 169.
38 Jackie Kay, 'A Writer's View', Booktrust, www.booktrust.org.uk/books/adults/short-stories/articles/a-writers-view-kay/ [Accessed 22 January 2015].
39 Jackie Kay, 'Why Don't You Stop Talking', *Why Don't You Stop Talking*, pp. 37–50 (p. 50).
40 Courttia Newland and Kadija Sesay (eds.), *IC3: The Penguin Book of New Black Writing in Britain* (2000; London: Penguin 2001), p. x.
41 Courttia Newland, 'Flight of Freedom', *Tell Tales: The Short Story Anthology*, vol. 2, ed. Rajeev Balasubramanyam (London: Tell Tales, n.d.), pp. 23–9 (p. 23).
42 Newland, 'Flight of Freedom', p. 29.
43 Paul March-Russell, *The Short Story: An Introduction* (Edinburgh: Edinburgh University Press, 2009), p. 256.
44 Salman Rushdie, 'Good Advice Is Rarer than Rubies', *East, West* (London: Jonathan Cape, 1994), pp. 3–16.
45 Salman Rushdie, 'The Courter', *East, West*, pp. 173–211 (p. 209).
46 Rushdie, 'The Courter', p. 211.
47 Bettina Schötz, 'The Exploration of Community in Hanif Kureishi's Fiction', *Literary London Journal*, 10.2 (Autumn 2013), www.literary london.org/london-journal/ autumn2013/schötz.html [Accessed 22 January 2015].
48 Hanif Kureishi, 'My Son the Fanatic', *Love in a Blue Time* (London: Faber, 1997), pp. 119–31 (p. 125).

49 Hanif Kureishi, 'We're Not Jews', *Love in a Blue Time*, pp. 41–51 (p. 45).
50 Kureishi, 'We're Not Jews', p. 51.
51 Syed Manzurul Islam, *The Mapmakers of Spitalfields* (1997; Leeds: Peepal Tree, 2003), p. 95.
52 Rehana Ahmed (ed.), *Walking a Tightrope: New Writing from Asian Britain* (London: Young Picador, 2004), p. 1.
53 Andrea Levy, 'Loose Change', *Underwords: The Hidden City*, ed. Maggie Hamand (London: Maia Press, 2005), pp. 67–76.

4

DAVID MALCOLM

The short story, identity, space and place

This chapter addresses links between the short story, identity and space-place from a number of angles.[1] It briefly discusses a basic aspect of space as it relates to short fiction, that is, the shortness of the short text; it considers one of the most influential discussions of the relationship of aspects of space and the short story, Frank O'Connor's *The Lonely Voice: A Study of the Short Story* (1962/1963); it sets out some theoretical positions as regards space in fiction and its meaning-bearing properties, and it shows how space operates in different types of short story to build and add meaning to the text, proposing a typology of spaces that occur in short fiction.

The shortness of the short story – its concrete and unavoidable spatial minimalism – is arguably the only viable definition of the form. Poe sees this clearly when he defines a tale as a text one can read 'at one sitting' over a relatively short period of time.[2] In his essay on 'The Short Story' (1896), Frederick Wedmore argues that short fiction rejects 'the *longueurs* of the conventional novel'.[3] Many other examples can be generated of this sense of the crucial spatial limitation of the short story. While arguing that the shortness of the short story is not just shortness, but 'a calculated brevity', Barbara Korte nonetheless acknowledges that '[t]he criterion of quantity is at the core of all attempts at definition' of short fiction.[4]

In Renate Brosch's *Short Story: Textsorte und Leseerfahrung* (2007), the author insists on the centrality of shortness or brevity to any understanding of what constitutes the short story, and on the effect of such a spatial configuration on the reader of the text. She argues that such abridgement compels the reader to a closer attention to the text.[5] The shortness of the short story encourages in the attentive reader an increased level of mental activity.[6] Gaps must be filled in, elisions amplified, points of indeterminacy imaginatively made concrete. There is a substantial encouragement of projective reading in the short story, which is much greater than in the case of novels.[7] As Korte remarks, short fiction 'invites a degree of reader participation not – or at least less frequently – found in longer pieces of narrative, or in other forms of short prose'.[8] Brosch sees such an invitation to imaginative engagement, such an encouragement to go beyond the immediate material of the text, as of considerable moral and educational importance.[9]

The spaces of *The Lonely Voice*

Frank O'Connor's study *The Lonely Voice* has had a salutary influence on short fiction's reception in the English-speaking world. In it, *inter alia*, O'Connor advances a thesis about the personnel, settings and places of production of the short story. The characters presented in the short story, O'Connor argues, have always belonged to a 'submerged population group'.[10] Such groups he locates spatially: 'Always in the short story there is this sense', O'Connor writes, 'of outlawed figures wandering about the fringes of society'.[11] The characters of the short story will, according to O'Connor, be marginalized and at the peripheries of metropolitan and establishment space: provincials, failures, ethnic others, women, the insane, the criminal.[12] In O'Connor's view, the place of production of the short story is particular, too. The short story has a 'peculiar geographical distribution': it flourishes in spaces without any strong community or belief in that community. It is about and from 'a society that has no signposts, a society that offers no goals and no answers'.[13] Thus, despite all his qualifications, O'Connor suggests that this is why short fiction is more important in Russia, Ireland and the United States than in England: because the short story comes from an unstable and atomized space.[14]

O'Connor's argument makes considerable sense within the context of the twentieth-century Irish short story. The central characters of many canonical Irish short fictions inhabit unstable borderlands, spaces and places that both express and condition their own parlous and marginalized identities. This is, for example, the case in Joyce's 'After the Race', from the collection *Dubliners* (published in 1914, although the stories were written before 1906).[15] The collection as a whole is concerned with Dublin as a provincial and colonized city that entraps its citizens, and the story material of 'After the Race' is characteristically organized around movement through space. It begins with a car race in the environs of the city and moves into Dublin itself, but the reader is also made aware of spaces beyond the city; the Continent, England and the United States, from which the protagonist's companions come. In all these spaces, Jimmy Doyle enjoys an uneasy position: Irish not English (although he has been partly educated in England); provincial not cosmopolitan (although he associates with persons from the great world); from Kingstown not from Dublin itself; well-off, but without the wealth and social rank of some of his companions. His status is provisional and precarious. At the end, the reader must surely ask whether he has lost too much money at cards, whether his family will be able to make the investment they plan, or whether, indeed, the gullible Irish provincial has been rooked by a bunch of cosmopolitan conmen.

The title of Seán Ó Faoláin's 'A Broken World' (1937) signals the fragmented nature of space in the story. It also indicates the damaging influence of place on its characters. 'That's a lonely place!' declares the priest in the text's first words, and the story goes on to present three central characters, priest, farmer and narrator (from the city), who inhabit a fallen world (all the more strikingly fallen, for this is a newly independent Ireland), and although normally isolated come together briefly in a train.[16] The priest is a man of status, but has been silenced by the Church hierarchy and is utterly dissatisfied with himself, his parish and his country. The farmer seems afraid of any intellectual stimulus, trapped in lethargy and a learnt timorousness. The narrator, a man of the city, walks anonymous streets, longing for a transformational revelation that will not come. The bleak and broken nature of the world these characters inhabit is made even clearer by the contrast, in the priest's story, both with the decent farms on good land and the ruined houses of the colonial gentry. But no one inhabits these good places, it seems, and all the characters live in a bleak and dissociative world.

Bernard MacLaverty's 'Walking the Dog' (1994) is set in one of Ireland's existential borderlands, Belfast at a time of murderous sectarian violence.[17] The protagonist, who may be Catholic or Protestant, is picked up by a murder squad who will not reveal their identity, although they attempt to elicit his. The interrogation in the back of a moving car takes place against a background of utter normality, and is all the more frightening for that reason. The protagonist does not know what to say, for he does not know who his captors are (although in the end, it seems that they are from a Protestant paramilitary). The reader never knows the protagonist's identity. He is a non-partisan everyman, trapped in a place where one may be killed for pronouncing the letter 'h' in a specific way.

One might adduce other examples of Irish short stories that exemplify O'Connor's points about unstable borderlands and their connection with character identity, including O'Connor's own short story 'The Shepherds' (1944).[18] When it comes to Irish short fiction, O'Connor is clearly on the money and his argument seductive.[19] However, it is a flawed argument, as one that associates a particular literary form with a nation or region (or ethnic group or gender) might be expected to be.[20] While there is much evidence to support it – not only Joyce's Dubliners, but also Elizabeth Bowen's transients and displaced in a bombed-out Second World War London, James Kelman's working-class Scots, Miriam Tlali's women of Soweto, and, on another level, the well-documented lack of prestige of short fiction in British publishing – the argument will not hold water. Many of the characters of short fiction are not marginalized or displaced, even if they are somewhat at odds with their environments. Such a description does not apply to the American family in Wilde's 'The Canterville Ghost', Stransom in Henry James's 'The Altar of the Dead', the scholars and antiquaries of M. R. James's ghost stories, the married couple in Katherine Mansfield's 'The Stranger' or the middle-class characters of Mollie Panter-Downes's wartime stories. Further, as O'Connor himself acknowledges, the argument ignores France and Germany, and surely distorts literary history.[21] In fact, two of the English-language writers whose *œuvre* consists almost entirely of short fiction – Rudyard Kipling and V. S. Pritchett – are both English.[22] The well-attested lack of status of short fiction over the past 200 years in Britain has literary and economic causes, and does not result from spatial incompatibility.[23]

Space in (short) fiction

There is a consensus that space in fiction, including short fiction, has not received the same theoretical and particular attention that narrator, time and intertextual reference have.[24] It is certainly true that neither Gérard Genette nor Franz K. Stanzel, in their now classic analyses of the workings of fiction, devote much space to spatial aspects of a fictional work. H. Porter Abbott also deals only briefly, if insightfully, with space, and combines it, as many do, with comments on time.[25]

Yet there is a strong and well-established formalist tradition of seeing space as a key feature of any fictional text, a feature that is semantically loaded and that, rightly read, opens out substantial interpretative possibilities. One of the most celebrated analyses of the semantic potential of space in fiction is that advanced by M. M. Bakhtin.[26] The chronotope is a fusion of time and space in a fictional text, to which Bakhtin ascribes substantial meaning. The chronotope, in which time is dominant, but in which space also plays a crucial role, defines genre, shapes the image of a character, and generates emotions and a sense of values.[27] Bakhtin points to the importance of the chronotope of the road, of the parlour and salon, and of the provincial town in the development of the novel,[28] and claims the chronotopes' significance as 'the organizing centres for the fundamental narrative events of the novel' to which 'belongs the meaning that shapes narrative'.[29]

Another important and illuminating discussion of the importance of space for the analysis and interpretation of a literary text is offered by Jurij Lotman in *The Structure of the Artistic Text* (1971). Space is a key element, along with, *inter alia*, frame, plot, persona/character and viewpoint in the 'Composition of Verbal Art'. The organization of space in a literary text is meaningful, Lotman argues, just as we understand the world through spatio-moral/social categories (top/bottom, closed/open, the boundary).[30] The structure of artistic space is related to plot and to point of view: the key feature in a narrated sequence of events is the crossing of a threshold or a boundary (leaving home, entering the house or the city), and the protagonist is the hero/heroine-agent who crosses that line of demarcation, while oppositions in the literary text are realized spatially.[31]

The Polish scholar Janusz Sławiński also argues strongly for the meaning-filled nature of space in the literary work. He writes of the spatial parameter of the world presented in a text, and calls space a centre of the work's semantics.[32] He sets out three levels of text-space: description ('opis'), scenery ('sceneria') and added meanings ('sensy naddane').[33] Sławiński insists that significant space in a text has to be actually present through some kind of description or reference.[34] The scenery presented in the text is multi-functional: it helps to establish a matrix of possible oppositions and interactions (here/there, church/inn, home/marketplace) and designates the type of territory ascribed to particular characters.[35] Space as scenery also shapes action (the road, the exotic voyage). Further, Sławiński argues that the presentation of space is a manifestation of narrator–receiver relations: elliptically presented space requires work on the part of the addressee; the opposite leaves him/her little room for independence.[36] Spatial elements in a text are also a source of added meanings – a connotational extension of action, suggesting longing, exclusions, mystery, enclosure.[37]

I have devoted some space to discussing theoretical assertions of the importance of spatial features in literature, both for their own sake, and also because space in fiction has not yet received the kind of analytic and interpretative attention that it merits.[38] The aforementioned approaches consider space in longer fiction, but *mutatis mutandis* – space in short fiction will almost inevitably be more elliptically and exiguously presented than in longer fiction – I would make similar claims for the value of looking at spatial features of short stories.

The spaces of short stories

Here I look at five different types of space in a range of twentieth-century short stories in English, in all of which spatial features are essential for a proper analysis and interpretation of that text. Space is always meaningful in the short story (as it is in the novel), but is, of course, meaningful in different ways, depending on the particular story or the particular conventions

The short story, identity, space and place

involved in that story. For convenience, I have distinguished five (not wholly consistently discrete) categories of space: mimetic or realist space; anti-mimetic space; fantastic space; non-mimetic space; and non-space.[39]

Mimetic/realist space

The overall title of Miriam Tlali's collection *Soweto Stories* (1989) announces the centrality of place and space in its texts. Indeed, space plays an important role in 'Fud-u-u-a!',[40] whose central theme is a train journey from Johannesburg to Soweto. Place names are used to establish the text's locale, its verisimilitude and subject matter. The reader is given the details of Friday evening travel back to Soweto: Park Station and the streets one can take to get there. Platform numbers are given and the destination of the protagonist Nkele's train. The text is located in a specific, documented place in South Africa, and is about the realia of life in apartheid Johannesburg.

The sheer crowdedness of spaces is emphasized constantly. The story's title refers to the noise commuters make when forcing their way onto an overcrowded train. 'It was never easy to make one's way through the hundreds of people, all competing for passing space', the narrator tells the reader, echoing Nkele's thoughts.[41] People and cars fill the way to the station. When the train whistle sounds, a 'torrent' of male passengers rushes for it, pushing and crushing Nkele and other women against the walls.[42] The trains themselves are packed, bodies crushed against each other; getting on a train and finding space to stand are victories.

Such space is one of danger for women, as women are subject to degrading sexual molestation on the trains. The trains and the station are a kind of '"front line" of a black woman's battle for mere existence in the bustling city of gold'.[43] They must defend their persons and their property constantly. Nkele uses the space of her body and clothing to make her purse safe from thieves. But, as Nkele tells the others of a previous journey: 'By the time the train got to Park Station, we [the women] were too hurt, too shamefully abused to speak.'[44] No one would listen anyway, she reflects. However, the dangerous space of the station does offer some security. The three central women characters find a corner, 'momentary shelter in the angle formed by the tall concrete pillar and the wall', in which they can converse.[45] The awful conditions prompt female solidarity and aid. Nkele and Ntombi can stand face to face on a train; their shopping bags clutched to their legs, and thus safe from thieves and abusers. The first battle for survival on a crowded train makes Nkele and Ntombi 'practically a team of comrades in action', and the narrator sees the offering of mutual help in adversity as a key feature of all women.[46]

Space is polarized in this story. There is white space: the less crowded streets and trains for tourists. It is also polarized in terms of gender. Men are able to push their way onto the trains; they are the molesters on the trains. Apartheid is, in this story, about space, as black South Africans are crowded into inhuman spaces. Black women are even more disadvantaged, pushed aside, crushed, abused, robbed. Female solidarity is a matter of surviving in this milieu. The semantic weight of location in this text is considerable: the evils of apartheid are conveyed spatially, and female resistance is marked as a struggle for standing room. In addition, verisimilar space gives the story a focus, authenticity and authority.

Anti-mimetic space

An anti-mimetic text always involves a confrontation of two orders of reality, and a revision of an empirical understanding of the world. This opposition must frequently involve a spatial opposition. The ghost or supernatural story is the paradigmatic anti-mimetic text. A vision of the world that precludes the supernatural is shown to be defective. The world of the dead, or the supernaturally monstrous, intrudes into the world of the living.

A particularly good and accessible example of anti-mimetic fiction with a strong spatial focus is Jean Rhys's 'I Used to Live Here Once' (first published in *Sleep It Off, Lady*, 1976). The text is about movement in space and begins with the protagonist (and point-of-view figure) standing by the river. She crosses the stream by stepping stones, listed in detail, that she remembers from the past. She notices changes as she moves on: the road is wider and its surface is newer, trees have been felled, the summerhouse has disappeared, the house to which she is moving 'had been added to and painted white'; a car stands in front of it, which the protagonist finds 'strange'.[47] But much is as she remembers it. One tree is still there; the lawn still looks the same. Then she encounters two children and tries to speak to them. They cannot see or hear her, but feel cold in her presence and run away, and the narrator suggests that the protagonist realizes she is a ghost.[48] The subject of the story is signalled by movement across a border, the river, which carries associations with the classical Styx. The protagonist's realization of her identity as a *revenante* ('That was the first time she knew')[49] is a steady passage through a landscape that is familiar and yet not. The reader is meant to assume, as the protagonist does, that this is a simple movement through mimetic space. In the end, however, both reader and protagonist realize that another journey has been made, and the empirical model of the world is revised.

One of the finest ghost stories in English, and one of the best examples of an anti-mimetic text that works primarily through space, is Rudyard

The short story, identity, space and place

Kipling's 'They' (published in *Traffics and Discoveries*, 1904). Time is not unimportant in 'They', as the text moves chronologically towards winter and darkness. But it is place that carries most meaning. The story is one of crossing borders. 'I had run myself clean out of my known marks,' the narrator declares at the beginning of the text.[50] 'Fancy a motor car coming into the garden!' remarks the proprietrix of the house.[51] The narrator himself is constantly addressed as being 'from the other side of the country', which is literally, but also metaphorically, true.[52]

The place into which he comes is loaded with meaning and associated with the past. The first journey there is into a landscape replete with the markers of English history. All the house's appointments, within and without, are ancient. It is also identified with nature. The children are associated with wild creatures and are certainly as elusive. The local people talk about an encounter with one's dead child as a walk in the wood. The house and the grounds are, further, of an extraordinary beauty, prompting the narrator to declare, 'I think it is the most beautiful place I have ever seen.'[53]

Yet the house is the centre of a strangeness. It lies beyond 'the confusing veils of the woods'.[54] It is hidden almost as soon as the narrator leaves it, it seems absent from any map, and it is a place of confusion, of mysterious utterances, half-seen children, their laughter and labyrinthine spaces. 'I could not see', says the narrator; 'Don't you understand?' asks the blind lady.[55] He clearly does not, until in the end – in a carefully orchestrated space inside the house, in the darkness, by the fire, in a shadowy hall – he realizes what is going on: the children are ghosts, and they include his own dead child. The story has been organized around space, and the narrator's gradual initiation (as in Rhys's story) is realized through experience of space.

Fantastic space

Just as an anti-mimetic text, a fantastic text involves a confrontation of two orders of reality, although in the case of the fantastic the hierarchy of the two is not resolved. Again, space is usually of considerable importance in the juxtaposition of orders of reality. Two particularly good examples of the use of space to present an unresolved ontological and epistemological enigma are one of the texts, '1934', in Keith Ridgway's recent collection of linked short crime stories *Hawthorn & Child* (2012), and Michèle Roberts's 'Flâneuse' from her collection *Mud: Stories of Sex and Love* (2010).

Set in contemporary London, *Hawthorn & Child* follows the frequently inconclusive investigations of two London policemen. Child is black and wears glasses; Hawthorn is white and gay. Apart from that the reader knows little about them. Place is very prominent in these texts. North London is a wasteland, desolate and abandoned, often empty of people. '1934' recounts an investigation into a seemingly random drive-by shooting. Although the story has a date in the title, from the very start two orders of spatial reality are juxtaposed. Sitting in the police car, Hawthorn dreams that he and Child are still while the city moves past the windows. He later sees it the other way round.[56] The story goes on to establish a mimetic textual world. Although this is achieved through non-spatial references, for example to the victim's appearance, it is also accomplished through providing documented North London place names. Other spatial elements, such as the description of the crime scene, and Hawthorn's detailed examination of the victim's bedroom, also give a strong impression of the realism of much crime fiction.

But this reality slips into another. As Hawthorn wanders Finsbury Park, Crouch End and Muswell Hill, the reader starts to see the city as a place of aimlessness, *accidie* and sorrow. The CCTV footage of the crime scene shows nothing definite, an empty street, some shapes. Hawthorn's investigation of the victim's bedroom slips into a gothic encounter with what seems to be the shape of 'a little old man', sniffing, reaching out towards him.[57] All becomes epistemologically ill defined. As a witness of the shooting says of the scene, 'There are pools of light, pools of shadow.'[58] Physical reality becomes unstable to the tired Hawthorn, as the victim's house no longer looks like a house, but rather some sinister abode of 'all the work and the toil and the pain of things'.[59] Uncertainty as to truth and reality is expressed spatially in the text: 'The case was elsewhere', Hawthorn thinks, '[t]he case was always elsewhere', and he subsequently declares, '[w]e are not at the centre of things'.[60] In '1934' space is multi-functional. It establishes a gritty mimetic world, but it also suggests how that world can slip into another. Space is thus used to evoke isolation, spiritual emptiness and an epistemological uncertainty and it is fantastic because the two orders of reality are never reconciled.

Space is fantastic, too, in Michèle Roberts's 'Flâneuse'. It is mimetic: a world of documented places in London, of a verisimilar contemporary theatre and apartment. This mimetic space itself bears meaning. Polly lives in South London, her lover in the north. William's emotional detachment from Polly is already indicated by where his home is. Space is used in this story metaphorically. The city is a body; its people are like blood being pumped through it; and divorce is seen as a space, a dark, sealed container.[61]

However, there is a border crossing into another space. This transgression is foreshadowed in the shortcut that Polly takes to get to the theatre: 'She chooses a backstreet route so that she crosses over into the unknown.'[62] Almost halfway through the story a more substantial transgression takes place: Polly passes from a twenty-first-century world into

The short story, identity, space and place

an eighteenth-century one. This movement is signalled by Polly's change in dress, but also by space: the streets, the weather, the darkness. This space is gendered: a young man may run freely; Polly may not. On the London streets, she is constantly taken for a harlot and cruelly insulted. The question of the reality of her travel into the past is not resolved. Polly asks herself if she has gone mad. Her lover clearly thinks it is all her imagination, but '[n]o, Polly says: it was real. That was why it was so strange.'[63] She has real enough blisters on her heels, apparently from eighteenth-century shoes. Which reality is real? Or are both? All she knows is that her sandals lie ready to take her to other places, to be a temporal and spatial 'flâneuse' whenever she wishes.[64]

As in '1934', space in 'Flâneuse' is multi-functional, used to embody Polly's sense of ill treatment at the hands of her lover, making her lover's use of her clear through the misogyny of the eighteenth-century street. Perhaps, also, her nightmare walk through eighteenth-century London expresses her own sense of and desire for abasement. But even if this is so, her temporal-spatial trespass becomes a source of freedom for her. She can defy her patronizing lover, and she can also become a 'flâneuse' whenever she wishes. Unsure whether the story's events are real or imagined, the reader is suspended between two models of the world.

Non-mimetic space

Non-mimetic texts present a world different from the empirical one, but a world that is not explicitly contrasted, within the text, with the empirical one. A good example of such a short story is Michael Moorcock's 'Jesting with Chaos' (1978). The protagonist, the albino warrior Elric of Melniboné, travels through a world radically different from the reader's and operates outside of realist conventions. The particularity of the non-mimetic world is marked by several features (events, characters' names and appearances), but much is achieved through spatial features of the text. Place names are undocumented – Oberlorn, the Caverns of Chaos, Kaneloon. The laws of space are not those of realist texts, as a green plateau and a forest can suddenly become a flat, stony plain, and vice versa. A 'great palace of greenstone' can appear before one, and, within, its walls may be of 'shifting flame'.[65] Space is fluid and polymorphic. Elric has the power of creation, and is able to amuse the Lords of Chaos by the wit of what he forges. Towards the story's end, it becomes clear that the reader is being presented with a metaphor of artistic creation. 'You are artists, indeed', says Elric to the Lords after an extraordinary masque of forms and beings.[66] Elric wins his freedom by his shrewd power to create something new. Thus, the story becomes one about art and artistry, although (or perhaps because) much of the text's attractiveness lies in its sheer exuberant inventiveness.

Creation is also at the centre of China Miéville's disturbing story 'Familiar' (2006). Here, too, the reader is presented with a world that is substantially different from the empirical one (which is never explicitly juxtaposed to it), and again, much difference is embodied spatially. This is a world in which witches and magic are possible. A familiar can and does exist. The familiar takes its form from the detritus of a canal, the municipal gardens of west London, a graveyard, an industrial sidings, a dump. It becomes a figure of the city it inhabits: 'It parsed the grammar of brick and neglected industry. [...] It was a Londoner.'[67] It fights for space with a more aged familiar, self-made on Victorian slag-heaps. In the end, it learns to speak, and draws heat from the sun-warmed surfaces of vehicles in a car wrecking yard. The familiar becomes a nightmarish (if rather sympathetic) incarnation of the junk, back yards, streets and post-industrial desolation of the great city.

Non-space

Non-space is an important type of fictional space, space that is anonymous or very exiguously designated. This space may belong to any of the aforementioned categories, but is most likely to overlap with mimetic/realist space. For example, Samuel Beckett's 'The End' (1954) is strikingly unspecified as regards space, and yet space is very prominent in the text.[68] Just as the story lacks many of the usual components of a narrative – character names, descriptions, certain kinds of events – so, too, it lacks the usual spatial designates. For example, where is the narrator expelled from in the opening pages? The reader knows it to be 'a charitable institution' and possessed of a 'cloister', but there are few other indicators.[69] The narrator is then, and suddenly, in a street. How did he get there? In what town or city is it? Why might it be familiar and yet unfamiliar to him? As is common in Beckett's prose texts, the narrator aims to 'go on', but where he gets to is left unclear.[70]

Nevertheless, space is very important in the story. The narrator is expelled from one place at the story's start and wanders through various settings – the city, lodgings, a basement room (from which he is also expelled), the country, a cave by the sea, a cabin in the mountains, a road, a shed and finally a boat – but these are not located on any map, real or imaginary, and remain nameless. The importance of space is underlined by the enclosed boat in which the narrator takes refuge, and the 'waters' over which he escapes, most likely into death.[71] Space is in fact used in this story to capture a sense of disorientation, loss and abandonment on the narrator's part. He is utterly powerless in the story's world, but goes on seeking some kind of refuge and escape. Impotence is marked by expulsions from space; refuge is spatially conceived (in the enclosed boat, for example). The lack of place names serves to generalize his plight. The action takes place nowhere, and thus anywhere or everywhere.

Conclusions

Spatial features of the short story are of great import in analysis and interpretation, particularly with a view to issues of identity. In varying categories of space, how that space is configured and how it is or is not designated carry meaning. Space can embody racial, social, gender and sexual identity, convey existential and epistemological unease, challenge the reader's understanding of reality and express metafictional interests. Finally, too, the sheer, ineluctable brevity of the short story and what that entails technically and semantically form a central spatial aspect of short fiction.

NOTES

1 In this chapter, I do not distinguish between place (e.g., London, Dublin, Johannesburg) and space (how the setting of the text is topographically configured). Although an important issue, it is not germane to my subject.
2 E. A. Poe, quoted in *Short Fiction and Critical Contexts: A Compact Reader*, eds. Eric Henderson and Geoff Hancock (Ontario: Oxford University Press, 2010), pp. 395–6.
3 Frederick Wedmore, 'The Short Story' (1896), quoted in 'Introduction', *Short Stories of the 'Nineties: A Biographical Anthology*, ed. Derek Stanford (London: John Baker, 1968), pp. 13–47 (p. 15).
4 Barbara Korte, *The Short Story in Britain: A Historical Sketch and Anthology* (Tübingen: Francke, 2003), pp. 4–5. For a fuller discussion of this matter see Adrian Hunter, *The Cambridge Introduction to the Short Story in English* (Cambridge: Cambridge University Press, 2007), pp. 1–4; and David Malcolm, *The British and Irish Short Story Handbook* (Malden, MA; Oxford: Wiley-Blackwell, 2012), pp. 36–8.
5 Renate Brosch, *Short Story: Textsorte und Leseerfahrung* (Trier: Wissenschaftlicher Verlag, 2007), p. 54.
6 Brosch, *Short Story*, p. 55.
7 Brosch, *Short Story*, p. 200.
8 Korte, *Short Story in Britain*, p. 5.
9 Brosch, *Short Story*, pp. 205–6.
10 Frank O'Connor, *The Lonely Voice: A Study of the Short Story* (Cleveland, OH; New York: Meridian, 1965), p. 18.
11 O'Connor, *Lonely Voice*, p. 19.
12 O'Connor, *Lonely Voice*, pp. 20–1.
13 O'Connor, *Lonely Voice*, p. 18.
14 O'Connor, *Lonely Voice*, pp. 19–21.

15 James Joyce, 'After the Race', *Dubliners* (Harmondsworth: Penguin, 1956), pp. 17–26.
16 Seán Ó Faoláin, 'A Broken World', *The Collected Stories of Seán O'Faoláin* (Boston, MA; Toronto: Little, Brown and Company, 1983), pp. 163–73 (p. 161).
17 Bernard MacLaverty, 'Walking the Dog', *Walking the Dog, and Other Stories* (London: Penguin, 1995), pp. 3–12.
18 Frank O'Connor, 'The Shepherds', *Collected Stories*, intr. Richard Ellmann (New York: Vintage, 1982), pp. 40 8.
19 Malcolm, *British and Irish Short Story*, pp. 48–9.
20 Hunter, *Cambridge Introduction*, p. 106.
21 O'Connor, *Lonely Voice*, p. 20.
22 I discuss this in more detail in Malcolm, *British and Irish Short Story Handbook*, pp. 48–50.
23 Hunter, *Cambridge Introduction*, pp. 6–7; Malcolm, *British and Irish Short Story*, pp. 3–4.
24 Brosch, *Short Story*, p. 123; Janusz Sławiński, 'Przestrzeń w literaturze: Elementarne rozróżnienia i wstępne oczywistości' [Space in Literaure: Elementary Distinctions and Introductory Obvious Points], *Przestrzeń i literatura: Studia z dziejów form artystycznych w literaturze polskiej*, eds. Michał Głowiński and Aleksandra Okopień-Sławińska (Wrocław: Ossolineum, 1978), pp. 9–22 (p. 9); H. Porter Abbott, *The Cambridge Introduction to Narrative*, 2nd edn (Cambridge: Cambridge University Press, 2008), p. 165.
25 Abbott, *Cambridge Introduction to Narrative*, pp. 160–5.
26 M. M. Bakhtin, 'Forms of Time and of the Chronotope in the Novel: Notes toward a Historical Poetics', trans. Carl Emerson and Michael Holquist, *Narrative Dynamics: Essays on Time, Plot, Closure, and Frames*, ed. Brian Richardson (Athens, OH: Ohio State University Press, 2002), pp. 15–24. My lack of Russian means that I have to use an English translation of this essay. I have also used an English translation of Jurij Lotman's writing (see note 30).
27 Bakhtin, 'Forms of Time', pp. 15–16.
28 Bakhtin, 'Forms of Time', pp. 17–20.
29 Bakhtin, 'Forms of Time', p. 22.
30 Jurij Lotman, *The Structure of the Artistic Text*, trans. Gail Lenhoff and Ronald Vroon (Ann Arbor, MI: University of Michigan Press, 1977), pp. 217–18; 229; 231.
31 Lotman, *Structure of the Artistic Text*, pp. 231; 233; 240–1; 237.
32 Sławiński, 'Przestrzeń w literaturze', p. 10.
33 Sławiński, 'Przestrzeń w literaturze', p. 16.
34 Sławiński, 'Przestrzeń w literaturze', p. 18.
35 Sławiński, 'Przestrzeń w literaturze', p. 19.
36 Sławiński, 'Przestrzeń w literaturze', p. 20.
37 Sławiński, 'Przestrzeń w literaturze', p. 21.
38 A recent exception to this neglect is David James, *Contemporary British Fiction and the Artistry of Space: Style, Landscape, Perception* (London; New York: Continuum, 2008).
39 In the following discussion, I rely on distinctions made by Andrzej Zgorzelski in his essay 'On Differentiating Fantastic Fiction: Some Supragenological Distinctions in Literature', *Poetics Today*, 5.2 (1984), 299–307. I have used these to discuss space, although, in Zgorzelski's formulation, they refer to other

features of the text as well (action and characters). I have added non-space to the types of space found in texts.

40 Miriam Tlali, 'Fud-u-u-a!' *Soweto Stories* (London; Sydney; Wellington: Pandora, 1989), pp. 27–42.
41 Tlali, 'Fud-u-u-a!', p. 27.
42 Tlali, 'Fud-u-u-a!', pp. 31–2.
43 Tlali, 'Fud-u-u-a!', p. 37.
44 Tlali, 'Fud-u-u-a!', p. 41.
45 Tlali, 'Fud-u-u-a!', p. 33.
46 Tlali, 'Fud-u-u-a!', p. 38.
47 Jean Rhys, 'I Used to Live Here Once', *The Collected Short Stories* (New York; London: Norton, 1987), pp. 387–8.
48 It is possible to read the story's conclusion in a different, but complementary, manner. The returning woman might not be a ghost, but an ethnic other. After all, the whiteness of the children is emphasized, perhaps implying the blackness of the protagonist. I owe this observation to my colleague Dr Monika Szuba.
49 Rhys, 'I Used to Live Here Once', p. 388.
50 Rudyard Kipling, 'They', *A Sahib's War, and Other Stories*, ed. Andrew Rutherford (Harmondsworth: Penguin, 1971), pp. 93–116 (p. 93).
51 Kipling, 'They', p. 95.
52 Kipling, 'They', pp. 97; 100; 110.
53 Kipling, 'They', p. 97.
54 Kipling, 'They', p. 93.
55 Kipling, 'They', pp. 99; 104.
56 Keith Ridgway, '1934', *Hawthorn & Child* (London: Granta, 2012), pp. 1–57 (p. 1).
57 Ridgway, '1934', p. 37.
58 Ridgway, '1934', p. 19.
59 Ridgway, '1934', p. 54.
60 Ridgway, '1934', pp. 25; 26.
61 Michèle Roberts, 'Flâneuse', *Mud: Stories of Sex and Love* (London: Virago, 2010), pp. 47–66 (pp. 48; 51).
62 Roberts, 'Flâneuse', p. 48.
63 Roberts, 'Flâneuse', p. 60.
64 Roberts, 'Flâneuse', p. 65.
65 Michael Moorcock, 'Jesting with Chaos', *Earl Aubec, and Other Stories* (London: Millennium/Orion, 1993), pp. 16–25 (pp. 20; 21–2).
66 Moorcock, 'Jesting with Chaos', p. 24.
67 China Miéville, 'Familiar', *Looking for Jake, and Other Stories* (London: Pan, 2005), pp. 79–96 (p. 89).
68 The text was first published in French as 'La fin' in *Nouvelles* in 1945.
69 Samuel Beckett, 'The End', trans. Richard Seaver in collaboration with the author, *The Complete Short Prose*, ed. S. E. Gontarski (New York: Grove Press, 1995), pp. 78–99 (pp. 78–80).
70 Beckett, 'The End', p. 78.
71 Beckett, 'The End', pp. 96–8; 98–9.

PART II
Periods

5

DAVID STEWART

Romantic short fiction

The Romantic period is frequently passed over in accounts of the rise of the short story, yet it was witness to a remarkable increase in its publication.[1] This suggests the existence of a critical blind-spot, but also the curious resistance Romantic stories have to absorption into narratives of, in Harold Orel's phrase, the 'development and triumph of a literary genre', the 'modern short story'.[2] James Hogg's three-volume novel *The Three Perils of Man* (1822) features a short story contest. There is no winner, and none of the characters can agree what form a story should take. After a story by Gibbie, the Laird of Peatstacknowe, another character, Tam Craik, pipes up: 'It is nae worth the name of a story that [...] for, in the first place, it is a lang story; in the second place, it is a confused story; and, in the third place, it ends ower abruptly, and rather looks like half a dozen o' stories linkit to ane anither's tails.'[3] The criticism, as Hogg hints, might be directed at his novel, but it might equally be directed at the whole culture of short story writing in the period. Writers wrote ever more short stories, and readers read them with great avidity, but no one could quite agree on what they were reading. One consequence of this is that critics have typically dated the establishment of the 'modern' short story in Britain to the late Victorian period. Another is that the Romantic period offers an extraordinary range of formal experiments opened up by the way writers considered what might be 'worth the name of a story'.

Short fiction in the Romantic period took many forms, and this seems to have counted against it. Edgar Allan Poe's remarkably influential definition of the story as a composition in which 'there should be no word written, of which the tendency, direct or indirect, is not to the one pre-established design' still sets the criteria by which the modern short story is defined against earlier examples of fiction which are simply short.[4] Tam Craik's description of a story that seems to inhabit all forms at once might be appealing, but the short fiction of this period is deemed to fail because it

DAVID STEWART

does not achieve a single form. For many, Walter Scott's 'The Two Drovers' (1827) is the first story which tells us 'one thing, and that, intensely'.[5] One might look for other writers in the early nineteenth century who offer hints of the form to come – R. J. Lyall finds one in Hogg, and Poe acknowledges the *'tales of effect'* in *Blackwood's Magazine* – but if the period's short fiction is to be celebrated adequately other critical models are necessary.[6] John Plotz has recently made the productive suggestion that we construct 'a "loser's history" of the genre, told by way of the evanescent experiments and unreprinted forays' of the period.[7] Examples of such forays could profitably be sought in the magazines of the eighteenth century and elsewhere, but in this chapter I will focus on the 1820s and 1830s. This period was crucial because it saw a sharp rise in the publication of short fiction in collections and periodicals, and also because it features such a rich array of fiction that is only now beginning to attract serious and sympathetic scholarly attention.

Varieties of Romantic short fiction

Tam Craik's response to Gibbie's story in *The Three Perils of Man* indicates two crucial factors in the development of short fiction in the Romantic period. First, short fiction in the period took no definite form, and, second, it was shaped by its close relation to its audience. Tim Killick's *British Short Fiction in the Early Nineteenth Century: The Rise of the Tale* offers the most important survey of the variety of fiction in the period.[8] He identifies a number of major strains, including the regional tale, the sketch and the moral fable. More might be added to the list because the field seemed constantly to proliferate. We can account for this by the fact that, as Killick notes, 'short fiction in the early nineteenth century was, to a large degree, defined by its market'.[9] Eighteenth-century magazines published much important short fiction, but in the early nineteenth century there were many more magazines directed at different sections of a diverse audience, and they published fiction more frequently, with greater prominence, and in a greater variety of forms. Writers increasingly published volumes containing 'tales', as Killick shows, but 'tale' could denote many different things. Readers picking up *Traits of Travel; or Tales of Men and Cities* in 1829 might wonder whether they would get moral fables, tales of fashionable 'silver-fork' life, factual travel narratives or something quite different. The book's advertisement describes the contents as a *'mélange'* of tales and sketches and ends by confessing that 'after sundry harassing efforts' to come up with a title, the writer gave up, and left it to his 'enterprising and experienced publisher'.[10] It is a telling joke that captures the reality for many writers who produced short fiction in diverse forms for an increasingly commercialized market.

The short fiction for this expanding market is characterized by a wilful spirit of experiment. Indeed, it is hard to know what to call it. The 'tale' was especially popular, but other forms likewise came into prominence: the sketch, the anecdote, novellas, fictional essays and other unclassifiable forms. Often these do not seem strictly to be short stories, but very little in the period conforms to, or shows any interest in, strictness. That least fixed of forms, the sketch, became fashionable. Washington Irving's *Sketch-Book of Geoffrey Crayon* (1820–1) was an enormous success in Britain, and one reason for this was its approximation of the miscellaneous form of the magazine.[11] Each part might be classified ('Rip van Winkle' as a story, 'Roscoe' as a critical essay), but the generic looseness implied by 'sketch' is the ruling mood. An encounter in Westminster Abbey ('The Mutability of Literature') with an old book that comes to life might be classed variously as cultural criticism, essayistic musing and a near-supernatural fiction. The sketch's indeterminate form was clearly attractive to many partly because it was far from clear what its parameters were. Theodore Hook's *Sayings and Doings: A Series of Sketches from Life* claims to offer glances at modern behaviour that illustrate (or undermine) the axioms of an older age.[12] This sounds much like the typological urban sketch of a later period: precise accounts of metropolitan phenomena which offer overwhelmed readers, as Martina Lauster has shown, an 'epistemology of the moment'.[13] There are certainly examples of this in the 1820s: Horace Smith's account of a counting-house poet, for example, was one among many sketches of new metropolitan 'types' in the *New Monthly Magazine*.[14] Yet Hook, like Irving, is far less precise. 'Danvers', the first sketch, offers an illustration of the axiom 'too much of a good thing is good for nothing', but it takes a 191-page history of a young man's progress and a series of colourful digressions (including a miscarriage caused by a large snake brought back to England by a nabob) to get there. 'Danvers' suggests in its plot and preoccupations later nineteenth-century comic tales like Thackeray's *Pendennis*, but it has neither the novel's baggy richness nor the taxonomic precision of the metropolitan sketch as Lauster describes it. Instead the sketch for Hook, as for Irving, is attractive for offering a tentatively poised mid-point between precise accounts of particular phenomena and the full balancing of mingled realities offered by the novel.

Mary Russell Mitford's *Our Village: Sketches of Rural Character and Scenery*, a hugely popular series of sketches published first in periodicals (beginning in the *Lady's Magazine* in 1819) and subsequently in a series of five volumes (1824–32), offers another set of modulations between the sketch's close detail and the novel's comprehensive embrace. The sketches are of rural characters and events – Lucy the gossiping servant, the whist-playing bachelor, village cricket – but they resist easy classification. They are not quite sketches, in the sense that Lauster has identified: Lucy is too fully drawn, too much an individual, to be a 'type' that we might recognize. Occasionally there is a narrative arch, such as 'Cousin Mary', which ends with her marriage. Yet the sketch is not driven by its conclusion: that Mary is, by the end, married, does not offer resolution because Mitford did not begin with a sense that there was something to be resolved. Instead, in all of these sketches, Mitford finds something curious, follows it, considers it, then stops. The picture she offers of 'Our Village' is remarkably atomized, for all its provincial closeness: characters almost never recur, and rather than build narratives from small details, she lets details stay details. The realities she enjoys are life's irrelevancies and accidents: a man with an adder under his hat, or the farmer who 'wore his dark shining hair combed straight over his forehead, and had a trick, when particularly merry, of stroking it down with his hand. The moment his right hand approached his head, out flew a jest'.[15] These moments, like the 'red-spotted leaves, and redder berries of the old thorns, the scarlet festoons of the bramble, the tall fern of every hue' that she sees on a walk, are drawn into no narrative arch, no pattern of explanation: they remain a 'brilliant mosaic'.[16] There is a motiveless lightness to the drift of these sketches, and that they are not aimed at some particular goal (fictional or factual) constitutes a large part of the charm they had for Mitford's many readers.

The very smallness of Mitford's details distinguishes her sketches from the novel as it began to be considered in this period. The most important figure in establishing the respectability of the novel is Walter Scott. The 'Waverley Novels' (published from 1814) are usually taken as providing a foil to the short story. Scott's novels combine a rambling multi-volume picture of the diverse realities of historical fact with the romance desire to find a full and comfortable resolution (a marriage, a death, the restoration of the ruling order). Scott is also praised for avoiding the diffuseness that characterizes his novels in the short stories – notably 'The Highland Widow', 'The Two Drovers' (both 1827) and 'Wandering Willie's Tale' (1824) – which offer the sharp illumination of a single incident. But Scott is more characteristic of his period than he is a prophet of the story to come. Santiago Rodriguez Guerrero-Strachan suggests productively that the whole series of 'Waverley Novels' 'resembles a collection of short stories'.[17] Throughout his career Scott was drawn to experiment with length. The three-volume novel became the norm, but forays into shorter forms, like 1816's single-volume

The Black Dwarf, offer fascinating glimpses of Scott's habit of opening things up.[18] The public liked three-volume novels, but Scott kept returning to shorter forms: in 1827 he produced a two-volume novel consisting of two short stories and *The Surgeon's Daughter*, which takes up the second volume. He wrote fiction for magazines and the annuals, and many novels contain inset tales. The novel, especially in Scott's hands, promises a rounding off of disparate facts into a conclusion that permits (to borrow *Waverley*'s famous formulation) 'real history' to continue, but his books are often far less consistently shaped.

'Wandering Willie's Tale' is often excerpted as a stand-alone story from the novel in which it appeared, *Redgauntlet*.[19] Such treatment seems appropriate: Willie's demotic language (the story is narrated in Scots) suggests that this is an excursion from the novel, a form that Scott clearly enjoys, but not one that the mature writer would indulge in fully. And yet, as so often in Scott, the story and its world will not stay neatly within its formal borders. The tale's short span creates a powerful sense of mysterious uncertainty and it depends on a full and sincere acceptance of supernatural explanations for events that Scott rarely permitted into the novel proper. The narrator, Darsie Latimer, presents it to his Edinburgh lawyer friend as a curiosity, but Willie always has the upper hand, and sees further. The effects of the story echo throughout the novel's primary plots, from Darsie's family romance to the speculative Jacobite rebellion. The uncertain truths glimpsed by its ghostly light hint at the ways the truths wrapped up by the novel are shadowed and left uncertain by other stories. The ending of *Redgauntlet* is notoriously simplistic in its easy resolution of personal and political difficulties, but perhaps Scott's heart wasn't in it. Despite his enormous success as a novelist, Scott, like many others in this period, often seemed to be seduced by the possibility of combining together shorter fictions.[20]

Despite the increasing popularity of the three-volume novel, writers found themselves drawn to short fiction seemingly against their will. Charles Robert Maturin's *Melmoth the Wanderer: A Tale* (1820) is usually classified as a novel, but it resists to the point of incoherence the absorption of its in-set stories into a connected narrative.[21] The set-up is familiarly gothic: a young Irishman named Melmoth visits his uncle's gloomy castle and receives a mysterious inheritance, including a cursed manuscript. The manuscript contains a mysterious tale which he begins to read, telling of an ancestor, also named Melmoth, with demonic powers. That story is interrupted when there is a shipwreck in which young Melmoth foolishly intervenes before being saved by a mysterious Spaniard, who tells his tale; that story brings us to the point where the Spaniard helps a Jewish scholar transcribe a tale set in the Indian

Ocean, which we hear, and that tale is interrupted by another tale, which itself contains a tale. This is a long novel (it takes up four volumes), but it reads less as a connected narrative than a series of partially connected fragments. Most of the tales are concluded, but we never hear how the Spaniard found his way to Ireland: in this respect, the tale never dies. In *Melmoth* stories multiply unstoppably and seem to hold the author, the narrator and the narrator's audience captive. As Sharon Ragaz has demonstrated, the text's hybrid mixture of novel and short fiction arose from a protracted series of negotiations between Maturin and his publisher Archibald Constable.[22] Constable proposed publishing it as a series of tales in his *Edinburgh Magazine*, and Maturin thought about following Thomas Moore's *Lalla Rookh*: a poem, 'connected by a prose narrative which is independent of, but *diffused between* the various poems'.[23] Maturin's novel shares with much Romantic fiction the desire to experiment within and between established forms, and also to attempt a fusion of them. *Melmoth* is the site of an unresolved battle between the desire for a cohesive narrative and the desire to fragment that narrative into shorter forms, all bound up in a complex negotiation between a writer and the expanding market for fiction.

Annuals and magazines

The short story requires a home, and usually its home is either the collection or the magazine. Authors increasingly published collections of stories in the 1810s and 1820s, and the same period was witness to a remarkable rise in the number and circulation of magazines. Writers had been publishing stories in magazines since the birth of the first magazine, the *Gentleman's Magazine*, in 1731, and in earlier periodicals like the *Spectator* before that, but this period is significantly different because the size of the market for magazines increased considerably and publishers began paying far more for contributions.[24] Publishers fed an appetite for entertaining short fiction in their increasingly domestic, increasingly female, middle-class audience. The best paying of all the magazines was Henry Colburn's *New Monthly Magazine*. Horace Smith, author of many short stories and semi-fictional essays in it (collected as *Gaieties and Gravities*, 1825), was paid two hundred pounds per year; Charles Lamb, who wrote semi-fictional essays for the *London Magazine* as well as the *New Monthly*, received sixteen guineas per sheet.[25] William Blackwood recognized the importance of fiction early on, and his *Blackwood's Edinburgh Magazine* published many of the most daring experiments in fictional forms, including the establishment of the practice of serialized novels. Blackwood paid writers well for doing so. Alongside the magazines were the annuals, elegantly bound books designed to be given as Christmas or New Year gifts, largely to young women. The trend in annuals began in 1823, and the market for them expanded enormously throughout the 1820s and 1830s before subsiding in the 1840s.[26] The market was competitive because it was potentially so lucrative. Publishers would spend lavishly on contributors (Scott was offered four hundred pounds for seventy pages) because they knew they would make their money back: the 1829 *Keepsake*, containing Scott's stories, sold between twelve thousand and fifteen thousand copies. Both the annuals and the magazines are crucial for short fiction: they provided a forum for it and helped define the form it would take.

Blackwood's Magazine was especially important, partly on account of the freedom with which it understood the boundary between fact and fiction.[27] The magazine published a great many stories, from David Stewart's episodic seafaring yarn 'The Man-of-War's Man' (September 1821–June 1826), to the 'Tales of Terror' that influenced Poe and others, to Caroline Bowles's carefully observed sentimental sketches 'Chapters on Churchyards'.[28] *Blackwood's* also disconcerted and delighted readers with reviews of books that did not exist, attacks and defences of Wordsworth written by the same writer, and the extraordinary *Noctes Ambrosianae*, a long-running series of semi-fictional conversations supposed to catch the writers for the magazine talking unguardedly over claret and oysters in an Edinburgh pub. The magazine offered writers the chance to experiment on the borders of fiction. Among the most successful was John Galt, whose *The Steam-boat* (February–December 1821) followed the popular *Ayrshire Legatees*, both of which were serialized in *Blackwood's*. Galt is interested less in serialization and more in producing an episodic collection of tales that mirrors the miscellaneous contents of the magazine in which they appeared. The narrator is Thomas Duffle, a Glasgow cloth merchant, who takes the boat down the Clyde to Greenock and back. In each episode he meets new characters who tell him tales. Duffle hears of a widow's search for her husband's grave at Waterloo, a tale of romance in high life in Poland, a comical 'wearyful woman' who talks constantly, a Norseman's gothic adventures and a biblical flood in Kentucky. Stories are cut off tantalizingly: the steam-boat has reached the dock, and the passengers disembark. As Caroline McCracken-Flesher observes, there is a 'simultaneous incompleteness and extensiveness' in Galt's writing, and this suggests the pleasures to be found in the mix of short inconclusive episodes that magazine publishing enables.[29] Each instalment permits Duffle's mind to wander into different genres (gothic, comic, historical, travel writing) and different dialects and styles

(Scots, American, Norwegian-accented English, a kind of prose Wordsworth uses in 'The Dumbie's Son'). His stories allow him to inhabit a different world without quite forgetting the pressure of reality. Duffle, like many magazine readers, is a leisurely man, but a man of business, and this made these short excursions especially germane. Magazines place limits on what a writer can write (space is restricted), but limitation, as Galt discovered, can be curiously freeing.

The magazines of the 1820s are most famously associated with the establishment of the personal essay by the likes of Charles Lamb, William Hazlitt, Leigh Hunt and Thomas De Quincey. Lamb claimed that he was happiest in 'the border-land' between 'the affirmative and the negative', 'content with fragments and scattered pieces of Truth', and magazine essays often mingled fact and fiction.[30] The essay format, a 'loose sally of the mind' in Samuel Johnson's definition, permits a movement between registers and between genres: it offers another way to essay experiments in short fiction. 'A Now, Descriptive of a Hot Day' by Leigh Hunt (assisted by John Keats) is a list of all the things that are happening 'now': 'Now ladies loiter in baths'; 'Now five fat people in a stage coach, hate the sixth fat one who is coming in'; 'Now blinds are let down, and doors thrown open'.[31] This series of hints seems waiting to blossom into stories, but the hints are also tantalizing narratives in their own right. Hazlitt's 'On the Conversation of Authors' in the *London Magazine* looks like a more conventional essay (the unpicking of a knotty cultural issue), but it permits dalliances on fictional ground. He is, he tells us, at Winterslow Hut, and he looks up from his window and lets his mind drift: he sees 'several poor women weeding the blue and red flowers from the corn', and has a reverie about the 'lively skirmishes at [the Lambs'] Thursday evening parties'.[32] Both the poor women and Lamb's merry wit were real, but in the space of the essay they take on the bright colouring of imaginative fiction. Hazlitt notes that 'lively sallies and connected discourse are very different things', but the pleasure of his essay lies in its capacity to glide between these modes as the essay evolves.[33]

Magazines offered writers a new freedom, but the annuals often seemed to place firm limits both on what writers could say and how they said it. Their stories tended to conform to a fairly rigid template: a moral or sentimental message rounded out in a few pages, sometimes written to 'embellish' one of the beautifully engraved prints that were a major selling-point of these volumes. The annuals take to an extreme the dominant role played by publishing constraints in the construction of much short fiction in the period, but their contents should not be written off as moribund or uniform. Not every annual was the same – the *Christian Keepsake* took a belligerent imperialist line, whereas the *Literary Souvenir* presented itself as principally aesthetic – and equally the stories are a miscellaneous collection. The Spanish writer Joseph Blanco White's 'The Alcazar of Seville, and the Tale of the Green Taper', for example, links together a series of short tales, travel writing, essayistic personal reminiscence, political commentary and a brilliantly suggestive discussion of apparitions.[34] Blanco White found in the annual a liberating fluidity in which competing forms mingle and echo each other, and he was not the only writer to do so. Walter Scott's four entries in the 1829 *Keepsake* are remarkable for their refusal to adopt a single genre: the shifting mixture of history, observation and gothic uncertainty clearly interested Scott, but it was also the sort of thing annual readers liked. Maria Jane Jewsbury wrote sentimental tales for various annuals, and she also developed a kind of observational sketch both historical ('The Hero of the Coliseum', *Amulet*, 1828) and contemporary ('The Military Spectacle', *Literary Souvenir*, 1825). Jewsbury, like Letitia Elizabeth Landon (or L.E.L.), the most prolific contributor to the annuals, and many other anonymous or forgotten annual writers, offers a rich and largely unexplored source of short fiction that has too often been dismissed.

Mary Shelley's stories have until recently been placed as a regrettable example of the consequences of a writer required to squeeze her ideas into the annual's commercial corset.[35] Shelley complained to Maria Gisbourne that 'I am worried to death to make my things shorter & shorter – till I fancy people think ideas can be conveyed by intuition.'[36] The stories typically end in romantic or tragic resolution, but the short form also allowed Shelley the kind of 'intuitive' half-knowledge that Lamb enjoyed in the essay form. The narrator of 'The Mourner' (*Keepsake*, 1830) confesses to Juliet, 'I ramble on in my narration as if I had a story to tell; yet I have little except a portrait – a sketch – to present, for your amusement or interest.'[37] The story begins with an account of a quite different painting of a regal river scene, but moves slowly away from it, evolving its forms as it goes. We get a kind of resolution, but the 'rambling' form suggests solving the mystery is not quite the point. Tales like 'The Invisible Girl' (*Keepsake*, 1833) and 'The False Rhyme' (*Keepsake*, 1830) begin with mysteries drawn from the engravings accompanying the stories; we get an explanation, but Shelley's narrative has moved beyond it, and the stories remain resistant to that kind of satisfaction. Her narrators often seem unsure of the tendency of their stories, but that is their strength: the lumpy unevenness of the form allows the slow working out of ideas. 'The Invisible Girl' opens with a confession: 'This slender narrative has no pretensions to the regularity of a story, or the development of situations and feelings; it is but a slight sketch.'[38] The annual story, whether a tale, a sketch, or something less easily defined, in its very 'slightness', might, Shelley realized, yield opportunities. We must learn to be guided by these hints that annual and magazine stories are not quite one thing – sketch, tale, anecdote – but that their form will emerge in the telling.

The debatable land

Romantic short fiction is so interesting, I have been suggesting, because it seems so uncertain of its own form. This makes it hard to theorize, but it is also a source of the fiction's vitality. I will conclude by considering the work of two writers, Allan Cunningham and James Hogg, who made more of this uncertainty than most. Both had relatively humble rural upbringings in the Scottish borders, and they knew and drew on oral folk tales in their stories, yet both were also ambitious literary men of the new era. Cunningham's 'Traditional Tales' and 'Twelve Tales of Lyddalcross' were published in the *London Magazine* (he also launched an annual, the *Anniversary*). Hogg wrote for magazines (especially *Blackwood's*) and annuals, and wrote novels that included or were composed of shorter stories. Both returned compulsively to short fiction, but neither could settle on a fixed form.

Hogg's 'The Renowned Adventures of Basil Lee', a gloriously diffuse tale that follows the careering path of a character incapable of sticking to any task, reminds its readers that it was first printed in a shorter form in Hogg's magazine, the *Spy*. Hogg's stories often seem to express Basil Lee's '*instability of mind*': some are short, barely explained anecdotes of a few pages, but 'The Bridal of Polmood' covers nearly 100 pages.[39] Many are modelled on folk history gathered in his native Borders, although he has no compunction about quoting Byron's scandalously successful new poem *Don Juan*.[40] His short stories in *The Shepherd's Calendar* (published first in *Blackwood's*) likewise move between forms and genres, and between tradition and modernity. 'Storms' begins like a piece of reportage, then moves into a mode of narrative description that cannot quite be called either fact or fiction. He stops for moments of sheer wonder at natural facts, such as the discovery of sheep after a snowstorm, 'all lying dead with their heads one way as if a flock of sheep had dropped dead going from the washing'.[41] He ends 'Storms' by dropping in a poem by a poet he much admires: himself. Stories expand and develop seemingly without the volition of the narrator and inhabit as many genres and moods as possible. His stories experiment with the limits of their form; he finds in them something of the essay's freedom to follow a path and respond to the impulse of the moment.

Allan Cunningham's stories, like Hogg's, often draw their readers into a habit of questioning and testing the way we might understand a set of events. 'The Mother's Dream' is a remarkable example. He begins with a modern narrator who warns us in clumsy prose that this is not 'a traditionary fiction'.[42] The story that develops is certainly hard to categorize: it follows no clear path, and although a rural prophecy is fulfilled, it is not clear what the characters ought to have done, although some moral conclusion is surely necessary. A tale of guilt offers us the extraordinary image, isolated with crystalline sharpness, of a ruined young man by the lakeside who, 'lifting up water in his palms, scattered it in the air; then dipping both hands again, showered the water about his locks like rain'.[43] As the tale rounds itself out, we have what seems to be an explanation of his fate, and we return to the lakeside. A figure runs around its bank in a tempest:

> His hat was found floating by the side of the water, but he was never more seen nor heard of – his death-lights, glimmering for a season on the lake, told to many that he had found, perhaps sought, a grave in the deepest part of the Ladye's Lowe.[44]

He may have done, and he may be the same young man we saw earlier: but all we have are the glimmering lights. Cunningham's story, likewise, glimmers away, concluded and yet not quite sure.

The Scottish Borders are, Cunningham reminds us, the 'debatable land', and in the stories this becomes not just a political or geographical condition, but an effect produced by storytelling.[45] 'Dubious' – in the sense of something not yet resolved – is a favourite word of Cunningham's, and it suggests well the effects of his stories. They drift between comic and serious modes, between the world of 'traditionary fiction' and the modern *London Magazine*, and between sincere attempts at explanation and a glimmering uncertainty. It is the same world that Hogg inhabits so successfully: his stories seem never quite sure how they will end when they begin, and always threaten to produce more stories. The same might be said of many others in these years who tested out the possibilities of a newly revitalized art. I began with Hogg's Tam Craik complaining about the story he had heard from Gibbie. Tam gets the chance to tell his own tale to his motley audience. Gibbie does not like it – 'it is turning out no tale at all' – the gushing Poet enjoys the romantic part, the warlike Charlie likes the duel, and the Friar offers formalist analysis: 'Lo, the tale is good [...] but it goeth here and there, without bound or limit.'[46] The range of responses captures well the nature of Romantic short fiction: it is intimately engaged with a diverse audience who want to hear it, try to dictate its form, cannot quite understand it, and yet see something new by its light. Its forms were varied, and had a tendency to shift and mutate in the telling, 'without bound or limit'.

These qualities make the field of Romantic short fiction difficult to map, but they are also what make it so fertile.

NOTES

1. Tim Killick, 'The Rise of the Tale: A Preliminary Checklist of Collections of Short Fiction Published 1820–1829 in the Corvey Collection', *Cardiff Corvey: Reading the Romantic Text* 7 (2001), www.cardiff.ac.uk/encap/journals/corvey/articles/cc07_n04.html [Accessed 20 November 2014].
2. Harold Orel, *The Victorian Short Story: Development and Triumph of a Literary Genre* (Cambridge: Cambridge University Press, 1986).
3. James Hogg, *The Three Perils of Man, or, War, Women, and Witchcraft: A Border Romance*, eds. Judy King and Graham Tulloch (Edinburgh: Edinburgh University Press, 2012), p. 244.
4. Edgar Allan Poe, *Essays and Reviews* (New York: The Library of America, 1984), p. 572.
5. V. S. Pritchett (ed.), *The Oxford Book of Short Stories* (Oxford: Oxford University Press, 2001), p. xi. See also Walter Allen, *The Short Story in English* (Oxford: Clarendon Press, 1981), p. 9. One should not, however, discount the story's relation to the two-volume novel in which it appeared, *The Chronicles of the Canongate*.
6. R. J. Lyall, 'Intimations of Orality: Scotland, America and the Early Development of the Short Story', *Studies in Short Fiction*, 36.3 (1999), 311–25. Poe, *Essays and Reviews*, p. 573.
7. John Plotz, 'Hogg and the Short Story', *The Edinburgh Companion to James Hogg*, eds. Ian Duncan and Douglas S. Mack (Edinburgh: Edinburgh University Press, 2012), pp. 113–21 (p. 114).
8. Tim Killick, *British Short Fiction in the Early Nineteenth Century: The Rise of the Tale* (Aldershot: Ashgate, 2008). Gary Kelly's *English Fiction of the Romantic Period, 1789–1830* (London: Longman, 1989) remains a very useful guide, notably his discussion of the 'quasi-novel', pp. 252–60.
9. Killick, *British Short Fiction*, p. 162.
10. Published anonymously by Thomas Colley Grattan, *Traits of Travel; or Tales of Men and Cities*, 3 vols. (London: Colburn, 1829), I: pp. vi, vii.
11. Washington Irving, *The Sketch-Book of Geoffrey Crayon, Gent*, ed. Susan Manning (Oxford: Oxford University Press, 2009).
12. Theodore Hook, *Sayings and Doings: A Series of Sketches from Life*, 3 vols. (London: Colburn, 1824).
13. Martina Lauster, *Sketches of the Nineteenth Century: European Journalism and Its Physiologies, 1830–50* (Basingstoke: Palgrave Macmillan, 2007), p. 22. Amanpal Garcha offers an insightful discussion of the rise of the sketch in the 1820s and its relation to plot: *From Sketch to Novel: The Development of Victorian Fiction* (Cambridge: Cambridge University Press, 2009), pp. 3–51.
14. 'The Poet's Supper', *New Monthly Magazine*, 10 (1824), 380–4. On this tendency in the *New Monthly*, see Mark Parker, *Literary Magazines and British Romanticism* (Cambridge: Cambridge University Press, 2000), pp. 139–51.
15. Mary Russell Mitford, *Our Village: Sketches of Rural Character and Scenery* (London: George B. Whittaker, 1824), p. 50.

Romantic short fiction

16 Mitford, *Our Village*, p. 269.
17 Santiago Rodriguez Guerrero-Strachan, 'Récit, story, tale, novella', *Romantic Prose Fiction*, eds. Gerald Gillespie, Manfred Engel and Bernard Dieterle (Amsterdam: Benjamins, 2008), pp. 364–82 (p. 369).
18 Walter Scott, *The Black Dwarf*, ed. P. D. Garside (Edinburgh: Edinburgh University Press, 1993). It was part of the appropriately named 'Tales of My Landlord', and was to have been one of four single-volume tales. Scott continued the 'Tales' across four 'series' of four-volume collections, making one set comprising a one-volume and a three-volume novel, one four-volume novel.
19 Walter Scott, *Redgauntlet*, eds. G. A. M. Wood and David Hewitt (Edinburgh: Edinburgh University Press, 1997).
20 See Scott, *The Shorter Fiction*, eds. Graham Tulloch and Judy King (Edinburgh: Edinburgh University Press, 2009) for further examples of Scott's stories in periodicals and 'detachable' stories included in novels.
21 Charles Robert Maturin, *Melmoth the Wanderer: A Tale*, ed. Victor Sage (London: Penguin, 2000).
22 Sharon Ragaz, 'Maturin, Archibald Constable, and the Publication of *Melmoth the Wanderer*', *Review of English Studies*, 57 (2006), 359–73.
23 Quoted by Ragaz, 'Maturin', 362–3.
24 See David Stewart, *Romantic Magazines and Metropolitan Literary Culture* (Basingstoke: Palgrave Macmillan, 2011).
25 Parker, *Literary Magazines*, pp. 12, 142 and Carol Polsgrove, 'They Made It Pay: British Short-Fiction Writers, 1820–1840', *Studies in Short Fiction*, 11.4 (1974), 417–21.
26 See Paula R. Feldman, 'Introduction', *Keepsake for 1829* (Peterborough: Broadview, 2006), pp. 7–25 for an excellent overview of annual culture.
27 On this quality, see Tim Killick, '*Blackwood's* and the Boundaries of the Short Story', *Romanticism and Blackwood's Magazine: 'An Unprecedented Phenomenon'*, eds. Robert Morrison and Daniel S. Roberts (Basingstoke: Palgrave Macmillan, 2013), pp. 163–74.
28 For an excellent overview of the range of fiction published in *Blackwood's* see Anthony Jarrells (ed.), *Selected Prose*, vol. 2, *Blackwood's Magazine, 1817–25: Selections from Maga's Infancy*, general ed. Nicholas Mason, 6 vols. (London: Pickering and Chatto, 2006), or Robert Morrison and Chris Baldick (eds.), *Tales of Terror from Blackwood's Magazine* (Oxford: Oxford University Press, 1995).
29 Caroline McCracken-Flesher, 'The Sense of No Ending: John Galt and the Travels of Commoners and Kings in "The Steam-Boat" and "The Gathering of the West"', *John Galt: Observations and Conjectures on Literature, History, and Society*, ed. Regina Hewitt (Lewisburg, PA: Bucknell University Press, 2012), pp. 73–92 (p. 75). See also Ian Duncan, 'Altered States: Galt, Serial Fiction, and the Romantic Miscellany', *John Galt*, pp. 53–71.
30 Charles Lamb, 'Jews, Quakers, Scotchmen, and Other Imperfect Sympathies', *London Magazine* (August 1821), 152–6 (153, 152).
31 Leigh Hunt, 'A Now, Descriptive of a Hot Day', *Indicator* (28 June 1820), 300–4 (301).
32 William Hazlitt, 'The Conversation of Authors', *London Magazine*, 2 (September 1820), 250–62 (252, 257).

33 Hazlitt, 'The Conversation', 260.
34 Published in *The Forget Me Not* (1825), 31–54.
35 Judith Pascoe offers a useful corrective in 'Poetry as Souvenir: Mary Shelley in the Annuals', *Mary Shelley in Her Times*, eds. Betty T. Bennett and Stuart Curran (Baltimore, MD: Johns Hopkins University Press, 2000), pp. 173–84.
36 *Selected Letters of Mary Wollstonecraft Shelley*, ed. Betty T. Bennett (Baltimore, MD: Johns Hopkins University Press, 1995), p. 256.
37 Mary Shelley, 'The Mourner', *Collected Tales and Stories*, ed. Charles E. Robinson (Baltimore, MD: Johns Hopkins University Press, 1976), pp. 81–99 (p. 87).
38 Shelley, 'The Invisible Girl', *Collected Tales*, pp. 190–202 (p. 190).
39 James Hogg, 'Basil Lee', *Winter Evening Tales*, ed. Ian Duncan (Edinburgh: Edinburgh University Press, 2004), pp. 3–74 (p. 4).
40 Hogg, 'Love Adventures of Mr George Cochrane', *Winter Evening Tales*, pp. 166–228 (p. 224).
41 James Hogg, 'Storms', *The Shepherd's Calendar*, ed. Douglas S. Mack (Edinburgh: Edinburgh University Press, 2002), pp. 1–21 (p. 4).
42 Allan Cunningham, 'The Mother's Dream', *Traditional Tales of the English and Scottish Peasantry*, ed. Tim Killick (Glasgow: Association for Scottish Literary Studies, 2012), pp. 112–28 (p. 112).
43 Cunningham, 'The Mother's Dream', p. 115.
44 Cunningham, 'The Mother's Dream', p. 128.
45 Cunningham, 'The Selbys of Cumberland', *Traditional Tales*, pp. 29–40 (p. 40).
46 Hogg, *Three Perils*, p. 266.

6

JOHN PLOTZ

Victorian short stories

Introduction: short stories, baggy novels

Walter Allen's magisterial *Short Story in English* begins with his version of the Mikado's little list.

> Everywhere in the world, whenever the short story is discussed, a handful of names crops up, Chekhov and Maupassant always, then Poe and Kipling and Joyce, and probably Katherine Mansfield and Hemingway as well.[1]

Allen presumably means modern readers whose taste is shaped by the standards Edgar Allan Poe enumerated in 1842: a story ought to be *unitary, compact* and achieve an *effect of immediacy* on the reader.[2] Those criteria held good in Poe's own day, and from Chekhov to the present they have also held sway. So perhaps only a Victorianist would fault Allen for omitting the heyday of British realist fiction from his list. Measure realism's golden age from Charles Dickens's *Pickwick Papers* in 1837 to George Eliot's *Daniel Deronda* in 1876 – or even stretch the era a bit to include quasi-naturalist novels like Thomas Hardy's *The Mayor of Casterbridge* (1886) – and only Kipling, whose first short stories were published in the mid-1880s, even comes close to writing within it.

Allen is not alone in skirting the British novel's heyday when compiling a short-story pantheon. This missing half-century is not mere happenstance, but a clue about the gap between Poe's criteria for short fiction's success and the formal attributes Henry James had in mind when he at once praised and disparaged his novelistic predecessors for writing 'large loose baggy monsters, with their queer elements of the accidental and the arbitrary'.[3] And when Somerset Maugham agrees that the 'long, unwieldy shapeless novels of the Victorian era' are England's chief contribution to world literature, he adds a revealing corollary: that 'English writers on the whole have not taken kindly to the art of the short story'.[4]

Scholars who agree with the Poe litmus test have often subscribed to the *delay* hypothesis – delay in Britain, that is, when compared to developments in the United States, France, even Russia. Korte, for example, argues that 'the short story "proper" emerged in Britain with considerable delay, not until the *late* nineteenth century'.[5] Dean Baldwin argues, along related lines, that 'the rise and fall of the British short story is intimately connected to the economics of writing and publishing' and that 'between 1880 and 1950 [but not before] the market for short fiction became sufficiently broad, deep, varied and flexible to accommodate all writers of talent and many of very limited abilities'.[6] From 1880 onwards, 'art and commerce [...] existed in creative tension, and [a surprising range of authors] turned the short story to their financial and artistic advantage'.[7] Taken together, the delay theory and Baldwin's economics-of-publishing argument militate against studying with too much attention the short stories of the early and mid-Victorian era.

Ever since Brander Matthews in 1901, canonizers have clung to Poe-inspired criteria for a short story's success and in doing so, consigned the internal critical norms of Victorian short fiction to comparative oblivion.[8] But success for the short story, like any artwork, is in the beholder's eye. A developmental lineage might be traced connecting Thomas De Quincey's 'The Household Wreck' (1838) to such jolly, macabre stories as Sheridan Le Fanu's 'The Ghost and the Bonesetter' (1838), 'The Drunkard's Dream' (1838) and 'Strange Event in the Life of Schalken the Painter' (1839). Stories by Dickens, Gaskell, Trollope, Thackeray, Collins and Oliphant, profoundly shaped by the aesthetic norms of the novel, also merit attention as clues to the time's shifting temper – as do once-popular works by such assiduous practitioners as sportsman-sketcher R. S. Surtees or the lachrymose Rhoda Broughton (known to her parodists as 'Rhody Dendron'). An investigation of what distinguished the norms of the mid-century might also focus on surging Victorian interest in *Arabian Nights* – betokened by the popularity of Lane's translation in the 1830s.[9]

Such a reassessment of Victorian criteria for fictional success should also tackle some surprisingly tricky boundary issues. Tim Killick has recently made a persuasive case about the generic categorization of short fiction in the early nineteenth century: 'short fiction does not fit into a single overarching agenda [...] the position and credibility of short fiction was by no means established. Consequently the boundaries of the genre had to be negotiated at every stage.'[10] Korte's remark about the 'proper' short story helpfully reminds us that boundary negotiation about the story's place, not just its publication record, continued throughout the era of the realist novel's apogee. If the short story 'proper' failed to thrive in mid-Victorian Britain, readers were nonetheless treated to many stories *within* the very genre that ostensibly put the short story into eclipse.

Pratt has argued that we ought to think of the modern short story as a permanently 'minor' genre, defined by its relationship (subordinate, contestatory) to the major prose fiction genre, the novel. What if we inverted Pratt's paradigm, however, and considered the realist novel, in all its bagginess, all its multiplottedness, not so much as a short story killer as an engulfer? The post – *Pickwick Papers* disappearance of the interpolated tale from the novel offers a very good clue for when that period of engulfment begins. Around 1837 (the year Victoria ascended the British throne), the realist novel starts to function as a repository of short stories. Although stories woven into novels by Dickens, Trollope, Thackeray, Brontë and others may lose one formal feature by no longer operating as stand-alone narratives, they retain many other key attributes of the short story. Incorporated into the larger form, we might say, such stories, in modern parlance, go viral.

1830–1840: the story of the sketch and a sketch of the story

In the few years before the volume publication of *Pickwick Papers*, significant changes occurred in the world of short fiction. Killick argues that 'for short fiction, in broad terms, the watchword during the 1830s was expansion', pointing out that twice as many short story collections appeared between 1830 and 1836 as during the entire 1820s.[11] This development spawns not just durable successes like Mary Shelley's 'The Mortal Immortal' (1834), but also oddball texts like 'The Rioters', dropped into Harriet Martineau's 1832 *Illustrations of Political Economy*. What happened during the subsequent half-century when realist novels ruled Britain's fictional roost has everything to do with the way that the Romantic-era *tales* of Hogg and Scott gave way not only to the short story as a recognizable category of fiction, but also to urban *sketches* – brief impressionistic or analytic descriptions of the city's physical and social geography.

Recent work by Lauster and Garcha has described the sketch as a crucial new form of short prose straddling the boundary between fiction and non-fiction, displacing the tale and shaping the new Victorian realist novel. Lauster focuses principally on French and German iterations of sketch publication, while Garcha studies British novelists who began as sketch writers, then imported their descriptive talents into long-form fiction. Both, however, emphasize what Lauster calls the 'cognitive' and Garcha the 'descriptive' work of the sketch.[12] Both see the sketch as an information-giving genre, one that forgoes experiential interiority in order to convey important aspects of the physical landscape or the social array of people one would likely meet on the streets of a city. For Garcha the sketch is a gateway towards descriptive totality in novels, whereas for Lauster the sketch itself allows readers to watch their own society's cultural classification apparatus at work.

The sketches and stories of the 1830s (and 1840s) are united in their desire to depict (mainly urban) types playing their customary roles – wearing 'character masks' in Lauster's useful formulation. But there is more to be said about the fictional forms that sprout up alongside the sketch in the 1830s. The short stories of the day (cf. John Galt's 1833 *Stories of the Study* and his 1834 'The Mem') contain a more complex cognitive system (to borrow Lauster's phrase) than the sketch itself readily permits. In those stories, characters can be classed as social types, but readers are also licensed to feel with characters – and such stories make use of forms of sympathy that often work most fully when characters are presented in the most incomplete, potentially frustrating ways. Such stories rebut an overly neat taxonomic division – sketches depict types, stories focus on affecting individuals – and provide a conjunction of the two.

Edgar Allan Poe's unsettling 'Man of the Crowd' (1840), for example, makes his appearance in that story as an abiding unclassifiable mystery only after the narrator has gone through dozens of urban types who rush past him on a typical London afternoon. The same duality that makes Poe's 'Man of the Crowd' so strikingly able to convey both typical knowledge about urban dwellers and a sense of mystery is also strikingly present in Charles Dickens's *Sketches by Boz* (1833–6). Even the earliest of those sketches demonstrate Dickens's dual commitment – on one hand to detailed empirical knowledge of city life and on the other to the shadowy spaces of individual feeling, site of the sort of lapidary effect Poe singles out as essential to the story.

For example, 'Our Next Door Neighbor' begins as a catalogue of the various types who live on Boz's street, and ends three pages later with Boz sitting at the deathbed of his newest neighbour, a boy recently arrived rosy-cheeked from the country. The sketch begins with a meditation on door-knockers and how well or poorly they describe the people who live behind them – which leads to a metonymic analysis of the avuncular hosts to be found behind 'the jolly face of a convivial lion' and the 'spare priggish' government clerk invariably found living at the house with a 'little pert Egyptian knocker'.[13] This is typological reading at its quickest and crudest, which offers an overly simplified and hence readily undermined form of urban legibility.

The arrival of a new next-door neighbour signals a shift, but the story still remains in the sketch world of types and their quirks. The landlord next door quickly proves incapable of reading typical urban cads – a task that Boz evidently views as indispensable for any physiognomically literate Londoner. First the landlord chooses to rent to a cheery young man who turns out to be a convivial drunk given to loud parties. Making a compensatory lurch, the landlord then rents to 'a serious man' – who promptly makes off with all the movables in the house on the first dark night. The simple reliable world where residents matched their knockers has been replaced by a shadowy (although still 'type'-ridden) zone where landlords are duped because young men of the new generation are so good at giving off misleading clues that their exteriors don't match their conduct. As readers ready themselves for a third laughable urban type, however, another more substantial narrative shift occurs: Boz unveils the pathetic tale of a dying young man and his solicitous mother. Within a page we are listening to the son's heartfelt plea:

> 'Mother! Dear, dear, mother – bury me in the open fields – anywhere but in these dreadful streets.' [...] He fell back, and a strange expression stole upon his features; not of pain or suffering, but an indescribable fixing of every line and muscle.
>
> The boy was dead.[14]

The final morbid moments likely strike modern readers as too lapidary to be truly moving. Still, Boz (who may initially seem to resemble the mid-Victorian journalist-turned-urban-ethnographer Henry Mayhew) is eager to move all the way from stock 'legible' city types to a deathbed where everyday urban experience is replaced by a 'you had to be there' kind of poignancy.

1840–1880: inside the whale

By many critical accounts, a mid-Victorian interregnum followed the era of Poe's apogee and the sketch's triumph. In his argument for the explosion of short stories as a separate genre post-1880, Baldwin proposes that short stories in mid-nineteenth-century Britain are dissatisfying because they aimed to be either merely descriptive sketches or 'brief novels'.[15] Baldwin's notion that the era's most successful writers calibrated their fiction for the long and not the short form may ring true if applied to short stories by the day's best known novelists. Anthony Trollope's 'Mrs. Brumby', a vitriolic and blunt attack on a female writer published as a stand-alone story in May 1870, pales in comparison to his complex character study of the novelist Lady Carbury inside *The Way We Live Now* (1875). But the relative paucity of Victorian stories that succeed when judged by the Poe yardstick does not mean that the readers of the day felt themselves bereft of short fiction. Ghost stories by Mary Elizabeth Braddon, Sheridan Le Fanu and others sold briskly, ethically uplifting tales like Geraldine Jewsbury's 'Agnes Lee' (1857) flourished, and there was a lively market for short stories for children: Frances Browne's *Granny's Wonderful Chair* (1857) and Lewis Carroll's 'Bruno' stories are only the iceberg's tip.[16]

Still, that Trollope-to-Trollope comparison suggests there may be a third way to locate, classify and analyze the short stories of the mid-Victorian era. That way begins by noting that Dickens's 1836 preface to the volume publication of *Sketches by Boz* – 'should they be approved of, he hopes to repeat his experiment with increased confidence, and on a more extensive scale' – proved prophetic in an unexpected way.[17] That extensive scale on which the experiment was to be repeated, it transpired, was housed within the realist novel itself.

Stories have always been at home within novels. The interpolated tale is a time-honoured novelistic device, predicated on the capacity of one fiction to contain another. Related to its container precisely by disjunction, such a tale is an image of the novel within the novel itself: the romance, fancy or tale that offers its characters just the same kind of interlude from their own reality that readers themselves enjoy by picking up a novel. The insertion of such tales implies three ontological levels: our extradiegetic world, the world of the depicted characters (Scheherazade the storyteller) and the world of the stories that they tell (Scheherazade's characters). Such characters from the age of Aesop through Boccaccio down to *Pickwick Papers* are generically barred from the world the storyteller inhabits.[18] In *Pickwick Papers*, old-school interpolation reigns, from 'the Stroller's Tale' in chapter 3 down to chapter 49, 'Containing the Story of the Bagman's Uncle'.[19] Even if readers were momentarily tempted to believe that the 'bagman's uncle' was a real person rather than a convenient fiction, the story itself is cast as a dream, existing only inside the head of the (presumably non-existent) uncle. At the climax of its action, '[m]y uncle gave a loud stamp in the boot in the energy of the moment and – found that it was gray morning, and he was sitting in the wheelwright's yard'.[20]

After *Pickwick Papers,* however, the interpolated tale vanishes almost entirely – not just from Dickens, but from British realist fiction.[21] Already early on in the serialization of *Oliver Twist* (August 1837, before *Pickwick*'s serialization itself had concluded) Dickens's chapter titles signal his intention to keep every story told on the same diegetic level. 'XIII. Some new Acquaintance are Introduced to the Intelligent Reader; Connected with whom Various Pleasant matters are related, appertaining to this story' introduces Bill Sykes and Miss Nancy – and although the matters related are anything but pleasant, they do fulfil the pledge of *pertinence* to the story.[22] *Oliver Twist* not only discards interpolated stories, it also offers up some significant early versions of a literary device that speaks volumes about Victorian notions of the role and place of the short story. From *Oliver Twist* on, Dickens makes liberal use of what we might call the *pseudo-interpolated story*. That is, a story introduced as if it were an interjection from another world instead proves to be a story directly linked to the novel's characters.

In the hands of Dickens and other mid-Victorian novelists, the pseudo-interpolated story is anything but simple. In *Oliver Twist*, Dickens uses pseudo-interpolation briefly (and awkwardly) to disclose Oliver's familial connections. Monks reveals Oliver's connection to Rose Maylie (his aunt) in a rambling, seemingly pointless story that temporarily omits names ('"The child", replied Monks, "when her father died in a strange place, in a strange name, without a letter, book or scrap of paper"') before suddenly making a story about a nameless girl pertinent by demanding, 'Do you see her now?'. The reply tumbles this story back into the mimetic frame: 'Yes, leaning on your arm.'[23] Deixis is the handmaiden of pseudo-interpolation. What seems to be a story from another world is suddenly made pertinent by a pointing finger: there stands the story's subject. Critics then and now have chided Dickens for the 'related after all!' pattern marked by such moments of pseudo-interpolation. But the tactic and a wide variety of related tropes, equally successful for Victorian novelists, attest to the centrality of the idea that every story told inside a novel must in some way 'appertain' to the characters who tell or hear it.

Dickens persistently uses such pseudo-interpolations to allow characters to reveal direct (damning, exonerating, delightful, dreadful) knowledge of others, and he also shares with his peers the tendency to disparage stories that propose a different way of imagining the relationship between tale and world. When Pip is given the nickname Handel by his friend Herbert, Herbert explains that he dislikes the name Philip because

> it sounds like a moral boy out of the spelling-book, who was so lazy that he fell into a pond, or so fat that he couldn't see out of his eyes, or so avaricious that he locked up his cake till the mice ate it, or so determined to go a birds'-nesting that he got himself eaten by bears who lived handy in the neighborhood.[24]

That joke turns on the failure of the moral tale (a rival genre) to be realistic – that is, its failure to tell a story that can be convincingly linked back to *this* real world, inhabited by these particular characters, who can see out of their own eyes, who don't lock up their cake and who live in neighbourhoods without handy bears. The realist novel then is predicated not on conquering the short story but on *assimilating* it, showing that any such story actually belongs to the same world within which it is told.

Pseudo-interpolation should also help us recognize another key aspect of storytelling in Dickens: that characters make sense of their mundane lives by framing (frequently mistaken) stories, about themselves and those around them. Pip's irrepressible tendency to invent stories that might explain his career and his desire for Estella, for example, lies at the heart of *Great Expectations*. That lends great significance to the moment Pip learns that in cold, hard reality he owes his wealth to the unsavoury convict, Magwitch, rather than Miss Havisham. The seeming rebuke to storytelling that is encoded in that moment takes an ironic twist when Dickens proves Pip's fantasy genealogy right, after a fashion. On Magwitch's deathbed, Pip re-sutures the plots through an unexpected byway, linking himself, via Magwitch, back to Estella ('You had a child once, whom you loved and lost.[...] She is a lady and very beautiful. And I love her!').[25] The story holds, we might say, but only because it is confirmed in the unlooked-for byways of life, rather than conforming to the banal clichés on which Pip had built his original storybook love for Estella.

Pseudo-interpolation, then, lies at the heart of a series of strategies that do not expel stories from the Dickensian novel, but instead generate a fictional landscape that restores all stories to the ontological plane on which the characters themselves reside. This incorporation of stories into novels via their application to the protagonists' situation – the swallowing up of stories – helps to explain some of the most distinctive features of the baggy, multiplotted Victorian realist novel. Even granting certain formal differences in how the interior stories are framed and related, Victorian realist novels can be usefully compared not only to eighteenth-century forebears like Defoe and Richardson, but also to the extensive story collections of earlier centuries: *Aesop's Fables, Arabian Nights, The Decameron, The Canterbury Tales*.

Other mid-Victorian novelists made equally avid use of pseudo-interpolated tales, weaving multiple plots together rather than setting embedded stories off as interjections from another world. In *Middlemarch*, for instance, even the furthest flung and most trivial-seeming anecdotes, moments of apparently pure interpolation, are eventually plucked in such a way that they resonate through the web. Take a forgettable early moment, when the young Doctor Lydgate and the Rev. Farebrother are getting acquainted. Farebrother informs Lydgate they have a mutual friend, Trawley, who has apparently forsaken his early ideas of retiring 'to the Backwoods to found a sort of Pythagorean community' in favour of 'practising at a German bath' and marrying a wealthy patient.[26] Lydgate greets this discovery with scorn, and Trawley appears no more in the novel. It would be easy to think for the subsequent 700 pages that he is only a topic to allow Farebrother and Lydgate to sound one another. In the novel's final pages, however, readers discover that Lydgate

> died when he was only fifty, leaving his wife and children provided for by a heavy insurance on his life. He had gained an excellent practice, alternating, according to the season, between London and a Continental bathing-place; having written a treatise on Gout, a disease which has a good deal of wealth on its side.[27]

Although readers cannot be certain Lydgate's bathing place is German, the application of Trawley's story is evident, and not at all what Lydgate had thought at twenty-five. Eliot remarks that '[t]he story [...] [of] men who once meant to shape their own deeds [...] coming to be shapen after the average and fit to be packed by the gross, is hardly ever told even in their consciousness.'[28] Trawley's story is not traced in his own consciousness, but readers nonetheless get glimpses enough of Lydgate's to register the irony of that superior scorn he had earlier heaped on Trawley.

Eliot's web of stories, then, works by showing Trawley and Lydgate alongside one another, and even showing us Lydgate looking at Trawley (future sad sell-out gazing at the present successful sell-out). Eliot needs such quasi-interpolated tales not only to give the reader a wide array of possible choices, but also to show us the mundane process whereby we, hearing the stories of others, try to find the application to our own lives – try, and sometimes, like the scornful Lydgate, fail to guess what sort of pertinence the future will actually reveal.

If there were a joke about how Victorian novels got their bagginess, the punch line might be: by swallowing short stories. During the half-century in which the Victorian realist novel held sway, short stories lived on (to steal a phrase from Orwell) inside the whale. Moretti has made the case that the *episodic* nature of nineteenth-century realist novels is a product of bourgeois sensibility: by his account the interweaving of mundane digressions and detours towards minor characters works to reduce every action to a merely aleatory set of occurrences, burying significance within trivia. If we take seriously the notion that the realist novel engulfs short stories and puts them to work within a larger multiplotted structure, then Eliot's aim in incorporating stories like Trawley's becomes clearer: to depict a world in which every story has a potential application to every person, even if how the story 'appertains' is presently obscure. Rather than being ways to forestall truly heroic action, as Moretti proposes, episodes and the stories of minor characters contained within those episodes mark ways daily life is not simply a backdrop to momentous events, but in some odd way actually comprises those moments of greatness, which are thereby revealed as essentially mundane as well.[29]

One reason that episodes operate as they do within nineteenth-century realist novels may be that stories are no longer *interpolated* into the novel's realm: instead, they belong *inside* that novel's world. Although that particular form of symbiosis between novel and story did not long endure, it had a strong influence on what followed in the final two decades of the nineteenth century, as freestanding stories seized a larger share of the (rapidly expanding) market for fiction. Rather than squelching the genre, the unusual co-existence of stories and novels in those mid-century decades may have given short stories an unusual space within which to mutate and develop in fascinating ways before emerging into the changed publishing environment and culture of the *fin de siècle*.

1880–1900: slips under the microscope

> I will begin by saying, for the encouragement of would-be writers, that there never was a greater opening for short stories than at present, for magazines multiply faster nowadays than do good writers.[30]

Scholars from diverse critical camps have proposed that in or around 1880 the British short story was (re-)born, pointing to works like Arthur Conan Doyle's Holmes stories (1891 onwards) and H. G. Wells's science fiction stories that began appearing in 1884. That breakout moment for British short fiction is, however, presaged in various ways: by, for instance, Robert Louis Stevenson's quirky cycle, *New Arabian Nights* (1878–80), and experimental prose works by Algernon Swinburne (e.g. 'Dead Love', 1862) and Walter Pater (e.g. 'Child in the House', 1878, and his subsequent 'Imaginary Portraits'). Nor can the volta in the mid-1880s be entirely explained by changes in the publishing world. Claire Hanson's explanation for the rupture may be incomplete,[31] but her underlying impulse is right: cultural developments require not only a fiscal but also a hermeneutic analysis. There are outward and inward pressures on how new forms of writing evolve, and even the outward may have their most enduring effects *indirectly*. The ways stories flourished *within* novels in earlier decades should suggest, however, that the increased cultural prestige that accrued to the freestanding short story at century's end resulted from some major transformations in how fiction's capacity and its role was imagined.

As the era of stories folded within realist novels waned, new kinds of stories waxed – stories that preserve Poe's ideas about concision and effect, but that also provide lapidary glimpses into mysterious or inaccessible interior states. If we assess the triumph of both down-market and upmarket stories from 1886 onwards, more similarities emerge than can be explained simply by new larger profits to be made everywhere.[32] The 1880s saw substantial shifts in notions about the essence of character or of action, and new ways of thinking about how impulsive, habitual and otherwise unwilled human actions could be explained.

Although intriguing links can be discerned, the hard-to-fathom inner spaces and potentially inexplicable inward impulses that crop up in *fin-de-siècle* fiction are sharply distinct both from Romantic-era tales and from the 'pertinent' or pseudo-interpolated stories at work within Victorian realist novels. Henry James's spectral experiment, 'The Turn of the Screw' (1898), depicts characters discovering unpredictable discrepancies between their experience of the world and the experience of those around them. Stories akin to James's psychological probings also crop up among British authors, especially those heavily influenced by Flaubert. Joseph Conrad's 1896 'An Outpost of Progress', for example, depicts two European traders destroyed not by the outward dangers of their Congo trading post, but rather by unforeseen inner attributes that the exigencies of their trading post draw to the surface. Early in the story, Conrad sketches them telling themselves seemingly harmless lies about their role in the ivory and slave trade, and the greatness of the cause they are pursuing. The narrator interjects:

> They believed their words. Everybody shows a respectful deference to certain sounds he and his fellows can make, But about feelings people really know nothing, We talk with indignation, or enthusiasm, we talk about oppression, cruelty, crime, devotion, self sacrifice, virtue – and we know nothing real beyond the words.[33]

Conrad points to the discrepancy between the seeming conventions and actual rules that govern our lives – but he offers no easy key by which those words can be folded back into a social context and successfully decoded.

Nor is such scepticism about everyday consensual reality confined to avant-gardists: in fact, the *fin-de-siècle* short story is built on doubt and slippage. Experiments with consciousness, perception and intention run through the science-fiction stories of H. G. Wells. His stories, funny, charming and swift as they are, work by suddenly, creepily uncovering alarming discrepancies between visible surfaces and only-guessable-at depths. Wells offers readers of middle-to-lowbrow periodicals tantalizing glimpses of various inaccessible worlds – at the bottom of the ocean, in the fourth dimension, beyond the edge of the universe. In his stories of the mid-1890s, Wells repeatedly explores moments in which a character finds his experience of the world divided into two. 'The Story of the Late Mr Elvesham' (1896), for example, features a soul-stealing old man who drugs a young medical student for the purpose of exchanging minds with him. At the terrifying heart of the story the young student finds his reality melting away and the old man's experience creeping in. At one point, he feels himself simultaneously walking down Regent Street and (impossibly) entering Waterloo Station:

> I put a knuckle in my eye and it was [again] Regent Street. How can I express it? You see a skillful actor looking quietly at you, he pulls a grimace, and lo! another person. Is it too extravagant if I tell you that it seemed to me as if Regent Street had, for the moment, done that?[34]

That motif of the suddenly doubled world recurs repeatedly in Wells. In 'The Plattner Story', (1896), a teacher is thrown by a strange explosion into 'the fourth dimension' which exists alongside but not quite congruent with the other three. After nine days spectrally spying on our world, he returns ostensibly unchanged, but with all his organs flipped to the other side of his body.

Even stories that describe a mental trip to the edge of the universe, or a quiet British officer's report of his bathysphere ride to the ocean's bottom are built on the presumption that Wells, his characters and his readers share a very ordinary world of knowable surfaces. Yet nearly all are shot through with the uneasy discovery that very ordinary people may prove susceptible to a totally divergent series of sensory inputs that can't readily be reconciled with that world. If the Victorian trope of the pseudo-interpolated tale prized pertinence and application above all, Wells's stories, like Conrad's, uncover hidden fissures that make shared experience impossible even in the most mundane of real-world settings. For Wells, a working-class student's involuntary motions under extreme psychological pressure (in 'A Slip under the Microscope', 1896) are just as worth plumbing as the fourth dimension, the depths of the South Pacific or the mind that feels itself in two places at once. The short story is a perfect medium for these explorations because it does not require the telling physiological, psychological or theological event to be placed as one pertinent episode among others, or to serve as a guide for how one character among many may have been built. Instead Wells looks for the moment when one kind of experience falls away, and another takes over.

The importance of that kind of unexpected small-scale discrepancy in the short fiction of the era offers a valuable hint about the genre's relationship to the new sort of novels heralded by Zola's 1880 manifesto, 'The Experimental Novel'. By Lukács's account, microscopic and macroscopic objects of attention supersede the medium or human-sized subjects in the naturalist novels inspired by Zola's manifesto.[35] That shift in scale resonates revealingly with the logic of short stories by Conrad and Wells in which the key epistemological issues are solved by peering very far inside an individual – or training new kinds of telescope on the distant cosmos. If the pseudo-interpolated tales in the realist novel suggested every event could ultimately be tied back to a single shareable social universe, these glimpses of the depths imply a different sort of commonality: experiential interiority that is the property of each of us, but is available only in isolation. Such scalar variations – when juxtaposed not only to the tales and sketches of the 1830s and 1840s, but also to the pseudo-interpolated stories of mid-Victorian novels – perhaps signal how wide a field falls under that unassuming tag, Victorian short stories.

NOTES

1 Walter Allen, *The Short Story in English* (Oxford: Clarendon Press, 1981), p. 3.
2 Edgar Allan Poe, Review of '*Twice-Told Tales*', *Essays and Reviews* (New York: Library of America, 1984) pp. 569–77 (p. 572).
3 Henry James, 'Preface', *The New York Edition of Henry James,* vol. 7 (New York: Charles Scribner's & Sons, 1908), pp. vi–xxii (p. x).
4 Quoted in Barbara Korte, *The Short Story in Britain: A Historical Sketch and Anthology* (Tübingen: Francke, 2003), p. 10.
5 Korte, *Short Story in Britain*, p. 9.
6 Dean Baldwin, *Art and Commerce in the British Short Story, 1880–1950* (London: Pickering & Chatto, 2013), pp. 1; 3.
7 Baldwin, *Art and Commerce*, p. 13.
8 Brander Matthews, *The Philosophy of the Short-Story* (New York: Longmans, Green, and Co., 1901).
9 See Peter Caracciolo, 'Introduction', *The Arabian Nights in English Literature*, ed. Peter Caracciolo (London: Macmillan, 1988), pp. 1–80. Rastegar argues, however, that it was only the best-selling new translations of the 1880s that really caused an upsurge in British readership. Kamran Rastegar, *Literary Modernity between the Middle East and Europe: Textual Transactions in Nineteenth-Century Arabic, English, and Persian Literatures* (London: Routledge, 2007).
10 Tim Killick, *British Short Fiction in the Early Nineteenth Century: The Rise of the Tale* (Aldershot; Burlington, VT: Ashgate, 2008), pp. 1–2. To Killick's point we might also add David Stewart's observation about 'the difficulties inherent in producing writing for a mass market, rather than particular readers' which made 'the Reading Public' into an inescapable preoccupation among Romantic-era writers. David Stewart, *Romantic Magazines and Metropolitan Literary Culture* (New York: Palgrave Macmillan, 2011), pp. 1–2.
11 Killick, *British Short Fiction*, pp. 157, 158–9.
12 Martina Lauster, *Sketches of the Nineteenth Century: European Journalism and Its Physiologies, 1830–50* (Basingstoke; New York: Palgrave Macmillan, 2007), p. 12. Amanpal Garcha, *From Sketch to Novel: the Development of Victorian Fiction* (Cambridge; New York: Cambridge University Press, 2009), p. 3.
13 Charles Dickens, 'Our Next-Door Neighbour', *Sketches by Boz* (London: Macmillan, 1892), pp. 37–43 (p. 37). The story originally appeared in the *Morning Chronicle* (18 March 1836).

14 Dickens, 'Our Next-Door Neighbour', p. 43.
15 Baldwin, *Art and Commerce*, p. 10.
16 See the illuminating *Broadview Anthology of Victorian Short Stories*, ed. Dennis Denisoff (Peterborough, ON: Broadview, 2004).
17 Dickens, *Sketches by Boz*, p. xv.
18 Borges's proposal that Scheherazade herself appears in one of the nested tales from the *1001 Nights*, thus making its structure truly Escheresque and recursive, is a revealingly postmodern innovation.
19 Aptly, the standard Oxford edition prints a cast of 'characters in the introduced stories' (*Prince Bladud* to *Maria Lobbs*), right after the dramatis personae of the novel itself. Charles Dickens, *The Posthumous Papers of the Pickwick Club* (Oxford: Oxford University Press, 1947), pp. 33; 681; xxiii.
20 Dickens, *Posthumous Papers*, p. 697.
21 One noteworthy exception is Wilkie Collins's *Queen of Hearts*, which, with shrewd commercial logic, transforms ten previously published short stories into a kind of novel by surrounding them with a frame-narrative and a love plot (London: Hurst & Blackett, 1859).
22 Charles Dickens, *Oliver Twist*, ed. Kathleen Tillotson (Oxford: Oxford University Press, 1966), p. 75.
23 Dickens, *Oliver Twist*, p. 355.
24 Charles Dickens, *Great Expectations*, ed. Margaret Caldwell (Oxford: Oxford University Press, 1993), p. 177.
25 Dickens, *Great Expectations*, p. 456.
26 George Eliot, *Middlemarch*, ed. David Carroll (Oxford: Oxford University Press, 1966), p. 169.
27 Eliot, *Middlemarch*, p. 821.
28 Eliot, *Middlemarch*, p.142.
29 Franco Moretti, *The Bourgeois: Between History and Literature* (Brooklyn, NY: Verso, 2013).
30 Anonymous, *Woman's Life*, 'How a Woman May Earn a Living. XV. – As a Short Story Writer', 21 March 1896. Quoted in Kate Krueger, *British Women Writers and the Short Story 1850–1930: Reclaiming Social Space* (Basingstoke; New York: Palgrave Macmillan, 2014), p. 1.
31 Clare Hanson, *Short Stories and Short Fictions, 1880–1980* (London: Macmillan, 1985), p. 8.
32 After summing up various factors increasing financial rewards for writers at the time, Baldwin astutely concludes that such market opportunities 'created conditions that contributed to the "culture wars" between traditionalists and Modernists, but also blurred the lines between these two camps', in Baldwin, *Art and Commerce*, p. 4.
33 Joseph Conrad, 'An Outpost of Progress', *Tales of Unrest* (New York: Doubleday, 1916), pp. 143–98 (pp. 178–9).
34 H. G. Wells, 'The Story of the Late Mr. Elvesham', *Thirty Strange Stories* (London: Harper, 1898), pp. 86–113 (pp. 96–7).
35 Georg Lukács, 'Narrate or Describe?', *Writer and Critic*, ed. and trans. Arthur Kahn (London: Merlin Press, 1970), pp. 110–48.

7

ANN-MARIE EINHAUS

The short story in the early twentieth century

Short stories of the early twentieth century can illustrate beautifully two key aspects of modernity: its tendency to increasing specialization and its constant tension between tradition and innovation. By the time the First World War broke out in August 1914 – defined by critics such as Paul Fussell and Samuel Hynes as the seminal event of the twentieth century – hundreds of increasingly specialized magazines were catering to the diverse tastes of modern audiences.[1] School stories in *Chums* and the *Captain*, romance, adventure and detective stories in *Blackwood's* or *Collier's Magazine*, modernist sketches and impressionist stories in a wide range of longer- and shorter-lived 'little magazines' – readers were spoilt for choice.[2] At the same time, there was considerable overlap in the realm of short fiction between two strands of literature that we now tend to think of as separate, the avant-garde and the mainstream. For instance, readers of the popular and lucrative *Strand Magazine* in April 1919 would have found within its covers a romantic tale like Keble Howard's 'Needs Must When Love Drives' (in which a disabled former officer and a music-loving young lady form tender bonds over lessons on a borrowed piano) rubbing shoulders with D. H. Lawrence's 'Tickets, Please' (a story that questions gender roles in relating the unsettling revenge wreaked by jilted female ticket collectors). On one hand, cash-strapped modernist short story writers like Lawrence or Katherine Mansfield reflect the experimental, innovative nature of their particular brands of modern literature by seeking to push the genre boundaries of the short story further, exploring the subtleties of storytelling and the social changes that were taking place around them. On the other hand, they had to acknowledge the need to meet the demands of the period's thriving commercial market for fiction, that other unavoidable aspect of modernity, in a bid to support themselves.

In his *Aspects of the Modern Short Story* (1924), A. C. Ward included a wide range of short story writers from literary to mainstream, such as George Meredith, Robert Louis Stevenson, Rudyard Kipling, H. G. Wells, Joseph Conrad, Arthur T. Quiller-Couch, Walter de la Mare, Arthur Conan

Doyle, H. C. Bailey, W. W. Jacobs, Stacy Aumonier, C. E. Montague, Anton Chekhov and Katherine Mansfield, in an endeavour to 'undertake an analytical survey of representative short stories by certain modern writers who have combined literary merit with a popular appeal'.[3] Despite the blurred boundaries and frequent overlaps between different types of short stories, the short story in the early twentieth century is still frequently equated with modernist short fiction. This perception persists despite the fact that the magazine market from the 1910s to 1930s was, if anything, more diverse and short stories more varied and successful at *all* cultural levels than ever before or since. While this *Companion* shows that the short story is not, as Walter Allen claimed in 1981, 'essentially a modern form', it was certainly a form that thrived in and was easily adapted to the modern period.[4] Magazines and periodicals catered for all kinds of reading tastes, and the short form and its magazine medium allowed for all manner of literary experimentation and exploration, whether in terms of form, content or both. While this chapter shows that modernist writers made new and innovative use of the short form, it will also look at the so-called magazine story, a kind of short story often perceived as based on craft rather than art.[5] Writers considered in this chapter range from modernist short story writers to so-called middlebrow exponents of the form, such as Stacy Aumonier and Elizabeth Bibesco, and popular magazine writers such as May Edginton. Besides linking these stories to the ongoing craft-versus-art debate in early-twentieth-century short story criticism, the chapter will also look at ways the short form responded to the social and political change of the 1910s and 1920s. While Ward in 1924 listed among his evaluative criteria for short fiction the quality and execution of plot, simplicity of style, characterization and a sense of 'progressive movement toward the end appointed', he also acknowledged that beside the traditional plot-driven story there was

> need to give patient and sympathetic attention to experiment and exploration and fresh endeavour, which involve trial and error, immaturity, and (it may be) certain factors not immediately intelligible to minds unprepared for experimental work.[6]

This chapter endeavours to do justice to both traditions of short story writing in the early twentieth century, and indeed to show that they cannot always be neatly separated from each other.

The short story as locus of experimentation and innovation

Opening his seminal study on modernist short fiction, Dominic Head observes, 'the short story encapsulates the essence of literary modernism, and has an enduring ability to capture the episodic nature of twentieth-century experience.'[7] This view echoes Ward's contemporary voice, who saw the short story as a genre well suited to conveying the 'jagged and blurred edges' of modern life and its 'hazy and indefinable outlines': 'The brief prose form', he claimed, 'lends itself readily to impressionistic effect; it affords a more suitable medium than the novel for excursions into the dim territory of the subconscious'.[8] According to Head's characterization, 'there is a stress on literary artifice in the short story which intensifies the modernist preoccupation with formal innovation', and he convincingly argues that 'the modernist short story, far from being "smaller and lesser" in any technical sense, actually exemplifies the strategies of modernist fiction'.[9] While Head does not suggest that this close relationship between the short form and modernism is necessarily an exclusive one, a survey of twentieth-century short story criticism suggests that there is at least an implicit equation of early-twentieth-century short fiction with modernism and/or formal experimentation. Although they offer detailed and in many ways carefully balanced accounts of the short story in the twentieth century, influential critics of the genre such as Clare Hanson, Valerie Shaw and Charles May include a larger selection of modernist than 'traditional' short story writers, and tend to leave out overtly commercial magazine fiction (with the exception of highly successful mainstream writers such as Rudyard Kipling, H. G. Wells and W. S. Maugham, or the Americans O. Henry and Bret Harte).[10] Critical distinctions between different types of short fiction hinge less on its situation in the literary marketplace, and more on the boundary between realist and experimental fiction. This is evident in studies such as May's *The Reality of Artifice*, where 'Nineteenth-Century Realism' is contrasted with 'Early-Twentieth-Century Formalism' in the very chapter structure.[11]

Modernist short fiction captured the attention of later-twentieth-century critics not least because it offered a seemingly radical break from traditional models of storytelling. As David Stewart shows in his contribution to this volume, the modernist sketch or stream-of-consciousness narrative has clear antecedents in the eighteenth-century and Romantic sketch. However, early-twentieth-century audiences and later critics alike perceived a departure from plot and from a stable narrative voice as the most striking and defining feature of new, avant-garde short fiction. As Head observes,

> In the stories of Joyce, Woolf and Mansfield [...] formal dissonance is both a yardstick of generic innovation and a vital key to interpretation. All three writers, in their different ways, expand the short story form to incorporate and express a complex view of the interaction between individual experience and social organization.[12]

It is perhaps unsurprising that short story critics past and present should be paying particular attention to what can be perceived as pushing boundaries, and undoubtedly the critical acclaim of modernist short story practitioners has done much – not least through endorsement by F. R. Leavis and the American New Critics – to boost the critical prestige of short fiction. The case for a close link between the short form and experimental modernism thus seems convincing; however, the implicit assumption that modernist short fiction has a monopoly on representing early-twentieth-century reality and the experience of modern life is flawed all the same, as it omits entirely the commercial and popular dimension of short fiction.

The short story as a commercial medium

There is more than one way of representing modern experience, and fragmentation and alienation are not the sole valid responses to modernity. Robert Scholes makes a valuable case for what he calls a modern literature of 'iridescent mediocrity', defined as 'writing that turns away from the realistic and distances itself from modernity in order to criticize it': a 'Light Modernism' that draws on high-cultural and canonical as well as popular models in its response to the challenges and frequent drabness and disillusionment of modern life.[13] The 'two key elements of the short story' that Head identifies – 'its intensity and its exaggerated artifice' – apply to many non-modernist short stories just as much as to modernist experimental short fiction.[14] Equally, Michael Joseph's dictum that '[t]here should be one outstanding "point" in a short story: one central incident, or climax, to which everything else in the story is strictly subordinate', can be applied with ease to the majority of modernist, experimental short stories, although perhaps not quite as Joseph had in mind.[15] Like modernist writers of short fiction, short story authors who wrote for mainstream magazines were writing to often exacting standards and set out to capture particular experiences of modernity, albeit of a different nature. While writing intended to be commercially successful (and in a sense, one might argue that most writing is) has to make concessions to readability and may have to do without radical experimentation to appeal to a broader readership, the editorial standards of many mainstream fiction magazines were restrictive and challenging in their own way. According to Michael Joseph's 1923 writing manual, *Short Story Writing for Profit*, the fiction editor of the *Strand Magazine* was looking for stories 'from three to seven thousand words in length, with plenty of plot and exciting incident, or of a light and entertaining nature [...] Payment is liberal for good work and is made on acceptance.'[16] Authors wishing to write for such liberal payment – which included, among others, D. H. Lawrence, Joseph Conrad and Arthur Conan Doyle – consequently had to work within narrowly defined boundaries, particularly with regard to word length, subject matter and accessibility.

Whether in the high-profile and generously paying *Strand Magazine* or elsewhere, short story writing in the early twentieth century was thus also a potentially very lucrative profession, provided writers were able to cater to the demands of particular magazines. In advice for and by writers of the period, tips on how to pitch one's short fiction abounds. In a 1922 letter to his friend William Townend, P. G. Wodehouse showed a particularly keen sense of literary positioning and the differences between different kinds of short fiction:

> All this sounds rather incoherent – but, well, look here: your story, *The Horse Thief*, was sure-fire for any magazine because the actual plot was so exactly right for any type of reader that it didn't matter that it was well written instead of cheaply. But *The Price of the Picture* was no good for popular magazines unless thoroughly cheapened.
>
> And I know what I am driving at is: When you get a plot, examine it carefully and say to yourself: 'Is this a popular magazine plot?' If it isn't, simply don't attempt to make it a popular magazine story. Just put all you know into it and write it the very best you can and confine its field to the really decent magazines like *Blackwood's*, the *Cornhill*, etc.[17]

Wodehouse himself here establishes clear distinctions between magazine stories of different calibre, from 'cheaply' written to 'decent' – the latter to be seen as primarily a judgement of quality, but potentially also implying a moral difference. His distinction does not, however, rest on a contrast of the plot-driven versus the psychological and plotless story, but on a sense of style and of the *quality* of plot.

Where the *Strand Magazine* and similar mainstream publications might be looking for a tightly knitted plot and educated but accessible language, the *English Review* – listed in the same writers' manual under the heading 'LITERARY' – is described more vaguely: 'Accepts occasional short stories (ordinary length) of literary merit', but with the revealing rider, 'Style important'.[18] Successful writers would contribute stories to very different magazines. Sticking with the contrasting examples of the *Strand Magazine* and the *English Review*, Stacy Aumonier is an example of an author who contributed short fiction to both magazines. His bittersweet wartime tale 'The Grayles' and his tragic story of a secret double life, 'The Friends', appeared in the *English Review*, while the *Strand Magazine* published stories such as 'The Match: Today and Yesterday' and 'A Source of Irritation'.[19]

While 'The Match' wistfully portrays two cricket matches, one pre-war and one wartime, to highlight the impact of the First World War on a rural community, the latter story is an exuberantly comic account of an old agricultural labourer who finds himself abducted from his Norfolk turnip field by a German aviator because he bears an astonishing resemblance to a famous German spy. As one might expect of a *Strand Magazine* tale, the gruff old man escapes, is celebrated as a hero by his highly amused countrymen, and taken back to Norfolk thanks to the modern convenience of a despatch airplane in time for his tea. It is a rather bizarre story, but it is well written and astonishingly manages to pull off its hair-raising plot without slipping into trite commonplaces or silliness. Aumonier's very versatility was indeed perceived as the key of his success, in a manner somewhat reminiscent of Wodehouse's emphasis on moulding one's fiction to the particular readership of whichever magazine one wished to publish in; Ward saw Aumonier's 'versatility and virtuosity' as insurance 'against the exclusive working of any one particular vein' and praised Aumonier on the grounds that he had arguably 'made himself acceptable to the magazine public without writing down to any presumed "magazine standard"', adding that '[i]f he has not the special powers which belong to a few of his contemporaries, he has, conversely, the advantage of not being a writer for an exclusive coterie'.[20]

In his versatility – although more firmly located on the craft rather than the art side of the fence – Aumonier somewhat resembles D. H. Lawrence, who likewise published in a range of different magazines and was excluded from Head's study of the modernist short story on the grounds that his stories are 'predominantly conservative in structure and form' and (particularly compared with his later work in the shape of fables) 'his work in the genre is distinct from the modernist short story proper, with its clear rejection of stable plotting'.[21] Aumonier's work is by no stretch of the imagination formally experimental, but it is arguably distinct from the average magazine story in its well-crafted style and often exquisitely comic tone. One of the assumptions of modernist critics critiqued by Scholes is their easy dismissal of 'traditional values' in literature, such as 'empathy with characters and concern for their fates in fiction, the pleasures of recognition and seeing freshly in visual art, and the defamiliarizing effects of poetic language', as well as 'wit and grace, whether verbal or visual'.[22] If, as Scholes suggests, '[t]he one thing that distinguishes the arts from other kinds of texts is that their aim is pleasure',[23] then Aumonier's witty approach to early-twentieth-century experience deserves to be given more critical attention – as, indeed, Kate Macdonald argues with regard to comic short fiction more generally in her contribution to this volume.

Social change, history and the short story

Although the very topicality of most short stories also contributes to their ephemerality, one of the greatest assets of short fiction is its ability to be close to the pulse of its time. Short stories published in early-twentieth-century magazines often responded with great immediacy to events, social or political developments and sentiments of the day. Although even a weekly magazine naturally needed to plan ahead when it came to its fiction contributions, and writers of fiction are, after all, not under the same obligations as journalists to deliver same-day news stories, short stories nevertheless frequently reveal or reflect their particular moment. The short story of the First World War is a case in point: within weeks of Britain's declaration of war, stories such as Arthur Machen's 'The Bowmen' (first published in the *Evening News* on 29 September 1914), appeared in newspapers and magazines.[24] By 1915, the war was not only dealt with as a momentous event in its own right, but had been absorbed as part of the backdrop for a host of romance, detective and adventure stories.[25] Arguably, the social changes that accompanied the war also had a beneficial effect on what short fiction could and did do. Reflecting on the effect of the Great War on the British short story, H. E. Bates noted:

> Writers, after the Great War of 1914–18, found themselves less fettered than at any time in history. They had suddenly a free pass to say and see and do and describe anything they wanted. No subject was now barred to a writer, to the last limit of physical experience. To the short-story writer, therefore, perhaps even more than to the novelist, a world of immense new possibilities was opened up.[26]

Although Bates wrote primarily of those post-war writers who 'saw no escape in the mechanical structure and consequent financial freedom in prosperous magazines',[27] magazine fiction also – if at a more cautious, gradual pace – reflected changing morals and conventions in the wake of the war.

Diversity

As we have seen, short stories at both the literary and the popular ends of the spectrum had their proponents, their respective philosophies of writing and belief in quality, although these are modelled on different understandings of what fiction in general and short fiction in particular ought to accomplish. In his introductory note to *Short Story Writing for Profit*, Joseph clearly delineated his audience as 'those who feel the need of a practical guide to short story writing'.[28] His principles for inclusion are equally straightforward and market-oriented, in that the 'majority of the authors quoted have been chosen as good working models for the writer who is anxious to produce a saleable story': the 'ultra-modern conception of the short story as a vehicle for brilliant writing will not help the would-be contributor to the magazines'.[29] However, modern readers might be surprised to find that Joseph saw not only the likes of Chekhov, Mansfield, Aldous Huxley and Henry James as unhelpful to aspiring magazine writers, but a range of less canonical writers now considered rather mainstream, such as Rebecca West, Walter de la Mare, Maurice Baring and Elizabeth Bibesco. Joseph clearly positions himself on the craft side of the art-versus-craft divide in observing that '[t]he man who contributes short stories to the magazines is every whit as useful a member of society as the man who manufactures furniture or cheap jewellery'.[30] There was clearly a difference, even in the eyes of pragmatists and apologists of writing as a trade like Joseph, between the formulaic and the merely mechanical, which Scholes characterizes as a distinction between craft and industry.[31]

A story may thus tap into literary formulae and yet not be a slave to mere repetition, or lack innovation. Equally, any short story may well pick up well-worn literary tropes and conventions and cast them in a new mould, as a comparison of four stories ranging from the modernist to the popular end of the literary spectrum may demonstrate. James Joyce's 'Clay' (1914) and Katherine Mansfield's 'Miss Brill' (1920) are prominent examples of early-twentieth-century short fiction, whereas Elizabeth Bibesco's 'Haven' (1922) and May Edginton's 'War Workers' (1917) are far less well known – yet all four deal with the position of the ageing, unmarried woman in a society poised between traditional values and rapid social and political change.[32]

The figure of the spinster is not, of course, a modern(ist) literary phenomenon, but the First World War in particular threw the predicament of the so-called surplus or superfluous woman into greater relief. The results of the 1921 National Census, which uncovered that there were 1,095 women for every 1,000 men in Great Britain (as opposed to 1,040 women for every 1,000 men in 1831), were met with considerable dismay and dramatic newspaper headlines, but more sober editorials admitted that 'the war [had] merely accentuated, though accentuated sharply, a long-established tendency'.[33] On one hand, the war effort meant that fears about unmarried women's economic destitution were somewhat allayed, as the war provided unprecedented opportunities for single women to support themselves. A 'Woman Correspondent' noted in *The Times* in 1916 that '[t]here seems no doubt that for the moment the demand [for women workers] exceeds the supply, a situation almost incredible to a generation brought up to talk glibly of "more than a million superfluous women"'.[34] Given their usually meagre salaries, the lot of unmarried female workers was not easy, especially once

The short story in the early twentieth century

they retired, but there were nevertheless increased opportunities for not only working-class but also 'genteel' women to enter a wider range of professions. On the other hand, the war also saw the deaths of a large number of eligible middle- and upper-class bachelors between eighteen and forty-two, and raised new concerns as to the marital prospects of young middle-class women in particular. Their plight – as described hauntingly in Vera Brittain's poem 'The Superfluous Woman' (1920) – was less an economic than an emotional one, since women like Brittain feared that their hopes for a family and fulfilling relationships might have been dashed by the war. The three short stanzas of Brittain's mournful poem are structured around three questions posed to her readers, pitched against descriptions of everyday life haunted by memories: 'But who will look for my coming?', Brittain's speaker asks, continuing with 'who will seek me at nightfall?' and closing with the poignant enquiry, 'who will give me my children?'[35] Brittain's poem thus laments lost companionship as well as voicing fears that a fulfilled family life has been made impossible by the war. The four stories under investigation, written before (Joyce), during (Edginton) and after (Mansfield and Bibesco) the First World War, tackle such fears of emotional precariousness and loneliness, rather than economic concerns. They engage with the plight of older unmarried women from a range of different angles that reflect the diversity of their writers' national, religious, social and gendered backgrounds. They approach their unmarried, ageing female characters from different perspectives, but also re-interpret the spinster trope for different audiences and in distinctly different styles.

Joyce's pre-war, Irish, working-class spinster, Maria, in 'Clay' seems economically secure enough, as she is able to support herself by working as a kitchen maid in a charitable institution for Dublin's 'fallen women'. It is emotional security and fulfilment she craves, however. Maria is introduced to the reader as a version of the ideal home-maker: the kitchen of which she is in charge is 'spick and span', and the barmbracks she has cut are so finely sliced that the cuts are imperceptible.[36] Maria's world is also full of substitutions for a family proper. At work, Maria 'had her plants in the conservatory and she liked looking after them' as one might look after and take pride in well-behaved children, and she acts much like a mother-substitute to the women living and working in the laundry, where '[e]veryone was so fond of Maria'.[37] Joe's family, whom she goes to visit for an All-Hallows-Eve party, is not her own either, although Joe likewise regards her as a substitute mother: 'She had nursed him and Alphy too; and Joe used often say: – Mamma is mamma but Maria is my proper mother.'[38] The story is also riddled with references to the perceived ideal of marriage that Maria has failed to attain. Not only does Maria fail to pick up the symbolic ring in traditional All-Hallows-Eve games at the opening and close of the story, she is also mocked by the girl in the cake shop who asks her spitefully 'was it wedding-cake she wanted to buy', and she experiences a parody of courtesy and flirtation with an inebriated older man on the tram, where 'none of the young men seemed to notice her'.[39] Although Maria herself repeatedly expresses her contentment – as when she 'had to laugh and say she didn't want any ring or man either' in return to a well worn joke – and clearly feels apprehensive about male volatility, particularly with regard to men and drunkenness, the overall impression conveyed by the narrative is one of regret for Maria's perceived lack on the part of those around her, if not necessarily Maria herself.[40] Told subtly from Maria's own naïve perspective, albeit in the form of a third person narrative, Joyce's story may thus be deliberately or unwittingly exposing the stereotypical view of spinsters at a time when 'benevolent people [...] would like to see every woman "a wife and mother"' despite the fact that, as one exasperated female letter-writer pointed out, women may equally be seen as 'that sex which, though traditionally counted more "dependent", is apparently better able than the other to be reasonably happy without marrying and adding to the population'.[41]

Mansfield's Miss Brill is a foreigner in London with no family ties in England whatsoever, and this story, like Joyce's, shows the main protagonist's feelings lavished upon a substitute object of affection, in this case her battered fur collar: the '[d]ear little thing' that is apostrophized and personified in Mansfield's free indirect discourse rendition of Miss Brill's fragile consciousness.[42] Miss Brill's sensation of 'something light and sad – no, not sad, exactly – something gentle' stirring 'in her bosom' could easily be read as a sense of regret at having to caress a dead animal as opposed to a live creature, and her loneliness becomes further apparent in her consistent focus on pairs and couples, from the elderly married couple seated next to her on her 'special seat' and recollections of last week's quarrelling husband and wife, to girls and soldiers walking out together, '[t]wo peasant women with funny straw hats', and finally the young couple whose careless remarks shatter her illusion of community and belonging.[43] Miss Brill's loneliness is intensified by her status as a foreigner, and she sympathizes seemingly naturally with another lonely, ageing woman, snubbed by a male acquaintance, while she appears a little wary of the 'cold, pale nun' whose solitariness is of her own choosing.[44] Her very sentimentality and need for belonging and recognition, for being somebody whose absence would be missed, mark Miss Brill as vulnerable. Her easily shattered illusions and vicarious enjoyment of company speak distinctly to the fears of loneliness in old age voiced in Brittain's poem and by concerned commentators in the papers and periodicals.

Bibesco's 'Haven', by contrast, approaches the plight of the lonely spinster in a more humorous and ultimately comforting way. Her protagonist Miss Wilcox is an English maiden lady past her prime, who has developed from 'a pretty, bouncing girl with bright blue eyes, bright pink cheeks and bright yellow hair' chased by 'all the young men in the neighbourhood', to frustrated middle age thanks to her misguided assumptions as to '"what men liked in a woman"'.[45] Not content to resign herself to the traditional spinster's fate of 'decorating the church and organizing village entertainments', Miss Wilcox impulsively seizes her chance of escape when an inheritance enables her to move to France and live happily ever after by posing as a tragically romantic widow, adorned with expensive mourning garb and a fake wedding band.[46] Bibesco adopts a more conventional tone of social satire and gentle, sympathetic mockery, as opposed to Mansfield's ability of putting her readers inside Miss Brill's wounded psyche; she offers us a rounded portrait of a small community surrounding her protagonist, whereas the poignancy of Mansfield's story rests precisely on the fact that we see Miss Brill in isolation. Bibesco also, however, deftly satirizes tropes of romantic magazine fiction, not only through Miss Wilcox's flowery fantasies of 'a huge man with whimsical, smiling eyes' on whose shoulder she can lay her head, but also by providing a happy ending that leaves Miss Wilcox happy with the pretence of married love rather than the (perhaps ultimately less appealing) reality of matrimony.[47]

Edginton's 'War Workers' – a prime example of popular magazine fiction – also takes a humorous approach, albeit one that closes with an actual marriage. The ladies on a small-town war relief committee are shocked to the core when they are sent a parcel of expensive lingerie by a wealthy well-wisher, to be sold to raise funds. The only two maiden ladies on the committee, however, take a secret fancy to the beautiful clothes and buy them in secret, or so they believe. The two friends gradually begin to dress a little more frivolously day by day and capture the attention of an eminently respectable local professor. The professor first decides to marry the one spinster whom he notices in her new attire, and then, when he finds out by accident that his new fiancée has given away all her nice underwear to her friend, he marries the friend. Edginton's story shows – before a topical wartime backdrop – that romance is not the preserve of the young, albeit rather tongue-in-cheek.

Conclusion

This chapter initially argued that early-twentieth-century short stories reveal two key aspects of modernity: increasing specialization on one hand and constant tension between tradition and innovation on the other. Traditional and experimental fiction existed side by side, and the boundaries between the two are often blurred. What, beyond the marital status of their protagonists, links such a diverse range of stories as the four spinster stories discussed in this chapter? They differ stylistically, were published in very different media with different audience appeal, and engage with different aesthetic approaches. Precisely because they range from the comic tale to the psychological sketch, however, these four stories bear witness to the increasing levels of specialization in early-twentieth-century short fiction, which follows on from developments in the magazine market that begin at least as far back as the Romantic period, as David Stewart and John Plotz show in their respective chapters. The short story occupies a shifting position between the twin poles of tradition and innovation not least because of its close links to this constantly developing periodical market.

Short stories of the early twentieth century reflect the diversity of their publishing environments just as much as they mirror the variety of modern experience. Topical and varied in their form, outlook and themes, short stories of the period offer a fascinating insight into a variety of aspects of modernity, from artistic and aesthetic debates to an increase in commercialization and consumerism. As we look at mainstream and coterie authors side by side, we can see that short fiction on both sides of the market may address very similar concerns or ideas, albeit in different ways and with different goals. To fully grasp the complexity of early-twentieth-century short fiction, we have to look beyond narrow categories such as modernist versus mainstream or literary versus popular fiction and take each story on its own terms as an expression of one particular facet of modern life.

NOTES

1. See Paul Fussell, *The Great War and Modern Memory* (London; Oxford; New York: Oxford University Press, 1975), and Samuel Hynes, *A War Imagined: The First World War and English Culture* (London: Bodley Head, 1990).
2. For a wide range of digitized 'little magazines', readers can refer to databases established by the American Modernist Journals Project (http://modjourn.org/) and the British Modernist Magazines Project (www.modernistmagazines.com/) [Accessed 12 March 2015].
3. Alfred C. Ward, *Aspects of the Modern Short Story: English and American* (London: University of London Press, 1924), pp. 7–8.
4. Walter Allen, *The Short Story in English* (Oxford: Clarendon, 1981), p. 3.
5. See, for example, Mary Louise Pratt, 'The Short Story: The Long and the Short of It', *New Short Story Theories*, ed. Charles E. May (Athens: Ohio University Press, 1994), p. 110.
6. Ward, *Aspects*, pp. 15; 16.

7 Dominic Head, *The Modernist Short Story: A Study in Theory and Practice* (Cambridge: Cambridge University Press, 1992), p. 1.
8 Ward, *Aspects*, pp. 16; 17.
9 Head, *Modernist Short Story*, pp. 2; 6.
10 In a chapter titled 'The Splintering Frame', Shaw addresses the status of the short story in the twentieth century and its relation to the fragmentation of modern experience by dividing 'a number of twentieth-century writers' into 'the broad categories, "realist" and "romantic"', depending on whether they are depicting faithfully or overtly challenging modern reality. See Valerie Shaw, *The Short Story: A Critical Introduction* (1983; London: Longman, 1995), p. 229. Hanson distinguishes more broadly between plotted short stories and plotless short fiction. See Clare Hanson, *Short Stories and Short Fiction, 1880–1980* (Basingstoke: Macmillan, 1985).
11 See Charles E. May, *The Short Story: The Reality of Artifice* (1995; New York; London: Routledge, 2002).
12 Head, *Modernist Short Story*, p. 139.
13 Robert Scholes, *The Paradoxy of Modernism* (New Haven, CT: Yale University Press, 2006), p. 193; 183.
14 Head, *Modernist Short Story*, p. 2.
15 Michael Joseph, *Short Story Writing for Profit*, 2nd edn (London: Hutchinson, 1923), p. 7.
16 Joseph, *Short Story Writing*, p. 204.
17 P. G. Wodehouse, *Performing Flea: A Self-Portrait in Letters*, intro. W. Townend (London: Jenkins, 1953), pp. 18–19.
18 Joseph, *Short Story Writing*, p. 217.
19 Stacy Aumonier, 'The Grayles', *English Review*, 22.88 (March 1916), 222–32; 'The Friends', *English Review*, 21.83 (October 1915), 253–71; 'The Match: Today and Yesterday', *Strand Magazine*, 52.307 (July 1916), 30–7; 'A Source of Irritation', *Strand Magazine*, 55.326 (February 1918), 99–107.
20 Ward, *Aspects*, p. 253.
21 Head, *Modernist Short Story*, pp. 34; 35.
22 Scholes, *Paradoxy*, p. xiii.
23 Scholes, *Paradoxy*, p. xiii.
24 Machen's story dealt with the British retreat at Mons and was subsequently collected in *The Angels of Mons: The Bowmen and Other Legends of the War* (London: Simpkin, Marshall, Hamilton, Kent & Co., 1915).
25 See, for example, Jane Potter, *Boys in Khaki, Girls in Print: Women's Literary Responses to the Great War 1914–1918* (Oxford: Oxford University Press, 2005), p. 76, and Ann-Marie Einhaus, *The Short Story and the First World War* (Cambridge: Cambridge University Press, 2013), chapter 2: 'The War in the Magazines'.
26 H. E. Bates, *The Modern Short Story: A Critical Survey* (1941; Boston, MA: The Writer, 1965), p. 133.
27 Bates, *Modern Short Story*, pp. 120–1.
28 Joseph, *Short Story Writing*, p. xiii.
29 Joseph, *Short Story Writing*, p. xiii.
30 Joseph, *Short Story Writing*, p. 3.
31 Scholes, *Paradoxy*, p. 10.

32 James Joyce, 'Clay', *Dubliners* (1914; London: Penguin Classics, 1992), pp. 95–102; Katherine Mansfield, 'Miss Brill', *Selected Stories* (Oxford: Oxford University Press, 2002), pp. 225–9; Elizabeth Bibesco, 'Haven', *Balloons*, 3rd edn (1922; London: Hurst & Blackett, n.d.), pp. 205–17; May Edginton, 'War Workers', *Strand Magazine*, 54 (October 1917), 386–94.
33 'Surplus Women', *The Times* (25 August 1921), p. 9.
34 'More Women Wanted', *The Times* (3 August 1916), p. 9.
35 Vera Brittain, 'The Superfluous Woman', *Testament of Youth: An Autobiographical Study of the Years 1900–1945* (1933; London: Virago, 2004), p. 490.
36 Joyce, 'Clay', p. 95.
37 Joyce, 'Clay', pp. 96; 95.
38 Joyce, 'Clay', p. 96.
39 Joyce, 'Clay', p. 98.
40 Joyce, 'Clay', pp. 97; 96; 99.
41 Eleanor F. Rathbone, 'More Women than Men', *The Times* (5 September 1921), p. 4.
42 Mansfield, 'Miss Brill', p. 225.
43 Mansfield, 'Miss Brill', pp. 225; 226; 227; 228.
44 Mansfield, 'Miss Brill', p. 227.
45 Bibesco, 'Haven', pp. 206; 207.
46 Bibesco, 'Haven', pp. 211–12.
47 Bibesco, 'Haven', p. 208. Mansfield of course also wrote different stories for different audiences throughout her career, from the biting satire of *In a German Pension* and sentimental (if still satirical) stories such as 'Marriage à la Mode', to more radically experimental sketches like 'Bank Holiday'. This variety reflects the fact that Mansfield produced short fiction for a range of periodicals, from avant-garde little magazines like *Rhythm* to mainstream story publications such as the *Story-Teller*.

8

VICTORIA STEWART

Mid-twentieth-century stories

In a review published in the *New Statesman and Nation* in January 1941, George Orwell lamented the current state of the short story:

> Something has gone wrong with this *genre*. [...] Nearly always the formula is the same: a pointless little sketch about fundamentally uninteresting people, written in short flat sentences and ending on a vague query. 'Mrs Whitaker parted the lace curtains above the geranium. The car was disappearing into the far distance.' '"You're a good kid," he whispered. Their lips met. But Maisie was thinking that they'd have to pawn Danny's dinner suit if the rent was to be paid this week.' There seems to be a sort of cult of pointlessness and indefiniteness, quite possibly covering, in many cases, a mere inability to construct a 'plot.'[1]

As Stephen Spender noted in his own assessment of the short story later the same year, Orwell's view of the form was both jaded and partial, omitting the 'very considerable achievement of some contemporary short story writers'.[2] While agreeing with some of Orwell's reservations about the works of H. E. Bates, Spender asserted that, 'as a fragmentary vision of a philosophy of life and of an experience, we would expect [the short story] to be one of the most vital forms of prose writing to-day. Given the world to-day, we can hardly expect writers to "see life steadily and see it whole."'[3] This sense that the short story as a form is particularly suited to representing the exigencies of living in wartime is one that is echoed by other commentators during this period; the 'indefiniteness' that Orwell identifies can be seen as a consequence of an attempt to capture a moment within a socio-political situation in constant flux. Even before the outbreak of the war, however, Elizabeth Bowen identified inconclusiveness as a particular attribute of the short story: 'free from the *longueurs* of the novel, [the short story] is also exempt from the novel's conclusiveness – too often forced and false: it may thus more nearly than the novel approach aesthetic and moral truth.'[4] In this context, the Second World War can be seen to have accelerated an existing tendency in the short story towards the kind of 'indefiniteness' that Bowen reflects on and Orwell critiques.

The ongoing aesthetic challenges of the short story form were compounded on the outbreak of war by problems of a practical kind. Many authors, and others involved in the publishing industry, faced mobilization, there were disruptions to printing, production and distribution, and paper rationing was introduced. Publishers' uncertainty initially led to what Robert Hewison has called 'a grand slaughter of magazines'.[5] A number of literary periodicals, including *New Stories*, the *Criterion* and the *Cornhill*, closed in 1939–40, but despite the ban on new journals imposed in May 1940, during the war, a wealth of new fora for short fiction established itself.[6] Soon after the end of the conflict, the situation shifted again; Elizabeth Berridge, reflecting in part on her husband, Reginald Moore's, publishing endeavours of the 1940s, including the journal *Modern Reading*, noted that by 1950 'the era of wartime anthologies' had come to an end.[7] The war provided both new subject matter and, perhaps unexpectedly, new opportunities for publication, but interest in the war as a topic began to diminish rapidly when the conflict concluded, and a publishing climate that had led to a boom in short fiction began to look less favourable to the kinds of publishing venture that had given many new writers a start. Certain issues, however, remained constant throughout this period: as Dan Davin commented some years later, 'the true problems of the short story are the same in war as they are in peace: because of the need for brevity, every comma, colon, full stop, paragraph, every word must be made to count.'[8] This chapter will show how the short story was adapted to the new circumstances of wartime, and how these circumstances in turn provoked experiments with form that had a continuing legacy in the post-war period.

The literary-historical context

Orwell's comments on the short story appeared in a review of, among other texts, a new volume of stories by H. E. Bates, an indication that single-authored short story collections continued to appear during this period, but a more usual route to publication, especially for new authors, was via journals or anthologies. The war necessitated creative thinking on the part of editors and publishers. For example, in his preface to the First Series of *English Story*, an anthology that appeared annually between 1941 and 1950, Woodrow Wyatt described the situation that had led to this publication's appearance. He identified a shortage of opportunities for the publication of what he described as the '"non-commercial"' short story, one 'which does not conform to the stereotyped pattern demanded by most magazine editors'.[9] Having initially intended to publish a bi-monthly magazine, Wyatt, together with his co-editor, his wife, Susan, instead struck a deal with Collins, so that what would have been 'the contents of two to three magazines' appeared in book form under the Collins imprint.[10] The Wyatts were thus able to combine the topicality of a magazine with the circulation and production values of a book.

A similar arrangement was negotiated between John Lehmann and Allen Lane of Penguin. Lehmann had begun publishing *New Writing* in 1936, and it continued into the war years, renamed *Folios of New Writing* in 1940, before becoming *New Writing and Daylight* the following year, appearing roughly twice a year in hard covers – a 'magazine in book form', as Françoise Bort describes it.[11] Meanwhile, from the end of 1940 until 1950, *Penguin New Writing*, in the same format as a paperback book, 'peacefully co-existed' with *Folios*, its circulation reaching seventy-five thousand copies by the end of 1941.[12] Alongside short stories, *Penguin New Writing* published poetry and essays, including art criticism and critical commentary such as Spender's reflections on the state of the short story. The publication had an international flavour, but, as for *English Story*, topicality and the nurturing of new talents were an important aspect of its remit. Some of the contributor biographies for each publication imply a connection between the war and beginning to write.[13] But authors who already had established reputations also took advantage of such new opportunities, with Elizabeth Bowen, for example, appearing in both, as well as in *Horizon*.

Unlike *Penguin New Writing* and *English Story*, *Horizon*, edited by Cyril Connolly, was a stand-alone journal that appeared from January 1940 until December 1949, and one that, like Lehmann's, published fiction, non-fiction and poetry. In its opening number, Connolly asserted: 'The aim of *Horizon* is to give to writers a place to express themselves, and to readers the best writing we can obtain. Our standards are aesthetic, and our politics are in abeyance.'[14] Connolly's apparent eschewal of politics did not mean a lack of engagement with current events on the part of his authors, however; Connolly was the first to publish Julian Maclaren-Ross's war stories, for instance. In the preface to the anthology *Horizon Stories* (1943), Connolly states a preference for stories 'with a beginning and an end', distinguishing these from the 'impressionist sketch or the reportage disguised as narrative'.[15] Despite these strictures, however, *Horizon*, like other journals mentioned here, included stories on a mixture of topics and in a wide range of styles. Characterizing the 'wartime story' is therefore difficult, but a consideration of selected stories from the war years, by both combatants and non-combatants, reveals some notable stylistic and thematic continuities.

War stories

Many authors in this period, both combatant and non-combatant, chose to write in a realist idiom, and in the case of journals which published fiction alongside non-fiction without indicating which was which, it is not always immediately obvious to the reader how a text should be categorized. Dividing authors into combatants and non-combatants also poses problems since during the Second World War the mobilization of civilians was more widespread than in previous conflicts, as the concept of the 'Home Front' indicates. Many authors wrote stories that focused on the contested borderland between different kinds of involvement in the war and on the tensions that could arise between the variously mobilized subjects in total war. In Graham Greene's 'Men at Work' (1940), the civil servant Skate, deprived by the war of both his family life, and, more significantly it seems, his ambitions to be a playwright, spends his time writing propaganda materials that are rendered instantly out of date by the progress of the war on the ground: 'Skate remembered how the minutes on who should write a "suggested" pamphlet about the French war-effort were still circulating while Germany broke the line, passed the Somme, occupied Paris and received the delegates at Compiègne.'[16] The story ends with Skate, barely managing to conceal a sense of the futility of his occupation from his colleague Hill, looking out of the office window: 'Far up in the pale enormous sky little white lines, like the phosphorescent spore of snails, showed where men were going home from work.'[17] Skate's ennui points towards the lack of consonance between his occupation and the 'work' that others are undertaking. Other stories provide a reminder that those on active service were once civilians too. As Mark Rawlinson has noted, 'Maclaren-Ross's stories in *The Stuff to Give the Troops* (1944) are the most entertaining and caustic contemporary narratives about conscripted civilians ensnared in the regulations of an autonomous and sovereign military regime.'[18] Maclaren-Ross's narrator, usually attempting to evade the demands made on him by the army, uses humour and the exposure of absurdity as means of rebellion.

If Greene and Maclaren-Ross represent the tensions between Home Front and active service by showing a single individual moving, or not, between the two positions, other authors employ the trope of the soldier going home on leave to similar ends. Sylvia Townsend Warner's 'English Climate' (1943) presents a striking critique of Home Front attitudes as it describes Gunner Brock setting off on leave. En route, Brock fantasizes about the pleasures of home, the solitude offered by his bedroom, and, most pleasurable anticipation of all, imagines running his hand along his bookshelf:

Which should it be? The fourth from the left was *Boswell's Life*, then the even ranks of *Fitzgerald's Letters*. In his fingers stirred a consciousness of how that bookshelf would feel: the orderly row, the smooth back, the sharp corners – a world away from that heap of flaccid derelicts by the door of the recreation hut.[19]

Townsend Warner conveys simultaneously the physical and intellectual shortcomings of army life that home can repair, but Brock's sensuous anticipation also warns the reader of his likely disappointment. Arriving at Dumbridge High Street he experiences 'a momentary impression that there had been an air-raid'; in fact, the assorted items of furniture and household goods stacked up on the pavements are a sign that the town is having a salvage drive, collecting items for re-use as part of the war effort.[20] The salvage also includes a 'book mile', which Brock examines despite his 'distress [...] reflecting on the kind of books Dumbridge could muster up: *The Scarlet Pimpernel*, *Hints to Fly Fishers*, *Anecdotes of European Courts*, and volumes of poetry called *Tally-Ho* or *By Quiet Waters*'.[21] But then he spots *The Collected Poems of Edward Thomas* and, struck by the familiarity of the 'well-read copy', discovers his own name on the flyleaf.[22] Stunned, Brock replaces the book and goes home to confront his mother, who seems oblivious to her apparent crime, justifying her actions by asserting: 'one must do something [...] we poor civilians in a poor old town that doesn't even get a bomb on it. Surely you wouldn't grudge a few old books for national salvage! Think what it means to the country.'[23] For Brock, the books represent a pre-war past, memories that provide an escape from the demands of army life: for his mother, the logic of the sacrificial rhetoric of the Home Front means that giving up her son to the armed forces is not enough. She must also make further material contributions. The story ends with Brock hesitating over whether to go and rescue his books, just as rain begins to fall. Even a bookish reader, however, might hesitate to sympathize unreservedly with Brock, whose fetishization of his book collection goes hand in hand with a degree of intellectual contempt both for his fellow soldiers and indeed for his mother. This story's emphasis on the loss of objects that symbolize the past, and specifically texts that have a memorial resonance, is echoed in Rose Macaulay's 'Miss Anstruther's Letters' (1942), which, drawing on Macaulay's own experience of losing almost all her possessions when her flat was destroyed in an air-raid, lays bare the distress of Miss Anstruther when she realizes that she has managed to save trivial items, but in her panic has left behind letters from her now-deceased lover: 'she had not yet re-read them; she had been waiting until she could do so without the devastation of unendurable weeping.'[24] Now, it is too late: only scraps and fragments remain.

A more explicitly politicized version of the clash between soldier and civilian is at the centre of Elizabeth Berridge's 'Subject for a Sermon' (1947), in which Lady Hayley's rousing of the local women to contribute to the war effort takes precedence over her son John's visit home on embarkation leave. John's time in the army has evidently raised his consciousness, and he interprets his mother's fund-raising and public speaking as a way for her to attempt to cement her social status: 'You wouldn't dream of letting the people round here organise their own schemes. [...] You're only interested in maintaining your own position, and seeing that they keep to theirs.'[25] Lady Hayley interprets these comments as evidence of how the army has 'coarsened' her son and dismisses his criticisms, asserting that she is 'a leader with generations of experience' behind her.[26] At the climax of the story, John decides to spend the remainder of his leave with a friend and drives off to the station, overtaking his mother who is cycling to another meeting. On Lady Hayley's arrival, Berridge allows the post-war reader a glimpse of an alternative perspective on her behaviour, when, having distributed the prizes at a produce show, Lady Hayley exclaims: 'Do you know, more than ever I feel so much – so much at *one* with you all.'[27] At this, the long-suffering Miss Pollett finds herself 'wishing with all her heart that Lady Hayley really meant it'.[28] 'Pulling together' across class boundaries on the Home Front is revealed as little more than a fiction, on both sides, and, on the part of Lady Hayley, a futile attempt to reinforce the status of a crumbling minor aristocracy.

Both Townsend Warner and Berridge employ the soldier as a focalizer for at least part of their narratives; in her post-war story '*Gravement Endommagé*' (1945), Elizabeth Taylor similarly depicts the after-effects of the war on a wife who stayed at home from the perspective of her husband, implying that her war experiences, including being bombed out of her home, were as traumatic for her as active service in 'the jungle' was for him.[29] Combatant authors also showed an awareness of what civilians might be going through. In 'They Came' (1941), by Alun Lewis (then serving with the Royal Engineers), a Welsh soldier, known only by his nickname Taffy, returns to his billet in a Hampshire village after a period of leave in a Welsh town. Several acquaintances ask, in the first part of the story, whether his leave was enjoyable. He replies 'automatically' at first that it was good, 'except for the raids'.[30] About a third of the way into the story, it is revealed to the reader that Taffy's wife, with whom he was spending his leave, was killed in one of these raids. Having dismissed several enquiries about his leave with this casual mention of the raids, Taffy eventually describes his ordeal to his friend Nobby; Taffy carries his wife back from the street where she was hit towards their ruined home:

> I carried her back in my arms. Over the fallen house. The fire wasn't bad by then. Took her home, see, Nobby. Only the home was on fire. I wanted her to

die all the time. I carried her over a mile through the streets. Fire hoses and water. And she wouldn't die. [...] I knew she was going to die. When they told me she was – I didn't feel anything. [...] What's it all for, Nobby? [...] I used to know what it was all about, but I can't understand it now.[31]

This harrowing account of his wife's death is the spur for a moment of restrained intimacy between Taffy and his friend: '[Nobby] put his hands on his mate's shoulders and let him lean against him for a bit.'[32] Nobby assures the bereaved man that he and his wife 'belong to each other for keeps, now', as though to retrieve a moment of transcendence from a profound loss.[33] At the conclusion of the story, Taffy stands alone, his perception of the 'calm and infinite darkness of an English night' punctuated by 'the violence growing in the sky' that signifies more raids.[34] The story is ultimately restorative, with Taffy emerging from the sharing of his loss with a renewed sense of purpose, but that 'violence growing in the sky' is a reminder to the reader that individual expressions of purpose or hope in wartime are always at the mercy of historical forces, even if the individual believes him self or herself to be acting in the service of a just cause. As in Greene's 'Men at Work', purposefulness is an easily shattered illusion, and what seems like closure can only ever be provisional.

A bleaker version of the scenario of the soldier home on leave witnessing death appears in 'How Sleep the Brave' (1943), one of a number of stories published during the war by H. E. Bates under the pseudonym 'Flying Officer "X"', after he was recruited to a public relations role with the RAF on the strength of his pre-war reputation as a short story writer; he rose to the rank of squadron leader. Allison is one of the narrator's bomber crew, and is still haunted by the experience of carrying the body of his dead child out of his bombed home, the survival of his wife offering no consolation: 'He would always go back, for ever to that moment; the moment when he carried the child from the house and up the street, himself like a dead person walking, until someone stopped him and took the child away.'[35] But once back at base, Allison does not speak of what has happened: 'All that could be felt, whether it was fear or terror or anger or the mutilation of everything normal in you to utter despair, must have already been felt by Allison. He was inoculated for ever against terror and despair.'[36] When the crew is shot down over the sea and left floating in a dinghy in the freezing cold, Allison's demeanour signals to the narrator that 'he did not care'; there is a brief moment of hope when Allison thinks he sees lights in the distance, but this soon dissolves and Allison is the first to succumb to the extreme conditions:

> I held him for the rest of that night, not telling even Ellis that he was dead. It was then about three o'clock. I felt that it was not the frost or the sea or the

wind that had killed him. He had been dead for a long time. He had been dead ever since he walked out of the bombed house with the child in his arms.[37]

The narrator's care for Allison's body echoes Allison's equally futile care for the body of his child, and reminds the narrator that he himself joined up as a way of escaping his wife and perhaps proving his bravery, while Allison, because he was a father, had a greater sense of purpose.

'Flying Officer "X"' focuses on exposing the reality of air force experience and critiquing its representation in the media.[38] Others on active service emphasized the disjunctiveness of their experiences by turning to formal experiment. Roald Dahl's story 'Death of an Old Old Man' (1946) uses first person narration to express the fears of an experienced pilot, but then switches to the third person as he bails out. The story culminates in a hallucinatory sequence in which, having hit the ground, the pilot has an out-of-body experience and sees his belongings being stolen from his body as he dies. This and other stories of Dahl's from this period illustrate how modernist experiments with narrative voice had filtered through into what are essentially realist narratives, but narratives which attempt to encompass events (in this instance, death in action) that are themselves at the limit of understanding.

A lack of certainty as to the boundaries between actuality and hallucination characterizes other stories that draw the reader into the strange new world of the war. Just prior to the outbreak of the war, Elizabeth Bowen had identified a trend in the short story towards 'inward, or, as it were, applied and functional fantasy, which does not depart from life but tempers it'.[39] Her own 'Mysterious Kôr' (1945) shows this process in action, as Pepita explains to her soldier lover Arthur how she escapes from bombed London into Kôr, Arthur later pondering, as might the reader: 'A game's a game, but what's a hallucination?'[40] William Sansom's story 'Fireman Flower', drawing on the author's own experience as a member of the Auxiliary Fire Service, makes a similar move from realism to hallucination. What begins as an account of a squad's attendance at a warehouse fire is gradually transformed into a symbolic encounter when, approaching what he believes to be the 'seat of the fire' as instructed by his training,[41] Fireman Flower finds not the source of the conflagration but his old friend Chalmers, inexplicably ensconced, in the midst of the burning building, in a room containing relics and mementoes from Flower's own past. Flower resists the lure of the past, represented by Chalmers, and by the end of the story, having found his way out of the building, feels at peace with his war-torn surroundings. Re-encountering and re-evaluating the past at a moment of danger, as Flower does, but turning nevertheless to face a potentially difficult future, was a task that became increasingly pressing as war gave way to peace.

Post-war

Writing in the wake of the war, P. H. Newby noted a tendency among authors to escape to the past through a focus on childhood, seeing this as a symptom of 'the state of unbelief or bewilderment' in which younger writers in particular found themselves.[42] As many of the stories discussed so far show, an engagement with past events at this period of historical crisis was not an uncommon tactic while the war was in progress, even among authors who, like Sansom, did not take childhood as a specific theme. Some, like V. S. Pritchett, employed narrators whose reminiscences, casting back to the pre-war, eschewed direct involvement with its pressures; others, like Frances Bellerby, in 'Pre-War' (1939; the war referred to here is the 1914–18 conflict) and 'October' (1940), evidence that a supposedly innocent past was itself often darkened by threats and forebodings.[43] The Scottish author J. F. Hendry's 'Chrysalis', first published in the New Apocalyptic anthology *The White Horseman* (1941), is similar in style to Sansom's work; supposedly homely objects, particularly a china dog on the mantelpiece of the family home, take on a sinister resonance in the imagination of the child protagonist, who escapes temporarily from his fears of punishment by making a shadow theatre out of the tissue paper from a loaf of bread, only for his anxieties to return when, moving the candle too close, he sets the paper alight.[44]

Where Bellerby and Hendry hint at the ways a child might gain, albeit indirectly, an awareness of mortality, this theme is dealt with more directly in A. L. Barker's 'The Iconclasts' (1947). This story centres on the fraught friendship between young Marcus and his slightly older friend Neil. The story has a wartime setting. Having tested Marcus's aircraft identification skills and found them wanting, Neil, in an incident reminiscent of one of Sansom's more fantastical tales, decides to climb up onto the sails of an abandoned windmill: 'It's a test, don't you understand – I have to test my nerve. I'm going to be a fighter-pilot, I've got to have nerve, I've got to be tough and take risks and keep cool.'[45] As Marcus watches Neil climb, the older boy is transformed in his vision: 'From being merely a subject for imitation, with contagious habits and rare knowledge, Neil had become a hero.'[46] After Neil falls and is fatally injured, he is unable to articulate the urgent need for Marcus to seek help, and Marcus himself is merely confused and disappointed that his hero is apparently unwilling to get up and play:

> Perhaps Neil would like his jacket as a pillow. He hesitated. [...] Neil would be contemptuous, and rightly so, if he went back for such a womanish gesture. Fighter pilots probably never used pillows but just stretched out on the hard

ground. Marcus was impressed by this Spartan routine, he knew he would find it very difficult to keep as still as Neil had for such a long time.[47]

Neil has taught Marcus too well, and it is notable that what he has taught him are what he himself believes to be the heroic, manly virtues. The power struggle enacted between the two boys raises the question of what values will be dominant in the post-war world, how the next generation will take its bearings. Marcus witnesses a death, but does not know that this is what he has seen; like the child protagonists of other stories in Barker's *Innocents: Variations on a Theme*, he has an experience that cannot be fully processed or understood, at least not within the boundaries of the narrative, and the consequences of this, similarly, exceed what the stories themselves can contain.

Even when the historical setting is less precise than in 'The Iconoclasts', the familiar progress from innocence to experience is given new point in the post-war period. Where Barker contemplates the potential effects of a wartime childhood on boys, Anna Kavan's 'Annunciation' (1950) focuses on female coming of age, in a story with an unspecified colonial setting. The description of Mary's experience of the menarche is framed with hints of hereditary madness and barely suppressed threat. Suddenly a woman at the age of ten, she barely understands her grandmother's explanation of what is happening to her, with only the dire warning that she must now avoid at all costs being taken advantage of by men registering in her consciousness: 'Most girls are much older before it happens – white girls, anyhow. It's like a nigger – disgusting. [...] As long as you're a good girl and do as I tell you you'll be all right. I shall protect you from everything.'[48] The story takes a turn towards the gothic at its conclusion, when Mary is seen at her bedroom window by some departing visitors: 'Mammoth arms closed round the figure at the window and lifted it bodily out of sight.'[49] There are echoes of Charlotte Brontë's Bertha Rochester in this story's disturbing equation between female sexuality, danger and madness.

A gothic turn is also discernible in Angus Wilson's 'Raspberry Jam' (1949). Wilson, one of the key new voices in the post-war period, shows Johnnie caught between his family, who encourage his friendship with the elderly sisters at the neighbouring farm, and the sisters themselves. At the climax of the story, the sisters reveal that they believe Johnnie has been sent to spy on them by his elders, and poke out the eyes of a captive bullfinch as a warning: '"We don't like spies round here looking at what we're doing. [...] When we find them we teach them a lesson so that they don't spy on us again."'[50] The friendship that has received a seal of approval of sorts from his parents is immediately sabotaged by the sisters themselves, leaving

Johnnie with his innocence damaged and in a state of isolation from all the adults around him. Newby was evidently nonplussed by Wilson, observing that 'many people have been distressed by what seems the queer relish he brings to his cruel material'.[51] Although a story like 'Raspberry Jam' seems to turn away from the historical contextualization that gives force to the relationship anatomized in, for instance, 'The Iconoclasts', the bewilderment conveyed in Wilson's story, and indeed in 'Annunciation', with regard to the status of apparently trustworthy representatives of an earlier generation seems of a part with a wider post-war reconsideration of authority and authoritarianism.

Conclusion

In a forum on 'The Future of Fiction' that appeared in *New Writing and Daylight* in 1946, Rose Macaulay suggested that the short story is 'far less exacting in form and content than of old [...] it can be an odd length chopped of a piece; any bit of a novel-in-progress will do; you merely cut and serve'.[52] Given the volume of short fiction published during the war years, and the need felt by some authors to preserve in an unembellished fashion the immediacy of their experiences, whether mundane or life-changing, Macaulay's cynicism is understandable. But many authors, including many of those discussed here, were continuing to digest the after-effects of modernism, and, as contact with writers on the Continent was re-established, new influences were absorbed. The appearance of Samuel Beckett's *Stories and Texts for Nothing* in 1958 confirmed the renewed focus on experiment that would characterize the next generation of short story writers.

NOTES

1 George Orwell, 'Review of *The Beauty of the Dead* by H. E. Bates; *Welsh Short Stories* selected by Glyn Jones; *The Parents Left Alone* by T. O. Beachcroft; *The Battlers* by Kylie Tennant', *The New Statesman and Nation* (25 January 1941). Reprinted in *The Complete Works of George Orwell Volume Twelve: A Patriot After All 1940–1941*, ed. Peter Davison (London: Secker & Warburg, 1998), pp. 371–4 (pp. 371–2).
2 Stephen Spender, 'Books and the War IV: The Short Story To-day', *Penguin New Writing*, 5 (April 1941), pp. 131–42 (p. 133).
3 Spender, 'Books and the War', p. 139.
4 Elizabeth Bowen, 'The Faber Book of Modern Short Stories' (1939), *The New Short Story Theories*, ed. Charles E. May (Athens: Ohio University Press, 1994), pp. 256–62 (p. 261).

5 Robert Hewison, *Under Siege: Literary Life in London 1929–45* (London: Quartet, 1979), p. 11.
6 Hewison, *Under Siege*, pp. 79–80.
7 Elizabeth Berridge, 'Afterword', *Tell It to a Stranger: Stories from the 1940s* (London: Persephone Books, 2000), pp. 165–74 (p. 173).
8 Dan Davin, 'Introduction', *Short Stories from the Second World War*, ed. Dan Davin (Oxford: Oxford University Press, 1984), pp. vii–xiv (pp. xiii–xiv).
9 Woodrow Wyatt, 'Preface', *English Story*, First Series, eds. Woodrow and Susan Wyatt (London: Collins, 1941), pp. 7–9 (p. 7).
10 Wyatt, 'Preface', p. 8.
11 Françoise Bort, 'A New Prose: John Lehmann and *New Writing* (1936–40)', *The Oxford Critical and Cultural History of Modernist Magazines: Volume I Britain and Ireland 1880–1950*, eds. Peter Brooker and Andrew Thacker (Oxford: Oxford University Press, 2009), pp. 669–87 (p. 678).
12 Bort, ' New Prose', p. 679. The exigencies of wartime publishing conditions meant that *Penguin New Writing* appeared irregularly during the mid-1940s. Rosamond Lehmann's short story 'Wonderful Holidays', approximately twenty thousand words long, appeared in serial form in issues 22–5, between late 1944 and late 1945, producing an unusually protracted reading experience.
13 For example, *Penguin New Writing* provided the following author note when it published Geoffrey Godwin's story 'Rescue' in issue 7, June 1941 (67–70): 'Geoffrey Godwin is nineteen years old, and is at present serving with the Marine Craft Section of the R.A.F., somewhere in England' (p. 142). The story itself evidently draws on this war service.
14 Cyril Connolly, 'Comment', *Horizon*, 1 (January 1940), 5–6 (5).
15 Cyril Connolly, 'Introduction', *Horizon Stories*, ed. Cyril Connolly (London: Faber & Faber, 1943), pp. 5–6 (p. 5).
16 Graham Greene, 'Men at Work' (1940), *Short Stories from the Second World War*, pp. 1–6 (p. 4).
17 Greene, 'Men at Work', p. 6.
18 Mark Rawlinson, 'Jocelyn Brooke and England's Militarised Landscape', *The Fiction of the 1940s: Stories of Survival*, eds. Rod Mengham and N. H. Reeve (Basingstoke: Palgrave, 2001), pp. 101–23 (p. 117). 'A Bit of a Smash in Madras', included in *The Stuff to Give the Troops*, first appeared in *Horizon*, 6 (June 1940), 434–55. The author's name was given as 'J. Maclaryn-Ross'.
19 Sylvia Townsend Warner, 'English Climate' (1943), *The Museum of Cheats and Other Stories* (London: Chatto & Windus, 1947), pp. 53–61 (p. 55). Townsend Warner was one of a number of British authors, including Mollie Panter-Downes and Elizabeth Taylor, who published stories in the *New Yorker* throughout the 1940s and 1950s.
20 Townsend Warner, 'English Climate', p. 56.
21 Townsend Warner, 'English Climate', pp. 56–7.
22 Townsend Warner, 'English Climate', p. 57.
23 Townsend Warner, p. 61. Jenny Hartley notes that during the war Townsend Warner worked 'sorting through books collected for pulping: she rescued rarities and books of use to the Blitzed Library Scheme'. See *Millions Like Us: British Women's Fiction of the Second World War* (London: Virago, 1997), p. 51.

24 Rose Macaulay, 'Miss Anstruther's Letters' (1942), *Wave Me Goodbye: Stories of the Second World War*, ed. Anne Boston (Harmondsworth: Penguin, 1989), pp. 65–73 (p. 71).
25 Elizabeth Berridge, 'Subject for a Sermon' (1947), *Tell It to a Stranger*, pp. 65–87 (p. 73).
26 Berridge, 'Subject for a Sermon', pp. 72; 75.
27 Berridge, 'Subject for a Sermon', p. 87.
28 Berridge, 'Subject for a Sermon', p. 87.
29 Elizabeth Taylor, '*Gravement Endommagé*' (1951), *Hester Lilley* (1954; London: Virago, 1990), pp. 111–19.
30 Alun Lewis, 'They Came' (1941), *Stories of the Forties*, eds. Reginald Moore and Woodrow Wyatt (London: Nicholson & Watson, 1945), pp. 47–59 (p. 49).
31 Lewis, 'They Came', p. 57.
32 Lewis, 'They Came', p. 57.
33 Lewis, 'They Came', p. 57.
34 Lewis, 'They Came', p. 58.
35 'Flying Officer "X"' [H. E. Bates], 'How Sleep the Brave' (1943), *Something in the Air* (London: Jonathan Cape, 1944), pp. 73–121 (p. 84).
36 'Flying Officer "X"', 'How Sleep the Brave', p. 85.
37 'Flying Officer "X"', 'How Sleep the Brave', pp. 107; 117.
38 See 'Flying Officer "X"', 'It's Never in the Papers' (1942), *Something in the Air*, pp. 11–18.
39 Elizabeth Bowen, 'The Faber Book', p. 261.
40 Elizabeth Bowen, 'Mysterious Kôr' (1945), *The Collected Stories of Elizabeth Bowen* (Harmondsworth: Penguin, 1983), pp. 728–40 (p. 738).
41 William Sansom, 'Fireman Flower' (1944), *Fireman Flower and Other Stories* (1944; London: Chatto & Windus, 1952), pp. 196–255 (p. 224).
42 P. H. Newby, *The Novel 1945–1950* (London: Longmans, Green, 1951), p. 10.
43 See for example V. S. Pritchett, 'The Saint', *Horizon*, 5 (April 1940), 274–88. Frances Bellerby, 'October', *English Story*, First Series, eds. Woodrow Wyatt and Susan Wyatt (London: William Collins, 1940), pp. 40–8; 'Pre-War', *Selected Stories*, ed. Jeremy Hooker (London: Enitharmon Press, 1986), pp. 17–21.
44 J. F. Hendry, 'Chrysalis', *The White Horseman* (London: Routledge, 1941), pp. 225–31.
45 A. L. Barker, 'The Iconoclasts', *Innocents: Variations on a Theme* (1947; London: Faber & Faber, 2009), pp. 56–86 (p. 75).
46 Barker, 'The Iconoclasts', p. 77.
47 Barker, 'The Iconoclasts', p. 86.
48 Anna Kavan, 'Annunciation', *English Story*, Tenth Series, ed. Woodrow Wyatt (London: William Collins, 1950), pp. 105–15 (p. 112).
49 Kavan, 'Annunciation', p. 115.
50 Angus Wilson, 'Raspberry Jam' (1949), *The Collected Stories* (Harmondsworth: Penguin, 1992), pp. 94–107 (p. 107). Wilson's first published story, 'Mother's Sense of Fun', appeared in *Horizon*, 95 (November 1947), 255–68.
51 Newby, *Novel*, p. 28.
52 Rose Macaulay, 'The Future of Fiction I', *New Writing and Daylight*, VII (September 1946), 71–5 (71).

9

MAEBH LONG

The short story from postmodernism to the digital age

In 1979 Declan Kiberd announced that '[f]or the past eighty years in Ireland, the short story has been the most popular of all literary forms with readers. It has also been the form most widely exploited by writers.'[1] Kiberd attributed the short story's popularity to the vibrancy of Ireland's folk tradition, and to the symmetry between the short story and oppressed or marginalized social groups, as its omissions and ellipses allow a subversion of dominant forms of expression.[2] Some forty years later Anne Enright reiterated this dynamic, linking hierarchies between nations to power discourses between genres by suggesting that if

> much of what is written about the short story form is actually anxiety about the unknowability of the novel (which we think we know so well), perhaps much of what is written about Irish writing is, in fact, anxiety about England. Sometimes, indeed, the terms 'England' and 'the novel' seem almost interchangeable.[3]

The perceived connection between Britain – England in particular – and the novel is not limited to the Irish, as while British publishers were reportedly happy to publish short fiction by Irish writers, they urged English authors to turn to the novel. British scholars compounded the short story's devaluation by concentrating academic attention on long forms of literary expression.[4] In an attempt to end the appraisal of the British short story as 'culturally redundant and economically unviable',[5] in 2004 *Prospect Magazine* pledged to publish a short story each month, and in 2005 the National Short Story Prize, which became the BBC National Short Story Award, was launched at the Edinburgh International Book Festival. The Sunday Times EFG Short Story Award was inaugurated in 2010, the Costa Short Story Award in 2012, and by 2015 the Booktrust website listed eighty-eight short story competitions. In 2004 Small Wonder, a literary festival dedicated to the short story, was launched in East Sussex, and Short Story Radio, which broadcasts recordings of short stories online, was founded in 2006. There

128

has been a concerted effort to provide avenues of publication and open scholarly debate on short fiction, which has served to continue the popularity of the short story in Ireland, and renew interest in it in Britain. As Carol Birch writes in the *Times Literary Supplement*,

> while publishers remain in general wary of the sales potential of short stories and often lean on their writers to 'move on' to writing a novel, creative writing classes and workshops are full of people experimenting with the form, and there is a constant healthy outpouring on the internet. The short story has perhaps never been more alive, more practised and more undervalued.[6]

Short story collections in Britain are slowly gathering more public and scholarly attention, causing Louise Doughty of the *Guardian* to declare that '[a] literary form declared dead on the slab a few years ago has proved to have a soft but resolutely pumping pulse.'[7]

Short stories from the 1960s to the contemporary in both Britain and Ireland have tended towards the realist, primarily remaining, as Malcolm and Malcolm write,

> within the conventions of social-psychological fiction, in which a story will be concerned to delineate a character's psychological state or development within a social milieu that is rendered according to the norms of literary realism.[8]

In Ireland until the 1980s the dominant style was realist, with some modernist influences; Seán Ó Faoláin explored the tensions between modernization and tradition, and Edna O'Brien's, William Trevor's and John McGahern's writings examined themes of paralysis, entrapment, repression and individual disillusionment. In Britain V. S. Pritchett wrote in a realist style, as did Muriel Spark, Jean Rhys and Bernard MacLaverty. While the basic formula for literary realism – specific characters acting as their personality and context would (relatively) logically decree, with plot, description and narration that enable the reader to envisage the action as if it were occurring rather than read – remains relatively stable, the conventions associated with the mimetic representation of reality change as technology, culture and socio-economic situations alter. The ubiquity of social media and the speed with which cross-cultural or international fertilization of concepts and style can occur over the Internet has led to a broad pool of influences, and contemporary writers inherit ever-expanding traditions. Many contemporary short story authors such as Deborah Levy, Michèle Roberts, James Kelman, Kevin Barry, Colin Barrett, Colum McCann and Mary Costello play with different perspectives in their writing, often orientating towards internal monologues that play on modernist stream of consciousness, lyrical prose that is strongly conscious of its writerly nature, or dialogue that speaks intimately to the spoken word and local speech patterns. Their fictions frequently remain within the broad definition of realism, but they work to reinvigorate the genre's conventions with different, frequently subtle, experiments in the evocation of mood, character and scene. As William Trevor observes,

> all writing is experimental. The very obvious sort of experimental writing is not really more experimental than that of a conventional writer like myself. I experiment all the time but the experiments are hidden. Rather like abstract art: You look at an abstract picture, and then you look at a close-up of a Renaissance painting and find the same abstractions.[9]

The short story, as a condensed, fragmented form ideally suited to an intensification of mood, an exploration of concepts, an experimentation with style, and a performance of self-referential closure or self-interrupting openness, is a form that lends itself to the avant-garde as well as to shards of realistic insight to events and characters.

Even the most conventionally realist of stories has an implied interrogation of the conventions of reality, which postmodern, and frequently contemporary, short fiction extended to question reality itself. As Roland Barthes writes:

> The real is not representable, and it is because men ceaselessly try to represent it by words that there is a history of literature [...] literature is categorically realist, in that it never has anything but the real as its object of desire; and I shall say now, without contradicting myself [...] that literature is quite as stubbornly unrealistic: it considers sane its desire for the impossible.[10]

It is with the insanity of the real that the postmodern text begins. Adrian Hunter sees the postmodern short story as a writing of 'the "afterlife" of the modernist short story',[11] and it is undeniable that short fiction from the 1960s to the contemporary retains many modernist traits. However, this section will look at the ways short story writers experimented with form and representation, and questioned meaning and reality, in ways quintessentially considered postmodern, moving on to look at the way these elements resonate in contemporary writing.

When Ihab Hassan provided a list of differences between modernism and postmodernism in 1982, he represented modernism as a writing of mastery, purpose, design and determinacy, and postmodernism as the play of chance, antiform, exhaustion, absence, desire and irony.[12] As problematized as these distinctions have been, postmodernism remains associated with openness, indeterminacy and an anarchistic play with conventions and traditions. It is seen as a period and style in which stable origins, the authority of the author and the concept of authenticity were abandoned or undercut. It is considered ironic, narcissistic and self-undermining, bound by schizophrenia, and what Fredric Jameson terms a 'new depthlessness [...] [with] a consequent weakening of history'.[13] Postmodern writings quintessentially embrace linguistic play, intertextuality and a strong self-reflexivity which questions assumptions about reality, knowledge and truth. As Jean-François Lyotard announced, 'I define *postmodern* as incredulity towards metanarratives';[14] the postmodern undoes the rules through which we determine the legitimate from the illegitimate, and rejects master narratives that serve to position and guide knowledge and behaviour, leaving people without frameworks through which to organize their lives. This vertiginous openness is a freedom and a nihilistic enslavement, and has been performed as both in postmodern fictions, often leading the postmodern to an excessive and undecidable oscillation between chaotic extremes. As Angela Carter replied, when asked once if she embraced opportunities for the overwritten: 'Embrace them? I would say that I half-suffocate them with the enthusiasm with which I wrap my arms and legs around them.'[15]

While British and Irish short story writers are associated with the heights of postmodernism far less regularly than their American and Canadian counterparts, exciting experiments did take place in short fiction on the European side of the Atlantic. B. S. Johnson's 'A Few Selected Sentences' (1973) begins and ends with an insistence on record-keeping, while establishing that no true version of an event exists independently of or prior to the act of recording, and that the truth created by the type and order of the records is wholly arbitrary: 'Do I want that to be the truth?'[16] There are no innocent, unbiased recordings, but choices that create arbitrarily the illusion of truth and consistency. In the absence of stable systems against which to measure the real or the true there is simply a proliferation of effects that ape depth in their surface referents, a contrivance that is often performed and ridiculed in the same text. As Johnson writes: 'A man taking pictures of a man taking pictures: there must be something in that.'[17]

Jean Baudrillard describes postmodernity as a time of hyper-reality and simulations, in which signs no longer signify reality, but conceal its absence.[18] The postmodern text is replete with this sense of artifice, in which the world comprises reproductions of reproductions without stable origin. J. G. Ballard's short stories repeatedly expose the simulations of modern life, while in Carter's 'Flesh and the Mirror' (1974) the narrator mimics life by performing rather than living, watching herself enact a role assembled from a cacophony of ideas of what a woman should be. So engaged is she in observing herself impersonate identities that she slips from the first to the third person: 'however hard I looked for the one I loved, she could not find him anywhere and the city delivered her into the hands of a perfect stranger.'[19] Identity in postmodern texts is never assured, as the postmodern typically rejects the notion of a strong, self-present subject, and sees the self as a fragmented and incomplete construct, eking out a partial existence. Fay Weldon's 'Weekend' (1978) shows the breaking down of the self by various social expectations, with paragraphs and sentences increasingly fragmented in tune with the protagonist's exhaustion. Formal experimentations within postmodern fiction operate not so much as questions of literary representation, but of existences in a demanding, yet counterfeit, world. As J. G. Ballard repeatedly asks, if the recounting of an existence can be reduced to the material form of a questionnaire in 'Answers to a Questionnaire' (1985), or an index in 'The Index' (1977), or a series of footnotes in 'Notes Towards A Mental Breakdown' (1976), then what does it mean to exist?

If the postmodern 'puts forward the unpresentable in presentation itself',[20] then Gabriel Josipovici's 'Second Person Looking Out' (1976) is an exemplary postmodern text, as it presents a tale of undecidable perspective through an unstable protagonist, and denies the reader the comfort of narrative progression, plot or characterization. Three times, in the first, third and second person, a story is told, in which the protagonist – who may or may not be the same person – abruptly shifts from being on the way to a house, leaving it, inside it, outside it, there for the first time and returning. Both the protagonist and the house are unfixed in space and time – the house can be seen in the distance from the windows of the house – and identity and meaning are indeterminate. This fluid existence stems from the multiplicity of perspectives that the house offers, as the guide explains: 'when you finally reach [the house], because you are constantly seeing fragments of it and imagining it when you can't see it, you've experienced it in a million forms.'[21] The only thing affording consistency to the protagonist and the house are narrative conventions, which get harder for the reader to rely on as the narrative progresses.

The most common performance of postmodernism in British and Irish short stories is metafiction, a form of writing that 'self-consciously and systematically draws attention to its own status as an artifact'.[22] This foregrounding of the narrative process can involve typographic play with the words on the page, direct addresses to the reader, commentary on the narrative process, or shifts in narrative framing, such as those performed in David Lodge's unfortunately named 'Hotel des Boobs' (1986). The story of Harry and Brenda is suddenly interrupted by a shift in narrative frame, and the reader realizes that Harry and Brenda are characters in a story which 'the author' has been writing in France. While the story of 'the author' is written in the third person, a further repositioning of the narrative reveals that the omniscient narrator is also 'the author', who, on the advice of his wife, has rendered himself a character in the story. But metafiction is not simply the formal play of metalepsis, which is a contamination between different layers of narrative reality, nor *mise en abyme*, in which a story is contained within a story, but the interrogation of the connection between fiction and reality. As Patricia Waugh writes, '[i]n providing a critique of their own methods of construction, such writings not only examine the fundamental structures of narrative fiction, they also explore the possible fictionality of the world outside the text.'[23] Josipovici's 'Mobius the Stripper' (1974) is an elaborate example of this exploration. On a page split horizontally, two stories are told; one of Mobius, who strips on stage in an attempt to find an authentic core, and one of an author frustrated by his inability to write anything real. However, each story not only loops in on itself, as the conclusion circles the reader back to the beginning – Mobius listens to the voices in his head, which are the voices narrating the story just read, while the writer begins to write a story about Mobius, which returns us to the first line of the writer's text – but, in the twisting connection of the Möbius strip, each story connects to the other. Thus, the ending of the story of the writer brings us to the beginning of the Mobius tale, as this is the tale he writes, and as Mobius listens to the voices in his head, he hears the writer say the opening lines of the writer's story.

The interlocking of Mobius's and the writer's stories points not only to the fabricated nature of their identities, but to the inevitable frustration of a search for authenticity and originality. Mobius tries to strip himself down, beyond his body and society's encoding of it, to find 'his essential self',[24] while the writer wishes 'that all the print which had ever been conveyed by my eye to my brain and thence buried deep inside me where it remained to fester could be removed by a sharp painless and efficient knife',[25] that is, to find the 'lost self' that existed prior to influence.[26] But as Mobius is a construct of the writer, and as the writer is a voice in Mobius's head, and as both are constructs of society – and of Josipovici, who is also a construct of his social context – there can be no authentic core, nor a clear distinction between fiction and reality.

Postmodernism is inextricable from this sense of reproductions without origins, a propagation which nullifies the concept of the unique. For Jameson this is evidence of the prevalence of the pastiche in postmodernity. Unlike a parody, an imitation which is predicated on the concept of a recognizable singular style, pastiche is a series of repetitions and fragmentations that dissolve any sense of the original or quotidian. The writers of postmodern pastiches not only present a composite assembly without care for original context, but 'no longer "quote" such texts as a Joyce might have done [...] [;] they incorporate them, to the point where the line between high art and commercial form seems increasingly difficult to draw'.[27] Adam

Mars-Jones's 'Structural Anthropology' (1981) apes the conventions of structuralism and Levi-Strauss's famous nature/culture opposition by performing an elaborate analysis of the themes of a domestic anecdote. John Berger's 'The Wind Howls Too' (1979) presents the contamination between the oral and the written, mixing the interruptions and conjunctions of an oral recounting with unconventional narrative structures. Stories from the past occupy the same narrative space as stories from the present, conversations are moved into and out of as listeners turn their heads from one side of the dinner table to the other, paragraphs change focus without warning or overt connection, and the story expands as it multiplies and fragments into the conjoined histories of the family. B. S. Johnson takes this to the extreme in 'Broad Thoughts from a Home' (1973), a chaotic assortment of references from Flann O'Brien to Shakespeare, Molly Bloom's monologue to fishing manuals, dictionary definitions to Jacobean playwrights. There is no stable style, as all is an intertextual web of quotation and imitation that mocks the illusion of a form other than copy and collage. Nor can such an assembly lead towards a single conclusion: of the four possibilities presented, one of which the reader must write herself, none take logical priority, and the text ends undecidably. Like Malcolm Bradbury's 'Composition' (1976), which provides three possible endings, the openness of a text's conclusion not only underpins the artifice of the text, but undercuts authorial authority, rendering the writer a conduit through which the reader can form his or her own text rather than the source of meaning and order.

The postmodern world is a riotous hybridity of cultures and traditions: 'Eclecticism is the degree zero of contemporary general culture: one listens to reggae, watches a western, eats McDonald's food for lunch and local cuisine for dinner, wears Paris perfume in Tokyo and "retro" clothes in Hong Kong.'[28] But this wealth of choice for self-determination is also the jungle of the shopping centre, the blandness of fast food, the corruption of multinational corporations and outsourced labour, the control of media saturation and the manipulation of planned obsolescence. Martin Amis's 'Career Move' (1992) is replete with people fatigued by flights and fine-dining, and in Ballard's 'The Intensive Care Unit' (1977) advances in technology have led people to incarcerate themselves in their homes, replacing contact with the camera: 'True closeness [...] was television closeness – the intimacy of the zoom lens, the throat microscope, the close-up itself.'[29] Alasdair Gray's 'Five Letters from an Eastern Empire' (1979) shows how dissent can be used to further a regime's ends, and the grotesque, corrupt system, personified by a hideous, two-foot-tall puppet emperor, is rendered permanent by the accidental complicity of a poet, whose protest against the system presents it as 'a simple, stunning, inevitable fact, [...] [with the Emperor] presented as

The short story from postmodernism to the digital age

a final, competent, all-embracing force, as unarguable as weather, as inevitable as death'.[30] The eclecticism and hybridity of postmodernism create a culture of 'anything goes', but this openness is not only a contextless appropriation of traditions and a potential denial of difference, but a fluidity that renders everything a commodity. As Lyotard writes, 'this realism of the "anything goes" is in fact that of money [...] Such realism accommodates all tendencies, just as capital accommodates all "needs", providing that the tendencies and needs have purchasing power'.[31] Salman Rushdie's 'At the Auction of the Ruby Slippers' (1992) is a cutting socio-political satire of this 'anything goes' realism, depicting a world in which neoliberal models of free-market capitalism are taken to the extreme. The Grand Saleroom of the Auctioneers is the 'courtroom of demand',[32] in which the ability to pay gives one the right to own, and the inability to pay gives one no rights at all. It is a simulacrum of freedom, choice and identity, masking the absence of any real liberty, power and selfhood.

The postmodern period coincided with the relaxation of repressive rules about sexual expression, which enabled women to explore their sexuality, but also led to the normalization of explicit objectification of their bodies and lives. From a contemporary vantage point, the sexism in many of the short stories of the period is tired, and tiring. Amis's 'Let Me Count the Times' (1981) is a puerile tale of a man who rediscovers masturbation, but while the story obsessively recounts Vernon's fantasies, at no point are we offered any insight to his wife's preferences. Lodge's 'Hotel des Boobs' may be a wry commentary on the way an author conceals his own desires behind a character's – the writer voyeuristically peers out through Harry's salaciousness – but the leering, which verges on the paedophilic, remains, as Harry ogles 'a pair of teenage girls [...] regarding their recently acquired breasts, hemispheres smooth and flawless as jelly moulds, with the quiet satisfaction of housewives watching scones rise'.[33] While Bradbury's protagonist in 'Composition' might, in the manner of Kingsley Amis's *Lucky Jim*, be weak and ineffectual, he remains the protagonist, with the female characters divided between objects of sexual attraction and objects of sexual disgust. The Margaret Peel of Bradbury's text is Miss Daubernethy, a crazed, ugly feminist – 'it seems that some diminution of sexual attractiveness is an entry qualification for graduate school'[34] – who is an unwelcome substitute for the 'fancy, fresh, forbidden bodies in his classes, for the flashing legs and mobile nipples under sweaters'.[35] Ian McEwan's collection *First Love, Last Rites* (1976) is a macabre collection of rape, paedophilia and murder, showing a predominance of men abusing women, but it is the fantastical, bloodless crime of 'Solid Geometry' that typifies the treatment of female characters: a male protagonist, through research, intelligence and dedication, bloodlessly rids himself of a nuisance, his wife, whose murder is represented as a purge rather than a crime.

In opposition to this was the feminist short fiction published in the period. Fay Weldon presents a witty, satirical look at women's roles in society, affording agency and insight to women in their emancipation and oppression. In 'Watching Me, Watching You' (1981) a man's third wife leaves him, and establishes a bond with his two previous wives, thereby escaping not only him, but the ghost of a woman who hanged herself when her husband betrayed her. Angela Carter's 'The Bloody Chamber' (1979) destabilizes the traditional roles and representation of women by rewriting the Bluebeard myth. Carter's narrator is not, or not merely, an innocent victim manipulated and trapped by an experienced sadist, but is also one who has to face the complicating factors of her complicity in her seduction, and engage with her potential for darkness and corruption. Importantly, this complicity is not a neutered relativism that seeks to condone abuse, but an effort to enable the reader to recognize the complexity of exploitative situations, and still attribute blame to the abuser. Carter's story is thus an engagement not merely with female arousal and sexual awakening, but a prescient contributor to contemporary debates on victim blaming. While short story writers in Ireland were engaging with feminist issues, their mode of engagement tended towards the realist, and they worked first to establish the abuses of women within deeply patriarchal systems, before they could undercut patriarchy in formally experimental ways. Thus, while Carter's narrator in 'Flesh and the Mirror' explored constructs of identity, two years later Maeve Kelly's protagonist in 'The Vain Woman' (1976) could see no identity at all when she looked in the mirror. Edna O'Brien's stories from the 1960s and 1970s were bleak; 'A Scandalous Woman' (1974) sees Ireland as 'a land of shame, a land of murder, and a land of strange, throttled, sacrificial women'.[36] But the 1980s saw a wave of Irish short stories destabilizing the Irish Catholic construction of family life and women's roles therein, from Mary Lavin, Mary Beckett and Ita Daly to Evelyn Conlon and Clare Boylan. In 1978 Leland Bardwell's *Different Kinds of Love* engaged with domestic violence and sexual abuse. Mary Dorcey's *A Noise from the Woodshed* (1989) has a strong lesbian element, with the sound in the woodshed not a trick from *Cold Comfort Farm*, but the sound of women making love echoing across the whole nation. Éilís Ní Dhuibhne embraces postmodern themes in 'The Wife of Bath' (1991), when Chaucer's Alisoun appears to the narrator, and forces her to reflect on the way women's identities are constructed and restricted by male traditions. Emma Donoghue's collection *The Women Who Gave Birth to Rabbits* (2002) shows women from various historical periods trying to find independence and voice within patriarchal societies.

For Lyotard the fragmented nature of postmodern form was born of a political imperative. As he wrote in 1982,

> [t]he nineteenth and twentieth centuries have given us as much terror as we can take. We have paid a high enough price for the nostalgia of the whole and the one, for the reconciliation of the concept and the sensible, of the transparent and the communicable experience. Under the general demand for slackening and for appeasement, we can hear the mutterings of the desire for a return to terror.[37]

While postmodernism has been accused of a sterility stemming from excess, and a lazy meaninglessness, the fear of the anaesthetizing effect of meaning figured as readily available and easily communicated was an important one, and marked much writing of the later postmodernist period. In 'A Guide to Virtual Death' (1992), Ballard presents a short story in the form of a television guide, whose programme explains that 'intelligent life became extinct in the closing hours of the 20th century'.[38] Pornography, consumerism, superstition, infantile game shows and voyeurism serve to numb rather than evoke debate or resistance, and in so doing they further corrupt and repressive power structures. Thus 3 PM sees 'Housewives' Choice. Rape, and how to psychologically prepare yourself',[39] while the 'Charity Hour' at 5 AM enables 'Third-World contestants [to] beg for money'.[40] Of course, the decades after postmodernism have seen the rhetoric of terror increase, the sense of social fragmentation grow, and a yearning nostalgia for an impossible self-presence abound. As Ali Smith writes, 'All short stories long',[41] and the short fiction of the early twenty-first century evinces broken-down cities and lives of yearning and frustrations. In Deborah Levy we find an emphasis on incompletion and a deep melancholy, as many mourn without a clear awareness of what they have lost. *Black Vodka* (2013) collects stories of outsiders, those who are alienated from themselves, displaced and haunted. When a character is asked what her first language is, she replies, untouchable and empty: 'There are so many languages.'[42]

This emptiness leads to the short story as symptomatic of the self-absorption of modern life. Kazuo Ishiguro's *Nocturnes: Five Stories of Music and Nightfall* (2009) is a collection of shards of events; shallow, temporary connections that stem from the chance meetings or arbitrary associations that arise in a mobile world. But these moments of exchange do not point to empathy between strangers, but to characters' self-preoccupation, as they rebound from one superficial point of contact to another. In 'Malvern Hills' the narrator retreats to the country to escape the superficiality of the London music scene. A moment of connection with other musicians leads neither to epiphany nor the conscious rejection thereof, but return to self: the narrator returns to the song he was playing, utterly self-involved. Will Self's 'Between the Conceits' (1994) proposes that London is controlled by eight people, whose powers are focused on small-minded self-interest; a story undecidably the maniacal self-delusion of the narrator or the revelation of a terrible truth. In China Miéville's 'Foundation' (2003), a man's ability to speak to buildings is born of his trauma of seeing Iraqi soldiers buried alive by the American army. When he returns home he realizes that in the foundations of every building are dead men, crushed together, alone and hungry: 'Every home is built on them. [...] Every house in every street.'[43] In 'Details' (2002), a dark reworking of *The Yellow Wallpaper*, the ability to read the meaning of seemingly random patterns is a terrible hazard, as it awakens the pattern to one's presence.

The hybridity, fragmentation and dispersal of contemporary short stories resonate with the experiences of marginalized communities. Salman Rushdie's 'The Courter' (1994) is a quiet love story between an ageing Indian *ayah* and a porter from an Eastern European country. Their companionship helps their exile in a disorienting, alien country, but after a violent attack the Indian lady finds herself torn between East and West. The sense of entrapment within indifferent systems shaped by deep inequality abounds. In Zadie Smith's 'The Embassy of Cambodia' (2013), Fatuo, an unpaid maid in London, is forced by her circumstances to ask herself if she is a slave. Shereen Pandit's 'She Shall Not be Moved' (2005) sees a woman, who used to be a freedom fighter in Africa, so enslaved by a culture of fear that she ignores an instance of racism on the bus, and is shamed when the Somalian woman targeted points out her imprisonment to her.

While excessive experimentations with form and subjectivity are less common in the contemporary short story in Britain and Ireland, metafiction remains present, and the constructed nature of fiction and reality is a continued theme. Form remains something to play with, and new technologies influence both the mode of presentation and the forms of representation. William Boyd's 'Adult Video' (2004) pauses, rewinds and fast forwards through events in the protagonist's life with the bored impatience of the television viewer. David Mitchell's 'The Right Sort' (2014) was published on Twitter over the course of seven days, and the plot's engagement with time travel and hiatus is performed in the immediacy and delays of online delivery. In 'Raw Material' (2002), A. S. Byatt writes of a writing teacher who tells his students 'to avoid falseness and strain. Write what you really know about. Make it new. Don't invent melodrama for the sake of it.'[44] Only one student, Cicely Fox, appears to take this advice, and writes beautiful prose pieces on cleaning. But the reality of her life is horror and degradation; she is viciously murdered, and there is evidence on her body of torture spanning decades. While the teacher is horrified, the class is delighted: 'Miss Fox belonged after all in the normal world of their writings, the world of domestic violence, torture and shock-horror. They could write what they knew, what had happened to Cicely Fox, and it would be most satisfactorily therapeutic.'[45] In Byatt's story reality is not quiet and calm, like Cicely's outward appearance, but nasty and brutish like the sustained torture she endured. This not only puts into focus the darkness of people's lives, the conventions of realism and the conventions of good short story writing, but contains a self-mocking twist, as Byatt's own story, which appears to place itself above the gruesome extremes of the class's stories, in the end is revealed as employing a plot as grisly as one they would write.

The modernist drive to make it new often finds postmodern and contemporary expression in a rewriting of the old. As David Lodge writes in *Thinks*,

> [i]n the first year of the new millennium Helen published a novel which one reviewer described as 'so old-fashioned in form as to be almost experimental'. It was written in the third person, past tense, with an omniscient and sometimes intrusive narrator.[46]

China Miéville's 'Report of Certain Events in London' (2004) comprises a series of letters, postcards, minutes, memos, papers, reports and booklets, but its experimentation with form is reminiscent of gothic novels such as Mary Shelley's *Frankenstein* and Bram Stoker's *Dracula*. Kevin Barry's 'A Cruelty' (2013), told in the present tense, tells of a vindictiveness that spoils the happy routine of a man with mental health issues with a clarity that calls to mind Katherine Mansfield's 'Miss Brill'. When Ali Smith's narrator asks in 'Erosive' (2003), 'What do you need to know about me for this story? How old I am? How much I earn a year? What kind of car I drive? Look at me now, here I am at the beginning, the middle and the end all at once,'[47] she plays not only on postmodern metafiction, but on Virginia Woolf's modernist rejection of Victorian realism: '"Begin by saying that her father kept a shop in Harrogate. Ascertain the rent. Ascertain the wages of the shop assistants in the year 1878. Discover what her mother died of. Describe cancer. Describe calico. Describe" – But I cried, "Stop! Stop!"'[48]

Where, then, do we leave the contemporary short story? Frank McGuinness describes it as a brick through a window, propelling itself into the reader's imagination,

> doing damage, external and internal, and, unlike most novels, not remotely bothered to care what consequent healing may be necessary. There is then a ruthlessness about the form, and its style is a matter of how that ruthlessness disguises itself.[49]

Within a culture of immediacy and disposability, it is possible that the short story is, paradoxically, too short: the slow unfolding of a novel makes even the loosest absorption of basic plot possible on a single reading, but the lyrical and tonal complexity of the short story's intensity means that it requires slow savouring, and re-reading, something not always pleasing to a modern audience. As Anne Enright considers:

> I am not sure whether the novel is written for our convenience, but it is probably written for our satisfaction. That is what readers complain about with short stories, that they are not 'satisfying'. They are the cats of literary form; beautiful, but a little too self-contained for some readers' taste.[50]

But the novel is, perhaps, growing tired in its general provision of satisfaction. In a speech given at the inauguration of the National Short Story Prize, Alexander Linklater said:

> The novel is a capacious old whore: everyone has a go at her, but she rarely emits so much as a groan for their efforts. [...] The short story, on the other hand, is a nimble goddess: she selects her suitors fastidiously and sings like a dove when they succeed. The British literary bordello is heaving with flabby novels; it's time to give back some love to the story.[51]

Ali Smith reworks Linklater's speech in 'True Short Story' (2005), in which two men, discussing the short story in a café, decide that while the novel is 'a bit used up, really a bit too slack and loose', the short story is 'a slim nymph. Because so few people had mastered the short story she was still in shape'.[52] In response to the male presentation of the short story in terms of objectified female bodies the narrator calls a female friend, and with scholarly reflections on short story writers' opinions on the form from Kafka to Bowen, they undo male discourse, finally concluding that the short story is indeed like a nymph, not because of its pristine, distant allure, but because it undercuts and subverts and disconcerts. That is, the short story is a nymph because 'the echo of it answers back'.[53]

NOTES

1. Declan Kiberd, 'Story-telling: The Gaelic Tradition', *The Irish Writer and the World* (Cambridge: Cambridge University Press, 2005), pp. 42–51 (p. 43).
2. Kiberd, 'Story-telling', pp. 43–4.
3. Anne Enright, 'Introduction', *The Granta Book of the Irish Short Story*, ed. Anne Enright (London: Granta, 2011), pp. ix–xxiii (p. xiii).
4. See T. O. Beachcroft, *The Modest Art: A Survey of the Short Story in English* (London: Oxford University Press, 1968); Cheryl Alexander Malcolm and David Malcolm, 'The British and Irish Short Story: 1945–Present', *A Companion to the British and Irish Short Story*, eds. Cheryl Alexander Malcolm and David

Malcolm (Chichester: Blackwell, 2008); Paul March-Russell, *The Short Story: An Introduction* (Edinburgh: Edinburgh University Press, 2009), p. 43.
5 Alexander Linklater, 'Reclaiming the story', *Prospect Magazine*, September 2005 www.prospectmagazine.co.uk/features/reclaimingthestory [Accessed 22 June 2015].
6 Carol Birch, 'Helen Simpson, Jackie Kay and the Life of the Short Story', *Times Literary Supplement*, 22 August 2012, www.the-tls.co.uk/tls/public/article 1108765.ece [Accessed 22 June 2015].
7 Louise Doughty, review of 'The Embassy of Cambodia', *Guardian*, 4 November 2013. www.theguardian.com/books/2013/nov/04/embassy-of-cambodia-zadie-smith-review [Accessed 22 June 2015].
8 Malcolm and Malcolm, 'British and Irish Short Story', p. 255.
9 William Trevor in interview with Mira Stout, 'The Art of Fiction No. 108', *Paris Review*, 110 (Spring 1989) www.theparisreview.org/interviews/2442/the-art-of-fiction-no-108-william-trevor [Accessed 22 June 2015].
10 Roland Barthes, 'Lecture in Inauguration of the Chair of Literary Semiology, College de France', *Oxford Literary Review* (1979), 31–44 (36).
11 Adrian Hunter, *The Cambridge Companion to the Short Story in English* (Cambridge: Cambridge University Press, 2007), p. 96.
12 Ihab Hassan, *The Dismemberment of Orpheus: Towards a Postmodern Literature* (Madison: University of Wisconsin Press, 1982), pp. 267–8.
13 Fredric Jameson, *Postmodernism, or the Cultural Logic of Late Capitalism* (London: Verso, 1991), p. 6.
14 Jean-François Lyotard, *The Postmodern Condition: A Report on Knowledge*, trans. Geoffrey Bennington and Brian Massumi (Manchester: Manchester University Press, 1984), p. xxiv.
15 John Haffenden, 'An Interview with Angela Carter', *Interviews with Writers*, ed. John Haffenden (London: Methuen, 1985), pp. 76–97 (p. 91).
16 B. S. Johnson, 'A Few Selected Sentences', *The Penguin Book of Modern British Short Stories*, ed. Malcolm Bradbury (London: Penguin, 2011), pp. 282–5 (p. 284).
17 B. S. Johnson, 'A Few Selected Sentences', p. 284.
18 Jean Baudrillard, *Simulacra and Simulation*, trans. Sheila Faria Glaser (Ann Arbor: University of Michigan Press, 1994).
19 Angela Carter, 'Flesh and the Mirror', *The Penguin Book of Modern British Short Stories*, pp. 362–8 (p. 364).
20 Lyotard, *Postmodern Condition*, p. 81.
21 Gabriel Josipovici, 'Second Person Looking Out', *New Stories 1: An Anthology*, eds. Margaret Drabble and Charles Osborne (London: The Arts Council of Great Britain, 1976), pp. 200–5 (p. 200).
22 Patricia Waugh, *Metafiction: The Theory and Practice of Self-Conscious Fiction* (London: Routledge, 1993), p. 2.
23 Waugh, *Metafiction*, p. 2.
24 Gabriel Josipovici, 'Mobius the Stripper: A Topological Exercise', *Mobius the Stripper* (London: Victor Gollancz, 1974), pp. 64–85 (p. 81).
25 Josipovici, 'Mobius the Stripper', p. 68.
26 Josipovici, 'Mobius the Stripper', p. 85.

27 Fredric Jameson, 'Postmodernism and Consumer Society', *The Anti-Aesthetic: Essays on Postmodern Culture*, ed. Hal Foster (Seattle, WA: Bay Press, 1983), pp. 111–25 (p. 112).
28 Lyotard, *Postmodern Condition*, p. 76.
29 J. G. Ballard, 'The Intensive Care Unit', *The Complete Short Stories Volume 2* (London: Harper Perennial, 2006), pp. 442–51 (pp. 449–50).
30 Alasdair Gray, 'Five Letters from an Eastern Empire', *Unlikely Stories, Mostly* (London: Penguin, 1984), pp. 85–133 (p. 132).
31 Lyotard, *Postmodern Condition*, p. 76.
32 Salman Rushdie, 'At the Auction of the Ruby Slippers', *East, West* (London: Vintage, 1995), pp. 85–104 (p. 99).
33 David Lodge, 'Hotel des Boobs', *The Penguin Book of Modern British Short Stories*, pp. 326–33 (p. 328).
34 Malcolm Bradbury, 'Composition', *The Penguin Book of Modern British Short Stories*, pp. 286–308 (p. 294).
35 Bradbury, 'Composition', p. 295.
36 Edna O'Brien, 'A Scandalous Woman', *The Love Object: Selected Stories* (New York: Little, Brown and Company, 2013), pp. 60–89 (p. 89).
37 Lyotard, *Postmodern Condition*, pp. 81–2.
38 J. G. Ballard, 'A Guide to Virtual Death', *The Complete Short Stories Volume 2*, pp. 757–9 (p. 757).
39 Ballard, 'A Guide to Virtual Death', p. 758.
40 Ballard, 'A Guide to Virtual Death', p. 759.
41 Ali Smith, 'The Third Person', *The First Person and Other Stories* (London: Penguin, 2009), pp. 55–70 (p. 57).
42 Deborah Levy, 'Vienna', *Black Vodka* (High Wycombe: And Other Stories, 2013), pp. 31–40 (p. 37).
43 China Miéville, 'Foundation', *Looking for Jake and Other Stories* (London: Macmillan, 2005), pp. 21–32 (p. 26).
44 A. S. Byatt, 'Raw Material', *Little Black Book of Stories* (London: Vintage, 2004), pp. 185–230 (p. 187).
45 Byatt, 'Raw Material', p. 229.
46 David Lodge, *Thinks* (London: Penguin, 2002), p. 340.
47 Ali Smith, 'Erosive', *The Whole Story and Other Stories* (London: Penguin, 2004), pp. 115–22 (p. 115).
48 Virginia Woolf, 'Mr Bennett and Mrs Brown', *Essentials of the Theory of Fiction*, eds. Michael J. Hoffman and Patrick D. Murphy (Durham, NC: Duke University Press, 1996), pp. 24–39 (p. 35).
49 Frank McGuinness, 'Brick', *Surge: New Writing from Ireland* (Dublin: O'Brien Press, 2014), pp. 13–16 (p. 13).
50 Enright, 'Introduction', p. x.
51 Michelle Pauli, 'Short Story Scores with New Prize and Amazon Project', *Guardian*, 23 August 2005, www.theguardian.com/books/2005/aug/23/news.michellepauli [Accessed 22 June 2015].
52 Ali Smith, 'True Short Story', *The First Person and Other Stories* (London: Penguin, 2009), pp. 1–18 (p. 4).
53 Smith, 'True Short Story', p. 17.

PART III
Genres

10

KATE MACDONALD

Comic short fiction and its variety

Humour in fiction functions as the salt that enhances taste, and crosses the boundaries of form and genre. It works impalpably in solution, disseminating through characterization, and as crystalline grains of joke, embedded in its medium. In short fiction, humour's protean quality has a stronger effect because it is less diluted. A humorous narrative voice will infuse an otherwise serious sequence of events with a comic perspective (John Buchan's 'The Frying-Pan and the Fire', 1928). Comedy delivers social shame for public enjoyment (Saki's 'Tobermory', 1911), and can reveal hidden meaning at the end of the narrative (Kevin Barry's 'Animal Needs', 2007). The pervasive but discreet quality of the comic in short fiction frequently disguises its workings, however, and makes it hard to identify as a convenient set of aesthetic characteristics.

We also cannot separate comic short stories from their medium. Short fiction is distinguished from the novel by its transmission in, historically, the magazine and the newspaper. The evolution of comic short stories through twentieth-century book history arrives in the age of the e-reader still linked closely to its medium, which offers digitized commute-length reading. The short story read in public becomes problematic when it causes involuntary laughter, since to smile or laugh out loud while reading is to lose control, and cease to inhabit a private space, by what Mary Beard calls 'an uncontrollable force that contorts the civilized body and subverts the rational mind'.[1]

Towards theorizing comic (short) fiction

Theoretical writing on comedy by its practitioners and critics is widespread, yet there are no major authors whose work is critically approved of *because* it is predominantly funny. Comic fiction is not academically respectable, unless produced by major authors who transcend genre and can lend their greatness to their humour: Charles Dickens and Rudyard Kipling are good examples of this phenomenon. The absence of critical attention may also be explained by comedy's status as a modal option for all genres of literature. It is not often considered as a form in itself, unlike tragedy. Critical analysis of comedy in the short story, rather than the novel, is rare. Isabel Ermida's *The Language of Comic Narratives: Humor Construction in Short Stories* (2008), although predominantly a linguistic study, contains chapters on the different markers and divisions within comedy and their application in the short story. It is the only full-length study available that covers fiction, its short form and comedy.

Establishing a critical foundation for comic short stories is possible by thinking in terms of a Venn diagram, to identify overlapping zones of commonality. The overlap zone is small because critical literature seems able to discuss only one area at a time. An extensive recent study of the British short story ignores humour completely; another barely acknowledges that 'Saki', an author usually considered a byword for witty short fiction, wrote to make people laugh.[2] Glen Cavaliero describes Dornford Yates and P. G. Wodehouse in his *The Alchemy of Laughter* as comic novelists, not noticing that their comedy was predominantly expressed in short stories.

This chapter attempts to offer an introduction to British comic short fiction and some of its authors, from the late Victorian period to the present day. It offers some suggestions of general principles, themes and trends over time. Definitions of the cognates and synonyms for 'comic short fiction' have changed during the period under discussion. Mark Twain – a powerful authority for British comic writers of his day – considered that 'the humorous story is American, the comic story is English, the witty story is French'.[3] Since Twain's dictum predates the humour of Bernard MacLaverty (Northern Irish) and the wit of 'Saki' (Anglo-Indian), this chapter feels free to extend the cultural field to embrace the in-joke, the parody, the pastiche, the satire, the tall story and their relations, since all these have been written, joyously, by 'English' writers. It will assume that the presence in short fiction of anti-climax, bathos, black humour, buffoonery, deflation, escalating farce, flippancy, facetiousness, irony, practical jokes, puns, sarcasm and word games can be counted as evidence of the long reach and multiple forms of the comic short story.[4] This chapter will use Twain's lead to show that 'comedy' and 'short story' are together much more than the sum of these separate elements, in how they reinforce each other. As a caveat, readers should note that this chapter does not use the theories of laughter deriving from Freud or Bakhtin, since they do not address comedy in short fiction. Short fiction from Caribbean, South African, New Zealand, Australian, East African, Indian or other Anglophone cultures outside North America, the United Kingdom and Ireland is also not discussed, since this would require a thorough knowledge of these cultures, impossible for one brief chapter.

Comic short fiction and its variety

Polonius's epigram 'brevity is the soul of wit' is usually understood as encouraging an intelligent person to be concise.[5] His words, contrasted with his character, also indicate that long-windedness and humour cannot co-exist: brevity is essential in the delivery of wit. Valerie Shaw notes that 'the short story is an intrinsically witty genre', and that 'being an essentially terse form, the short story can exploit the fundamental wittiness of making a character say a great deal about himself in a small number of words'.[6] Clare Hanson observes that the comic short story carries a strong stylization of form and 'depends for much of its effect on the reader's familiarity with the code employed and on his ability to recognise departures from it'.[7] This innate understanding of the rules and the necessity of expressive brevity both have their foundation in the techniques that Mark Twain described in 1897, whose markers of the comic short story are summarized next:

- To string incongruities and absurdities together in a wandering and sometimes purposeless way, innocently unaware that they are absurdities;
- The slurring of the point, ensuring that the point of the joke is half-hidden, as if the narrative voice does not realize its importance in the story;
- The dropping of the studied remark apparently without knowing it;
- The pause, to crank up suspense and anticipation;
- The narrative voice adopting a serious mask, concealing any sense that his story is funny, let alone outrageous.[8]

These markers show how humour can be produced in discursive prose that intends to entertain. They also show how the reader is expected to react to the narrative voice, which is essential because the reader's assumed responses determine the mode of delivery. Twain's categories are also helpful as a way of identifying typologies of comic short story, and noticing twentieth-century adjustments to this *fin-de-siècle* model.

Some forty years later A. P. Herbert, the British journalist, humourist and Member of Parliament, gave names to the theoretical models of comic writing:

- the Relative Theory of Risibility: the need to know the circumstances, scene and audience before an event can be funny;
- the Sub-doctrine of Surprise: incongruity between words and actions, surroundings or character;
- the Marginal Theory of Incongruity: something happening out of place.[9]

Isabel Ermida's linguistic approach equally enables her to formulate some definitions of how comedy works from a theorist's perspective. After considering the 'conceptual satellites'[10] of laughter, wit and irony, she offers these theories to explain some characteristics of humour in short fiction, although not asserting that these constitute the only or total approach:

- Disparagement theory: this connects laughter with scorn, laughing at rather than with someone, and invokes the emotions of envy, hostility and superiority;
- Release theory: this allows an escape from social inhibitions, producing pleasure in the liberation of the emotions against oppressive forces;
- Incongruity theory: this produces laughter from surprise, deriving from the breaking of, or temporary freedom from, social rules.[11]

Twain, Herbert and Ermida all follow Aristotle and Kant in noting the central role of incongruity in comedy, showing the longevity of the reasons for human laughter. Ermida also draws on Quintilian's observation that laughter is close to derision, and pre-Freudian thought in identifying laughter as a release.[12] These rules and indicators can be summarized as one universal theory: that Anglophone comic short fiction ambushes the expectations of the auditor and reader, and breaks their anticipated pattern of behaviour, just as the Vorticists demanded in *Blast*.[13]

An example of this is black comedy, a mordant humour that challenges the boundaries of taste, and an important and common feature in British and Irish comic writing. M. Beth Meszaros, writing about disability humour, notes that this dark comedy

> discovers humor in pain, suffering, and even terror. An edgy, disquieting mode, it has no truck at all with decorum or sentiment. Even to our cool, postmodern sensibility, it hovers just one short step this side of bad taste. It is discordant, subversive, impolite. Black comedy appropriates, as its own special province, subjects that are usually off-limits, subjects that it often dismantles with casual cruelty, flippancy, sometimes even brutality.

The differentiating effect of black comedy is that it does not produce 'the restorative laughter of comedy', since it continues to bite after the story has finished, leaving the reader a little shocked, but laughing despite the rules of good taste.[14] Kevin Barry's 'The Penguins' (2007), an airy report of the aftermath of an air crash on pack ice, fills these criteria admirably. The reader laughs and is horrified, and instinctively responds by trying to reformulate the horror as admiration for the insouciant writing style, or the wit in the dialogue, rather than gaze at the central premise of the terror of not knowing who will die.

Taste is crucial in how comedy is received. Robert Bernard Martin notes that the emergence of a sense of humour as a desirable character trait 'seems to have made its appearance in the nineteenth century' in Britain, since

Comic short fiction and its variety

Leslie Stephen noted its existence in 1876 'as one of the cardinal virtues'.[15] Before this date, humour was suspect to Victorian taste (although not in the early, post-Regency years of the nineteenth century) since it denoted 'the obscene, and the religious, and [was] a sign of insobriety and unseriousness': laughter in or at fiction signified social impropriety, and was not approved of for 'the innocent', among whom we should also include the untaught, the uneducated and those socially conditioned to be priggish.[16] This attitude to laughter made humour in nineteenth-century fiction problematic, and derives partly from the eighteenth-century Hobbesian theory of superiority, which 'makes laughter condescending and aggressive', an invitation to *schadenfreude*. Comedy's incongruities may also reflect an insecure society.[17] After the public embrace of musical comedy as joyous and respectable entertainment – epitomized by the Savoy Operas of Gilbert and Sullivan from the 1870s – the Victorians allowed themselves to read in the open pursuit of amusement.

Prestige and publishing environment

Nineteenth-century comic short fiction is tied to its means of publication. There were many lightly comic stories in the fashionable annuals of the 1820s and 1830s, and magazines such as *Blackwood's Magazine* and the *New Monthly Magazine* were important disseminators of light or comic writing. But because Victorian comic short fiction was written to amuse, rather than to move and instruct, it had a low cultural value. In magazines it was a filler, in contrast to the 'central commodity' of the long novel.[18] This sense of the short story deriving inferiority from its medium was compounded by the industrial production of late Victorian romance fiction magazines, or novelettes, which offered mass-produced and indistinguishable short fiction to an undiscriminating readership.[19] The longevity and wide circulation of mass-market fiction magazines, from the Victorian period to the Second World War, continued to withhold critical approval from comic short fiction, although individual authors were extolled.[20] Valerie Shaw observes that in the 1930s, 'for cultural critics like Q. D. Leavis', magazines and newspapers downgraded the reputation of the short fiction they carried because they were 'mass market and populist, and thus by extension could not carry any literature of the kind of literary merit she and the Leavisites promoted'.[21] The reader was also a problem for cultural judgements. The low literacy and limited income of the readers of cheap fiction periodicals would have connoted a lower-class readership for Victorian short fiction.

P. G. Wodehouse is an excellent example of a comic writer intimately connected to the magazine medium. He began his career writing comic short stories for the *Boys Own* market from 1901, publishing most of them in a rival magazine, the *Captain*. He made his name as a comic writer from 1911, with his Reggie Pepper and Jeeves and Wooster stories, writing in New York where he was also working in musical theatre. His stories' success depended on the contrast between their British tone and humour and the North American settings. His work appeared concurrently in New York evening newspapers and British monthly fiction magazines, so the evolution of his success from his pre-war stories of Mike and Psmith, to becoming the British comic writer *par excellence* of the war years and the 1920s and 1930s, has a great deal to do with the early reception of his work as a foreigner. The easy duplication of markets for the comic short story also suggests an increasing homogeneity of national senses of humour after the war and through to the 1930s and 1940s.

Wodehouse's use of multiple platforms for the same story, routinely reissuing magazine stories as collected episodes in books, was dependent on multiple markets in the United States and the United Kingdom. Between the wars, the fiction magazine market fractured into genre publication, and new humour magazines emerged. It was not uncommon for a Wodehouse story to be used as a lure to attract readers to the first issue, even if his stories never appeared there subsequently. Magazine historian Michael Ashley observes that 'the *Happy Mag.* was one of the many humorous fiction magazines that flourished during the twenties and its success encouraged imitators such as *The Merry* and *The Jolly*'.[22] The *Happy Mag.* (1922–40) launched Richmal Crompton's *Just William* stories; the short-lived *Jolly Mag.* (1927) carried a regular feature written and illustrated by the comic cartoonist H. M. Bateman; the *Merry Mag.* (1924–30), like the *Happy*, used contributions from the music hall in its fiction, and published light romances laced with simple humour. This range, and the embrace of different forms for the publication of humour, indicates the whole-hearted acceptance of light reading in British leisure time. *Gaiety* (1921–7) advertised itself as a humour magazine, and carried four or five comic short stories in each issue, with contributors such as Stacy Aumonier and George C. Birmingham.[23] Comic short fiction writers in the *Sunny Mag.* (1925–33), the companion to the *Happy*, included C. C. Andrews, Phyllis Hambledon, Evadne Price's 'Jane Turpin' stories about the female 'Just William', May Edginton, Ursula Bloom (as Mary Essex) and Michael Kent. *Pan* (1919–24), formerly a Bohemian fiction magazine and a humour miscellany, began to print short stories rather than skits from the mid-1920s. It was one of the first fiction magazines to 'genrefy' its content, after which only about 10 per cent of its stories were categorized as 'humour'.[24]

Comic short fiction and its variety

Like their Victorian counterparts, Edwardian and Georgian readers no longer considered the humour in short fiction high quality when it was written 'down' to overworked factory hands and office clerks. Edwin Pugh noted in 1908 that magazine editors advertised for new short stories to 'provide them with comic relief from the dolours and squalors of the ordinary literary stock-pot', but that the Edwardian comic short story writer – with some important exceptions – was largely deficient in skill, originality and taste.[25] This sense of reducing standards in the pursuit of sales affected the cultural value of short stories as a medium. Endorsement by authors of serious merit might heighten the comic story's prestige, yet it was not uncommon for literary and now canonical writers to ignore or suppress their comic writing because of its association with a lack of maturity. Katherine Mansfield told her agent that she did not want *In a German Pension* (1911) reissued because it was 'most inferior' and contained too much 'youthful extravagance of expression and youthful disgust'.[26] *In a German Pension* is a remarkable example of dark stories deploying the popular British trope of anti-German humour of the period. The narrative voice dwells on the vocal health and bodily complaints of the German boarding-house guests. The stories are exercises in the grotesque, where the humour depends on the reader sharing the narrator's sense of English superiority over German cultural values. Mansfield's vicious descriptions are curiously undercut by the characters' innocence of their appalling habits. Yet these stories are relentlessly funny. Mansfield expertly paces the revelations and delicately dissects characters in free indirect speech, producing comic exposure by an apparently artless voicing of the thoughts of the foolish and the arrogant in their own words.

Critics, too, often denigrate the comic writing of an author better known for the weighty and lofty. Rudyard Kipling is probably the only major twentieth-century author whose comic short stories are valued as highly as his other fiction. Kipling had been publishing almost exclusively short fiction since the 1880s, beginning with comic tales of British Army rankers in India. In the Edwardian period he constructed highly wrought farcical short stories that target arrogance through the assumed superiority of the narrative voice, in bitter, ironic situations revelling in social disgrace. 'The Village that Voted the Earth Was Flat' (written in 1914) is uproarious and cruel, a comedy of persecution and rule breaking. The distance between Kipling's narrative voice and the reader gives the comic events authority and makes them funnier, but the story ends with public humiliation. This is comic short fiction at its most punitive. In contrast, Arnold Bennett's short stories are characteristic for their 'gentle humour [...] a sophisticated incongruity between tone and subject'.[27] 'His Worship the Goosedriver' (1905) shares the tone of his comic novel *The Card* (1911) in its blunt cheerfulness in the face of social anxieties, and shrewd appreciation of how to deal with human nature.

The 1890s had seen the rise of the British New Humour, serving the requirements of conservative, mainstream readers who preferred safer and more familiar fiction than the fashionable writing of *fin-de-siècle* decadence and aestheticism. John D. Cloy notes that the New Humour modernized the well-established heartiness of Muscular Christianity, producing 'high-quality, pro-British, morally unobjectionable stories that appealed to the large segment of the English public who detested decadence in any form'.[28] Adding humour to earnest high Victorian moral codes 'gave fresh perspective to a flagging literary form'.[29] Middle-class humourists like Jerome K. Jerome, Barry Pain and W. W. Jacobs were considered 'wholesome' and thus respectable. They were also very widely read: 'never had such a body of writing been within the reach of such a large group of consumers.'[30] Their short stories and novels made the lower classes human for middle-class readers, and they showed lower-class readers how middle-class values could be accessible through a sense of humour. Margaret Stetz has observed that New Women writers of the New Humour were similarly invested in ameliorating relations between the sexes. They favoured 'a version of humor that recognised the inevitability of an ongoing relationship with the masculine objects of their laughter, as well as the need to reform and improve the character of that relationship'.[31]

In the First World War, British comic short fiction became grimly facetious, rather than frivolous or socially satirical. It is notable for its use of black humour in processing appalling experiences, and mediating their horror and emotional drain to the civilian readers at home. Cyril McNeile, writing as 'Sapper', was possibly the most effective of these short story writers, but British trench journals of the period contain many outstanding anonymous examples of the same art, written by soldiers. The novelist Ian Hay (John Hay Beith) wrote episodes of army life from the front for *Blackwood's Magazine* that were both comic and sentimental, later collected as *The First Hundred Thousand* (1915). These stories use a forced intimacy that makes the reader's emotions vulnerable to sudden attack by pathos. Dornford Yates also followed this fashion and developed 'Sapper's' facetiousness into a signature form of his own, in which he balanced the fashion for swooningly romantic episodes with witty banter between the sexes, and vituperative invective that followed Shakespearean models to balance his characters' rhetoric. Yates was a leading contributor of short stories and serialized novels to the *Windsor Magazine* for decades, and influenced a distinctive sector of the market. His stories' popularity encouraged Barry Pain, Hugh Walpole,

E. F. Benson, A. M. Burrage, Hugh de Sélincourt, Hylton Cleaver, Richmal Crompton, Horace Annesley Vachell and E. M. Delafield to write similarly light-hearted fiction, more or less comic, set in what Michael Ashley calls 'formulaic chocolate-box village life in Britain in the twenties and thirties [...] the world the *Windsor* wished to project'.[32]

Following the Second World War, post-war austerity exacerbated existing conditions that needed to be laughed at or escaped from in fiction. The Irish writer Frank O'Connor produced hundreds of short stories of rural and small-town Irish Catholic life, and is revered as a comic writer, although those unfamiliar with these cultures may struggle to find humour in these bleak depictions of constrained lives. His affinity with the Irish clergyman produces his most deeply felt comic works, particularly 'First Confession' (1951) and 'My Oedipus Complex' (1952). The Anglo-Indian novelist Lawrence Durrell, meanwhile, had a very well regarded career as an expatriate commentator on modern mores and post-war life, and was considered for the Nobel Prize for Literature in 1961 and 1962. He reissued his comic stories as collections in the 1970s, twenty years after their first magazine appearance in the late 1950s, when they were relatively unconsidered. The episodes in *Esprit de Corps: Sketches from Diplomatic Life* (1957) and its two sequels are told in the first person by Antrobus, a Foreign Office diplomat, recalling stories from his career to his unnamed former colleague. They are farcical and mildly smutty, describing catastrophic consequences for British diplomats in central Europe, with the humour resting on private understanding battling with a public inability to admit this without losing official status. 'Frying the Flag' (1957) is probably his finest comic work, orchestrating a perfectly balanced crescendo of language jokes and puns based on inappropriately misplaced letters.

Farce, satire and parody

Durrell's younger brother Gerald was also an accomplished author, and hardly published any short stories that were not funny in his long career as a writer, naturalist and zookeeper. His collection *Fillets of Plaice* (1971) – the title a deliberate parody of his brother's more serious collection of travel essays, *Spirit of Place* (1969) – is a particularly rich collection of comic short stories. 'A Question of Promotion' and 'A Transport of Terrapins' show Durrell's power as a farceur, creating chaos out of carefully positioned events and actions. The situation and his mode of narration were essential for his humour.

John Buchan applied farce to a Stevensonian plot in 'A Lucid Interval' (1910), in which a vengeful cook adds an extra ingredient to the curry for a political dinner-party, bringing about a catastrophic change of politics in the grand old men and rising stars of the House of Commons. Buchan was willing to use humour maliciously to expose the arrogant and pompous, but there is a restraint in his writing that may also have restricted his use of the form. For the peerless satirist, such as Max Beerbohm, all human foibles should be available for ridicule. Glen Cavalicro calls Beerbohm's faux-autobiographical sketches 'dizzyingly persuasive',[33] among which 'Savonarola Brown' (1919) is a perfect literary and historical pastiche, whose influence can be seen in the sketch writing of Monty Python fifty years later. Edmund Wilson admires Beerbohm's 'talent for impersonation', noting in particular the short stories 'Enoch Soames' and 'Not That I Would Boast' as 'the virtuoso pieces of a parodist'.[34] Fellow satirist, erstwhile journalist and war correspondent 'Saki' (Hector Hugh Munro) published his short stories in the first fifteen years of the twentieth century, and developed a unique line in satirical short fiction about amoral young men and the comedy of comeuppance. His genius for social commentary through ironic deflation gave him a distinctive literary voice that was expressed almost wholly in black humour, with a porous line between horror and wit. He epitomizes Aristotle's definition of wit as 'educated insolence'.[35]

While 'Saki' and Beerbohm had been the main, if not the only, pre-war British satirists, satire became highly popular in British comic writing after the First World War, especially in its less aggressive form of parody. The detective fiction critic and satirist Father Ronald A. Knox was pessimistic about the relationship between satire and humour, writing in 1928 that 'our habituation to humorous reading has inoculated our systems against the beneficent poison of satire'.[36] Valentine Cunningham suggests that every British author will use satire at one time or another, since it is a natural aspect of British humour to produce, often very unexpectedly, 'an outburst of hot spleen against some just perceived abuse or occasion of offence'.[37]

Parodies are the most common examples of comic short fiction on the satirical continuum: burning up fast and brightly, in contrast to the slow deliberate smoulder of the satirical novel, which can be humourless in its pursuit of a lengthy savage rendition. E. F. Benson, for example, could satirize perfectly in his celebrated Lucia novels, but his short fiction on the same theme is flat and comparatively unfunny. The fashion for short parodies in the 1930s had satirical intent, but a limited range. Rachel Ferguson's *Celebrated Sequels* (1934) and Leonard Russell's anthology *Parody Party* (1936) parody other writers only by pointing affectionately at weaknesses in their victims' writing styles, not at anything more socially relevant. Evelyn Waugh's short stories are in the same style as his novels: sardonic and bleakly facetious with an air of thoughtless anarchy that produces social chaos in place of order. His 'Love in the Slump' (1932) and 'On Guard' (1934) evoke upper-class heartlessness and idiocy in the 1930s with a very black wit.

Best known for their work in the fantasy and horror genres, Terry Pratchett and Neil Gaiman are contemporary multi-genre parodists who use comedy to satirize modern life and art, through the fantastical in the everyday. An excellent example of Neil Gaiman's comic short fiction is 'Forbidden Brides of the Faceless Slaves in the Secret House of the Night of Dread Desire' (2005), a parody of gothic fiction that also critiques the denial of legitimacy to the unfashionable and unserious. Pratchett's comedy relies on the sustained unfolding of related jokes, and the puns and referential jokes in his novels occur less successfully in his shorter fiction, as if he needs to build up a head of creative steam before his intensely situational humour can emerge. 'Turntables of the Night' (1989), in which an obsessive record collector encounters the one collector – Death – who will outdo him, relies on the reader's previous exposure to the main protagonist to fully appreciate the humour.

Women's comic short fiction

Comic writing, particularly from the beginning of the twentieth century, is routinely dismissed if written by women. Talia Schaffer notes that

> humor signalled the writer's light, charming point of view, which guaranteed that the work would not have serious political ideas or literary pretensions. The humor requirement was a way of demanding that women's literature be second-rate.[38]

Schaffer was describing the New Woman who dared to be witty, but her comments are echoed in E. M. Delafield's self-deprecating magazine columns that would become *Diary of a Provincial Lady* (1930).

In post-war Britain, where gender roles were policed with vigour, women writers knew that laughing at society was more effective than railing at it. They pushed with renewed energy and purpose at the convention, noted earlier, that women may not laugh and also be taken seriously. Margaret Stetz writes that women writers of comedy have 'created situations that will make their readers laugh, while also demonstrating, through their fictional characters' conduct, that they know it is wrong (or, at least, considered so) for women to indulge in making jokes, or in showing that they find something funny'.[39] As an example, the great British actor and author Joyce Grenfell is characteristic of the social and entertainment forces that enabled twentieth-century women writers to be funny as performers, but did not permit them to be wits. Grenfell's short monologues are celebrated as works of comic genius, but they are written for the stage, not as fiction.

Women writers drawn to comedy found that the way to be accepted and published was to be self-effacing. The novelist Barbara Pym created a superbly balanced, barely there comic style that was nonetheless devastating in its ridicule of the arrogant and overbearing. Margaret Stetz describes her as a writer of 'situations where [the heroine] must be subjected to the hilariously inappropriate behaviour of those with greater social privilege and advantages, yet feel "unable to laugh"'.[40] Suppression of the protagonist's amusement is a necessary part of Pym's approach, to show how powerful the social forces must be that will not let a woman laugh when she wants to. Her short story 'Goodbye Balkan Capital' (1940s) is a story of the comic rivalry between sisters, undercut with sly understatement to show the minute detail of the things that women laugh at.

A growing body of work in the 1970s and 1980s by British women writing comic short stories reflected feminist politics and critiques of capitalism. This humour was as deeply felt as black humour can be, using the reader's recognition that these stories produce catharsis, in showing that previously hidden subjects were no longer considered shameful. Gloria Kaufman describes the new feminist comedy that 'clarifies vision with the satiric intent of inspiring change'.[41] Fay Weldon's story 'Polaris' (1978) is a bleak exposure of the ridiculousness of life as a navy wife on a submarine base, in which exasperation at life's disappointments produces a constant unwilling laughter. Her feminist politics work within her fiction to raise awareness of oppression and ludicrous patriarchy that clearly demands change, resisting an undercurrent of hopelessness. Penelope Lively's dark humour in 'A Long Night at Abu Simbel' (1984) derives from the chaos produced when a holiday courier abandons her tiresome charges in Egypt, producing social disintegration. In her Oxford satire 'Presents of Fish and Game' (1978) she retells Jane Austen's masterly reduction of an inheritance from *Sense and Sensibility*, in which exhausted and ambitious academics manipulate university business management, producing the wry laughter of recognition and despair.

At the turn of the twenty-first century, feminist comic writing embraced the horror of middle-class desperation. Helen Simpson's stories in *Four Bare Legs in a Bed* (1990) and *Hey Yeah Right Get a Life* (2000) expose the wasted lives of young middle-class professionals trapped on maternity leave. Her humour is delivered through intricate narrative patterns and storytelling that court gasps of unexpected laughter from recognition as well as horror. Her 'Burns and the Bankers' (2000) is a clear-eyed condemnation of all that is ridiculous about professional Scotsmen. Ali Smith's 'The Child'

(2001) is written with an everywoman narrative voice that reinforces its situation comedy. A demon child appears in her supermarket shopping trolley and no one will believe that he is not hers, so the reader's horrified recognition of the grotesqueness of the mother who rejects a child whom no one would ever want is enhanced by the comedy of exasperation. Jackie Kay's 'Bread Bin' (2012) is a retelling of the traditional tale of sexual conquests from a lesbian perspective, producing humour by manipulating the reader's expectations from the jaunty first-person narration.

As this chapter has shown, the varieties of comic short stories in the British Anglophone tradition are innumerable. The strength and effectiveness of comic short fiction come from its precision under the limitation of length. Thus we see that the medium dictates the form, and the form brings forth the economy of wit, a mutual reinforcement of all the short story's elements. Although the strategies employed and topics explored vary widely, British comic short fiction at its best challenges the rules and confounds the reader's assumptions with comedy that shocks and humour that cannot be anticipated.

NOTES

1. Mary Beard, *Laughter in Ancient Rome: On Joking, Tickling and Cracking Up* (Berkeley: University of California Press, 2014), p. 40.
2. David Malcolm, *The British and Irish Short Story Handbook* (Oxford: Wiley-Blackwell, 2012); Emma Liggins, Andrew Maunder and Ruth Robbins (eds.), *The British Short Story* (Basingstoke: Palgrave Macmillan, 2011).
3. Mark Twain, 'How to tell a Story', *How to Tell a Story and Other Essays* (1897; New York: Oxford University Press, 1996), p. 3.
4. See Frank Muir (ed.), *The Oxford Book of Humorous Prose: From William Caxton to P. G. Wodehouse* (Oxford: Oxford University Press, 1990) for excellent and detailed discussions of these terms.
5. *Hamlet*, II.2.91.
6. Valerie Shaw, *The Short Story: A Critical Introduction* (London; New York: Longman, 1983), pp. 11, 115.
7. Clare Hanson, *Short Stories and Short Fictions, 1880–1980* (London: Macmillan, 1985), p. 6.
8. Twain, 'How to Tell a Story', p. 3.
9. A. P. Herbert, 'The Monkey and the Bishop', *General Cargo* (1939; London: House of Stratus, 2001), pp. 33–7, 34–5.
10. Isabel Ermida, *The Language of Comic Narratives: Humor Construction in Short Stories* (Berlin; New York: de Gruyter, 2008), p. 6.
11. Ermida, *Language of Comic Narratives*, pp. 15–30.
12. Aristotle, *Rhetoric*, 3.11; Immanuel Kant, *The Critique of Judgement*, trans. J. C. Meredith (1790; Oxford: Oxford University Press, 1952), p. 199; Quintilian, *De Oratore* 2.236; see also Beard, chapter 2.
13. Beard, *Laughter in Ancient Rome*, p. 30.

14 M. Beth Meszaros, 'Enlightened by Our Afflictions: Portrayals of Disability in the Comic Theatre of Beth Henley and Martin McDonagh', *Disability Studies Quarterly*, 23.3-4 (Summer 2003), n.p. http://dsq-sds.org/article/view/433/610 [Accessed 27 November 2014].
15 Robert Bernard Martin, *The Triumph of Wit: A Study of Victorian Comic Theory* (Oxford: Clarendon Press, 1974), p. 6.
16 Martin, *Triumph of Wit*, pp. 9-10.
17 Martin, *Triumph of Wit*, p. 19.
18 Harold Orel, *The Victorian Short Story: Development and Triumph of a Literary Genre* (Cambridge: Cambridge University Press, 1986), p. 2.
19 Kate Macdonald and Marysa Demoor, 'Borrowing and Supplementing: The Industrial Production of "Complete Story" Novelettes and Their Supplements, 1865–1900', *Publishing History*, 63 (2008), 67–95.
20 See, for example, Edwin Pugh's extravagant praise of W. W. Jacobs in his 'The Decay of the Short Story', *The Fortnightly Review*, 52.537 (October 1908), 631-42.
21 Shaw, *Short Story*, p. 7.
22 Michael Ashley, *The Age of the Storytellers: British Popular Fiction Magazines, 1880–1950* (London: British Library and Oak Knoll Press, 2006), p. 87.
23 Ashley, *Age of Storytellers*, p. 252.
24 Ashley, *Age of Storytellers*, pp. 87, 100, 123, 156-8.
25 Pugh, 'Decay of Short Story', p. 640.
26 Claire Tomalin, *Katherine Mansfield: A Secret Life* (London: Penguin, 2012), p. 208.
27 Liggins et al., *British Short Story*, pp. 124, 125.
28 John D. Cloy, *Muscular Mirth: Barry Pain and the New Humor* (Victoria, BC: University of Victoria, 2003), p. 7.
29 Cloy, *Muscular Mirth*, p. 9.
30 Cloy, *Muscular Mirth*, p. 10.
31 Margaret D. Stetz, *British Women's Comic Fiction, 1890–1990: Not Drowning, but Laughing* (Aldershot: Ashgate, 2001), p. 11.
32 Ashley, *Age of Storytellers*, p. 228.
33 Glen Cavaliero, *The Alchemy of Laughter: Comedy in English Fiction* (Basingstoke: Macmillan, 2000), p. 50.
34 Edmund Wilson, 'An Analysis of Max Beerbohm', *The Surprise of Excellence: Modern Essays on Max Beerbohm*, ed. J. G. Riewald (Hamden, CO: Archon Books, 1974), pp. 38-46, 42.
35 Aristotle, *Rhetoric*, 2.12.
36 Ronald A. Knox, *Essays in Satire* (London: Sheed & Ward, 1928), p. 42.
37 Valentine Cunningham, 'Twentieth-Century Fictional Satire', *A Companion to Satire Ancient and Modern*, ed. Ruben Quintero (Oxford: Wiley-Blackwell, 2011), pp. 400-33 (pp. 402-3).
38 Talia Schaffer, *Forgotten Female Aesthetes: Literary Culture in Late Victorian England* (Charlottesville: University of Virginia Press, 2000), p. 8.
39 Stetz, *British Women's Comic Fiction*, p. ix.
40 Stetz, *British Women's Comic Fiction*, p. x.
41 Cited in Stetz, *British Women's Comic Fiction*, p. xi.

11

MARTIN PRIESTMAN

The detective short story

Of all fictional genres, detective fiction is perhaps the most recognizable 'brand'. Whether under this name or its near-cognates 'mystery' or 'crime fiction', a narrative structure involving the solving of a mystery – usually criminal – by someone who detects the truth from small indications and then reveals it towards the end, accounts for a sizeable proportion of the fiction read, watched and listened to for the past century and a half. With its clear formula and its own extensive spaces in bookshops and drop-down menus, it is a brand happy to distinguish itself from the rest of 'literary fiction', over which its mystery-clue-resolution structure has nonetheless often had a massive influence. And from 1840 to 1920, both its basic form and the new single-hero series structure underlying much of its success were established, not in novels but in short stories.

From Poe to Doyle: the reign of the short story

It is a fact universally acknowledged that the first fully formed detective story was Poe's 'The Murders in the Rue Morgue', published in the Philadelphia *Graham's Magazine* in 1841. Numerous recurrent features of the subsequent genre can be traced directly back to it: the genius-detective who keeps his deductions to himself until near the end; the awestruck companion-narrator; the trail of clues; the baffled policemen; the conflicting witness reports; the crime committed in an apparently locked room; the mixture of bloody gore with a certain cheerful (not to say heartless) lightness of tone. Other subsequently generic features appear in two further Dupin stories: 'The Mystery of Marie Rogêt' features the armchair deductions of a detective who does not even bother to visit the crime scene, and 'The Purloined Letter' offers both the genius-criminal who is almost the hero's double and the paradox whereby, at a certain level of cleverness, the best-hidden solution sometimes turns out to be the most obvious.

No study of British detective fiction can sidestep the American Poe's foundational influence. But if we now shift focus more specifically to nineteenth-century Britain, it becomes clear that the rising interest in tales of crime and detection has other roots, too, still with the short narrative structure to the fore. Under the 'bloody code' of eighteenth- and early-nineteenth-century Britain, public executions for crimes from murder to simple robbery were a common feature of life, attracting crowds whose feelings might range from ghoulish vengefulness to various degrees of sneaking sympathy. A whole subculture of broadside ballads and criminal life-stories grew up, and from 1728 a series of books collectively known as the *Newgate Calendar* started to appear, consisting of short criminal biographies whose stern moral warnings failed to dilute the more basic fascination with daring exploits which makes the *Calendar* such staple reading for Fagin's gang in Dickens's *Oliver Twist* (1838).[1]

Although *Twist* allied Dickens with other 1830s 'Newgate novelists' increasingly attacked for showing too much sympathy for the poverty-driven criminal classes,[2] he was also a leading figure in the subsequent shift from the straightforward narration of crime to a more distancing structure based on its detection. His admiring portrayal of Detective Inspector Bucket in *Bleak House* (1852–3) was preceded by a series of short articles in *Household Words* (1850), lauding the achievements of the new plainclothes Detective Police founded in 1842 and led by Inspector Charles Frederick Field, on whom Bucket is transparently based. Particularly in 'Three Detective Anecdotes', Dickens begins to shape his general enthusiasm for the new detective force into well-paced short narratives of their exploits, narrated by themselves in a style effectively blending working-class directness with high intelligence and an almost aesthetic appreciation of the 'artful' and 'beautiful' skills required on both sides of the legal fence.

The ground for such narratives of successful detection was partly laid by the hugely popular 1828 translation of the *Mémoires* of François Eugène Vidocq, an ex-thief who rose to become head of the French *Sûreté*. Whatever their differences of emphasis, short 'true crime' narratives from the *Newgate Calendar* to Vidocq's or Dickens's reports of dramatic arrest have a satisfyingly clear shape which already links them closely to the enjoyments of fiction, and it is perhaps only a short step sideways from this tradition to William E. Burton's significantly early tale of detection, 'The Secret Cell' (1837).[3] Although Burton published it in the Philadelphia *Gentleman's Magazine* (where Poe in fact soon replaced him as editor), it is set in his native London, where a girl goes missing and the police detective L– follows a winding trail of contacts to the solution, assisted by his sharp-eared wife, a range of disguises and the girl's loyal dog.

About twenty years later another, more confident step was taken towards making detection the centre of interest, developing Poe's embryonic series idea into a complete run of stories, supposedly told by the real-life police detective 'Waters'. 'Waters' was actually a fiction created by the journalist William Russell, but the claim to authenticity in his *Recollections of a Detective Police Officer* (1856) brings out the thin line separating fiction from Dickens's celebrations of Field and his team as a politically equalizing force: Waters goes out of the way to defend 'Peace Soldiers' like Field against a judge's class-based insults in a Preface bristling with contempt for the upper orders who are themselves only jumped-up descendants of land-grabbing 'cattle-stealers on a considerable scale'.[4]

Despite the Preface's egalitarianism, many of the stories revolve around the entrapment of upper- or middle-class characters by lower-class gangs, with the rescue of the former often outweighing the demands of impartial justice. This partly reflects the fact that, although a public service in one sense, in practice the early police force often acted on behalf of specific 'prosecutors' who tended to be well off and to have their own families' needs at heart. In Russell's first story, 'One Night in a Gaming House', Waters's task is partly to catch a gang of forgers and illegal gamblers, but more specifically to break their grip on the aristocratic Mr Merton, whose involvement in their world arguably criminalizes him too. Having himself been earlier led astray by the main villain, Waters's task takes on an added tinge of revenge as he worms his way into the gamblers' trust and manoeuvers them into staking all their ill-gotten gains on a single rigged card game with the hapless Merton, at whose climax they are arrested. If not much to do with trails of clues (since it is clear 'whodunnit' from the first), there is real tension in the way Waters uses his own inner grasp of gambling psychology to spring his trap.

How far Russell was aware of Poe's 'tales of ratiocination' is uncertain; but around the same time such awareness is very clear in the short stories of Wilkie Collins. In 'The Diary of Anne Rodway' (1856), as in 'Rue Morgue', the killer is tracked from evidence clutched in the victim's hand; and in 'The Lawyer's Tale of a Stolen Letter' (1856), the eponymous lawyer's recovery of a compromising letter from a blackmailer's room owes just about everything to Poe's 'The Purloined Letter'.[5] But it could be argued that in both these stories the characters simply seem too large for their plots, or the plots too trifling for the characters. The meat of Anne Rodway's story lies in her moving diary of the hard life which drove her best friend to laudanum addiction, compared to which the precise causes of the latter's death seem almost a melodramatic irrelevance; while the meat of 'A Stolen Letter' lies in the warm-hearted curmudgeonliness of the lawyer Boxsious's narration, snapping such things at the reader as: 'You want to know her name, don't you? What do you think of Smith?'[6] Arguably the reader wants to know more about Anne and Boxsious in ways which their rather thin plot-lines don't satisfy, but which a novel-length tangle of several such plot-lines would, and it is as just such a satisfying tangle that Collins's later *The Moonstone* (1868) stands out as the best nineteenth-century *novel* of detection.

Both Collins's referencing of Poe and his early use of a woman detective figure have echoes in the work of a much weaker – although still interesting – writer probably called James Redding Ware, who used the *nom de plume* Andrew Forrester, Jr. Despite its business-like title, Forrester's *The Revelations of a Private Detective* (1868) is a mixed bag with no fixed narrative persona; in one story – 'Arrested on Suspicion' – the narrator seems less a professional sleuth than a bookish Poe addict simply trying to clear his sister from a charge of theft. Slavishly copying the Dupin of 'The Purloined Letter', but with none of his *chutzpah*, he eventually finds a coded letter which the culprit simply dropped next to her chair, before deciphering it on the exact lines of another Poe story, 'The Gold Bug'.[7] *Revelations*' style is often incoherent and there are yawning plot holes, but Forrester did take detective fiction a significant way forward a year later with *The Female Detective* (1864).

'Who am I?': the start of Forrester's introduction impressively opens out one of the key issues confronting fictional female detectives: can they let themselves be completely subsumed in the role of 'detective' as male protagonists routinely are, or must they first be defined in terms of age, looks, class and above all the marital status that would normally be indicated by their very name? Forrester's female detective coolly sidesteps the whole issue of 'whether I am married or single, old or young' and moves straight on to a spirited defence of her chosen profession and a denial of its supposed 'hard-heartedness'.[8] This last claim is put strongly to the test in the impressive first story, 'Tenant for Life', where some chance conclusions drawn from a chat with working-class friends lead her to track down, become employed by and then effectually entrap a well-to-do brother and sister, the latter of whom has bought an unwanted baby from a passer-by to ensure an inheritance. Like her unknowing brother and supposed niece, the sister is a thoroughly good person apart from this single deed, and the 'rightful' heir is an unfeeling swine; nonetheless the Female Detective has no doubts at all of her duty to reveal all to the latter with no hope of personal reward, and only a lucky heart attack enables the good family to keep what they so clearly deserve. While amply displaying the heroine's deductive brilliance, this story thus

The detective short story

raises real issues about morality versus law, as well as a non-judgemental grasp of the social reasons why a poor woman might be desperate to sell her baby to the first comer.

Elsewhere in *The Female Detective*, Forrester simply patches in accounts where the heroine hardly features, and even the first story has a bumpy start where it seems to be heading into another case altogether. But throughout there is a sense of a flawed but interesting writer, trying to do something really original with the detective form. This is less clearly the case with the other outcome of what was evidently a bumper year for female detectives, the anonymously published *Revelations of a Lady Detective* (1864), probably written by William Stephens Hayward. Perhaps because she does have a name, Hayward's Mrs Paschal is more often mentioned as an early breaker of gender moulds than Forrester's anonymous heroine, but her adventures really belong more to the realm of gothic melodrama than the nose-to-the-ground attention to detail on which detective fiction was coming to depend.

Many of the narratives we have looked at so far might be seen as trying the detective form on for size. Along with some awareness of the bar set by Poe, there is also a fair amount of sloppy writing and much uneasy slippage between the claims of melodrama, 'true crime' authenticity, ripe characterization and comedy. Arguably, one of the great achievements of Doyle's Sherlock Holmes series was to find a good balance between all these elements; but in the 1860s and 1870s some significant steps were taken in this direction by two Scottish writers: the real-life police detective James McLevy and his fictional counterpart James McGovan, actually the creation of a violinist, William Honeyman. In dramatizing his own past cases with some nicely written dialogue laced with broader reflections on social morality, McLevy's tone extends from pawky humour to grimmer narratives such as 'The Dead Child's Leg', where the finding of a severed leg in a drain leads to the exposure of the mother's desperate attempt to conceal a stillbirth.[9] Using the freedom of fiction to construct more intricate chains of connection while projecting a similar professionalism, 'McGovan' produces a much more comical tale of a leg, this time brought to the police by some boys first seen fighting over it as a valuable piece of meat, and eventually traced to a thief shot in the shin during a burglary, and the breezily unconcerned medical student who performed an amputation on him.[10]

Arthur Conan Doyle's prime inspiration in constructing Sherlock Holmes was certainly Poe's eccentric genius Auguste Dupin and the dim friend who narrates his adventures, but there is also a fair touch of Edinburgh in the mix, from the deductive methods borrowed from Doyle's early medical instructor Dr Joseph Bell to a number of detective narratives first published in that city: 'Waters' in the 1850s as well as McLevy in the 1860s and 'McGovan' in the 1870s. Brought up in Edinburgh and then travelling widely, Doyle moved to London only after he had created that iconic Londoner, Sherlock Holmes, in 1887, in two novels whose modest fame was hugely outstripped when he re-emerged from 1891 in short-story series form in the *Strand Magazine*. It is arguable that Holmes's truly massive impact from then on greatly depended on the series form that Doyle himself claimed as his virtual invention, after it struck him and the *Strand* editors that 'a single character running through a series, if it only engaged the attention of the reader, would bind that reader to that particular magazine'.[11] And although Holmes is vividly remembered for his gothic encounters with speckled bands, luminous hounds and the nemesis-like Moriarty (who in fact only appears in a single story), the heart of the series arguably lies in the quirkier urban tales where he and Watson 'hover over this great city, gently remove the roofs, and peep in at the queer things which are going on', criminal or not.[12] As with McLevy or McGovan, a bafflingly bizarre title often points the way to a labyrinth of memorable – sometimes comic – encounters linked through unexpectedly sideways connections: the Fleet-Street-swamping redheads and mad business model of 'The Red-Headed League', or the theologian's opium-addicted brother, Chinese lascar and suspiciously deformed beggar of 'The Man with the Twisted Lip'.

Doyle's were not the only successful detective series stories between 1890 and the First World War. Detectives whom more than one anthology calls 'Rivals of Sherlock Holmes' included C. L. Pirkis's Loveday Brooke, Arthur Morrison's Martin Hewitt and Horace Dorrington and G. K. Chesterton's Father Brown.[13] The first significant woman detective actually created by a woman, Loveday Brooke works in a private detective agency consisting just of herself and a boss who thoroughly respects her; like the earlier Female Detective she is 'altogether nondescript' and her femininity unemphasized. In her most frequently anthologized adventure, 'The Murder at Troyte's Hill' (1894), the trail of clues surrounding a country-house murder give Loveday ample chance to show her detective skills before these are made almost superfluous by the frank confession of the quietly insane murderer, a respectable old philologist whose obsession with the primal sources of speech has filled him with an urge to compare the dying cries of a dog, a man and – but for a last-minute rescue – a female detective.[14]

The author of several penetrating novels about working-class London, Arthur Morrison constructed his regular series detective Martin Hewitt as a somewhat drabber version of Sherlock Holmes, complete with his own 'methods' and Watsonesque narrator-friend, but often with rather creaking plots revolving more round chance pieces of recondite knowledge than complex clue-trails. Morrison's flair for social critique appears to better advantage in a series of seven stories featuring a detective with all the colour Hewitt lacks, who also happens to be a swindler, thief and occasional would-be murderer. Horace Dorrington is a cheerful, round-faced friend-to-all who uses genuine detective skills to worm out secrets which he then unscrupulously turns to his own advantage. Forced to flee the country for a cold-blooded attempted murder, he leaves behind him a 'deed-box' of past cases where his bending of rules is used to glance satirically at the get-rich-quick mentality of late Victorian Britain. In the best of these, the new cycling craze inspires the manager of one bicycle company to set up a fraudulent rival concern built entirely on advertising.[15] Dorrington's Holmesian deduction of the culprit from a trace of sticking-plaster caught in a metal chair leads to a satisfying showdown in the sham factory, where the manager's attempt to murder Dorrington – who has suavely blackmailed his way into half the proceeds – leads to an explosion, causing the 'Avalanche Bicycle Company' to collapse appropriately in a shower of falling masonry.

Starting two decades after Holmes, perhaps the best known of the latter's short-story 'rivals' is G. K. Chesterton's apparently unassuming little priest, Father Brown. As with Agatha Christie's elderly spinster Miss Marple, the trick of introducing barely noticed figures into a crime scenario which they then effortlessly unravel can produce great narrative and comic dividends, while running the danger of dwindling credibility as their success rate inexorably mounts. Known for his love of paradox, Chesterton handles Brown's quiet seizing of the spotlight well in the first few stories at any rate, matching them with similar reversals in the roles of two other far more dramatic figures, a master-criminal and a master-detective, the former of whom eventually becomes Brown's Watson-like assistant. In the brilliant second story, 'The Secret Garden', a fantastically clever way of concealing a beheaded victim's identity in a garden with no exits is tied in with the full-blooded pro-Catholic propaganda round which many of these stories are constructed.[16] The dramatic paradox of the atheistic detective's fall from grace is led up to through the skilful misdirection of suspicion around a sizeable circle of well-differentiated suspects, collected together in a way Doyle's more linear narratives rarely attempt in the confines of the short story, but at which Chesterton excels.

Between the World Wars: the rise of the novel

After the First World War, a thumbnail history of the detective genre would be justified in firmly shifting focus from the short story to the novel. With Agatha Christie's *The Mysterious Affair at Styles* (1920) a formula emerged which added many satisfying new intricacies to the single-mystery focus first developed in shorter tales. If Chesterton's handling of multiple suspects marks a great advance on Doyle's, neither comes near the complexities of constantly shifting suspicion achieved in the new 200-page detective-novel form pioneered above all by Christie.

However, despite the novel's rise, almost all its best-known practitioners also wrote short stories, often still featuring their star detectives. As early as 1923, the *Sketch* magazine commissioned several Christie stories featuring *Styles'* detective Hercule Poirot, some of which manage to cram the multiple-suspect formula into the shorter form with great ingenuity. Thus 'The Submarine Plans' artfully allows four or five people access to a room from which some vital plans have disappeared, before narrowing the focus down to a highly suspicious adventuress, and then finally producing a 'least-likely' culprit in the shape of the theft's apparent victim, who goes on to become prime minister.[17]

Miss Marple, Christie's other lead detective, also featured in several short stories. In one of the best, 'Tape-Measure Murder', Miss Marple displays her 'harmless old lady' manner at its finest, using the familiar rhyme about it being lucky to 'see a pin and pick it up' to focus attention on a single pin found at a murder scene, and thence deducing that only the dressmaker – an apparently innocent witness – could have had the kind of unquestioned physical access to the victim's neck to allow for a quick strangulation by tape measure.[18]

Christie's engagement with the short story's particular qualities emerges most clearly with a detective duo specifically designed for the form: the observant Mr Satterthwaite and his elusive, half-unreal alter ego Harley Quin, in the stories collected as *The Mysterious Mr Quin*.[19] Typically, Satterthwaite finds himself in a situation which puzzles him, until some specific detail is pointed out which leads to a solution involving a reunion of lovers, a death or both. The pointer-out is Mr Quin, who tends to turn up as if from nowhere, amid strange tricks of light evoking the mask-and-diamond patterns of the traditional harlequin costume – a constantly hinted parallel which becomes actual identification in 'Harlequin's Lane'. In one of the best, 'The Soul of the Croupier', detection takes second place to Quin's carefully planned reunion of a croupier and his rags-to-riches-and-back-again ex-wife. The ex-wife's insane pride of casually lighting her ex-husband's cigarette with the casino winnings which he has risked his job to give her constitutes a rather magnificent climax.[20] While Quin's not-quite-real character would find difficulty in surviving the exhaustive elucidations of the novel form, his evanescent appearances and vanishings fit well with the more liminal possibilities of the short uncanny tale.

The detective short story

Of other inter-war writers, Dorothy L. Sayers produced a different kind of short-story-only detective in the shape of Montagu Egg, a wine salesman whose shrewd deductions are comically bound up with such humdrum pronouncements from *The Salesman's Handbook* as 'Whether you're wrong or whether you're right, it's always better to be polite' (in a case hinging on a poisoning butler's bad manners).[21] Although this kind of implicit condescension to his class precludes him from novel-hero status, Egg arguably makes a more agreeable short-story companion than Sayers's usual novel-series detective, Lord Peter Wimsey, whose learned mannerisms tend to overwhelm the fair number of tales in which he also appears. Most of the short stories discussed so far first appeared in periodicals, only re-emerging in book form once their authors had established their distinctive 'brands'. In some cases, a good sense of the intended initial readership can be gathered from a glance at the relevant journals: as Knight argues, Holmes's middle-class sympathies and strong London focus tally well with the bustling thoroughfare connecting the workaday City with the smart West End after which the *Strand Magazine* is named;[22] and Christie's early Poirot stories find a natural home amidst the high-society reportage of the *Sketch*, whose well-known cartoons by H. M. Bateman exactly pinpoint the kind of small deviation from 'good form' on which so many of Poirot's and Marple's deductions are based.

Since the Second World War: the role of the anthology

While the shorter cases of the best-known detectives continued to migrate from periodicals to book-length collections, the massive success of the genre as a whole also ensured a rising tide of detective anthologies, ranging from periodical anthologies specifically publishing new crime fiction to collections of 'best detective stories', out of which some semblance of a 'canon' began to emerge, away from the iron demands of the single-hero series. One beneficiary of both these structures was Roy Vickers, whose occasional stories featuring 'The Department of Dead Ends' migrated from the influential periodical anthology *Ellery Queen's Mystery Magazine* (featuring British as well as American authors in the 1940s and 1950s) into frequent 'best of' anthologization. 'Inverted' from a whodunnit point of view,[23] Vickers's tales usually start with a grimly humdrum account of the main crime before some inconclusive piece of trace evidence stored in the eponymous (and imaginary) Scotland Yard 'Department' is suddenly thrown into focus by its indirect links with another case, through a mixture of sideways thinking and sheer blind luck. Straddling the Second World War and putting its actual detectives in second place to their department, the 'Dead Ends' series intertwines two new strands which were to become increasingly dominant in post-war writing: the 'procedural' revolving around unshowy police work, and the focus on the psychology of rather pathetic domestic crimes of the type ambivalently lamented in George Orwell's famous essay 'The Decline of the English Murder'.[24]

Different 'Dead Ends' stories appear in two 'best stories' anthologies which between them give a good flavour of the shifting tastes of the post-war period up to the 1980s, when the genre was arguably groping its way between old-style playfulness and a more contemporary focus on criminal psychology. Edmund Crispin's *Best Detective Stories* (1959) bears out Crispin's definition of a detective story as a thoroughly artificial 'machine for reading in',[25] with plot-twisting tales such as Anthony Gilbert's story of an upper-class game of 'Murder in the Dark' played for real, or his own 'Who Killed Baker?', which wraps what is basically a lateral-thinking exercise up in an atmosphere of Senior Common Room brain-teasing. Crispin's Preface is partly written as a riposte to an early article by Julian Symons, arguing for more realistic or imaginative treatments of the psychology of crime, and these arguments are implicit in Symons's own later *Penguin Classic Crime Omnibus* (1984), where classics by Poe, Doyle, Christie and even Crispin himself sit alongside far edgier works by Roald Dahl and Ruth Rendell.[26] Between the two anthologies, Symons had crystallized the views attacked by Crispin in his magisterial *Bloody Murder: From the Detective Story to the Crime Novel* (1972): one of the few critical studies to give due weight to the historical transition from stories to novels, as well as a significant shift of emphasis from pure detection to crime itself.[27]

The anthologizing strands discussed previously have continued into more recent times: from 1969 to 1986, the British periodical anthology *Winter's Crimes* published specially written stories by Colin Dexter, P. D. James, Ellis Peters, Ruth Rendell and many others, while the more recent *OxCrimes* (2014) contains new works by established authors such as Ian Rankin, Val McDermid and Mark Billingham. Meanwhile the 'best of' tradition of selecting stories published more evanescently elsewhere is currently being amply served by Maxim Jakubowski, in a continuous flood of volumes starting with *The Mammoth Book of Best British Mysteries* (2008) and continuing as successive numbers of *The Mammoth Book of Best British Crime*, already reaching volume 11 by 2014. If much of this work has been under the radar of the series-novels which dominate the crime genre, these stories demonstrate how successfully many contemporary writers grasp the essentials of the short story form. While some bring in their usual novel-detectives to tackle cases whose few suspects allow for satisfyingly quick closure, others seize the opportunity to draw us into the minds of driven protagonists

The detective short story

whose mounting impulses towards murder and mayhem would be harder to empathize with at novel length.

Thus, in the first group, Ian Rankin's now-retired Inspector Rebus unpicks a long-hidden murder in the gap between a guided brewery tour and his return for a second quietly sympathetic chat with the killer; a child's discovery of a dead Santa Claus is handled by Mark Billingham's Inspector Thorne with less final focus on the (obvious) solution than the delicate problems of negotiating round the boy's belief in Father Christmas; and the investigation of a young man's death by John Harvey's Inspector Resnick is more interesting for the miserable tensions it brings out within a dead-end Nottingham youth culture than for its deliberately ambiguous, unclimactic conclusion.[28] In a very different vein, Neil Gaiman resurrects Sherlock Holmes in both a literary and literal sense, in a delightful tale of oriental beekeeping and the quest for eternal life.[29]

If such detective-centred works return us to the origins of the genre in Poe's Dupin stories, others have more echoes of the tales of gothic obsession – such as 'The Black Cat' or 'The Tell-Tale Heart' – for which Poe is equally famous. Often we are let bit by bit into a mind whose emotional openness attracts initial sympathy, only to find ourselves sharing a journey to murder into which it is easier to relax because at least we know it will be brief. Two of the best stories in *Winter's Crimes* are by Lionel Davidson, the first the apparently bland narration of a child who turns out to be a compulsive killer unable to grasp the unconscious roots of his disturbance because he has been brought up not to 'dwell' on things he does not understand; the second a tale of attempted murder whose dependence on the minutiae of fly-fishing ought to render it impenetrable, but where these very minutiae shield the would-be killer from the emotional undertows also echoed in the turbulent river whose fatal currents provide the *leitmotif* throughout.[30] More recent stories include several examples of 'Tartan Noir', where a gleefully transgressive Scots gusto wafts us towards some truly horrible goings-on.[31] Thus Val McDermid intertwines a steamily graphic lesbian affair with a deadly battle of blackmail and murder, and Allan Guthrie embroils two bickering Siamese twins in a botched theft and ridiculously self-defeating homicide. Meanwhile Stuart MacBride opens a story with a junkie blindly searching for heroin in a turd-filled septic tank where he is soon joined by the corpse of his murdered girlfriend, and lets things broadly go downhill from there.[32]

Over the edge: postmodern detection

Far though some of these stories may push the envelope of the genre, they still at least deal with actual detectable crime. However, there are other

169

stories which deliberately build up our genre expectations of a rational solution only to suddenly dematerialize them: a postmodern conjuring trick developed in such classics as Jorge Luis Borges' 'Death and the Compass',[33] but also evident in several interesting British works. To be effective, such 'anti-detective stories' often have to sound convincingly flat, deliberately eschewing the build-up of emotional impressions we might associate with normal fiction in favour of a detective-like insistence on concrete details, so that the final subversion of our genre-expectations comes to feel like an assault on objective materiality itself.[34] This 'flat' effect is certainly to the fore in much of John Fowles's 'The Enigma' (1974), where the massing of evidence surrounding a Member of Parliament's disappearance is exhaustive to the point of plodding until eventually derailed by the detective's love affair with a witness, whose theory that they and all the other characters might be fictitious soon takes over as the most feasible explanation.[35] With less of an explicitly 'detective' framework but a similarly unruffled style, Nicholas Royle's 'Continuity Error' uses a range of carefully specified London locations to build up a convincingly three-dimensional picture of small domestic ups and downs, until the eponymous 'continuity' of the murder-obsessed protagonist's thoughts and actions starts to fracture increasingly alarmingly, and finally leaves us imagining the absolute worst.[36]

From early reportage and tales of ratiocination, through the increasingly skilful blends and craftings of the Holmes era and into the long years of fighting back against the novel, short stories have often been the crucibles for new directions and experiments in the detective genre, particularly at its more playful and dangerous edges. In the absence of the demand for exhaustiveness endemic to the novel, such tales can either revel in the nuts and bolts of whodunnits as pure 'machines for reading in', or push their readers' readiness for a brief, provisional immersion in crime over the edge, into the darkly sad, the mad or the self-reflexively uncanny.

NOTES

1 Charles Dickens, *Oliver Twist* (Harmondsworth: Penguin, 1966), p. 196.
2 See Lyn Pykett, 'The Newgate Novel and Sensation Fiction, 1830–1868', *The Cambridge Companion to Crime Fiction*, ed. Martin Priestman (Cambridge: Cambridge University Press, 2003), pp. 19–40.
3 William E. Burton, 'The Secret Cell', *Gentleman's Magazine* (Philadelphia, 1837, issues 4–5), first reprinted in Michael Sims's invaluable *The Dead Witness: A Connoisseur's Collection of Victorian Detective Stories* (London: Bloomsbury, 2012), pp. 1–38.
4 'Waters', *Recollections of a Detective Police Officer* (London: J. & C. Brown & Co., 1856), p. v.

The detective short story

5 Wilkie Collins, 'The Diary of Anne Rodway', *Household Words*, XIV.330–1 (19 and 26 July 1856); Sims, pp. 99–140. Wilkie Collins, 'The Lawyer's Story of a Stolen Letter', *After Dark* (London: Smith, Elder & Cornhill, 1856), pp. 87–119 (p. 88).
6 Collins, 'The Lawyer's Story', p. 88.
7 Andrew Forrester, Jr., 'Arrested on Suspicion', *The Revelations of a Private Detective* (London: Ward Lock, 1858), pp. 289–320.
8 Andrew Forrester, Jr., *The Female Detective* (London: Ward Lock, 1864), 'Introduction', pp. 1–5 (p. 1.); 'Tenant for Life', pp. 6–96.
9 James McLevy, 'The Dead Child's Leg', *McLevy the Edinburgh Detective* (Edinburgh: Mercat, 2001), pp. 20–30.
10 'James McGovan' [William Honeyman], 'The Mysterious Human Leg', *The McGovan Casebook: Experiences of a Detective in Victorian Edinburgh* (Edinburgh: Mercat, 2003), pp. 1–11.
11 Arthur Conan Doyle, *Memories and Adventures* (Cambridge: Cambridge University Press, 2012), p. 95.
12 Arthur Conan Doyle, 'A Case of Identity', *The Penguin Complete Adventures of Sherlock Holmes* (London: Penguin, 1981), p. 191.
13 Hugh Greene and Nick Rennison have both edited collections under this name.
14 Catherine Louisa Pirkis, 'The Murder at Troyte's Hill', *The Experiences of Loveday Brooke, Lady Detective* (London: Hutchinson, 1894), pp. 15–30.
15 Arthur Morrison, 'The Affair of the Avalanche Bicycle and Tyre Co., Ltd.', *The Dorrington Deed-Box* (London: Ward Lock, 1897), pp. 153–97.
16 G. K. Chesterton, 'The Secret Garden' (1911), *The Penguin Complete Father Brown* (Harmondsworth: Penguin, 1981), pp. 23–39.
17 Agatha Christie, 'The Submarine Plans', *Sketch*, 1606 (7 November 1923), 297–8; xxvi; *Poirot's Early Cases* (London: Collins, 1974), pp. 229–51.
18 Agatha Christie, 'Tape-Measure Murder', *Miss Marple's Final Cases & Two Other Stories* (London: Book Club Associates, 1980), pp. 45–61.
19 Agatha Christie, *The Mysterious Mr Quin* (London: Collins, 1930).
20 Agatha Christie, 'The Soul of the Croupier', *The Mysterious Mr Quin*, pp. 82–98 (p. 98).
21 Dorothy L. Sayers, 'The Poisoned Dow "08"', *Hangman's Holiday* (1933; London: New English Library, 1978), pp. 91–100 (p. 100).
22 Stephen Knight, *Form and Ideology in Crime Fiction* (Bloomington: Indiana University Press, 1980), pp. 70–1.
23 A tradition started in R. Austin Freeman's 'inverted' stories featuring Dr Thorndyke in *The Singing Bone* (London: Hodder & Stoughton, 1912).
24 George Orwell, 'Decline of the English Murder', *Tribune* (15 February 1946), reprinted in *The Decline of the English Murder and Other Essays* (Harmondsworth: Penguin, 1965), pp. 9–13.
25 Edmund Crispin (ed.), *Best Detective Stories* (London: Faber, 1959), p. 13.
26 Julian Symons (ed.), *The Penguin Classic Crime Omnibus* (Harmondsworth: Penguin, 1984).
27 Julian Symons, *Bloody Murder: From the Detective Story to the Crime Novel* (London: Faber, 1972).
28 Ian Rankin, 'The Very Last Drop', *The Mammoth Book of Best British Crime*, vol. 8, ed. Maxim Jakubowski (London: Robinson, 2011), pp. 3–13; Mark

Billingham, 'Underneath the Mistletoe Last Night' and John Harvey, 'Not Tommy Johnson', both in *OxCrimes*, eds. Mark Ellingham and Peter Florence (London: Profile Books, 2014), pp. 339–411, 215–27.

29 Neil Gaiman, 'The Case of Death and Honey', *OxCrimes*, pp. 33–55.
30 Lionel Davidson, 'I Do Dwell', *Winter's Crimes*, 16, ed. Hilary Hale (London: Macmillan, 1984), pp. 53–72; 'Indian Rope Trick', *The Best of Winter's Crimes*, vol. 1, ed. George Hardinge (London: Guild Publishing, 1986), pp. 132–45.
31 A term invented jointly by Ian Rankin and James Ellroy: see Ian Rankin, 'Rough Justice in Tartan Noir', *Dead Sharp: Scottish Crime Writers on Country and Craft*, ed. Len Wanner (Uig, Skye: Two Ravens, 2011), p. 3.
32 Val McDermid, 'I've Seen that Movie Too', *OxCrimes*, pp. 75–91; Allan Guthrie, 'The Killer Beside Me', *The Mammoth Book of Best British Mysteries*, ed. Maxim Jakubowski (London: Robinson, 2008), pp. 488–95; Stuart McBride, 'The Ballad of Manky Milne', *Mammoth Book of Best British Crime 8*, pp. 106–19.
33 Jorge Luis Borges, 'Death and the Compass', *Labyrinths*, eds. D. A. Yates and J. E. Irby (Harmondsworth: Penguin, 1970), pp. 106–16.
34 See Michael Holquist, 'Whodunit and Other Questions: Metaphysical Detective Stories in Post-War Fiction', *New Literary History*, 3.1 (Autumn 1971), 147.
35 John Fowles, 'The Enigma', *The Ebony Tower* (London: Vintage, 1996), pp. 185–240.
36 Nicholas Royle, 'Continuity Error', *Mammoth Book of Best British Mysteries*, pp. 322–47. See also Nicholas Royle, *The Uncanny* (Manchester: Manchester University Press, 2002).

12

LUKE THURSTON

The gothic in short fiction

'Our modern attraction to short stories', wrote G. K. Chesterton in 1906,

is not an accident of form; it is the sign of a real sense of fleetingness and fragility; it means that existence is only an impression, and, perhaps, only an illusion.[1]

The keyword here is *modern*: Chesterton has in mind above all the literary and aesthetic revolution of the 1890s, a period during which artistic innovation combined with – indeed *grew out of* – the industrial transformation of publication and communication to constitute a defiant rejection of the perceived solidity and complacency of Victorian culture, a culture seen as incarnated in the ponderous bulk and stately narrative of the three-volume novel. The revival of the gothic in the nineteenth century, reaching its apogee in the delirious neogothic fantasies of the *fin de siècle*, was wholly bound up with the epochal shift in the dissemination of culture during that period, a period that saw the introduction of the telegraph (1840s) and the telephone (1880s) as well as huge changes in the production and consumption of cultural commodities. As Roger Luckhurst notes, '[e]conomics as much as aesthetic taste was the factor that killed off the three-volume novel in 1893. By 1897, only four three-volume novels were printed in England, a remarkably sudden transformation.'[2]

By the end of the nineteenth century an explosion of print culture was serving a much wider readership, partly the result of the 1870 Education Act that had produced a new generation of literate citizens of different classes. It is here that we can give Chesterton's observation a historical context: what he sees as the link between short fiction and 'fleetingness and fragility' may be less to do with existential insecurity than with the 'modernity' of the late Victorian culture industry, its new technologies and new, fast-moving marketplace. For if novels were still being written at the end of the nineteenth century (now in single volumes, as potential 'bestsellers'), at the same time the huge expansion of magazines demanded new forms, specifically

173

ones pitched to an expanded range of readers, many of whom simply lacked time for the leisured perusal of novels. The 'characteristic form' of the 1890s, writes Ian Fletcher, thus became the short story, a form conveniently suited to the rapid delivery and restricted page space of a weekly or daily magazine.[3] Fletcher quotes H. G. Wells on this golden dawn for the short story:

> The nineties was a good and stimulating period for a short story writer. Mr Kipling had made his astonishing advent with a series of little blue-grey books, whose covers opened like windowshutters to reveal the dusty sun-glare of the east; [...] The *National Observer* was at the climax of its career of heroic insistence upon lyrical brevity and a vivid finish. [...] No short story of the slightest distinction went for long unrecognised. The sixpenny popular magazines had still to deaden down to the conception of what a short story might be to the imaginative limitation of the common reader – and a maximum length of six thousand words. Short stories broke out everywhere.[4]

Wells seems to offer a hard-nosed rebuke to Chesterton's airy talk of the short story's 'sense of fleetingness and fragility', stressing the editorial realities of what was possible and what would sell. His account, though, is shot through with class-based and imperialist prejudices: Kipling's work opens a window in some imperial citadel onto a dazzling and unsettling (i.e. heavily ideological) orient; and while Wells praises a middle-class magazine for fostering the poetic virtue of 'lyrical brevity', by contrast he derides cheaper publications that merely 'deaden down' literary culture to the level of a semi-literate 'common reader'. These ideological implications are inflected, in a sense significant for this discussion of the gothic and the short story, in an essay by Wells of 1911:

> A short story should go to its point as a man flies from a pursuing tiger: he pauses not for the daisies in his path, or to note the pretty moss on the tree he climbs for safety. But the novel by comparison is like breakfasting in the open air on a summer morning: nothing is irrelevant if the writer's mood is happy.[5]

The opposition playfully sketched by Wells here is worth pausing over. While the novel inhabits a fantasy world of aristocratic leisure – and the picture of someone 'breakfasting in the open air on a summer morning' would certainly have seemed such to Wells's hard-pressed urban readers in 1911 – by contrast the short story emerges from a dangerous encounter with something outside the bounds of everyday normality, something as terrifying and romantic as a tiger. The short story, that is, is driven by a nervous intensity, an impulsive energy bordering on panic that is fundamentally at odds with an English literary culture exemplified by the stately edifice of the three-decker novel with its subtleties of social commentary. If the novel thus

The gothic in short fiction

supposedly embodied the heart of true Englishness, the short story would be its heart of darkness.

This notion of the short story – and with it, as we will see, crucial features of the gothic – as somehow essentially non-English, part of an alien culture lying threateningly and alluringly beyond the feudal pale of the leisurely novel, has been remarkably long-lived. For H. E. Bates, writing in 1934, the short story was no more than 'a kind of orphan slavey' to the English novel, and as late as 1980 V. S. Pritchett noted that Victorian readers 'preferred to graze on the larger acreage of the novel', adding that 'even tales by Dickens or Thackeray or Mrs Gaskell strike us as being unused chapters of longer works'.[6] The true source of the Anglophone short story for such commentators was undoubtedly America, with the figure of Poe, theorist and master practitioner of the 'tale of terror', almost an emblem of the strangeness and uncanny inventiveness of the form. Poe had famously prescribed 'unity of effect' as the governing principle of literary creation, stipulating that a proper 'tale of terror' should be consumable in a single sitting, its effect 'unblemished, because undisturbed', with the reader barely allowed to pause for breath, let alone for a leisurely breakfast.[7] The rapidity of the short story, in this sense, was a sign of the desire to *impact* the reader's mind, not merely engage her in polite conversation; and in this, it also betokened (what was perceived as) a fundamentally non-English unsubtlety.

It is here that the imaginary convergence of the short story and the gothic begins to be unavoidable. If Poe, with his mid-nineteenth-century ruminations on how to terrify readers, had laid down a shocking challenge to the genteel self-image of the English literary estate, he had been preceded earlier in the century by another ambiguous semi-colonial likewise fascinated by non-English literatures: namely Walter Scott. Scott's 1827 article on Hoffmann was one of the first coherent efforts to reflect, both theoretically and in terms of writerly technique, on the precarious negotiation between literary enjoyment and affective excess or terror. This fundamentally gothic question is treated with exemplary clarity by Scott:

> [T]he supernatural in fictitious composition requires to be managed with considerable delicacy, as criticism begins to be more on the alert. The interest which it excites is indeed a powerful spring; but it is one which is peculiarly subject to be exhausted by coarse handling and repeated pressure. It is also of a character which it is extremely difficult to sustain, and of which a very small proportion may be said to be better than the whole. The marvellous, more than any other attribute of fictitious narrative, loses its effect by being brought much into view. The imagination of the reader is to be excited if possible, without being gratified.[8]

This passage will echo throughout subsequent writings on the gothic and the ghost story, most notably in influential statements by M. R. James. What we might call the libidinal economy of the supernatural, as sketched here by Scott, will repay closer scrutiny. It is haunted by the Burkean analysis of the sublime, and thus centred above all on the key significance of 'obscurity', of semiotic fragmentation or non-closure. Scott's crucial Burkean insight into gothic fictionality is that *excess* representation will cancel, rather than augment, its effectiveness: so that, as with the sublime, it is signifying *inadequacy* here that generates aesthetic power. It is this essentially metonymic aspect of the genre, in which 'a very small proportion may be said to be better than the whole', that H. G. Wells will reformulate a century later as a contrast between short story and novel. While for Wells the novelist may legitimately lay claim to an all-encompassing realism where nothing is irrelevant, the true story writer 'pauses not for the daisies in his path'. Indeed, should he slip mistakenly into *the wrong kind of realism* (and the history of the ghost story is littered with examples of this stylistic error), the essential magic of the story, its sublime power to grip and terrify, will rapidly evaporate.

Around the same time as Scott, another famous gothic novelist, Ann Radcliffe, was also theorizing the supernatural in fiction; but her approach is significantly closer to modern psychology. Radcliffe focuses on the emotional states induced by gothic literature or theatre, crucially distinguishing between two of these: 'Terror and horror', she writes, 'are so far opposites, that the first expands the soul, and awakens the faculties to a high degree of life; the other contracts, freezes, and nearly annihilates them'.[9] This binary opposition is clearly structured by Radcliffe as an ideological hierarchy, with terror the privileged term and horror its debased antithesis: thus terror is linked to the Burkean sublime, to what is 'seen in glimpses through obscuring shades',[10] while horror is the result of a desublimating overexposure, a ghastly excess of representation that borders on the obscene or the ridiculous. Indeed, with this contrast between an obscure and an explicit supernatural, linked in turn to a vertiginous expansion of the psyche or its claustrophobic shrinkage, Radcliffe in effect predicts the full aesthetic gamut of gothic cultural production, from the refined sensibilities of the Edwardian ghost story to the pornographic video nasties of our time.

Writing the supernatural, then, for both Scott and Radcliffe was a matter that required 'considerable delicacy', an art of subtle shades and nuances. Literary terror was an essentially fragmentary genre, where too much or too clear representation could entail a stylistic catastrophe, making a sublime story seem ridiculous – or worse, taking it into the salacious, unspeakably vulgar domain of horror. The thing that works the gothic magic in a text, the

The gothic in short fiction

secret source of its hypnotic power over readers, was thus a dangerous thing that needed to be strictly disciplined and constrained, in terms shot through with class and gender politics; and at the same time it was an *alien* thing, an invader from beyond the familiar 'realistic' features of an imaginary literary England. Writing in the 1820s, Scott and Radcliffe were still at some distance from the explosion of magazine culture and literacy that by the end of the century would spell the end of the three-decker novel. But nonetheless what they observe – the essential incompatibility of supernatural terror with ordinary 'English' novelistic discourse, the psychical obscurity and aesthetic rapidity of fear – provides in effect a map for the future genre of the Victorian ghost story, where the apparent constraints of writing for magazine publication would turn out to have a hugely beneficial effect on literary style. For it was precisely the brevity and stylistic economy of the ghost story – features enforced by ruthless magazine editors – that would come to define the genre at its best.

To get a sense of the diverse ways to write the supernatural that opened up with the rise of the nineteenth-century ghost story, we will start by looking at two very different examples: one from early in the genre's development – Walter Scott's 'The Tapestried Chamber' (1829); and another from the era of Victorian mass magazine culture – Joseph Sheridan Le Fanu's 'Squire Toby's Will' (1868). Scott's story comes only a few months after his article on Hoffmann and the supernatural quoted earlier; and its publishing environment is strikingly different to Le Fanu's forty years later. In 1828, Scott was asked to contribute a story to the *Keepsake*, a literary annual published every Christmas for a genteel circle of readers, by its proprietor Charles Heath. This was an invitation to join a literary elite: Heath had already secured contributions from Wordsworth, Coleridge and Southey, as well as both Percy and Mary Shelley. What identified Heath's annual as a lofty literary endeavour were the enormous fees he could offer his contributors: Scott received the staggering sum of five hundred pounds for a single story (the equivalent of many thousands of pounds today). By contrast, when in 1868 the debt-ridden Le Fanu had his story published in the monthly periodical *Temple Bar*, he earned no more than a few pounds. From Scott in 1829 to Le Fanu in 1869, we move from the refined, elitist world of Regency publishing to the fast-moving and ruthless marketplace of the Victorian magazine. And the contrast between these milieux is clearly legible in the stories themselves.

For V. S. Pritchett, we recall, the cultural dominance of the English novel in the nineteenth century meant that when novelists wrote short stories they were often in effect producing only draft chapters of a longer work. [Editor's note: Pritchett's proposition is complicated in this volume by John Plotz's chapter.] In the case of 'The Tapestried Chamber', such an observation may be partly justifiable – the text has little of the urgency or stylistic coherence of the best Victorian ghost stories. For David Blair, Scott's tale is merely 'an incident, not a story', its protagonist little more than a stylistic exercise, 'a rather desultory device for reworking the gothic *topos* of spectral female iniquity'.[11] The story certainly has a leisurely narrative pace, with lavish descriptions of its aristocratic setting and refined social exchanges. The encounter with the ghost is coded, according to conventional 'male gothic' heteronormativity, as a test of manhood in the face of a deviant femininity: General Browne is more or less molested in his bed by a spectral hag and has to confess that 'all firmness forsook me, all manhood melted from me like wax in the furnace'.[12] This detumescence of the masculine centre of the narrative is thus how Scott's text gives an ideological sense to the proximity of the abject, horrifying Thing, whose presence for Radcliffe 'contracts, freezes, and nearly annihilates' the faculties of the soul. One way to read 'The Tapestried Chamber', indeed, is as an unconscious effort by the genteel literary culture of the 1820s to ward off the coming stylistic catastrophe of the ghost story, to constrain and frame the horrific intruder within the patriarchal bounds of novelistic decorum.

By 1868, with Le Fanu's 'Squire Toby's Will', those polite discursive borderlines have been thoroughly trounced. In Le Fanu's stories, writes E. F. Bleiler, 'the supernatural is an unconscious element in the mind and it may leap into emergence when the barriers protecting the conscious ego are temporarily broken down'.[13] The story's setting – the ruinous Gylingden Hall with 'the howl and sobbing of the wind through its empty galleries' – forms a stark contrast to the well-managed estate of Woodville Castle in Scott's tale.[14] If the latter symbolically confined its ghost to a single room, Le Fanu's ghost has fully invaded the text, as it were: both plot and style are suffused with an uncanny, unaccountable vitality. The initial scenario is produced by the death of the perverse 'father of enjoyment' Squire Toby Marston, triggering the mortal rivalry of the two sons Charlie and Scroope (the latter just a twisted letter away from Scrooge, the haunted miser of *A Christmas Carol*, the 1843 Dickensian text that had launched the Victorian craze for ghost stories). Squire Toby's ghost is one of the 'rollicking animal spirits'[15] that haunt Le Fanu's narrative, a force of abject, disruptive energy that constantly blurs and jeopardizes the border between self and other, between human and animal. Charlie suffers nightly hallucinations of his father's ghost in the form of an animal-human hybrid, a 'semi-human brute':

> In these visions the dog seemed to stretch himself up the side of the Squire's bed, and in dilated proportions to sit at his feet, with a horrible likeness to the pug features of old Squire Toby, with tricks of wagging his head and throwing up his chin.[16]

The gothic in short fiction

Like his father, Charlie is thus 'dogged',[17] possessed by an intractable desire that refuses to die or submit to the rational parameters of human identity. The surreal, hallucinatory distention of the story's surface realism here can be seen as an emblem of the warping energy of Le Fanu's writing itself, its furious stretching of stylistic possibilities. In this ghost-invaded world, nothing is undoubtedly itself: there is a frantic tumult of mixed identities and hybrid discourses, as if the presence of the ghost has made discursive realism of the traditional novelistic kind impossible. This is vividly shown by a moment late in the story when the hapless housemaid Mrs Beckett has her prayers twisted into 'threats and blasphemies' by furious ghost-voices:

> What these voices said, Mrs Beckett could never quite remember one minute after they had ceased speaking; one sentence chased another away; gibe and menace and impious denunciation, each hideously articulate, were lost as soon as heard. And this added to the effect of these terrifying mockeries and invectives, that she could not, by any effort, retain their exact import, although their horrible character remained vividly present in her mind.[18]

The ghost-voices come *ex nihilo*, and vanish on the instant: they do not occupy the discursive space-time of realism, where events and ideas can be represented and remembered. The proximity of the horrific Thing – the cause of psychical contraction in Radcliffe, of masculine detumescence in Scott – here impacts the textuality of realism itself, surreally bending its signifying laws, dragging its lucid discourse into a carnivalesque mish-mash of voices and noises. Le Fanu's ghost-voices thus anticipate the Freudian unconscious ('The compositions which constitute dreams', writes Freud, 'are barren of the qualities which would make it possible to remember them' – exactly like Mrs Beckett's voices);[19] no less than they foretell the experimental vagaries of modernism, where likewise 'one sentence chased another away' in a dream-writing or Joycean 'traumscrapt' that defies the old rules of discursive rationality.[20]

The oneiric modernity of Le Fanu's writing in 'Squire Toby's Will' is clearly bound up with the mid-Victorian modernization of communication technology, above all with the rapid spread of mass publications. We could even interpret the ghostly voices of the story – with 'gibe and menace and impious denunciation, each hideously articulate' – as a metaphorical version of the jostling, competitive mass of new magazines, where 'one sentence chased another away' in a rapid, aggressive journalistic discourse far removed from the genteel conventions of the three-volume novel. The Victorian ghost story is thus split between its formal modernity, as a print commodity seeking innovative ways to grab the reader's attention, and its gothic or archival lineage, its preoccupation with the past (Le Fanu's story is set in the late eighteenth century). If the ghost story seemed traditional, supposedly harking back to ancient oral storytelling and ancestral crimes, it was in fact ultramodern, a formally sophisticated brand of magazine entertainment.

One effect of this generic split between tradition and modernity is the emergence, among the cluster of stylistic traits that begin to define the Victorian ghost story, of a curiously *anti*-gothic rhetoric. This rhetoric, often coming at the opening of a story, characteristically marshals a modern, empiricist scepticism against the supposedly archaic and outmoded world of gothic superstition. Thus, when Edward Bulwer-Lytton publishes a ghost story in *Blackwood's* in 1859, he deliberately shifts the haunted setting from ruined castle to humdrum modern dwelling ('on the north side of Oxford Street, in a dull but respectable thoroughfare'), as if to mock the Brontëesque excesses of recent gothic writing.[21] And Bulwer-Lytton's narrative begins by stating the story's modernity: 'Excuse me – I have no desire to be ridiculed as a superstitious dreamer – nor, on the other hand, could I ask you to accept on my affirmation what you would hold to be incredible without the evidence of your own senses.'[22] The ghost story can thus have it both ways, it seems – both repudiating gothic superstition in the language of modern science and invoking the domain of the occult, because, as Bulwer-Lytton writes in a preface to his story, 'science itself has not yet disenchanted that debateable realm of its haunted shadows'.[23] This equivocal position of the ghost story, poised between modern scepticism and gothic distrust of science, will constantly return in the scenarios and debates staged by the genre. In Amelia Edwards's 'The Phantom Coach', published in the Christmas 1864 edition of Dickens's *All the Year Round*, the narrator begins with an empiricist rebuttal of theory: 'I want nothing explained away. I desire no arguments. My mind on this subject is quite made up, and, having the testimony of my own senses to rely upon, I prefer to abide by it.'[24] But later in the same story this reliance on empirical evidence will be subverted by a thoroughly gothic condemnation of science:

> 'The world,' he said, 'grows hourly more and more sceptical of all that lies beyond its own narrow radius; and our men of science foster the fatal tendency. They condemn as fable all that resists experiment. [...] Against what superstition have they waged so long and obstinate a war, as against the belief in apparitions?'[25]

In this sense, the Victorian ghost story can be presented as a critique of a modernity led astray by the scientific drive to disenchant the world and impoverish the imagination. The ghost thus returns from a richer lifeworld of the past to rebuke the sterile present, just as the miserly Scrooge is chastised in *A Christmas Carol* by spirits from an idealized Dickensian tradition of hospitality and social undividedness.

'From the beginning', writes Alison Milbank, 'Dickens's writing is replete with an amazing range of demonic and exciting Gothic villains'.[26] It is hard to overstate the importance of Dickens in the development of the Victorian gothic. If his imagination was, as Milbank suggests, gothic from the outset, he was able to use it in both his innovative practice as writer and as magazine editor to create the cultural environment in which the English ghost story would come to flourish. The Christmas editions of Dickens's journals, above all, were to give the ghost story a permanent place in English popular culture (in 'Christmas Books' intended, for the first time in the late 1840s, to be given as gifts).[27] The ghosts in *A Christmas Carol*, of course, are not primarily terrifying spectres, but bearers of Dickens's moralistic message to the Victorian public. When Robert Louis Stevenson first read the book, he told a correspondent, it moved him to tears and made him 'want to go out and comfort someone', give money to charity and so on.[28] This was precisely what Dickens had intended: his Christmas gift was meant to teach, as well as to entertain.

But it was the sheer entertainment value of the gothic, of course, that led to the overwhelming success of *All the Year Round*, above all at Christmas (in 1867, the special festive edition sold more than three hundred thousand copies). And the stories that appeared there were not always as Dickensian in their moral outlook as Dickens might have liked, although as editor – or self-styled 'conductor' – he kept a close eye on everything in the magazine and tried to push contributors towards what he called his '*Carol* philosophy'.[29] After Dickens's death in 1870, when the magazine editorship passed to his son Charles Junior, the stories published begin to seem less Dickensian in their narrative content, as is clear if we compare Edwards's 'The Phantom Coach' (1864) – marked, as noted previously, by a comforting critique of modern rationality – to Mary Braddon's 'The Shadow in the Corner' (1879), whose very un-Dickensian plot features the abuse and suicide of a blameless doe-eyed female.

And yet almost Dickens's last act as editor of *All the Year Round* was to publish one of the least heart-warming ghost stories ever written: his own 'No. I Branch Line: The Signal-man' (1866). Critics have seen in this text both a radical artistic response to trauma (namely the 1865 railway accident at Staplehurst which Dickens was lucky to survive) and a foretaste of the cryptic withdrawal of authorial presence in modernist writing.[30] Between *A Christmas Carol* and 'The Signal-man', we might say, lies the full spectrum of the ghost story: at one end earnest, ultimately comforting moral didacticism; at the other extreme, compelling artistic bewilderment.

If the gothic in short fiction after Dickens continued to move within that spectrum, its most significant texts would follow the lead of 'The Signal-man' in subversively challenging whatever remained of *Carol* philosophy'. By the 1890s, the gothic was being freely adapted for avant-garde literary experiment, in the famous novels of Wilde and Stoker, but also in shorter forms. Vernon Lee's *Hauntings* (1890) envisages the supernatural in terms of aestheticist philosophy, as the source of an uncanny beauty irreducible to 'the wisdom of these modern ghost-experts', as Lee dismissively labels the advocates of Psychical Research.[31] Such an aestheticized uncanny was at once a re-affirmation of gothic anti-enlightenment and a subversive celebration of perverse enjoyment. When the narrator of Lee's 'A Wicked Voice' (1890) finally hears the exquisite ghost-voice of his fantasy, 'I felt my body melt even as wax in the sunshine, and it seemed to me that I too was turning fluid and vaporous, in order to mingle with theses sounds'.[32] The liquefaction of the male subject, which had been the horrific nadir of Scott's 'The Tapestried Chamber' in 1829, thus returns in Lee's *fin-de-siècle* writing as a voluptuous rapture, an orgasmic self-evacuation deliberately intended to outrage Victorian family values.

In promoting alternative selves and sexualities, this aestheticist gothic was part of the 'modern' assault on patriarchal tradition being championed – although often in very different moral terms – by New Woman writers and suffragists. The idea that the ghost story could have feminist implications also appealed to more conventional writers in the 1890s. In Edith Nesbit's 'Man-Size in Marble' (1893), a metropolitan couple's move to a charming rural cottage is ruined by the legend of the 'things that walked', statues in the local church that come alive every Halloween. It is clear that these spectres correspond to the symbolic return of a premodern violence – a time of 'fierce and wicked men, marauders by land and sea' – in effect as a punishment of the rootless and superficial lifestyle of the modern couple, who live on the wife's earnings as a magazine writer while the husband idles away his time painting.[33] If Nesbit's story may thus seem a conservative lament for a defunct patriarchal order, it is made clear when the female breadwinner is finally killed and symbolically raped by a spectre that in Nesbit's view the victims of this modern dereliction of patriarchal tradition will undoubtedly be women.

The gothic of the *fin de siècle* is very often a combination of the innovative and the conservative, the modern and the nostalgic. The famous 'antiquarian' ghost stories written by M. R. James from the mid-1890s could freely raid the archive of gothic tropes – in 'Oh, Whistle, and I'll Come to You, My Lad' (1904) a sceptical professor is confronted by an apparition that severely dents his rationalist outlook – while displaying a distinctly modern concern with the inner-worldly and the sexual. It is impossible to ignore the sexual connotations of much of the imagery in James, as when the protagonist of 'Casting the Runes' (1904) reaches down to touch 'a mouth, with teeth, and with hair about it, and [...] not the mouth of a human being'.[34] An abject, radical force of horror – corresponding, as Radcliffe argued in 1826, to psychical contraction or detumescence – clearly haunts the margins of M. R. James's ostensibly genteel modern gothic. It is thus that his stories are sometimes classed as 'weird tales' and grouped with the work of Arthur Machen or the American H. P. Lovecraft, writers associated with the subgenre of supernatural horror.

Machen's early writing brilliantly tapped into the *fin-de-siècle* craze for fantasy gothic, with the sensational success of 'The Great God Pan' (1890). The narrative, heavily influenced by Stevenson and Wilde, has deranged scientist Dr Raymond attempt to bridge the gulf between matter and spirit with some magical brain surgery:

> I am perfectly instructed as to the possible functions of those nerve-centres in the scheme of things. With a touch I can complete the communication between this world of sense and – we shall be able to finish the sentence later on.[35]

The great modern breakthrough that will heal the rift between nature and culture is uninscribable, with only myth – the revelation of the god Pan – left as a symbolic resource, although as such it remains metaphorical and thus removed from the thing itself. Machen's writing returns obsessively to the figure of the transgressive, Faustian discovery of things as they really are, a mysterious other world kept invisible by a repressive everyday reality.

What was sensational about Machen's work was thus its rhetoric of transgression, of breaking through a surface reality to a deeper, more vital – if horrific – truth. The fact that this closely coincided with the Freudian discovery of the unconscious should alert us to the true significance of Machen's writing: it centres on precisely what conventional realism had always repressed, namely the sexual. If the ghost story, as we saw with M. R. James, often touches on the sexual 'thing itself', verging on Radcliffean horror before recoiling into the less explicit register of terror, Machen's work opens up a new vein of sexualized gothic horror, to be developed by authors from Angela Carter and Peter Ackroyd to Stephen King and Anne Rice.

Carter's *The Bloody Chamber* (1979) is at once part of this gothic horror subgenre, with its sensational plot twists and lurid imagery, and a postmodern deconstruction of the gothic as a set of literary conventions and effects. This postmodern gothic thus pushes to an extreme the citational irony of the late Victorian ghost story, where the stylistic repertoire of gothic literature could be both playfully disavowed and surreptitiously put to work. The reader is invited by Carter into a mock-gothic world that is both derisory and uncanny:

> You are always in danger in the forest, where no people are. Step between the portals of the great pines where the shaggy branches tangle about you, trapping the unwary traveller in nets as if the vegetation itself were in a plot with the wolves who live there, as though the wicked trees go fishing on behalf of their friends.[36]

The analogy between scary forest and text, once it has been pointed out to the reader, can no longer be taken seriously: Carter's writing mocks the fairytale-gothic it nonetheless invokes. The style thus becomes a self-conscious pastiche of its own gothic artifice, its horrific or erotic content shot through with a metafictional irony that makes reading it more amusing than horrifying. For Fred Botting, it is this metafictionality that gives postmodern gothic its political significance:

> In turning over expectations and conventions, 'The Bloody Chamber' exposes the artifice of social and symbolic meanings and refuses any preservation of credulity at a fictional level, significantly disrupting the credibility of the ideological framework in which any tale is given meaning.[37]

Short fiction, Carter argued in 1974, 'interprets everyday experience through a system of imagery derived from subterranean areas behind everyday experience'.[38] We can see *The Bloody Chamber* as part of that critique of unreflecting realism, its pastiche of the gothic complicating the reader's enjoyment by playfully making her aware of the groundlessness of any literary claim to be representing the world as it really is.

NOTES

1. G. K. Chesterton, *Charles Dickens* (1906; London: Methuen 1911), p. 85.
2. Roger Luckhurst, 'Introduction', *Late Victorian Gothic Tales* (Oxford: Oxford University Press, 2005), p. xvi.
3. Ian Fletcher, 'Introduction', *British Poetry and Prose 1870–1905* (Oxford: Oxford University Press, 1987), p. xxxiii.
4. Fletcher, 'Introduction', p. xxxiii.
5. H. G. Wells, 'The Contemporary Novel' (1911), *Henry James and H. G. Wells: A Record of their Friendship, their Debate on the Art of Fiction, and their Quarrel*, eds. Leon Edel and Gordon Ray (Urbana: University of Illinois Press, 1958); quoted in Valerie Shaw, *The Short Story: A Critical Introduction* (Harlow: Longman, 1983), p. 48.
6. H. E. Bates, 'Notes on the English Short Story', *Lovat Dickson's Magazine*, II (February 1934), p. 145; V. S. Pritchett, *The Tale Bearers: Essays on English, American and Other Writers* (London: Chatto & Windus, 1980), p. 164.

The gothic in short fiction

7 Edgar Allan Poe, 'On Unity of Effect', *The Portable Edgar Allan Poe*, ed. J. Gerald Kennedy (London: Penguin, 2006), p. 529.
8 Walter Scott, 'On the Supernatural in Fictitious Composition; and Particularly on the Works of Ernest Theodore William Hoffmann', *Foreign Quarterly Review*, I (1827), pp. 60–98 (p. 63).
9 Ann Radcliffe, 'On the Supernatural in Poetry' (1826), *Gothic Documents: A Sourcebook, 1700–1820*, eds. E. J. Clery and R. Miles (Manchester: Manchester University Press, 2000), pp. 163–72 (p. 168).
10 Radcliffe, 'On the Supernatural', p. 169.
11 David Blair, 'Introduction', *Gothic Short Stories* (London: Wordsworth, 2002), p. xiii.
12 Walter Scott, 'The Tapestried Chamber', *Gothic Short Stories*, pp. 40–51 (p. 48).
13 E. F. Bleiler, 'Introduction', *The Best Ghost Stories of J. S. Le Fanu* (New York: Dover, 1964), p. viii.
14 J. S. Le Fanu, 'Squire Toby's Will', *The Best Ghost Stories of J. S. Le Fanu*, pp.1–28 (p. 2).
15 Le Fanu, 'Squire Toby's Will', p. 5.
16 Le Fanu, 'Squire Toby's Will', p. 10.
17 Le Fanu, 'Squire Toby's Will', p. 10.
18 Le Fanu, 'Squire Toby's Will', p. 20.
19 Sigmund Freud, *The Interpretation of Dreams* (London: The Hogarth Press and The Institute of Psycho-Analysis, 1953), SE IV–V, p. 44.
20 James Joyce, *Finnegans Wake* (1939; London: Penguin, 1999), pp. 623–36.
21 Edward Bulwer-Lytton, 'The Haunted and the Haunters: or, the House and the Brain', *The Penguin Book of Ghost Stories: From Elizabeth Gaskell to Ambrose Bierce*, ed. Michael Newton (London: Penguin, 2010), pp. 39–66 (p. 40).
22 Bulwer-Lytton, 'The Haunted and the Haunters', p. 39.
23 Bulwer-Lytton, Preface, quoted from *The Penguin Book of Ghost Stories*, p. 377.
24 Amelia Edwards, 'The Phantom Coach', *The Oxford Book of English Ghost Stories*, eds. Michael Cox and R. A. Gilbert (Oxford: Oxford University Press, 1986), pp. 13–24 (p. 13).
25 Edwards, 'The Phantom Coach', p. 18.
26 Alison Milbank, 'Victorian Gothic in English Novels and Stories, 1830–1880', *The Cambridge Companion to Gothic Fiction*, ed. Jerrold E. Hodge (Cambridge: Cambridge University Press, 2002), pp. 145–66 (p. 155).
27 See Tara Moore, 'Christmas Books and Victorian Book Reviewing', *Victorian Periodicals Review*, 45.1 (Baltimore, MD: Johns Hopkins University Press, 2012), pp. 49–63 (p. 52).
28 Robert Louis Stevenson in *The Dickensian*, 16 (1920), p. 200; quoted in Michael Slater, Introduction to Charles Dickens, *The Christmas Books Volume 1: A Christmas Carol / The Chimes* (London: Penguin, 1971), p. vii.
29 Dickens to Charles Forster, quoted in Catherine Waters, 'Gender, Family and Domestic Ideology', *The Cambridge Companion to Charles Dickens*, ed. J. O. Jordan (Cambridge: Cambridge University Press, 2001), pp. 120–35 (p. 121).
30 J. L. Matus, 'Trauma, Memory and Railway Disaster: The Dickensian Connection', *Victorian Studies*, 43.3 (Spring 2001), 413–36; Luke Thurston, *Literary Ghosts from the Victorians to Modernism: The Haunting Interval* (New York: Routledge, 2012), pp. 34–49.

31 Vernon Lee, Preface, *Hauntings* (1890; Milton Keynes: Dodo Press, 2010), p. i.
32 Vernon Lee, 'A Wicked Voice', *Hauntings*, pp. 107–31 (p. 129).
33 Edith Nesbit, 'Man-size in Marble', *The Oxford Book of English Ghost Stories*, pp. 125–36 (p. 128).
34 M. R. James, 'Casting the Runes', *Collected Ghost Stories*, ed. Darryl Jones (Oxford: Oxford University Press, 2011), pp. 145–64 (p. 155).
35 Arthur Machen, *The Great God Pan* (1890; London: Martin Secker, 1926), p. 13.
36 Angela Carter, 'The Company of Wolves', *The Bloody Chamber* (London: Victor Gollancz, 1979), pp. 129–39 (p. 130).
37 Fred Botting, 'Aftergothic: Consumption, Machines, and Black Holes', *The Cambridge Companion to Gothic Fiction*, pp. 277–300 (p. 286).
38 Quoted in Helen Simpson, 'Introduction', *The Bloody Chamber*, p. vii.

13

ANDREW M. BUTLER

The British science fiction short story

Introduction

There is a moment in Andrew Ross's analysis of science fiction (sf) when he claims that

> [i]n the pulp star system, it was usually the magazines, or their formulae, and seldom the writers themselves (however highly paid), who were the major actors. For the SF cognoscenti, the magazine editors played the starring role; consequently it is Gernsback and John W. Campbell, editor of *Astounding Stories* from 1937 to 1971, who are commemorated as the 'fathers' of science fiction, not Verne, Wells, Capek or even E. E. 'Doc' Smith, creator of the 'space opera'.[1]

The contours of the field of sf have been shaped by editors and economics, as well as the emergence of particular writers. From the 1920s to the 1960s, the genre was defined by pulp magazines published in North America, which were dominated by American and Canadian contributors, although British authors such as John Wyndham and Arthur C. Clarke were able to sell to them. Most sf would be published in magazine form before books and most sf novelists began by publishing short stories, novellas and novelettes.

Proto-sf

While the identity of the first sf novel is contested, Brian W. Aldiss's championing of Mary Shelley's *Frankenstein* (1818) provides a useful starting point. Her nested tale of a scientist who fails to take adequate care of his creation cemented an archetype of the genre and demonstrated an ambivalence towards science and technology that characterizes much British sf. Her depiction of the landscapes – of Germany, Britain and the Arctic – also points to an interest in the pastoral and the natural world, under threat from the Industrial Revolution. Her only other sf novel, *The Last Man* (1826), displays a pessimism and sense of decline that was also to pervade the British form. Shelley's career was hampered by the politics of her family life; after the death by drowning of Percy Bysshe Shelley she had to borrow money from her father-in-law, Sir Timothy Shelley, against her son, Percy Florence's, inheritance. Sonia Hofkosh argues that Shelley 'recognizes an economics of the marketplace, wherein production and consumption are compelled and constrained by publishers, editors, and readers'.[2] She published in the annuals, ornate gift books that contained vignettes, poetry, accounts of the previous year and engravings. The first annual had been *Forget-Me-Not: A Christmas and New Years Present for 1823* (1822), but the *Keepsake* (1827–57) was more successful. In Shelley's 'Mortal Immortal' (*Keepsake*, 1833), protagonist Winzy becomes immortal as he accidentally drinks an alchemist's potion and then watches his lover Bertha as she ages and dies. It is tempting to read this (like *The Last Man*) autobiographically, with the dead Percy forever twenty-nine and Mary subject to the ravages of time and economic struggle.

There then seems to be a fifty-year gap: ghost, horror and fantasy short stories, but no sf. Charles Dickens invokes the supernatural in 'The Signalman' (1866), but as Norris Pope observes, the story 'has never been seriously considered [...] within the context of railway signaling technology, the system for providing advance information about traffic and line conditions on which railway safety depended'.[3] Technology was increasingly present in fiction, but there was no short British sf. The situation changed with the anonymous publication in *Blackwood's Magazine* of 'The Battle of Dorking' (May 1871) by Sir George Tomkyns Chesney. This describes, from a perspective fifty years on, a Prussian invasion of the south of England that defeats the army and dismantles the empire. The issue was reprinted seven times and the story sold tens of thousands of copies in pamphlet form. Chesney, a lieutenant general of Anglo-Irish background, had fought in India's First War of Independence and cautioned against complacency in the armed forces. The Liberal Prime Minister William Gladstone feared the story would undercut Britain's reputation and the story was debated in Parliament, magazines and newspapers. It inspired sequels and imitations, such as *The Battle of Dorking, a Myth: England Impregnable* (1871), in both chapbooks and novels. The trend stopped only with the outbreak of the First World War.

The fiction magazine market in Britain, selling through railway station bookstalls and newsagents, was joined by George Newnes's *Strand Magazine* (1891–1950). While the *Strand* became best known for Sherlock Holmes stories (July 1891–April 1927) and other detective fiction, it also published weird fiction, some of it sf, such as Canadian Grant Allen's 'The Thames Valley Catastrophe' (December 1897) in which London is destroyed

The British science fiction short story

by a volcanic eruption. J. B. Harris-Burland's 'Lord Beden's Motor' (1901) describes a car journey where the passengers encounter a steam-driven automobile that seems to require no steering, and L. de Giberne Sieveking's 'The Prophetic Camera' (1927) features a device that can take pictures of the future.

H. G. Wells also contributed stories such as 'The New Accelerator' (December 1901), 'The Country of the Blind' (April 1904), 'The Empire of the Ants' (December 1905), 'The Land Ironclads' (December 1903) and a serialization of *The First Men in the Moon* (November 1900–August 1901), but his early stories had appeared in a rival magazine, *Pearson's Magazine* (1896–1939), for example 'In The Abyss' (August 1896), 'The Valley of Spiders' (March 1903) and a serialization of *The War of the Worlds* (April–December 1897). Wells also wrote sf for other magazines, such as 'The Crystal Egg' (*New Review*, May 1897) and 'The Star' (*Graphic*, December 1897). In the latter, a celestial body, apparently a star, is spotted near Neptune heading for Earth. As it approaches, various unnamed characters react to the possible catastrophe with degrees of panic, whereas cynics point to the millennial panics of 1000 A.D. Night is increasingly replaced by day and the temperature rises, melting the ice caps. In the end, the star passes through the atmosphere, causing floods, volcanoes and earthquakes, but there are a few survivors. What is chilling about the story is the distance from which it is told, matched by the view of the Martian astronomers at the end of the story – humanity is a speck of insignificance within the cosmos. This echoes the vast timescales of *The Time Machine* (1895) and is one of the first sf narratives about the Earth being hit by a celestial body.

The Anglo-Indian writer Rudyard Kipling wrote across a range of genres, including sf, occult and fantasy – as Janet Montefiore argues, 'Kipling was amongst the first English writers to respond to the revolutionary technologies of the early-twentieth century – radio, cinema, motor cars and air travel.'[4] In 'Wireless' (USA: *Scribner's Magazine*, August 1902), the nameless narrator's interest in Guglielmo Marconi's radio experiments leads him to a chemist's shop where they are attempting to send messages between there and Poole, Dorset. One of the chemists, John Shaynor, appears to be dying of tuberculosis and has drunk a cocktail of cardamoms, ground ginger, chloric-ether and alcohol as they are adjusting the equipment and he seems temporarily possessed by the spirit of the Romantic poet John Keats. There is a curious sense of one-way and failed communication – Shaynor ventriloquizes the dead Keats as he is slowly dying and the radio apparatus picks up two battleships in Portsmouth failing to understand each other. 'With the Night Mail: A Story of 2000 A.D.' (USA: *McClure's*, November 1905; UK: *Windsor Magazine*, December 1905) is told from the point of

ANDREW M. BUTLER

view of a journalist on board a dirigible travelling from London to Quebec. Just as in Kipling's listing of drugs and chemicals in 'Wireless', here he describes the details of the engines driving the airship and the actions of the men at work in keeping them running. Further authenticity comes from the various materials appended to the story: details of lighthouses; news of the missing and the dead; answers to correspondents; a book review and a number of adverts. The story is not only modern in subject matter, imagining the coming power of air transport even if it was planes that came to the fore, but modern in form. '"As Easy as A.B.C.": A Tale of 2150 A.D.' (*London Magazine*, March–April 1912) is a sequel set in the same milieu of air power, but is more dystopian in tone, with the Aerial Board of Control revealed as a technocratic élite. It has at its disposal various electrical weapons and control mechanisms with which it enforces the proscription of democracy and the gathering of crowds.

Crossing the Atlantic

Meanwhile, in America, a specialist genre of sf was being created. Hugo Gernsback devised the term 'scientifiction' for his pulp magazine *Amazing Stories* (1926 onwards), aiming for a mix of scientific teaching and adventure narratives, to educate and entertain the generation of people exposed to the mass media world of radio, cinema, cars and telecommunications – he had previously edited titles such as *Modern Electrics* (1908, sold 1913, merged with *Electrician and Mechanic* in 1914) and *Practical Electrics* (1921–4, renamed *Electrical Experimenter*, in 1926 merged with *Science and Invention*, 1920–31). The first issue of *Amazing Stories* reprinted American writers George Allan England, Austin Hall, Edgar Allan Poe and G. Peyton Wertenbaker, part one of Jules Verne's 'Off on a Comet' and H. G. Wells's 'The New Accelerator' (1901). Reprints of 'The Crystal Egg', 'The Star', 'The Man Who Could Work Miracles', 'The Empire of the Ants', 'In the Abyss' and serializations of Wells's novels followed. The scientist Julian Huxley, with 'The Tissue-Culture King' (1927; from *The Yale Review* and *Cornhill Magazine*, April 1926), seems to have been the only other British writer to appear until 1932. Huxley's story is the account of the capture of a biologist, Hascombe, by an African tribe, and his bargain with an elder, Bugala, to use his science to help the latter gain power via his religion. Unfortunately the cloned tissue samples enable Bugala to telepathically control the population.

The British writer John Wyndham first appeared with 'The Lost Machine' (April 1932) under the by-line John Beynon Harris, one of many variant pseudonyms of John Wyndham Parkes Lucas Beynon Harris. The story is

The British science fiction short story

about first contact between humans and a robot, the only survivor of a Martian space mission to Earth. The encounter is one of mutual incomprehension – the robot being too complex for the humans to understand, the humans being too primitive for the robot. It sees Earth as a world of madness and destroys itself. Wyndham had already published 'Worlds to Barter' (May 1931) in *Wonder Stories* (1929–55), and was to continue to publish in it under the editorship of Gernsback, who was also to publish the obscure British writers Ralph Stranger, W. P. Cockcroft and Festus Pragnell.

A competitor to *Amazing Stories* was *Astounding* (1930 onwards), initially edited by Harry Bates, but best known for the editorship of John W. Campbell (1938–71). Bates published stories by John Russell Fearn such as 'The Man Who Stopped the Dust' (March 1934), the cautionary tale of a device that removes all dust and causes an apocalypse, and 'Mathematica' (February 1936), in which two scientists use an alien metal to summon (or imagine) an extra-terrestrial who explains to them that the universe is mathematics and transports them to a highly advanced society. On their return to Earth, they realize they have arrived in a parallel world. British sf stories that Campbell published in *Astounding* included Arthur C. Clarke's 'Loophole' (April 1946) and Eric Frank Russell's 'Allamagoosa' (May 1955). The latter won the first Hugo Award for Best Science Fiction Story; Clarke won the award the following year for 'The Sentinel' (*Infinity Science Fiction*, November 1955). For more than four decades *Astounding* was the leading market of hard science fiction.

Britain was slow to copy the sf pulps, although fiction magazines continued. In 1934, Pearson's began a weekly tabloid-sized magazine, *Scoops*, aimed at boys, which included (often pseudonymous) sf and quasi-scientific information. Fearn ('Invaders from Time', #12, May 1934) appeared, but the magazine closed in June. The next British sf magazine started as a fanzine, *Novae Terrae* (1936–9), initially edited by Maurice K. Hanson, with Arthur C. Clarke and John Carnell as co-editors from issue 17. William F. Temple – whose novel *Four-Sided Triangle* was to appear in *Amazing* (November 1939) – edited numbers 25–9, before Carnell became editor and changed the name to *New Worlds*. There was an attempt to launch this as a professional magazine in 1939, but that was delayed until 1946 under Pendulum Publications. Pendulum went bankrupt in 1947 and Frank Edward Arnold, Carnell, Walter Gillings, Eric C. Williams and John Wyndham set up Nova Publications to continue the magazine under Carnell's stewardship. In 1951, Carnell took over editorship of *Science Fantasy*, which Gillings had started. Carnell developed a stable of writers, few of whom are remembered today. John Boston is largely critical of them in his extended survey of the magazine; the better writers sold to the more lucrative American markets, publication there often preceding appearance in the United Kingdom.[5] Carnell was the first to publish J. G. Ballard, with 'Escapement' (*New Worlds*, December 1956) and 'Prima Belladonna' (*Science Fantasy*, December 1956), and he published some of Michael Moorcock's early stories. But by the early 1960s, the magazine market was in decline on both sides of the Atlantic and Carnell decided that the future of *New Worlds* lay as a paperback original.

New Worlds's competitors in the 1950s included *Nebula Science Fiction* (1952–9), edited by Peter F. Hamilton, and *Vargo Statten Science Fiction Magazine* (1954–6). *Nebula* was based in Glasgow and published the first sales of Brian W. Aldiss ('T' in #18, November 1956, although by then he had published elsewhere) and Bob Shaw ('Aspect' in #9, August 1954). When Hamilton took over as owner, he started printing the magazine in Dublin and built up a sizeable readership, mostly outside of Britain. Unfortunately, increased excise duties in Britain and import limits in Australia and South Africa meant that he could not afford to continue. *Vargo Statten Science Fiction Magazine* was an attempt by the publisher Scion to cash in on the remarkable success of the scores of novels by John Russell Fearn it published under the pseudonym Vargo Statten. The first seven issues were edited by Alistair Paterson and included Statten's 'Beyond Zero' and Fearn's 'March of the Robots', under the pseudonym Volsted Gridban. After Scion was prosecuted for publishing a pornographic novel, the company restarted as Scion Distributors, but debts meant that the magazine passed into the hands of the printers Dragon Press. Fearn took over as editor under his pseudonym Statten, but a printers' strike bankrupted the magazine. The journal was juvenile in tone and, aside from early stories by Kenneth Bulmer and Barrington Bayley, it produced little of note. It looked backwards rather than forward.

The New Wave and its aftermath

By the mid-1960s, sf had changed. *Amazing* and *Astounding* had focused on what they saw as extrapolation from hard science, emphasizing mind-expanding ideas over characterization and prose style – which veered between the functional and the purple. Competitors such as the *Magazine of Fantasy and Science Fiction* (1949 onwards) and *Galaxy* (1950–80) strove for more literary values and were interested in sociology and psychology, as well as some experimentation in form. In Britain, John Wyndham had become a bestseller with *The Day of the Triffids* (1951) and *The Midwich Cuckoos* (1957), and Arthur C. Clarke with *Childhood's End* (1953). Meanwhile, astronomical and space exploration were reducing the likely habitable spaces within the solar system and a desert Mars or swamp Venus

The British science fiction short story

could no longer be imagined with a straight face. In May 1962, Ballard had written a guest editorial in *New Worlds*, calling for sf that would explore inner rather than outer space – and in 1964 *New Worlds* became a venue for just that kind of story. Maclaren & Sons, who had bought Nova Publications in 1954, sold the magazines to Roberts & Vintner, who gave the twenty-four-year-old Moorcock a choice of one to edit. He chose *New Worlds* and, while he continued to publish some of Carnell's stable, he set about widening the possibilities of what an sf magazine was interested in – William S. Burroughs, Jorge Luis Borges, Salvador Dalí, pop art, the media landscape, modernist techniques, cut-ups and sexual desire in all its forms.

New Worlds became the centre of New Wave sf, a term clearly borrowing from French and British New Wave cinema, which attempted to redefine the genre. J. G. Ballard was the key writer, with titles such as 'The Assassination Weapon' (April 1966) and 'The Assassination of John Fitzgerald Kennedy Considered as a Downhill Motor Race' (March 1967) – which drew on Alfred Jarry's 'The Crucifixion Considered as an Uphill Bicycle Race' (1965). Ballard had fragmented male protagonists, motivated by paraphilic drives, and his imagery drew on both the surrealism of Salvador Dalí and Max Ernst and the pop art icon deconstructions of Andy Warhol and Richard Hamilton, although he was as likely to appear in *Science Fantasy*, now under the editorship of Kyril Bonfiglioli and retitled *Impulse* from March 1966, then *SF Impulse* (August 1966 to February 1967, when it merged with *New Worlds*). Ballard was briefly its editor, but was more at home as prose editor of the more experimental *Ambit* from 1967, where he experimented with collages, advertisements and questionnaires in his testing of the short story form. Other writers who featured in the pages of *New Worlds* included Barrington Bayley, M. John Harrison, Langdon Jones, R. W. Mackelworth and Moorcock himself. The latter's Nebula Award–winning 'Behold the Man' (September 1966) is a potentially blasphemous account of troubled time traveller Karl Glogauer's visit back to the first century AD, where he is crucified as Christ. Colin Greenland calls it 'a classic of New Wave sf: physics is thrust into the background and psychology dragged to the fore'.[6] It was a rich exploration of the messiah figure as saviour and willing victim.

While the New Wave broke down taboos about what sf could be, it was still a male preserve. The few contributions by British women included Daphne Castell's 'Emancipation' (October 1965), 'Entry from Earth' (February 1966) and 'Rumpelstiltskin' (May 1966) and Hilary Bailey's 'The Fall of Frenchy Steiner' (July 1964), 'Be Good Sweet Man' (October 1966), 'Dr. Gelabius' (April 1968), 'Agatha Blue' (March 1970), 'A Chronicle of Blackton' (January 1972) and 'Bella Goes to the Dark Tower' (September 1973).

Circulation was low, with Roberts & Vintner pulling out in late 1966, but an Arts Council grant negotiated by Aldiss and Moorcock's prolific writing schedule kept the magazine afloat until 1970. However, the adult nature of the content led to newsagents John Menzies dropping it and W. H. Smiths leaving the decision to stock the magazine to individual shops. The two hundredth was the last regular issue, as Moorcock shifted to a paperback original format with publishers Sphere and Corgi for ten volumes (1971–6); five more magazine issues appeared between 1978 and 1979. After April 1969 editorial duties were shared with or devolved to Hilary Bailey, David Britton, Michael Butterworth, Graham Charnock, Graham Hall, Langdon Jones, R. Glyn Jones or Charles Platt.

The New Wave had been promoted by American editor and writer Judith Merril, who put together an anthology, *England Swings SF* (1968), which explicitly linked the New Wave to swinging London. The contents included stories by Aldiss, Bailey, Ballard, Bayley, Bonfiglioli, Castell, Jones, David I. Masson, Moorcock, Platt, Christopher Priest and by visiting Americans Thomas Disch and Pamela Zoline, alongside poetry by George MacBeth, Michael Hamburger and Peter Redgrove. Langdon Jones edited *The New S.F.: An Original Anthology of Modern Speculative Fiction* (1969), with stories by Aldiss, Butterworth, Giles Gordon, Maxim Jakubowski, MacBeth, Moorcock, Platt and James Sallis, visiting Americans Disch, Zoline and John Sladek and poetry by Moorcock and D. M. Thomas. All these writers were pushing at the edges of what sf could be.

Carnell, meanwhile, published twenty-one volumes of *New Writings in SF* (1964–73), including a number of writers associated with the New Wave – he had printed some in *New Worlds*, of course – and some who had rarely or never found a place in Moorcock's *New Worlds*. Keith Roberts appeared regularly, as did Sydney J. Bounds, Colin Kapp, Douglas R. Mason/John Rankine and Priest. In his first editorial, Carnell declared the volume

> [a] radical departure in the field of the science fiction short story. As the name implies, not only *new* stories written for the series as well as s-f stories which would not normally be seen by the vast majority of readers, will appear in future editions, but *new* styles, ideas, and even *new* writers who have something worth contributing to the *genre*, will be presented. (emphases in the original)[7]

Brian W. Aldiss was in volume one, but his more experimental work appeared as a series of frankly baffling 'Three Enigmas' when Kenneth Bulmer took the series on for nine more volumes (1973–8) after Carnell's death. Mike Ashley argues that the *New Writings* 'remained the last

The British science fiction short story

bastion of traditional Britishness against the onslaught of the New Wave. It was to all intents a continuation of the *New Worlds* of the 1950s' and claims '[i]t was comfortable, enjoyable and occasionally old-fashioned – the kind of book that helped you relax rather than made you feel you were on a crusade'.[8] This is a little unfair, as Carnell pushed sf beyond the hard sciences to genetics, medicine, politics, psychology, sociology and religion.

There were other British anthologies through the 1970s – fan, editor, anthologist and space advocate George Hay produced *The Disappearing Future* (1970), which mixed fiction and essays, *Stopwatch* (1974) and two volumes of *Pulsar* (1978, 1979), and Peter Weston produced three volumes of *Andromeda* (1976–8). Aldiss judged a short story competition leading to *Gollancz – Sunday Times Best SF Stories* (1975); the winning story, Garry Kilworth's debut 'Let's Go to Golgotha', was a blasphemous account of time-travelling tourists visiting the crucifixion. Christopher Priest edited *Anticipations* (1978), which included Ian Watson's ideas-dense 'The Very Slow Time Machine', in which the time traveller is observed growing younger and more presentable as the years progress; the following year Priest and Robert Holdstock co-edited *Stars of Albion* (1979) for the British World Science Fiction Convention in Brighton, with reprinted stories by Aldiss, Ballard, Bayley, John Brunner, David S. Garnett, Holdstock, Masson, Priest, Keith Roberts, Josephine Saxton, Bob Shaw and Watson.

About the only professional British magazine of the era was *Science Fiction Monthly*, edited for twelve issues in 1974 by Patricia Hornsey and then for sixteen issues to April 1976 by Julia Davis. It was published by New English Library in tabloid format, drew on its picture library, and included authors such as Holdstock, Kilworth, Shaw and Brian Stableford, as well as a number of American authors and Polish sf writer Stanisław Lem.

The late 1970s seemed optimistic for British sf. In an all-British special issue of the New York – based *Magazine of Fantasy and Science Fiction*, Brian Aldiss listed the professional sf writers as including Mark Adlard, Barrington Bayley, D. G. Compton, Michael Coney, Edmund Cooper, Richard Cowper, Philip Dunn, M. John Harrison, Robert Holdstock, Laurence James, Duncan Lunan, Chris Morgan, Christopher Priest, Bob Shaw, Andrew Stephenson, Ian Watson and Angus Wells.[9] *Star Wars* (dir. George Lucas, 1977), *Close Encounters of the Third Kind* (dir. Steven Spielberg, 1977) and *Doctor Who* (1963 onwards) all suggested that sf was more popular than ever. But for many of the British professionals, their best years were behind them or they had to turn to fantasy to thrive. American magazines became the main market for short fiction.

ANDREW M. BUTLER

The *Interzone* years

The next professional magazine arrived amid some controversy. A science fiction convention, Yorcon II, made a profit and, rather than refunding it to the members, Leeds-based organizers Alan Dorey, Graham James, Simon Ounsley and David Pringle decided to set up a magazine. Meanwhile, Malcolm Edwards, who worked for the publisher Gollancz, suggested to Dorey, then chair of the British Science Fiction Association, that they set up a fiction magazine, with critics and writers such as John Clute, Colin Greenland and Roz Kaveney as associate editors. The two groups came together and established *Interzone*. Taking its name from William S. Burroughs, a beat novelist who had been championed by J. G. Ballard in *New Worlds*, the publication inevitably drew comparisons with the earlier magazine; indeed, the first editorial suggested that it would be a *New Worlds* for the 1980s. The publication of stories by New Wave British writers such as Aldiss, Ballard, Bayley and Harrison, alongside Angela Carter, as well as a focus on cultural icons in the tradition of *New Worlds*'s pop art sensibilities, cemented such a reputation. Peter Nicholls and Mike Ashley declared that '[i]t has slowly become clear that this one magazine, despite its slender resources and comparatively small readership, has been largely (if not solely) responsible for catalyzing a second new wave of UK sf'.[10] Certainly there has been no magazine that has had anything like the same effect on the British sf scene. It was perhaps a little better than *New Worlds* in nurturing women writers, but its all-female issue 42 (December 1990), with Gwyneth Jones's 'Forward Echoes' as the only British contribution, drew some criticism. Steve Grover suggested the issue was 'patronizing, sexist and counter-productive', while Gordon van Gelder, then working at St Martin's Press and later editor of *Fantasy and Science Fiction*, argued: 'I don't believe women and men are yet equal, but I do believe that pigeonholing members of either group will do nothing to further the cause for equality.'[11]

By then, the initial editorial collective had gone. Pringle and Ounsley became the main editors from #13 (Autumn 1985) to #41 (November 1991); from #42 (December 1990) until #106 (April 1996) Pringle's co-editor was, with some exceptions, Lee Montgomerie. The magazine was supported in 1984 by a donation from Sir Clive Sinclair, at the height of the boom of Sinclair home computers, and then grants from the Arts Council of Great Britain and other arts organizations. As sales ebbed and flowed, the schedule varied from an initial quarterly appearance in spring 1982 to a bi-monthly format from #25 (September/October 1988) and monthly publication from #35 (May 1990). To boost readers and subscriptions, crossover issues

The British science fiction short story

were arranged with other magazines. *Interzone* #47 (May 1991) reprinted the contents of an issue of *Aboriginal Science Fiction* (1986–2001), while *Interzone* #51 (September 1991) reprinted some of the contents of issue #5 of *Million: The Magazine of Popular Fiction* (#1, January 1991– #14, March 1993). *Million* was also edited by Pringle and was subsumed into *Interzone*. Some subscribers, especially if they also subscribed to *Aboriginal* or *Million*, felt short-changed. *Interzone* had guest editors, such as *New Worlds* stalwart Charles Platt (#94, April 1995) and Nicholas Royle (#114, December 1996), and Pringle was later joined by Paul Brazier, who had edited three issues of *SF Nexus* (#1, April 1991 to #3, spring 1993). This brought a radical redesign to the layout of *Interzone*.

Alongside New Wave and other British sf writers – such as Richard Cowper, Gwyneth Jones, Garry Kilworth, Brian Stableford and Ian Watson – *Interzone* nurtured several generations of new authors who went on to become significant writers. These included Stephen Baxter, Keith Brooke, Eric Brown, Richard Calder, Neil Ferguson, Dominic Green, Nicola Griffith, Peter F. Hamilton, Simon D. Ings, Graham Joyce, Ian R. MacLeod, Paul McAuley, Ian McDonald, Kim Newman (co-writing with Eugene Byrne), Alistair Reynolds, Charles Stross and Liz Williams. As cyberpunk became the dominant subgenre of sf, cyberpunk advocate Bruce Sterling used the pages of *Interzone* to publish some of his polemics. The role of Pringle in sustaining the British sf short market is incalculable and in 2005 he was recognized with a special Hugo Award at the World Science Fiction Convention in Glasgow. Pringle retired only with #193 (Spring 2004), when the magazine was taken over by Andy Cox of TTA Press, who had previously published the horror magazine *The Third Alternative* (April 1993 to summer 2005, thereafter *Black Static*).

Occasional competing magazines included the Northern Ireland – based *Extro Science Fiction* (#1, February–March 1982 to #3, July–August 1982), edited by Paul Campbell; *Back Brain Recluse* (#1, June 1984 to #23, 1997), edited by Chris Reed firmly within the small press scene in Sheffield; *The Gate* (#1, May 1989 to #3, December 1990), edited by Maureen Porter for two issues and then by Cardinal Cox; *Amaranth* (#1 September/October 1990), edited by Rob Jeffrey; *Odyssey* (#0, September 1997 to #7, November/December 1998), edited by Liz Holliday; *Spectrum SF* (#1, February 2000 to #9, November 2002), edited and funded by Paul Fraser; *3SF* (#1, October 2002 to #3, February 2003), edited by Liz Holliday; and *Postscripts* (#1, spring 2004 to #17, winter 2008), edited first by Peter Crowther and from #5 (Autumn) by Crowther and Nick Gevers. *Postscripts* was part of Crowther's highly successful P. S. Publishing imprint that specialized in limited edition hard back and paperback editions of novellas, beginning with James Lovegrove's *How the Other Half Lives* (1999) and Graham Joyce's *Leningrad Nights* (1999), and continuing with titles by authors such as Nina Allan, Baxter, Brown, Michael Marshall Smith, Ian R. MacLeod, Ken MacLeod, McAuley, McDonald, Newman, Reynolds, Adam Roberts, and Ian Whates. *Postscripts* continued as an anthology (#18, May 2009 to #30/31, August 2013), edited by Crowther and Gevers.

Brave new worlds?

The problem that all these professional sf magazines faced was the ability to grow a readership. The British magazine market had all but abandoned fiction, while there were numerous body-building, computer, cooking, film and other hobby magazines. Bookshop chains were no longer clear as to where they should stock fiction magazines as there were no comparable periodicals. Equally, in order to supply shops that had increasingly centralized distributors, publishers would have to print large runs. Magazines were dependent on subscriptions and a few specialist bookshops, unless they could be cross-financed from other enterprises. The magazine *3SF* was published by novelist Ben Jeapes's small press Big Engine, who felt that '*Interzone* was safely into magazine middle age, no longer turning out new talent with quite the frequency it once did but relying on staple producers of fiction'.[12] There was not enough cash flow and the magazine and publisher closed while issue #4 was in preparation. P. S. Publishing tackled the same problems by a clever use of limited editions, with some of its early novellas republished in dos-à-dos formats and then in omnibuses of four by Gollancz.

There had been other attempts at anthologies and anthology series after 1980. The Women's Press released *Despatches from the Frontiers of the Female Mind* (1985), edited by Jen Green and Sarah Lefanu, featuring British women authors such as Margaret Elphinstone, Mary Gentle, Gwyneth Jones, Tanith Lee, Naomi Mitchison and Josephine Saxton alongside Americans Joanna Russ, Raccoona Sheldon, Lisa Tuttle and Pamela Zoline. Robert Holdstock and Christopher Evans co-edited three volumes of *Other Edens* (1987–9), focusing on British or Britain-based writers. David S. Garnett edited three volumes of *The Orbit Science Fiction Yearbook* (1988–90) and two of *Zenith* (1989–90) before gaining permission to revive *New Worlds* (four volumes 1991–4), but even the cultural capital of that name was insufficient, with a final – to date – volume coming out in 1997 from the Georgia, US publisher White Wolf that specialized in role-playing games.

Other small presses have brought out themed anthologies. Jurassic London, led by Anne C. Perry and Jared Shurin of the Kitschie Awards, edited a series of themed anthologies such as *Pandemonium: Stories of the Apocalypse* (2011), inspired by artist John Martin; *Pandemonium: Stories of the Smoke* (2012), inspired by Charles Dickens; and *Pandemonium: 1853* (2013), alternate histories set in 1853. NewCon Press, run by author Ian Whates, published anthologies including *Celebration: Commemorating the 50th Anniversary of the British Science Fiction Association* (2008) and *Fables from the Fountain* (2011), a homage to Arthur C. Clarke's collection *Tales from the White Hart* (1957).

Some newer writers have been better known for their short stories than novel-length fiction and these are usually published by a small press, not necessarily British. Dave Hutchinson had released four short story collections, beginning with *Thumbprints* (1978) with Abelard-Schuman. After a career in journalism, he began writing fiction again with 'The Trauma Jockey' (*Interzone*, 117, March 1997); his first sf novel was *Europe in Autumn* (2014). Chris Beckett also appeared in *Interzone*, 'A Matter of Survival' (40, October 1990), with two well-regarded short story collections, *The Turing Test* (2008) and *The Peacock Cloak* (2013). Nina Allan has been publishing since 'Best Friends' (*Dark Horizons*, 41, spring 2002), but argues that 'all my short fiction to date has been a kind of apprenticeship in novel-writing. I've been trying to stretch my technical skills and the scope of my subject matter to that point where I have the ability to write a novel that will satisfy me as a complete work of fiction.'[13] Her first novel, set in a present-day and near-future version of Hastings, is *The Race* (2014).

Despite Allan's assertion and the boom in British sf since the late 1990s, it feels as if the short story is less an apprenticeship for novel writing than an opportunity for an established writer to produce work at shorter length. Iain M. Banks, Ken MacLeod, China Miéville, Jeff Noon and Adam Roberts all debuted with novels rather than stories. It seems either as if the short story has become a loss-leader that gives a reader a taste of their talents, or it can be used to raise money for a cause or to make a political point. For example, Farah Mendlesohn's anthology *Glorifying Terrorism, Manufacturing Contempt* (2006) featured stories written to protest against and break the UK Terrorism Act (2006) which introduced a new offence of condoning or glorifying terrorism. E-commerce and the increasingly virtual world of the sf community have helped small publishers to thrive, although recent changes in VAT legislation will make business more complex for them. The annual fan – Hugo and BSFA – and professional – Nebula – awards have continued to draw attention to the most-liked stories of various lengths. Increasing numbers of writers are bypassing the traditional magazine or publisher route in favour of self-publishing, although it is unclear as yet how many significant writers can emerge from the resulting cacophony. Equally, with the willingness of some anthologies – for example the annual *Best of British Short Stories* (2011 onwards) edited by Nicholas Royle – and prizes – for example the Edge Hill Prize – to take genre fiction seriously, the genre boundaries may well be evaporating again.

NOTES

1 Andrew Ross, *Strange Weather: Culture, Science and Technology in the Age of Limits* (London; New York: Verso, 1991), p. 106.
2 Sonia Hofkosh, 'Disfiguring Economies: Mary Shelley's Short Stories', *The Other Mary Shelley: Beyond Frankenstein*, eds. Audrey A. Fisch, Anne K. Mellor and Esther H. Schor (New York; Oxford: Oxford University Press, 1993), p. 205.
3 Norris Pope, 'Dickens's "The Signalman" and Information Problems in the Railway Age', *Technology and Culture: The International Quarterly of the Society for the History of Technology*, 42.3 (2001), 436–61.
4 Janet Montefiore, *Rudyard Kipling* (Tavistock: Northcote House, 2007), p. 123.
5 See John Boston and Damien Broderick, *Building New Worlds, 1946–1959: The Carnell Era, Volume One* (San Bernardino, CA: Borgo Press, 2012). See also the two follow-up volumes by the same authors, *Strange Highways: Reading Science Fantasy, 1950–1967* (Borgo, 2012), and *New Worlds: Before the New Wave, 1960–1964: The Carnell Era, Volume Two* (Borgo, 2013).
6 Colin Greenland, *The Entropy Exhibition: Michael Moorcock and the British 'New Wave' in Science Fiction* (London: Routledge and Kegan Paul, 1983), p. 129.
7 John Carnell, 'Foreword', *New Writings in SF 1* (London: Dobson, 1964), p. vi.
8 Mike Ashley, *Gateways to Forever: The Story of the Science Fiction Magazines from 1970 to 1980* (Liverpool: Liverpool University Press, 2007), p. 118. Also note the preceding volume, Mike Ashley, *Transformations: The History of the Science-fiction Magazines from 1950 to 1970* (Liverpool: Liverpool University Press, 2005).
9 Brian W. Aldiss, 'The Gulf and the Forest: Contemporary SF in Britain', *Fantasy and Science Fiction*, 54.4 (1978), 4–11.
10 Peter Nicholls and Mike Ashley, 'Interzone' (28 September 2014), *The Encyclopedia of Science Fiction*, eds. John Clute, David Langford, Peter Nicholls and Graham Sleight, www.sf-encyclopedia.com/entry/interzone [Accessed 25 May 2015].
11 'Interaction', *Interzone*, 45 (March 1991), 5. My thanks to Paul Kincaid for checking his copies.
12 Ben Jeapes, '3SF, and the Beginning of the End' (2013), www.benjeapes.com/index.php/2013/05/3sf-and-the-beginning-of-the-end/ [Accessed 25 May 2015].
13 Seregil of Rhiminee, 'An Interview with Nina Allan', *Rising Shadow* (1 June 2013), www.risingshadow.net/articles/245-an-interview-with-nina-allan [Accessed 25 May 2015].

14

MARC BOTHA

Microfiction

The history of narrative brevity

Now!

'The short story form, in its brevity and condensation, fits our age', writes Michèle Roberts in her aptly brief introduction to Deborah Levy's collection *Black Vodka* (2013). It fits 'the short attention span of modern readers, the gaps and fragmentedness of modern consciousness'.[1] If this is true of the short story, how much truer might it be of the *very* short story? Is the increasing prominence of microfiction as a contemporary literary genre indicative of the fact that even the short story cannot convey the speed and immediacy of contemporary life, and that only the extremities of narrative scale are able to communicate the relentless intensity of the present and future? If the short story is the genre of today, might the very short story – which is as comfortable on the screen as it is on the page, matching the shifting media and ever-accelerating pace of the present – be the genre of tomorrow?[2]

Although the capacity of microfiction to communicate the immediacies of the present has seen it increasingly embedded in the infrastructures of academic criticism, the publishing industry and competitive writing in recent years, miniature narrative genres are by no means new to the literary scene. Even a cursory survey of literary history reveals that a great variety of very short forms have emerged in different periods and cultural contexts,[3] each bringing with it a singular set of aesthetic concerns while also exemplifying a shared commitment to the relationship of minimal scale to maximal intensity which allows us to trace a certain generic unity across distinctive species of microfiction.

Names

Literary genres do not emerge fully formed – as immutable laws, stable structures or established sets of texts – but are the product of an ongoing process of differentiation. What defines the health of a particular genre at any point is the degree to which it is disputed, and the extent to which its boundaries prove permeable and its conventions responsive to the shifting contexts and demands of literary production and reception. The very short form is thriving in this sense. Ongoing debate around its origins and generic precursors, its formal and stylistic features, its optimal length, how it might best be named, and its relation to the changing media of publication and dissemination complicate matters further.[4]

Far from empty rhetorical posturing, critical debate around names and naming often has considerable historical and ideological implications. The various terms offered to describe contemporary short fictional forms – very short story, short-short story (or often just short-short), shorter and shortest story, skinny fiction, curt fiction, sudden fiction, flash fiction, quick fiction and microfiction – constitute a polemical field; one which is further intensified by the long and complex histories of antecedents of the contemporary genre which include the aphorism, parable, fragment, digression, paradox, anecdote, joke, riddle, epigram, exemplum, emblem, myth, fable, tale, tableau, vignette, character, sketch, prose poem, miniature and, indeed, short story. This chapter uses the term *microfiction* – which is maximally descriptive but minimally prescriptive – to refer to the overall field of very short fiction, and it uses more specific terms where necessary to pinpoint certain historical practices. A conjunction of the Greek *mikros* (small) and the Latin *fictio* (formation), microfictions are small literary forms, either historical or contemporary, which are suited to representing a wide range of subjects while remaining responsive to the shifting contexts of literary production and reception.

Precursors

While there is general consensus that oral folk forms such as the tale and parable, or the even more concise proverb and anecdote, are the precursors to contemporary microfiction,[5] there exist a range of views regarding the precise moment at which extreme narrative brevity becomes a technique consciously employed by writers with a specific effect in mind. For some, this point is located as far back as the exemplum and fable of Classical antiquity,[6] while others trace it to the medieval genres of the fabliau, nouvelle and lai.[7] The Renaissance certainly brought an intensified interest in the miniature, with the exceptionally fine detail of Hilliard's tiny portraits reflected in the controlled prose of Thomas Overbury's *Characters* (1614) and the didactic microcosms of Francis Quarles's *Emblems* (1635).[8] The intermittent prominence of a variety of very short forms in diverse contexts – the *Athenaeum* fragments of the Jena Romantics (1798–1800), the vignettes of Anton Chekhov (1880s), the prose poetry of Gertrude Stein's *Tender Buttons* (1914) or the minimalist stories of Raymond Carver's *Will You Please Be Quiet, Please?* (1976) – confirms that the complex genealogical network of contemporary microfiction is both transhistorical and transcultural. The point at which brevity becomes significant in itself, rather than simply as an attribute of a specific work, is tied to the subsumption of these diverse miniature forms under the banner of the short story, which, despite its popularity through much of the nineteenth century, entered the twentieth century as a genre largely ancillary to the expansive aesthetic sensibility of modernity.

Modern microfiction

Microfiction demonstrates well the depth of the rift between high and low cultural forms in modernist aesthetics. Despite, or perhaps on account of, a 'notable boom in the "short short" story for magazines from the 1920s through the 1940s',[9] very short narrative forms receive scant critical attention. Yet, at the margins of a marginalized genre, microfictions possess a disruptive force which frequently places them at the experimental cusp of the avant-garde. Iconic modernist microfictions emerge at significant nodes of narrative innovation: the tense patterns of incremental repetition and angular discontinuity in the miniature sketches of Stein's 'Three Portraits of Painters' (1912) open paths of verbal patterning explored by experimentalists as different as Samuel Beckett and Charles Bernstein; the unadorned, declarative prose of Kafka's parable, 'Before the Law' (1915), reveals a conceptual sophistication which influences writers from Jorge Luis Borges to J. M. Coetzee; the overlap of sense, affect and imagination in the diminutive but dense verbal icons of Virginia Woolf's post-impressionistic 'Blue and Green' (1921) resonate in the tableaux of stylists as varied as Alain Robbe-Grillet and Jeanette Winterson; and the robust, plain speaking of Ernest Hemingway's 'A Very Short Story' (1924) informs a range of work from Carver's minimalism to Tao Lin's ultra-hip realism.

Resurgence

Despite its credibility as an ancient folk form and its modernist experimental currency, microfiction takes root in the public literary imagination as an independent genre only in the wake of the experimentalism of the 1950s and 1960s. Among the numerous, magisterial, and strikingly diverse very short works from this period, pulsating with the 'spirit of experiment and wordplay',[10] we might count Borges' metafictional masterpieces in *Ficciones* (1956), Samuel Beckett's 'Texts for Nothing' (1950-2), which constitute an important minimalist turn in his *oeuvre*, the phenomenological exemplars of Robbe-Grillet's *Snapshots* (1962), the ludic intertextuality of Robert Coover's 'Seven Exemplary Fictions' (1969), and J. G. Ballard's virtuosic arrangement of fragments in *The Atrocity Exhibition* (1970).

The upsurge of microfictional forms is arguably symptomatic of a more fundamental cultural shift which the philosopher Jean-François Lyotard famously refers to in terms of the disintegration of the historically legitimated grand narrative of human progress into multiple, local, contingent and competing accounts of the world as it is experienced in practical terms.[11] Transposing this insight to the literary sphere, the proliferation of new forms is indicative of the diversification of narrative strategies required to come to grips with what McHale terms a shift in *dominant* from the modernist to postmodernist aesthetic.[12] The emergence into an increasingly diverse narrative field of autonomous, microfictional forms thus points to a sustained challenge to the progressive logic of the formation of the autonomous subject (*Bildung*). A growing number of prominent publications promote very short forms: a 1976 'Minute Stories' special issue of *TriQuarterly* edited by Coover constitutes the first successful attempt to gather together narrative miniatures;[13] while *Esquire* and the *New Yorker* championed emerging minimalist writers including Raymond Carver, Amy Hempel, Mary Robison, Ann Beattie and Tobias Wolff.[14]

This resurgent interest in short narrative forms in the 1970s and 1980s was by no means limited to the United States. Alongside the continued influence of short works by British and Irish writers such as Beckett, Ballard and Muriel Spark emerged an exciting younger generation which included such figures as Ian McEwan, Kazuo Ishiguro and Angela Carter; the last, in particular, penning numerous and strikingly original miniatures. Indeed, significant works reflecting a spectrum of approaches to the very short narrative form are published across the Anglophone world by, among many others, Canada's Alice Munro, New Zealand's C. K. Stead, South Africa's Nadine Gordimer and Australia's David Malouf. However, the sustained attention devoted to minimalist and microfictional forms by writers, critics, educationalists and publishers in the United States places it consistently at the vanguard of the evolution of this enigmatic and protean genre. Significant anthologies of very short stories – stories included or excluded on the quantitative measure of word count – begin to appear in the 1980s.[15] Irving and Ilana Howe's *Short Shorts* (1982) set its limit at 2,500 words and gathered an admirable historical and international selection of canonical microfiction,

Microfiction

and Robert Shapard's and James Thomas's *Sudden Fiction* (1986), *Sudden Fiction International* (1989) and *New Sudden Fiction* (2007), all with limits of 1,500 words, quickly became standard works in literature and creative writing courses. *Flash Fiction* (1992), *Flash Fiction Forward* (2005) and *Flash Fiction International* (2015) – edited in various combinations by Robert Shapard, James and Denise Thomas, Tom Hazuka and Christopher Merrill – set their upper limit at 750 words, while Jerome Stern's *Micro Fiction* (1996) included only works of 300 words or less. These collections remain prominent points of access to contemporary microfiction.

Pressing short narrative forms towards their minimal extreme remains an abiding concern for many writers, and the rapidly evolving media of literature present both challenges and opportunities in this respect. Digital technology in particular effects a radical shift both in the structures of communication and in the speed at which literary miniatures are created, published, accessed and processed. The ongoing shift from page to screen, with its concomitant incorporation of linear and non-linear processes of reading, occasions a radical reconsideration of the ways verbal material is organized into literary form. Websites and blogs continue to provide fertile ground for the composition and archiving of miniature works, albeit often of extremely variable quality, as do various mobile communication technologies. Nicholas Royle draws attention to the first mobile application developed to host '[q]uick fictions' which aims 'to take us to the very quick of things' in order to discover 'the writing of our time'.[16] It should not be forgotten, however, that the serialized mobile phone novel – consisting of chapters limited by a fixed number of characters to which readers can subscribe and which are distributed principally by text messaging – had already aimed at achieving a similar sense of immediacy and accessibility. Another recent development in this format uses social media platforms and micro-blogging tools such as Twitter to explore both serialized forms – Jennifer Egan's 'Black Box' (2012) and David Mitchell's 'The Right Sort' (2014) are the most prominent examples – and single tweets limited to a miniscule 140 characters.

That the miniature is increasingly seen as a professional genre – taught widely as part of creative and professional writing courses, as well as a category in an increasing number of writing competitions – has resulted in a rapid increase in both the number of very short stories written and published (often online), and in the didactic material addressing the writing of various types of flash-, quick- and microfiction. Stern's *Micro Fictions* was the first anthology compiled entirely from competition pieces, with more recent anthologies emerging from Calum Kerr's and Valerie O'Riordan's UK *National Flash-Fiction Day*, which has to date culminated in the publication of *Jawbreakers* (2012), *Scraps* (2013) and *Eating My Words* (2014).

Although its present commercial success is likely to wane over time, microfiction has proved itself a resilient and adaptable genre and one likely to discover significant expressive routes in the future.

The aesthetics of shortness

Shortness

According to Howe, '[t]he one thing we can be sure of is that the short short [story] is shorter than the short story'.[17] Yet, on closer inspection, even this truism proves problematic: how might we distinguish the exact point at which *merely* short becomes *very* short? The question of brevity has been taken up in two substantial critical pieces, Norman Friedman's epochal 'What Makes a Short Story Short?' and William Nelles's more recent 'Microfiction: What Makes a Very Short Story Very Short?'. Both are principally concerned with the techniques through which brevity is achieved, rather than with the conceptual problem of shortness itself, although Friedman speculates in this regard. Thus, it is not entirely surprising that although writers, critics, publishers and readers disagree widely on what distinguishes short from very short, the tendency in anthologizing very short work has been to emphasize the purely quantitative measure of word count.

Along with regularly renaming and redefining the genre, editors have prescribed progressively lower word limits for inclusion, from the 2,500 words of Howe's short-shorts in 1982, to the 100 words of Kerr's and O'Riordan's microfictions in 2012.[18] In the shadows of the totalizing economic logic of late capitalism, the qualities of these stories are all too often reduced to fixed quantitative measures – word count, the amount of space a text occupies or the time it takes to be read – which focus attention on what Friedman contends are the 'symptoms rather than the causes'[19] of brevity. While Friedman recognizes that certain narrative conditions are hospitable to shortness – principally the representation of 'intrinsically small' events, or larger events 'reduced in length' by various techniques of reduction[20] – shortness itself proves curiously resistant to direct description. To Friedman, what is most significant about shortness is that it involves a principle of parsimony, and hence an economy which cannot be quantified in absolute terms: a short story should not 'exceed [...] the needs of [its] effect'.[21]

Scale

In short fiction, and even more so in very short fiction, quantity becomes the essential quality of the work in question, and yet one which cannot be expressed in terms of a fixed, quantitative measure. The concept of *scale* provides the most convincing means of grasping quantity as part of an ongoing process of quantification. Scale is a relative measure of both spatial and temporal quantity, a relation of size and duration which applies equally to the literary work itself and to the contexts of its production and reception. As in the case of the visual arts, it is helpful to distinguish between internal and external scale. Internal scale describes the relation of parts to other parts, and of parts to the whole or the form of the work in question and is often described in terms of the proportion of parts to one another.[22] The question of proportion applies to literature at both a formal and representational level: characters, action and plot must be proportioned so as to constitute a narrative which is either believable or appropriate to a work's aesthetic aims.[23] External scale describes the relation of the work in question to other works and forms, to readers and the contexts of reading, and to genre, medium and other markers of literature as a world system.[24]

In microfiction, the internal scale of the work accounts for the manner in which many very short works appear to be 'like most ordinary short stories, *only more so*',[25] differing in 'degree but not in kind'.[26] Hemingway's 'Mr. and Mrs. Elliot' (1925) and Graham Greene's 'Special Duties' (1954) both offer highly condensed accounts of strained marital relationships, yet retain the narrative structures and proportions which make them comparable to longer forms. Internal scale, established by the relation of their parts, must remain relatively stable as these stories diminish in length in order for them to maintain the coherence of their storyworlds – the models of 'who did what to and with whom, when, where, why and in what fashion'.[27] When such internal scale is disrupted, microfiction ceases to conform to conventional narrative rules: it 'begin[s] to exhibit qualitative differences'[28] which do not derive solely from crossing a quantitative threshold, as Nelles appears to suggest,[29] but arise because of a shift from questions of internal to those of external scale.

At this threshold – between shorter and shortest – microfiction becomes overwhelmingly concerned with conveying a sense of immediacy or immanence. Much as with minimalist visual art, the most minimal microfiction achieves its sense of immediacy through a symmetrical manipulation of physical and temporal scale, so that 'the duration of the story event described closely corresponds to the length of time required to process the discourses in which those events are presented'.[30] Rin Simpson's 'Inked' (2012) takes approximately thirty seconds to read, for example – a realistic temporal scale for the brief, nervous pause it depicts in its 150 words, as a tattooist is about to tattoo her first customer. Pressed further, the shortest microfiction presents itself in terms of singularities which evade easy classification, and which by their extremity come to constitute events in their own right, often evoking an aesthetics of the sublime.

Minimal sublime

The sublime refers to a specific type of 'negative pleasure'[31] which arises when we encounter phenomena of extreme scale. Initially experiencing a sort of terror in the face of apparently imminent threat,[32] the capacity of the mind to conceptualize the idea of the infinite, and to assert it above even the most overwhelming sensory experiences, reasserts human agency and autonomy. Pleasure is derived from the sublime 'not because [it] arouses fear, but because it calls forth our strength'.[33] The aesthetics of the sublime provide an imperfect means of presenting that which cannot be represented – the absolute.[34] In this sense, the extremities of scale associated with the aesthetics of the sublime are ciphers for the absolute. Pivotal to the present argument is Susan Stewart's assertion that '[s]mall things can be sublime as readily as the grand material phenomena of nature and human making'.[35]

The minimal sublime – the most radical pole of smallness, shortness and brevity evoked in contemplating disappearance, absence, nothingness and the void – informs an aesthetic movement towards the infinitesimal. Its literary manifestations are numerous and diverse: at one extreme the material experiments of micrographia explore the sublime extreme of minimal scale through tiny writing;[36] at the other extreme, we find microfictions such as Beckett's 'Fizzle 5' (1973–5), which examines the liminal point at which concept, experience, language and knowledge threaten to collapse into one another, exemplifying the conditions under which microfiction proves its aptitude to the sublime task of 'presenting the unpresentable',[37] to recall Lyotard. The elliptical fragments and aphorisms of Friedrich Schlegel, Friedrich Nietzsche and Chekhov often grapple with the minimal sublime, at the levels of both form and content. Equally evocative in this respect are self-reflexive and recursive miniatures such as John Barth's celebrated 'Frame-Tale' (1968), which, if read correctly, endlessly loops its single phrase, 'ONCE UPON A TIME THERE WAS A STORY THAT BEGAN'; Borges' 'The Library of Babel' (1941), which demonstrates the paradoxical capacity of miniature works effectively to represent infinity alongside the infinitesimal; and Dave Eggers's 'There Are Some Things He Should Keep To Himself' (2004), the four blank pages of which communicate both the sublime threat of absolute absence – death – and the sublime promise of the infinite and infinite possibility.

The minimal scale of much microfiction is able to *intensify* the immanence of the work, constituting a type of sublime access to a reality which transcends the work even as it points to the very heart of its aesthetic. In successful microfiction *scale* and *intensity* operate in tandem: as the scale of the work decreases, so its intensity increases, reflecting the aesthetic logic of the aesthetic maxim, *multum in parvo*, or *more in less*.

Towards a contemporary typology of microfiction

Relation

The question of how readers relate to microfiction, and how microfictional stories relate to one another, is central to understanding its ongoing development. Microfiction is a sociable genre. It is comparatively rare to find a very short story published in isolation. Reasons vary, from Johnson's rather cynical but practical assessment that '[e]ditors like [microfiction] [...] because it means we can publish several titles in a single issue, thereby creating the illusion of diversity on the contents page',[38] to Baxter's idealism, which, in regarding microfiction as a 'fiction-of-proximity', is able to claim that its stories reveal 'something about the scale of our lives, not so much that diminishment has occurred but that intimacy and community have increased'.[39] What is crucial in both cases is a sense that at the heart of the microfictional enterprise is the question of relation: of works to one another, of works to readers, and finally of readers to one another, as these works collectively address a reading public which is marked by divergent views on the nature, limits, merits and effects of the genre.

The rapid proliferation of microfiction as a professional genre – one taught in many creative writing courses, codified in numerous textbooks, published in lucrative literary journals and magazines, the subject of international writing competitions and festivals such as the United Kingdom's *National Flash Fiction Day*, and embedded within an ever-proliferating number of online platforms – has meant that a great number of its best works have been written with a specific set of relations in mind. Such relations often involve revisiting historical forms, as exemplified in Borges' or Carter's use of folklore and fable. Equally prominent are the intertextual relations commonly used by writers of microfiction to 'increase the function or interpretive reach of a story'.[40] Consider, for example, Teju Cole's Twitter fictions, *Seven Short Stories about Drones* (2013),[41] a series of short tweets, each of which begins with the opening line of a celebrated novel, followed by an incisive phrase carefully conceived to convey the brutal futility of drone warfare.

Particularly significant are the increasingly numerous longer cycles from leading authors which demonstrate both continuity and diversity. Jim Crace's *The Devil's Larder* (2002) is one of several compelling microfictional cycles – others include Stein's *Tender Buttons*, Carter's *The Bloody Chamber* (1979), Alasdair Gray's *Lean Tales* (1985), Robert Olen Butler's *Severance* (2006) and Jonathan Kemp's *Twentysix* (2006) – which weave together distinct miniature narratives by shared threads of motif, theme, style or formal constraint. Kemp's is a bold and inventive cycle – unapologetically philosophical, self-consciously writerly, yet also visceral and explicit in its narration of twenty-six homosexual encounters, each of which confronts the capacities and limits of language as it attempts to mediate the overwhelming intensity of the body and erotic experience. These stories exemplify many of the most compelling qualities of contemporary microfiction.

Event

In Kemp's 'L' (2006), for instance, the reader encounters a single event beginning *in medias res*, as is often the case in microfiction. A transgender prostitute, Ruby, humorously narrates oral sex with 'her latest trade' to an attentive audience cruising for sex in a public park.[42] Yet this single event is carefully situated in a generic field, allowing minimal verbal patterns to imply a great deal of detail. Rapidly oscillating between quite distinct narrative techniques and styles allows Kemp to incorporate several typical tropes of the miniature. The aphoristic philosophical reveries with which the piece begins and ends – 'I must have a body because some obscure object lives in me', and '[i]t is thus not a question of language or the body, but language *and* the body' – contrast sharply with Ruby's monologue, which takes the form of a joke, replete with the punchline, 'the bastard wouldn't even swallow', demonstrating the proclivity in much microfiction for twists, surprises and inversions.[43] Yet the force of this work emerges from a third narrative register. Through minimal but suggestive detail, Kemp carefully balances the sense of contemporaneity and the present, so central to microfiction,[44] with the historical details of Ruby's 'former life' as Rudy, a life spent with his 'Chelsea hooligan mates' and amplified by its symbolically charged 'scars where the British Bulldog and Union Jack tattoos have been removed'.[45] This tension allows the narrator to polarize feminine and masculine, emphasizing the moments when 'Rudy makes an appearance, and Ruby's feminine demeanour disappears in a vapour of violence', all in order to mark the epiphanic event – the 'moment when who she wants to be and who she appears to be coincide [...] gloriously'.[46]

Such events are sources of radical novelty and change, powerful as they are fleeting, and in their singularity call to be witnessed, to be represented, even as they remain essentially inassimilable to any system or order. Microfiction grapples with the singularity of events in several ways, with many of its

Microfiction

best works taking up the sublime challenge of presenting the unpresentable. Centred on the motif of an empty white room – the *tabula rasa* upon which potential events erupt, and upon which consequences of these events are traced, elliptically and uncertainly – Jeanette Winterson's 'The White Room' (2004) weaves together short meditations on the interpenetration of temporality, affect, memory and phenomenological experience in order to represent the 'caught moment opening into a lifetime'.[47] Exemplary of numerous of the most significant aesthetic subtleties of microfiction, 'The White Room' exposes the event as a threshold upon which the distinction between poetry and prose, contraction and expansion, determinism and chance, fragility and resilience, and nostalgia and avant-gardism are rendered problematic.[48]

Events are equally important to microfiction in thematic terms, often taking the form of epiphanic moments such as the one in Kemp's 'L', or unexpected revelations, as in the case of Ballard's 'Track 12' (1958), where a long-standing but largely sublimated rivalry between two men, one of whom is having an affair with the wife of the other, suddenly gives way to a murder. The representation of liminal events – and particularly of death – is often linked to a pursuit of technical virtuosity. According to Francis, '[w]riters have always challenged themselves to absolute reduction, skeletons. They tempt death',[49] while for Royle, the accelerations of the contemporary miniature or 'quick fiction' constitute a curious species of life-writing.[50] In the headlong race to the impossible experience of death, this writing witnesses the paradoxical appearance of 'the life-giving drop [...] that will spread an intensity on the page'[51] in the disappearance of the *longue durée* of traditional narrative time as it approaches zero. Much microfiction addresses the sublime intensity of the space between life and death – the event which in its unrepresentability always calls to be represented; the intuition of 'very little ... almost nothing'[52] in the uneasy search for last words in works as different as Beckett's 'Imagination Dead Imagine' (1965) and Patrick White's late miniature, 'The Screaming Potato' (1987).

Miniature

If, as Stewart suggests, 'the miniature is the notation of the moment and the moment's consequences,'[53] its aesthetic fate is closely tied to that of the event. However, where the event constitutes a point of intensified dynamism, the miniature seeks stasis: 'a world of arrested time [...] to create a tension or dialectic between inside and outside, between private and public [...] [and] between the space of the subject and the space of the social.'[54]

By abstracting the essential and subtracting the inessential, the miniature intensifies the representational capacity of literature through its diminution of scale and remains perhaps the most pervasive microfictional type. Its techniques are closely tied to the emergence and development of the art tale in the nineteenth and twentieth centuries as distinct from its folk predecessors,[55] and also to a transhistorical range of experiments with micrographic forms of tiny writing.

Miniatures which involve a diminution in their external scale tend to take a concrete form, exhibited most overtly in the production of physically tiny micrographia – miniature books and tiny writing – which are 'emblematic of craft and discipline',[56] and to this extent invested with a symbolic force and ritual significance which recalls the ancient religious association of inscription and power.[57] This power symbolically transforms the micrographic work into a microcosm – a world in miniature – the intensity of which is intimately connected to the medium through which it is given its shape. The 'limits of bodily skill in writing'[58] are significantly extended by the increased precision of technologies of printing, itself radicalized by the rise of digital technology. In digital writing the material distinction of short and long texts is minimal, and both are habitually transposed into the virtual world of cyberspace which blurs any clear distinction between macrocosm and microcosm, infinite and infinitesimal. Yet micrographic experimentation thrives in this medium. Christine Wilks's *Underbelly* (2010), for example, is a self-contained multimedia anthology of microfictional fragments which explore the untold history of women in mining, dragging the reader interactively through the subterranean microcosm of a nineteenth-century Yorkshire coal mine.

Miniatures which involve a diminution in their internal scale resemble longer narrative forms with respect to their parts and proportions, relying on careful omissions, contractions and condensations to convey a great deal of implicit information. In short, '[w]hat is minimal [...] is the *means*, not the end'.[59] Drawing on notable precursors such as Chekhov and Hemingway, minimalist and postminimalist writers – including Raymond Carver, Mary Robison, Amy Hempel, Ann Beattie, Donald Barthelme, Tobias Wolff, Richard Ford, Bobbie Ann Mason, Lydia Davis, Jayne Anne Philips, Bret Easton Ellis and Dave Eggers – use miniature forms as 'containers of compressed meaning'.[60] While longer narrative forms rely on establishing complex and detailed patterns to convey their sense, the miniature deploys generic characters and situations, historically and culturally specific events or objects which act as ciphers for large amounts of implicit information.[61]

Many of the stories in Crace's *The Devil's Larder* draw on a nostalgic attachment to familiar images and practical wisdom, revivifying the traditional patterns of the folktale, parable and anecdote. The cycle interrogates food in all its material manifestations, together with its associated spheres of hunger, craving, satiety and excess, a spectrum of culinary customs, habits and rituals, and their role as bearers of individual, social and cultural memory. In a rather caustic account of contemporary health fads, Crace's '37' (2002) recounts the eating habits of a 'regimented, well-organized, reliable' man who centres his diet around a variety of 'foods to see off death', a ritual saturated with irony inasmuch as he follows this diet 'without a break, until the day he die[s]'.[62]

The small scale of microfiction is thus adept at representing both the everyday and the epiphanic, and both are capable of functioning as 'emblem[s] of the universal',[63] demonstrating that 'what might be seen as a microcosmic tendency is macrocosmic as well'.[64] Miniature stories do not dispense with detail, but rather displace it, establishing a 'distance between the context at hand and the narrated context'[65] which enables them to clarify the correspondences between narrative structure and the external world, and thus to depict a reality which exists at an equal or even greater intensity to that of longer narrative forms.

Fragment

The fragment proves particularly apposite to the task of addressing the essential contingency of reality, offering a radical and compelling alternative to the encompassing logic of totalizing systems. Reaching across history, the fragment as literary form occupies a position both terminal and foundational, its words at once the scattered remnants of fractured wholes, and points of inception for new configurations of thought.[66] The fragment disrupts any straightforward distinction between philosophy and literature, and although always limited in scale, it is nonetheless characterized by an 'essential incompletion'[67] which indicates 'that it should forever be becoming and never be perfected'.[68] In this sense, it is a genre always 'tending' – one way towards the finite, the other towards the infinite.[69]

In this respect we might counterpose the fragmentary lessness of Beckett's late novella, *Worstward Ho* (1983), arrived at through an immense deconstructive labour, to the fragmentary parataxis of Robison's *Why Did I Ever?* (2001), a novel wrought from extensive reconstructive labour as its author battled a decade of writer's block. Indeed, there is great variety in fragmentary writing: Stein's *Blood on the Dining Room Floor* (1933/1982) is a murder mystery, Ballard's *The Atrocity Exhibition* a cycle of fragments, while Richard Brautigan's *I Watched the World Glide Effortlessly By* (1956), John Cage's *Empty Words* (1975) and Steve McCaffery's *Panopticon* (1984) defy easy generic description altogether. Yet it is the detached fragment which, 'like a miniature work of art, has to be entirely isolated from the surrounding world and be complete in itself',[70] that best captures the transhistorical eclecticism of microfiction.

Indeed, March-Russell holds that the short story generally conforms to a logic of fragmentation, a 'breaking or separating off from an imposed limit'.[71] What very short forms reveal is that this fragmentation is not merely a relation of part *to* whole, but also of part *as* whole. This was certainly the aim of the Jena Romantics, whose self-reflexive fragments aim to expose the capacity for singular works to instantiate a universal logic. The varied fragmentary and aphoristic works of, among others, Nietzsche, Chekhov, Søren Kierkegaard, Arthur Schopenhauer, August Strindberg, Oscar Wilde, Walter Benjamin, Maurice Blanchot and Fernando Pessoa expose a wider conception of fragment,[72] capable of grounding parables and proverbs, epigrams and epigraphs, digressions and allegories, anecdotes and jokes.

The remarkably diverse work of Lydia Davis explores a range of fragmentary forms, including the question-and-answer format of 'Jury Duty' (2001), the eclectic sequence, 'Marie Curie, So Honourable Woman' (2001) and the self-reflexively witty 'Honouring the Subjunctive' (2001) which reads: 'It invariably precedes, even if it do not altogether supersede, the determination of what is absolutely desirably and just.'[73] Alasdair Gray concludes his *Lean Tales* with a witty and progressively contracting series of fragments which terminate in the autopoietic gem, 'Having beguiled with fiction until I had none left I resorted to facts which also ran out.'[74] Don Patterson has published three volumes of aphorisms, which include timely provocations – 'You've made a *blog* ... Clever boy! Next: flushing'[75] – alongside tiny but meaningful meditations on freedom and autonomy – 'Fate's book, but my italics.'[76]

In its insistence on the capacity of singular works to convey universal truths, the fragment instantiates a threshold upon which clear distinctions of part and whole, closure and openness, and microcosm and macrocosm are undermined.[77] Indeed, the fragment emerges at a 'point [...] continuously fluctuating between self-creation and self-destruction'[78] – a sublime point that reflects the radical contingency at the heart of every literary event, its plurality and reinterpretability.

Medium

The evolution of the literary medium – which has for the most part been progressive, emphasizing greater durability, accessibility and portability – is inextricable from technological transformation. It begins with inscription on stone and clay, continues through the paper and vellum of scrolls and manuscripts, is revolutionized by the genesis of printing and the rise of the age of the book, and radically compressed and accelerated by the dawn of digital technology. Every innovation introduces a shift in the scale and intensity of our connection to the world through literature.[79] Sensitive to these shifts, microfiction has tended to embrace experimental forms and media in order to gain an increasingly immediate access to the world, and to expose an irremissible sense of presence at the heart of the work. This is exemplified in the clear, but still largely unremarked, parallel progression of microfictional forms and the technological advancement of literary media. Perhaps because visual perception offers our most immediate access to the world, these forms have tended to take their cue from visual techniques – from sketch, to snapshot, to flash fiction.

The balance of impression and expression achieved in sketching by visual artists aiming to capture the dynamism of experience is matched by the immediacy of verbal sketches by such masters as Dickens, Hemingway and Woolf. The latter's 'Blue and Green' – written in 1921 and discussed previously – aims for an immediate access to the complexities of sensory experience, creating a liminal region in which word and world bleed into one another in recollecting and projecting into language an impressionist melange of sensation and affect. Another fine, albeit very different type of sketch is Ian Hamilton Finlay's 'Break for Tea' (1952), which although brief and descriptive – it depicts two fishermen drinking tea around a small fire as mist gathers and rain begins to fall – is also highly evocative of a mood which allows Finlay to interrogate the nuanced relationship between location and the local, to measure customary behaviour against the singularity of the moment sketched.

A great deal has been written of the disruptive effect of photography on the traditional economies of mimesis, including its paradoxical ability to abstract the dynamic immediacy of existence to a static point. It is this situation, weighed against Merleau-Ponty's assertion that our access to the world always arrives through a dynamic process of perception,[80] that concerns Robbe-Grillet's early fiction in *Snapshots* (1962). The three interconnected microfictions of 'In the Corridors of the Underground' significantly extend the logic of the sketch by focusing attention on specific objects or events of perception – a giant advertisement on a wall and an escalator journey, for instance – in order to draw attention to the capacity of the literary medium to grasp stasis and movement simultaneously and immediately, which is the precise capacity of the snapshot. The intensity of these small-scale works reflects a literary drive towards a 'reality [which] would no longer be permanently situated elsewhere, but *here and now*',[81] and the immanence of the snapshot is important to the work of a range of writers including Gabriel Josipovici, Beckett, Patrick White, John Barth, Charles Bukowski and Raymond Carver.

A flash is a moment of immediate insight and of immanent access – a point of appearance, but also of disappearance. Not merely a question of intensified access, however, flash fiction is also a genre of transition. In the genealogy of mediatized microfictional forms, flash fiction follows the sketch and snapshot, taking shape in the wake of the digital revolution that began in the 1950s. Although many flash fictions have neither a thematic nor a material connection to digital technology, they nonetheless reflect the epochal shift marked by the rise of digital culture, and exhibit an intuitive connection to new media thinking: the 'convergence of two separate historical trajectories: computing and media technologies', gives rise to 'graphics, moving images, sounds, shapes, spaces, and texts that have become computable'.[82]

If the advent of new media technologies offers unprecedented opportunities for the democratization of knowledge, and indeed of the literary system in general, it also precipitates a predictable yet significant cultural anxiety regarding the future of literature. These are most emblematically captured in debates around attention: Carr holds that we are witnessing an erosion of the deep reading through which the communicative function of writing becomes tied to increased attention and even complex understanding; Hayles is more cautious, so that while she acknowledges that digital and hypermedia alter aspects of reading and information retention, she argues persuasively that such alteration should not simplistically be conflated with degradation.[83] Similar anxieties manifest with respect to the transformation of the literary field – not only by the ubiquity of digital technology and the rise of electronic literature, but particularly by the effects of digital communication technologies such as cellular phones, tablets and laptops, along with the modes of communication associated with social media platforms and tools such as text messaging, Twitter, Facebook and blogging.

Flash fiction, in both printed and digital form, proves particularly adept at responding to the need for simultaneous intensification and acceleration marked by new media. As Bellamy suggests, while readers possess 'shorter attention spans than previously, they are also well-equipped to process information quickly',[84] and arguably the media of microfiction are perfectly adapted to the task of evoking a sublime intensity where our access to the work and to the world is identical. This task is by no means straightforward since, as Royle recognizes, '[i]f we live in the age of the short attention span, we are by the same token caught up in a history or histories of speed.'[85] The vocation of microfiction resides not merely in matching the speed of the everyday, but in 'what Hélène Cixous [...] calls "find[ing] the slowness inside the speed"'.[86] Although microfiction is in some sense an opportunistic genre increasingly framed by commercial and utilitarian concerns, this vocation remains at its heart inasmuch as its best works reflect a deep commitment to responding proactively to the pace of the contemporary condition. The effectiveness of this response hinges in large part on discovering a scale of expression appropriate to our contemporary sense of life, and it is to this scale that microfiction remains oriented. Finally, the 'fundamental quality [of microfiction] [...] is life' itself,[87] and in exploring the minimal scale but maximal intensity of these works we discover a means to 'see fast [but] dwell long'.[88] It is precisely in this sense that microfiction 'fits our age'.[89]

NOTES

1 Michèle Roberts, 'Introduction', Deborah Levy, *Black Vodka* (High Wycombe: And Other Stories, 2013), pp. vii–viii (p. vii).
2 See William Nelles, 'Microfiction: What Makes a Very Short Story Very Short', *Narrative*, 20.1 (2012), pp. 87–104 (p. 88).
3 See Charles Johnson and Stuart Dybeck in 'Afterwords', *Sudden Fiction*, eds. Robert Shapard and James Thomas (Layton: Gibbs Smith, 1986), pp. 233; 241 respectively.
4 See Stephen Minor in 'Afterwords', *Sudden Fiction*, eds. Shapard and Thomas, p. 235.
5 Karl-Heinz Stierle, 'Story as Exemplum – Exemplum as Story: On the Pragmatics and Poetics of Narrative Text', *The New Short Story Theories*, ed. Charles E. May (Athens, OH: Ohio University Press), pp. 15–43 (p. 21).
6 Jack Matthews in 'Afterwords', *Sudden Fiction*, eds. Shapard and Thomas, p. 235.
7 See Nelles, 'Microfiction', pp. 92; 97.
8 See Ralph Rugoff, 'Homeopathic Strategies', *At the Threshold of the Visible: Miniscule and Small-Scale Art, 1964–1996*, ed. Ralph Rugoff (New York: Independent Curators Incorporated, pp. 11–71 (pp. 55–6); Susan Stewart, 'At the Threshold of the Visible', ibid., pp. 73–85 (pp. 73–4); Robert Kelly in 'Afterwords', *Sudden Fiction*, eds. Shapard and Thomas, p. 241.
9 Nelles, 'Microfiction', p. 90.
10 Robert Shapard, 'Introduction', *Sudden Fiction*, eds. Shapard and Thomas, pp. xiii–xvi (p. xiv).
11 Jean-François Lyotard, *The Postmodern Condition*, trans. Geoffrey Bennington and Brian Massumi (Manchester: Manchester University Press, 1984), pp. 33–6.
12 Brian McHale, *Postmodernist Fiction* (London; New York: Routledge, 2004), pp. 6–11.
13 See Shapard, 'Introduction', p. xiv, and Gordon Lish in 'Afterwords', *Sudden Fiction*, eds. Shapard and Thomas, p. 255.
14 Kim A. Herzinger, 'Introduction: On the New Fiction', *Mississippi Review*, 40/41 (1985), pp. 7–22 (p. 7); see also Michael Marton, 'Selling Short Stories', *Mississippi Review*, 40/41 (1985), 58–61.
15 See Nelles, 'Microfiction', pp. 89–90.
16 Nicholas Royle, 'Quick Fiction: Some Remarks on Writing Today', *Mosaic*, 47.1 (2014), 23–39 (p. 27).

17 Irving Howe, 'Introduction', *Short Shorts: An Anthology of the Shortest Stories*, eds. Irving Howe and Ilana Wiener (New York: Bantam Books, 1983), pp. ix–xv (p. x).
18 See Nelles, 'Microfiction', p. 89.
19 Norman Friedman, 'What Makes a Short Story Short?', *Modern Fiction Studies*, 4.2 (1958), pp. 103–17 (p. 104).
20 Friedman, 'What Makes', p. 117.
21 Friedman, 'What Makes', p. 109.
22 See Frances Colpitt, *Minimal Art: The Critical Perspective* (Seattle: University of Washington Press, 1990), pp. 74–5; Friedman, 'What Makes', p. 115.
23 Friedman, 'What Makes', pp. 114–17.
24 See Colpitt, *Minimal Art*, pp. 75–8. For important discussions of scale in relation to literary genre and the world literature paradigm, see Nirvana Tanoukhi, 'The Scale of World Literature', *New Literary History*, 39.3 (2008), 599–617 (pp. 604–6; 612–14); Wai Chee Dimock, 'Genres as Fields of Knowledge', *PMLA*, 122.5 (2007), 1377–88 (pp. 1382–3) and Emily Apter, *Against World Literature: On the Politics of Untranslatability* (London; New York: Verso, 2013), pp. 39–43; 328–9.
25 Howe, 'Introduction', p. x.
26 Friedman, 'What Makes', p. 104.
27 David Herman, 'Storyworld', *Routledge Encyclopedia of Narrative Theory*, eds. David Herman, Manfred Jahn and Marie-Laure Ryan (London; New York: Routledge, 2005), pp. 569–70 (p. 570)
28 Nelles, 'Microfiction', p. 91.
29 See Nelles, 'Microfiction', pp. 88; 91.
30 Nelles, 'Microfiction', p. 93.
31 Immanuel Kant, *Critique of Judgment*, trans. Werner S. Pluhar (Indianapolis, IN; Cambridge, MA: Hackett, 1987), p. 98.
32 See Kant, *Critique*, p. 129; Edmund Burke, *A Philosophical Enquiry into the Origin of Our Ideas of the Sublime and Beautiful* (Oxford: Blackwell, 1987), p. 39.
33 Kant, *Critique*, p. 121.
34 See Jean-Francois Lyotard, 'The Sublime and the Avant-Garde', *The Inhuman: Reflections on Time*, trans. Geoffrey Bennington and Rachel Bowlby (Cambridge: Polity, 1991), pp. 98–9 (pp. 89–107).
35 Susan Stewart, *On Longing: Narratives of the Miniature, the Gigantic, the Souvenir, the Collection* (Durham, NC; London: Duke University Press, 1993), p. 75.
36 See Stewart, *On Longing*, pp. 37–9; 41–3.
37 Jean-Francois Lyotard, 'Presenting the Unpresentable: The Sublime', trans. Lisa Liebmann, *Artforum*, 20.8 (1982), 64–9 (p. 64).
38 Johnson in 'Afterwords', *Sudden Fiction*, eds. Shapard and Thomas, p. 232.
39 Baxter, 'Introduction', p. 22.
40 Nelles, 'Microfiction', p. 96.
41 Teju Cole, 'Seven Short Stories about Drones', *The New Inquiry*, 14 January 2013, http://thenewinquiry.com/blogs/dtake/seven-short-stories-about-drones/ [Accessed 2 June 2015].
42 Jonathan Kemp, 'L', *Twentysix* (Brighton; London: Myriad, 2011), p. 57

Microfiction

43 Kemp, 'L', pp. 57; 58. See also Nelles, 'Microfiction', p. 97.
44 See Royle, 'Quick Fiction', pp. 27–9.
45 Kemp, 'L', p. 57.
46 Kemp, 'L', p. 58.
47 Jeanette Winterson, 'The White Room', *Guardian*, 17 July 2004. www.theguardian.com/books/2004/jul/17/originalwriting.fiction1 [Accessed 2 June 2015].
48 See Chappell, Davis, Dybek and Kelly in 'Afterwords', *Sudden Fiction*, eds. Shapard and Thomas; Nelles, 'Microfiction', p. 90; Baxter, 'Introduction', pp. 20–1; 23.
49 H. E. Francis in 'Afterwords', *Sudden Fiction*, eds. Shapard and Thomas, p. 231.
50 Royle, 'Quick Fiction', p. 29.
51 Joy Williams in 'Afterwords', *Sudden Fiction*, eds. Shapard and Thomas, p. 257.
52 Simon Critchley, *Very Little ... Almost Nothing: Death, Philosophy, Literature* (London; New York: Routledge, 1997), p. 180.
53 Stewart, *On Longing*, p. 46.
54 Stewart, *On Longing*, pp. 67–8.
55 See Paul March-Russell, *The Short Story: An Introduction* (Edinburgh: Edinburgh University Press, 2009), pp. 9–11.
56 Stewart, *On Longing*, p. 38.
57 See Berjouhi Bowler, *The Word as Image* (London: Studio Vista, 1970), pp. 7–9.
58 Stewart, *On Longing*, p. 37.
59 John Perreault, 'Minimal Abstracts', *Minimal Art: A Critical Anthology*, ed. Gregory Battcock (New York: Dutton, 1968), pp. 256–62 (p. 260).
60 Cynthia Whitney Hallett, *Minimalism and the Short Story – Raymond Carver, Amy Hempel, and Mary Robison* (Lewiston, NY: Edwin Mellen, 1999), p. 11.
61 See Baxter, 'Introduction', p. 25; Nelles, 'Microfiction', p. 93; Howe, 'Introduction', p. x.
62 Jim Crace, '37', *The Devil's Larder* (London: Penguin, 2002), p. 112.
63 Howe, 'Introduction', p. xi.
64 Stewart, *On Longing*, p. 63.
65 Stewart, *On Longing*, p. 48.
66 See Heather McHugh, 'Broken English: What We Make of Fragments', *Broken English: Poetry and Partiality* (Middletown, CT: Wesleyan University Press, 1993), pp. 68–86 (p. 70).
67 Philippe Lacoue-Labarthe and Jean-Luc Nancy, *The Literary Absolute: The Theory of Literature in German Romanticism*, trans. Philip Barnard and Cheryl Lester (Albany: State University of New York Press, 1988), p. 42.
68 Friedrich Schlegel, Athenaeum Fragment 116, *Philosophical Fragments*, trans. Peter Firchow (Minneapolis; London: University of Minnesota Press, 1991), p. 32.
69 McHugh, 'Broken English', p. 69.
70 Schlegel, Athenaeum Fragment 206, *Philosophical Fragments*, p. 45.
71 March-Russell, *Short Story*, p. 167.
72 See Gitte Mose, 'Danish Short Shorts in the 1990s and the Jena-Romantic Fragments', *The Art of Brevity: Excursions in Short Fiction Theory and Analysis*, eds. Pet Winther, Jakob Lothe and Hans H. Skei (Columbia: University of South Carolina Press, 2004), pp. 81–95 (p. 87).

73 Lydia Davis, 'Honoring the Subjunctive', *The Collected Stories of Lydia Davis* (London; New York: Penguin, 2009), p. 377.
74 James Kelman, Agnes Owens and Alasdair Gray, *Lean Tales* (London: Vintage, 1995), p. 282.
75 Don Patterson, *The Blind Eye: A Book of Late Advice* (London: Faber, 2007), p. 35.
76 Patterson, *Blind Eye*, p. 59.
77 See Maurice Blanchot, 'The Athenaeum', *The Infinite Conversation*, trans. Susan Hanson (Minneapolis; London: University of Minnesota Press, 1993), pp. 351–9 (p. 356).
78 Schlegel, Athenaeum Fragment 51, *Philosophical Fragments*, p. 24.
79 Marshall McLuhan, *Understanding Media: The Extensions of Man* (London; New York: Routledge, 1964), pp. 8–9.
80 See Maurice Merleau-Ponty, *Phenomenology of Perception*, trans. Colin Smith (London; New York: Routledge, 2002), pp. 77–83.
81 Alain Robbe-Grillet, 'On Some Outdated Notions', *Snapshots and Towards a New Novel*, trans. Barbara Wright (London: Calder and Boyars, 1965), pp. 58–74 (p. 68).
82 Lev Manovich, *The Languages of New Media* (Cambridge, MA; London: MIT Press, 2001), p. 20.
83 See Nicholas Carr, *The Shallows* (New York and London: W. W. Norton, 2010), pp. 63–5; 90–1; N. Katherine Hayles, *How We Think: Digital Media and Contemporary Technogenesis* (Chicago; London: Chicago University Press, 2012), pp. 62–8.
84 Joe David Bellamy in 'Afterwords', *Sudden Fiction*, eds. Shapard and Thomas, p. 238.
85 Royle, 'Quick Fiction', p. 30.
86 Royle, 'Quick Fiction', p. 29.
87 Shapard, 'Introduction', *Sudden Fiction*, eds. Shapard and Thomas, p. xvi; see also Royle, 'Quick Fiction', p. 27.
88 Kelly in 'Afterwords', *Sudden Fiction*, eds. Shapard and Thomas, p. 241.
89 Roberts, 'Introduction', p. vii.

GUIDE TO FURTHER READING

Short story theory and genre criticism

Allen, Walter. *The Short Story in English*. Oxford: Clarendon Press, 1981.
Bonheim, Helmut. *The Narrative Modes: Techniques of the Short Story*. Cambridge, MA: Brewer, 1992.
Hanson, Clare (ed.). *Re-reading the Short Story*. Basingstoke: Macmillan, 1989.
Hanson, Clare. *Short Stories and Short Fiction, 1880–1980*. Basingstoke: Macmillan, 1985.
Lohafer, Susan. *Coming to Terms with the Short Story*. Baton Rouge: Louisiana State University Press, 1983.
Lohafer, Susan, and Jo Ellyn Clarey (eds.). *Short Story Theory at a Crossroads*. 1989; Baton Rouge: Louisiana State University Press, 1998.
March-Russell, Paul. *The Short Story: An Introduction*. Edinburgh: Edinburgh University Press, 2009.
May, Charles E. (ed.). *Short Story Theories*. Athens: Ohio University Press, 1976.
(ed.). *New Short Story Theories*. Athens: Ohio University Press, 1994.
The Short Story: The Reality of Artifice. 1995; London; New York: Routledge, 2002.
Shaw, Valerie. *The Short Story: A Critical Introduction*. 1983; London: Longman, 1995.
Winther, Pet, Jakob Lothe and Hans H. Skei (eds.). *The Art of Brevity: Excursions in Short Fiction Theory and Analysis*. Columbia: University of South Carolina Press, 2004.

Short story criticism by practitioners

Bates, H. E. *The Modern Short Story: A Critical Survey*. 1941; Boston, MA: The Writer, 1965.
Lounsberry, Barbara, Susan Lohafer, Mary Rohrberger, Stephen Pett and R. C. Feddersen (eds.). *The Tales We Tell: Perspectives on the Short Story*. Westport, CO: Greenwood, 1998.
May, Charles E. (ed.). *Short Story Theories*. Athens: Ohio University Press, 1976.
O'Connor, Frank. *The Lonely Voice: A Study of the Short Story*. 1963; Hoboken, NJ: Melville House, 2004.
Pritchett, V. S. *The Tale Bearers: Essays on English, American and Other Writers*. London: Chatto & Windus, 1980.

GUIDE TO FURTHER READING

Regionally or nationally specific studies of the short story

Awadalla, Maggie, and Paul March-Russell (eds.). *The Postcolonial Short Story: Contemporary Essays*. Basingstoke: Palgrave Macmillan, 2013.
D'Hoker, Elke, and Stephanie Eggermont (eds.). *The Irish Short Story: Traditions and Trends*. Bern: Peter Lang, 2015.
Ingram, Heather. *A History of the Irish Short Story*. Cambridge: Cambridge University Press, 2009.
Malcolm, Cheryl Alexander, and David Malcolm (eds.). *A Companion to the British and Irish Short Story*. Oxford: Wiley-Blackwell, 2008.

Historical and period-specific studies of the short story

Ashley, Michael. *The Age of the Storytellers: British Popular Fiction Magazines, 1880–1950*. London: British Library and Oak Knoll Press, 2006.
Baldwin, Dean. *Art and Commerce in the British Short Story, 1880–1950*. London: Pickering & Chatto, 2013.
Einhaus, Ann-Marie. *The Short Story and the First World War*. Cambridge: Cambridge University Press, 2013.
Hanson, Clare. *Short Stories and Short Fiction, 1880–1980*. Basingstoke: Macmillan, 1985.
Head, Dominic. *The Modernist Short Story: A Study in Theory and Practice*. Cambridge: Cambridge University Press, 1992.
  (ed.). *The Cambridge History of the Short Story in English*. Cambridge: Cambridge University Press, 2016.
Hunter, Adrian. *The Cambridge Introduction to the Short Story in English*. Cambridge: Cambridge University Press, 2007.
Iftekharrudin, Farhat, Joseph Boyden, Joseph Longo and Mary Rohrberger (eds.). *Postmodern Approaches to the Short Story*. Westport, CT: Praeger, 2003.
Killick, Tim. *British Short Fiction in the Early Nineteenth Century: The Rise of the Tale*. Farnham: Ashgate, 2008.
Korte, Barbara. *The Short Story in Britain: A Historical Sketch and Anthology*. Tübingen: Francke, 2003.
Liggins, Emma, Andrew Maunder and Ruth Robbins. *The British Short Story*. Basingstoke: Palgrave Macmillan, 2010.
Orel, Harold. *The Victorian Short Story: Development and Triumph of a Literary Genre*. Cambridge: Cambridge University Press, 1986.
Sacido, Jorge (ed.). *Modernism, Postmodernism and the Short Story in English*. Amsterdam; New York: Rodopi, 2012.

Subgenre-based criticism

Ashley, Mike. *Gateways to Forever: The Story of the Science Fiction Magazines from 1970 to 1980*. Liverpool: Liverpool University Press, 2007.
  Transformations: The History of the Science-fiction Magazines from 1950 to 1970. Liverpool: Liverpool University Press, 2005.
Ermida, Isabel. *The Language of Comic Narratives: Humor Construction in Short Stories*. Berlin; New York: de Gruyter, 2008.

Hallett, Cynthia Whitney. *Minimalism and the Short Story: Raymond Carver, Amy Hempel, and Mary Robison*. Lewiston, NY: Edwin Mellen, 1999.
Symons, Julian. *Bloody Murder: From the Detective Story to the Crime Novel*. London: Faber, 1972.

Practice-based criticism and writing manuals

Bailey, Tom (ed.), *On Writing Short Stories*. Oxford: Oxford University Press, 2000.
Cox, Ailsa (ed.). *Teaching the Short Story*. Basingstoke: Palgrave Macmillan, 2011.
Cox, Ailsa. *Writing Short Stories: A Routledge Writer's Guide*. London; New York: Routledge, 2005.
Lewis, Carolyn. *The Short Story: A Guide to Writing Short Stories*. Bristol: SilverWood, 2012.
Lounsberry, Barbara, Susan Lohafer, Mary Rohrberger, Stephen Pett and R. C. Feddersen (eds.). *The Tales We Tell: Perspectives on the Short Story*. Westport, CT: Greenwood, 1998.

INDEX

3:AM (magazine), 24

Aboriginal Science Fiction, 197
Academy, The, 15
Ackroyd, Peter, 183
Adlard, Mark, 195
Aesop, 92
 Fables, 94
affect, 28, 33, 175, 203, 211, 215
Ahmed, Rehana, xxiii, 52
Alderman, Naomi, 22
Aldiss, Brian W., 187, 192, 194, 195, 196
Allan, Nina, 19, 198, 199
Allen, Grant, 188
Amaranth, 197
Amazing Stories, xviii, 190, 191
Ambit, 24, 193
Amis, Kingsley, 135
Amis, Martin, 134, 135
Andrews, C. C., 150
anecdote, 75, 82, 94, 134, 202, 212, 214
Anniversary, The, 82
annuals, 9, 77, 78, 79, 80, 81, 82, 149, 177, 188
 annual story, 81, 82
anti-climax, 146
Apartheid, 61, 62
aphorism, 202, 208, 214
apps, 23, 24. See also digital media
Arabian Nights, The, 88, 94
Aristotle, 148, 154
Arnold, Frank Edward, 191
artistry, 16, 66
Asham Trust, 20
Astounding Stories, 187, 191, 192
Atkinson, Kate, 20
audience, 6, 7, 22, 23, 74, 78, 83, 101, 103, 109, 112, 140, 147
Aumonier, Stacy, xviii, 102, 105, 106, 150

Austen, Jane, 156
Australia, 192
avant-garde, 24, 97, 101, 103, 130, 182, 203, 211. See also coterie

Back Brain Recluse, 197
Bailey, H. C., 102
Bailey, Hilary, 193–94
Baileys Women's Prize for Fiction, 19. See also literary prizes
Bakhtin, M. M., 59, 146
Ballard, J. G., xxi, 131, 132, 134, 137, 192, 193, 194, 195, 196, 204, 211, 213
Banks, Iain M., 199
Bardwell, Leland, 136
Baring, Maurice, 108
Barker, A. L., xx, 123–24
Barker, Pat, xxii, 38
Barrett, Colin, 129
Barry, Kevin, 19, 129, 139, 145, 148
Barstow, Stan, 35–36, 37, 38
Barth, John, 208, 215
Barthelme, Donald, 212
Barthes, Roland, 29, 130
Bates, H. E., 2, 107, 115, 116, 121, 175
Baxter, Stephen, 197, 198
Bayley, Barrington, 192, 193, 194, 195, 196
BBC National Short Story Award, xxiii, 20, 21, 25, 128. See also Literary prizes
Beattie, Ann, 204, 212
Beckett, Chris, 19, 199
Beckett, Mary, 136
Beckett, Samuel, xxi, 66–67, 125, 203, 204, 208, 211, 213, 215
Beerbohm, Max, 154
Beith, John Hay, 152
Bellerby, Frances, 123
Benjamin, Walter, 214

INDEX

Bennett, Arnold, 34, 151
Benson, E. F., 153, 154
Berger, John, xxi, 134
Bergson, Henri, 35
Berridge, Elizabeth, 116, 119–20
Best American Short Stories, 25
Bibesco, Elizabeth, xviii, 102, 108, 109, 111
Bierce, Ambrose, 2
Billingham, Mark, 168, 169
Birmingham, George C., 150
Black Static, 197
Blackwood's Edinburgh Magazine, xvi, 8, 78, 79, 82, 179, 187. See also *Blackwood's Magazine*
Blackwood's Magazine, xvii, xxi, 74, 79, 101, 105, 149, 152. See also *Blackwood's Edinburgh Magazine*
Blanchot, Maurice, 214
Blast, xviii, 15, 148
blogs, 205, 214, 216
Bloom, Ursula, 150
Boccaccio, Giovanni, 92
Bonfiglioli, Kyril, 193, 194
Bookseller, The, 17
Borges, Jorge Luis, 170, 193, 203, 204, 208, 209
Bounds, Sydney J., 194
Bowen, Elizabeth, xx, 1, 58, 115–16, 117, 122, 140
Bowles, Caroline, 79
Boyd, William, 138
Boylan, Clare, 136
Boys Own Magazine, The, 150
Bradbury, Malcolm, xxii, 134, 135
Braddon, Mary Elizabeth, 92, 181
Brautigan, Richard, 213
Bray, Carys, 20, 24
Bridport Prize, xxi, xxiii, 20. See also literary prizes
British Science Fiction Association Award, 199. See also literary prizes
Brittain, Vera, 109, 110
Britton, David, 194
Brontë, Charlotte, 89, 124
Brontë sisters, the, 180
Brooke, Keith, 197
Broughton, Rhoda, 88
Brown, Eric, 197, 198
Browne, Frances, 92
Brunner, John, 195
Buchan, John, 145, 153–54
Bukowski, Charles, 215
Bulmer, Kenneth, 192, 194

Bulwer-Lytton, Edward, 180
Burke, Edmund, 30, 176
Burnside, John, 19
Burrage, A. M., 153
Burroughs, William S., 193, 196
Burton, William E., 160–61
Butler, Robert Olen, 210
Butterworth, Michael, 194
Byatt, A. S., 138–39
Byrne, Eugene, 197
Byron, George Gordon, Lord, 82

Cage, John, 24, 213
Calder, Richard, 197
Campbell, John W., 187, 191
canon, the, 3, 5–6, 20, 88, 104
Canterbury Tales, The, 94
Capek, Karel, 187
Captain, The, 101, 150
Carnell, John, 191–2, 193, 194–5
Carroll, Lewis, 92
Carter, Angela, xxi, 131–2, 136, 183–4, 196, 204, 209, 210
Carver, Raymond, xxi, 21, 22, 203, 204, 212, 215
Castell, Daphne, 193, 194
Chaplin, Sid, xx, 36
Charnock, Graham, 194
Chekhov, Anton, 2, 87, 102, 108, 203, 208, 212, 214
Chesney, George Tomkyns, 188
Chesterton, G. K., 164, 165, 166, 173, 174
Christian Keepsake, The, 80
Christie, Agatha, 165–6, 167, 168
Chums, 101
Civil and Military Gazette, The, 44
Cixous, Hélène, 216
Clarke, Arthur C., 187, 191, 192, 199
Cleaver, Hylton, 153
Clute, John, 196
Cockcroft, W. P., 191
Coetzee, J. M., 203
Cole, Teju, xxiii, 209
Coleridge, Samuel Taylor, 177
Collier's Magazine, xvii, xx, 4, 101
Collins, Wilkie, 88, 161–2
Compton, D. G., 195
Coney, Michael, 195
Conlon, Evelyn, 136
Conrad, Joseph, xvii, 45–6, 52, 97, 98, 101, 105
Cooper, Edmund, 195
Coover, Robert, 204

226

INDEX

Coppard, A. E., 34
Cornhill Magazine, The, xvi, xix, xx, xxi, 105, 116, 190
Costa Short Story Award, xxiii, 20, 22, 128. *See also* literary prizes
Costello, Mary, 129
coterie, 106, 112
Cowper, Richard, 195, 197
Crace, Jim, 209, 212–13
Crackanthorpe, Hubert, xvii, 33
Crackanthorpe's, 35
craft versus art, 102, 106, 108
Crane, Stephen, 2
Crispin, Edmund, xxi, 168
Criterion, The, xviii, xix, 116
Crowther, Peter, 19, 197–98
Cunningham, Allan, 82–83
cyberpunk, 197

Dahl, Roald, 122, 168
Daly, Ita, 136
Davidson, Lionel, 169
Davin, Dan, 116
Davis, Julia, 195
Davis, Lydia, 17, 212, 214
de la Mare, Walter, 101, 108
De Quincey, Thomas, 80, 88
Decameron, The, 94
Delafield, E. M., 153, 155
Dexter, Colin, 168
Dhuibhne, Éilís Ní, 136
Dickens, Charles, xvi, 30–31, 32, 87, 88, 89, 90–91, 92–94, 145, 160, 161, 175, 178, 180, 181–82, 188, 199, 215
digital media, 9, 24, 205, 212, 215, 216
Disch, Thomas, 194
Dorcey, Mary, 136
Doyle, Arthur Conan, 96, 101, 105, 163–64, 165, 166, 168
Dunn, Nell, xxi, 35, 37–38
Dunn, Philip, 195
Durrell, Gerald, 153
Durrell, Lawrence, xx, 153
Dyson, Jeremy, 19

Edge Hill Prize, xxiii, 18, 19, 20. *See also* literary prizes
Edginton, May, 102, 108, 109, 111, 150
Edwards, Amelia, 180, 181
Edwards, Ken, 19
Eggers, Dave, 21, 208, 212
Eliot, George, 87, 94–95

Eliot, T. S., 51
Ellery Queen's Mystery Magazine, xix, 167
Ellis, Bret Easton, 212
Elphinstone, Margaret, 198
England, George Allan, 190
English Review, The, xvii, xix, 105
English Story, 116, 117
Enright, Anne, 128, 140
ephemerality, 17, 107
epigram, 147, 202, 214
Evening News, The, 107
exemplum, 202
exotic story, 43
Extro Science Fiction, 197

fable, 74, 94, 106, 202, 209
Fantasy and Science Fiction, Magazine of, xx, 192, 195, 196
Fearn, John Russell, 191, 192
feminism, 7, 135, 136, 156–57, 182
Ferguson, Neil, 197
Ferguson, Rachel, 154
fin de siècle, 96, 97, 147, 152, 173, 182, 183
Finlay, Ian Hamilton, 215
First World War, xviii, 101, 106, 107, 108, 109, 152, 154, 164, 165, 188
flash fiction, xxiii, 24, 202, 205, 215, 216
Flash: The International Short-Short Story Magazine, xxiii, 20
Flying Officer 'X'. *See* Bates, H. E.
Folio Prize, 17. *See also* literary prizes
folk tale, 82
Ford, Richard, 212
formula, 4, 5, 6, 108, 115, 129, 159, 165, 166, 187
formulaic, 153
Forrester, Andrew, Jr., 162, 163. *See* Ware, James Redding
Fowles, John, 170
fragment, 78, 80, 132, 202, 203, 204, 208, 212, 213–14
Freud, Sigmund, 146, 148, 179, 183

Gaiety, 150
Gaiman, Neil, 155, 169
Galaxy, 192
Galsworthy, John, 34
Galt, John, xvi, 79–80, 90
Garnett, David S., 195, 198
Gaskell, Elizabeth, 31, 32, 88, 175
Gate, The, 197
gender, 7, 8, 58, 62, 65, 67, 101, 109, 155, 163, 177, 210

genre fiction, 3, 19, 24, 200
Gentle, Mary, 198
Gentleman's Magazine, The, xv, xvii, 78, 160
Gilbert, Anthony, 168
Gilbert, Zoe, 22
Gillings, Walter, 191
Gissing, George, 28, 31–32, 33, 38
Gogol, Nikolai Vasilievich, 2
Gordimer, Nadine, xx, 204
Graham's Magazine, 159
Granta, 22
Gray, Alasdair, 134–35, 210, 214
Green, Dominic, 197
Greene, Graham, 118, 121, 207
Greenland, Colin, 193, 196
Grenfell, Joyce, 155–56
Gridban, Volsted, 192. See also Fearn, John Russell
Griffith, Nicola, 197
Guthrie, Allan, 169

Hadley, Tessa, 21
Hall, Austin, 190
Hall, Graham, 194
Hall, Sarah, 18, 21, 22
Hambledon, Phyllis, 150
Hamburger, Michael, 194
Hamilton, Peter F., 192, 197
Hanson, Maurice K., 191
Happy Magazine, The, xviii, xix, 150
Hardy, Thomas, 87
Harris, Joanne, 16
Harris, John Beynon, 190
Harris-Burland, J. B., 189
Harrison, M. John, 193, 195, 196
Harte, Bret, 103
Hawthorne, Nathaniel, xvi, 2, 17
Hay, Ian. See Beith, John Hay
Hayward, William Stephens, 163
Hazlitt, William, 80
Hemingway, Ernest, 87, 203, 207, 212, 215
Hempel, Amy, 204, 212
Hendry, J. F., 123
Henry, O., 103
Henty, G. A., 43, 44
Herbert, A. P., 147, 148
Hoffmann, E. T. A., 175, 177
Hogg, James, 73, 74, 82, 83, 89
Holdstock, Robert, 195, 198
homosexuality, xxi, 8, 63, 209

Honeyman, William, 163. See also McGovan, James
Hook, Theodore, 75
Horizon, xix, xx, 117
Howard, Keble, 101
Hugo Award for Best Science Fiction Story, 191, 199. See also literary prizes
Hunt, Leigh, 80
Hutchinson, Dave, 199
Huxley, Aldous, 108
Huxley, Julian, 190

impressionism, 89, 101, 103, 117, 203, 215
Infinity Science Fiction, 191
Ings, Simon D., 197
Internet, the, 6, 9, 10, 24, 25, 129
Interzone, xxi, 196–97, 198, 199
Irving, Washington, xvi, 2, 75
Ishiguro, Kazuo, xxiii, 137–38, 204
Islam, Manzu, xxii, 51

Jacobs, W. W., 102, 152
Jakubowski, Maxim, xxiii, 168, 194
James, Graham, 196
James, Henry, xvii, 59, 87, 97, 108
James, Laurence, 195
James, M. R., 59, 176, 182–83
James, P. D., 168
James, Peter, 19
Jarry, Alfred, 193
Jena Romantics, the, 203, 214
Jerome, Jerome K., 152
Jewsbury, Geraldine, 92
Jewsbury, Maria Jane, 81
Johnson, Adam, 22
Johnson, B. S., 131, 134, 208
Jolly Magazine, The, 150
Jones, Gwyneth, 196, 197, 198
Jones, Langdon, 193, 194
Jones, R. Glyn, 194
Josipovici, Gabriel, xxi, 132, 133, 215
Joyce, Graham, 197, 198
Joyce, James, xviii, 35, 57–58, 87, 103, 108, 109–10, 133, 179

Kafka, Franz, 140, 203
Kant, Immanuel, 148
Kapp, Colin, 194
Kavan, Anna, 124
Kaveney, Roz, 196
Kay, Jackie, xxiii, 19, 48–49, 51, 157
Keats, John, 80, 189
Keegan, Claire, 19

INDEX

Keepsake, The, 79, 81, 177, 188
Kelly, Maeve, 136
Kelman, James, 38–39, 58, 129
Kemp, Jonathan, 210, 211
Kent, Michael, 150
Kierkegaard, Søren, 214
Kilworth, Garry, 195, 197
King, Stephen, 183
Kipling, Rudyard, xvii, 32, 43–45, 46, 52, 59, 62–63, 87, 101, 103, 145, 151, 174, 189–90
Kitschies, the, 24. *See also* literary prizes
Kureishi, Hanif, xxii, 49, 50–51

Lady's Magazine, The, 75
Lamb, Charles, 78, 80, 81
Lambert, Zoe, 19–20
Landon, Letitia Elizabeth, 81
Lane, Allen, 117
Lasdun, James, 22
Lavin, Mary, 136
Lawrence, D. H., xix, 35, 38, 101, 105, 106
Le Fanu, Sheridan, 88, 92, 177, 178–80
Lee, Tanith, 198
Lee, Vernon, xvii, 182
Lehmann, John, 117
Lem, Stanisław, 195
lesbianism, 136, 157, 169
Levy, Andrea, 52
Levy, Deborah, 129, 137, 201
Lewis, Alun, xix, 120–21
Lin, Tao, 203
literary prizes, 17, 19, 20, 21, 22, 24, 25
Literary Souvenir, The, 80, 81
Lively, Penelope, 156
Lloyd, Tom, 19
Lodge, David, 132–33, 135, 139
London Magazine, The, xv, xvi, 8, 78, 80, 82, 83, 190
Lovecraft, H. P., 183
Lovegrove, James, 198
Lunan, Duncan, 195
Lyons, Neil, 34–35
Lyotard, Jean-François, 131, 135, 137, 204, 208

Macaulay, Rose, 119, 125
MacBeth, George, 194
MacBride, Stuart, 169
Machen, Arthur, 107, 183
Mackelworth, R. W., 193
Maclaren-Ross, Julian, xx, 117, 118

MacLaverty, Bernard, xxii, 58, 129, 146
MacLeod, Ian R., 197, 198
MacLeod, Ken, 198, 199
Mademoiselle, 4
magazine fiction, 9, 29, 82, 102, 103, 105, 106, 107, 111, 150
Maitland, Sarah, 22
Malouf, David, 204
Man Booker Prize, 17, 19. *See also* literary prizes
Mansfield, Katherine, xvii, xviii, 15–16, 59, 87, 101, 102, 103, 108, 109, 110, 111, 139, 151
Mantel, Hilary, xxiii, 16
Markham, E. A., 48
Mars-Jones, Adam, 133
Martineau, Harriet, xvi, 89
Mason, Bobbie Ann, 212
Mason, Douglas R., 194. *See also* Rankine, John
Masson, David I., 194, 195
Matthews, Brander, xvii, 15, 88
Maturin, Charles Robert, 77–78
Maugham, W. Somerset, 43, 87, 103
Maupassant, Guy de, 2, 87
McAuley, Paul, 197, 198
McCaffery, Steve, 213
McCann, Colum, 129
McClure's, 189
McDermid, Val, 168, 169
McDonald, Ian, 197, 198
McEwan, Ian, xxi, 135–36, 204
McGahern, John, 129
McGovan, James, 163, 164. *See also* Honeyman, William
McGregor, Jon, 21
McGuinness, Frank, 139
McLevy, James, 163, 164
McNeile, H. C., 152. *See also* Sapper
McSweeney's, xxii, 8, 21
Meredith, George, 101
Merleau-Ponty, Maurice, 215
Merry Magazine, The, 150
metafiction, 67, 132–33, 138, 139, 184, 204
Miéville, China, xxiii, 66, 138, 139, 199
Million: The Magazine of Popular Fiction, 197
miniature, 201, 202, 203, 204, 205, 208, 210, 211–13
Mitchell, David, 18, 138, 205
Mitchison, Naomi, 198
Mitford, Mary Russell, xvi, 75–76

INDEX

Modern Reading, 116
modernism, 28, 35, 102–04, 125, 130, 179
Montague, 102
Moorcock, Michael, xxii, 65–66, 192, 193, 194
Moore, Thomas, 78
moral fable, 74
moral tale, 29–30, 93
More, Hannah, 30, 32
Morgan, Chris, 195
Morrison, Arthur, xvii, 28, 31–33, 34, 35, 38, 39, 164–65
Mort, Graham, 19
Mosse, Kate, 16
Munro, Alice, 17, 204
Munro, Hector Hugh, 154

National Flash-Fiction Day, 205, 209
National Flash-Fiction Day, xxiii
National Observer, The, 174
naturalism, 28, 32, 33, 87, 98
Nebula Award, 193, 199. *See also* literary prizes
Nebula Science Fiction, 192
Nesbit, Edith, 182
New Criticism, 4, 7, 104
New Monthly Magazine and Literary Journal, The, xvi, 75, 78, 149
New Statesman and Nation, 115
New Stories, 116
New Woman, 152, 155, 182
New Worlds, xix, 191, 192, 193, 194, 195, 196, 197, 198
New Writing, xix, 117
New Writing and Daylight, 125
New Yorker, The, xviii, 4, 22, 204
Newgate Calendar, The, xv, 160
Newland, Courttia, 26, 49
Newman, Kim, 197, 198
Nietzsche, Friedrich, 28, 214
Nobel Prize for Literature, xvii, xxi, 17, 153. *See also* literary prizes
Noon, Jeff, 24, 199
Northwest Short Story Network, 20
Novae Terrae, xix, 191. *See also* New Worlds
novel, 5, 6, 8, 9, 10, 16, 17–18, 19, 22, 56, 59, 60, 75, 76–77, 78, 87, 88, 89–96, 98, 103, 115, 128, 129, 139, 140, 145, 146, 149, 159, 165–66, 168, 169, 170, 173, 174, 175, 176, 177, 188, 199, 205
three-decker novel, 2, 9, 29, 76, 77, 173, 174, 177, 179

novelette, 149, 187
novella, 5, 8, 75, 187, 197, 213

Ó Faoláin, Seán, 58, 129
O'Brien, Edna, 129, 136
O'Brien, Flann, 134
O'Connor, Frank, xxi, 22, 56, 57, 58–59, 153
Odyssey (magazine), 197
Oliphant, Margaret, 88
Orange Prize for Fiction, 19. *See also* literary prizes
Orwell, George, xx, 95, 115–16, 168
Overbury, Thomas, xv, 202
Oyeyemi, Helen, 22

Pain, Barry, 152
Pan (magazine), 150
Pandit, Shereen, 138
Panter-Downes, Mollie, 59
parable, 31, 45, 202, 203, 212, 214
Paraxis, 24
Pater, Walter, 96
Patterson, Don, 214
Penguin New Writing, xx, 117
Perrin, Alice, 44
Pessoa, Fernando, 214
Peters, Ellis, 168
Philips, Jayne Anne, 212
Pioneer, The, 44
Pirkis, C. L., 164
Platt, Charles, 194, 197
plotlessness, 1, 37, 38, 105
Poe, Edgar Allan, xvi, 2, 4, 15, 17, 21, 56, 73, 74, 79, 87, 88, 90, 91, 96, 159–60, 161–62, 163, 168, 169, 175, 190
postcolonialism, 3, 8, 9, 21, 42–43, 47, 48
postmodernism, 3, 9, 130–35, 137–39, 204
Postscripts, 197–98
Power, Chris, 17, 18
Pragnell, Festus, 191
Pratchett, Terry, 155
Price, Evadne, 150
Priest, Christopher, 194, 195
Pringle, David, 196, 197
Pritchett, V. S., 59, 123, 129, 175, 177
prose poem, 1, 202
Prospect Magazine, 128
proverb, 202, 214
Pugh, Edwin, 151
Pym, Barbara, 156

230

INDEX

Quarles, Francis, xv, 202
quick fiction, 202, 211
Quiller-Couch, Arthur T., 101
Quintilian, 148

racism, 7, 47, 50, 51, 138
Radcliffe, Ann, 176–77, 178, 179, 183
Rankin, Ian, xxiii, 168, 169
Rankine, John, 194. *See also* Mason, Douglas R.
Redgrove, Peter, 194
regional tale, 74
Rendell, Ruth, 168
Reynolds, Alistair, 197, 198
Rhys, Jean, xxi, 62, 63, 129
Rhythm, xvii, 15
Rice, Anne, 183
Ridgway, Keith, xxiii, 63–64
Robbe-Grillet, Alain, 203, 204, 215
Roberts, Adam, 19, 198, 199
Roberts, Keith, 194, 195
Roberts, Michèle, xxiii, 19, 63, 64–65, 129, 201
Robison, Mary, 204, 212, 213
Rogers, Jane, 21
Royle, Nicholas, 25, 170, 197, 200, 205, 211, 216
Rushdie, Salman, xxii, 49–50, 51, 135, 138
Russ, Joanna, 198
Russell, Eric Frank, 191
Russell, Leonard, 154
Russell, William, 161
Russian formalism, 19

Saki, 145, 146, 154. *See also* Munro, Hector Hugh
Sallis, James, 194
Sansom, William, xx, 122, 123
Sapper, 152. *See also* McNeile, H. C.
Saturday Evening Post, The, 4
Saunders, George, 17, 21
Save Our Short Story campaign, xxiii, 25
Savoy, The, xvii, 15
Saxton, Josephine, 195, 198
Sayers, Dorothy L., 167
Schlegel, Friedrich, 208
Schopenhauer, Arthur, 214
Science Fantasy, 191, 192, 193
Science Fiction Monthly, xxi, 195
Scoops, 191
Scott, Sir Walter, 74, 76–77, 79, 81, 89, 175–76, 177–78, 179, 182

Scribner's Magazine, 189
Second World War, xix, xx, 35, 47, 51, 58, 115, 118, 149, 153, 167
Self, Will, 138
Sélincourt, Hugh de, 153
Selvon, Samuel, xx, 47, 51
sexism, 19, 135, 196
SF Impulse, 193
SF Nexus, 197
Shaw, Bob, 192, 195
Sheldon, Raccoona, 198
Shelley, Mary, 81–82, 89, 139, 177, 187–88
Shelley, Percy Bysshe, 177, 188
Short story, renaissance of, 16, 17, 18
short-short story, 202, 206
Shriver, Lionel, 21, 22
Sieveking, L. de Giberne, 189
Sillitoe, Alan, xxi, 33, 35, 37, 38
Simpson, Helen, 156
Simpson, Rin, 207
sketch, 8, 15, 30, 74, 75–76, 81, 82, 89–91, 99, 101, 103, 115, 117, 202, 215, 216
 psychological sketch, 1, 112
Sketch (magazine), 166, 167
Sladek, John, 194
slice-of-life, 28
Small Wonder festival, xxiii, 20, 128
Smith, Ali, 18, 137, 139, 140, 156–57
Smith, E. E. 'Doc', 187
Smith, Horace, 75, 78
Smith, Michael Marshall, 198
Smith, Zadie, 22, 138
social media, 10, 23, 24, 129, 205, 216
Southey, Robert, 177
Spark, Muriel, 47, 129, 204
Spectator, The, xv, 78
Spectrum SF, 197
Spender, Stephen, 115, 117
Stableford, Brian, 195, 197
Stead, C. K., 204
Steel, Flora Annie, 44
Stein, Gertrude, xviii, 203, 210, 213
Stephenson, Andrew, 195
Sterling, Bruce, 197
Stevenson, Robert Louis, xvii, 96, 101, 153, 181, 183
 New Arabian Nights, 96
Stewart, David, 79
Stoker, Bram, 139, 182
Strand Magazine, The, xvii, xx, 101, 104, 105, 106, 164, 167, 188

231

INDEX

Stranger, Ralph, 191
Strindberg, August, 214
Stross, Charles, 197
Structo, 24
Sunday Times EFG Short Story Award, xxiii, 20, 22, 128. *See also* literary prizes
Sunny Magazine, The, 150
Surtees, R. S., 88
Swinburne, Algernon, 96
Symons, Julian, xxii, 168

tableau, 202
tall story, 146
'Tartan Noir', 169
Taylor, Elizabeth, 120
Telegraph, The, 17
temperance tract, 29
Temple, William F., 191
Temple Bar, The, 177
Thackeray, William Makepeace, 75, 88, 89, 175
Third Alternative, The, 197
Thomas, D. M., 194
Times, The, 108
Times Literary Supplement, 129
Tlali, Miriam, xxii, 58, 61–62
Tóibín, Colm, 19
Townend, William, 105
Townsend Warner, Sylvia, 118–19, 120
Tremain, Rose, 22
Trevor, William, 129, 130
TriQuarterly, 204
Trollope, Anthony, 15, 88, 89, 91, 92
Tuttle, Lisa, 198
Twain, Mark, 146, 147, 148
Twitter, 24, 138, 205, 209, 216. *See also* social media

unity of effect, 4, 73, 87, 96, 175

Vachell, Horace Annesley, 153
Vargo Statten Science Fiction Magazine, 192

Verne, Jules, 187, 190
Vickers, Roy, 167–68
Vidocq, François Eugène, 160
vignette, 188, 202

Wallace, David Foster, 21
Walpole, Hugh, 152
Ware, James Redding, 162–63
Warwick Review, The, 24
Watson, Ian, 195, 197
Waugh, Evelyn, 154–55
Weldon, Fay, 132, 136, 156
Wells, Angus, 195
Wells, H. G., xvii, 34, 96, 97–98, 101, 103, 174, 176, 187, 189, 190
Welsh, Irvine, xxii, 39
Wertenbaker, G. Peyton, 190
West, Rebecca, 108
Whates, Ian, 198, 199
White, Joseph Blanco, 81
White, Patrick, xxii, 211, 215
Wilde, Oscar, 59, 182, 183, 214
Wilks, Christine, 212
Williams, Eric C., 191
Williams, Liz, 197
Wilson, Angus, 124–25
Wilson, D. W., 22
Windsor Magazine, The, xvii, xix, 152, 189
Winterson, Jeanette, 203, 211
Wodehouse, P. G., xviii, 105, 106, 146, 149–50
Wolff, Tobias, 204, 212
Wonder Stories, 191
Woolf, Virginia, 34, 103, 139, 203, 215
Wordsworth, William, 79, 80, 177
Wyndham, John, 187, 190, 191, 192

Yale Review, The, 190
Yates, Dornford, 146, 152–53
Yellow Book, The, xvii, 15

Zola, Emile, 32, 98
Zoline, Pamela, 194, 198

Cambridge Companions to...

AUTHORS

Edward Albee edited by Stephen J. Bottoms
Margaret Atwood edited by Coral Ann Howells
W. H. Auden edited by Stan Smith
Jane Austen edited by Edward Copeland and Juliet McMaster (second edition)
James Baldwin edited by Michele Elam
Beckett edited by John Pilling
Bede edited by Scott DeGregorio
Aphra Behn edited by Derek Hughes and Janet Todd
Walter Benjamin edited by David S. Ferris
William Blake edited by Morris Eaves
Boccaccio edited by Guyda Armstrong, Rhiannon Daniels and Stephen J. Milner
Jorge Luis Borges edited by Edwin Williamson
Brecht edited by Peter Thomson and Glendyr Sacks (second edition)
The Brontës edited by Heather Glen
Bunyan edited by Anne Dunan-Page
Frances Burney edited by Peter Sabor
Byron edited by Drummond Bone
Albert Camus edited by Edward J. Hughes
Willa Cather edited by Marilee Lindemann
Cervantes edited by Anthony J. Cascardi
Chaucer edited by Piero Boitani and Jill Mann (second edition)
Chekhov edited by Vera Gottlieb and Paul Allain
Kate Chopin edited by Janet Beer
Caryl Churchill edited by Elaine Aston and Elin Diamond
Cicero edited by Catherine Steel
Coleridge edited by Lucy Newlyn
Wilkie Collins edited by Jenny Bourne Taylor
Joseph Conrad edited by J. H. Stape
H. D. edited by Nephie J. Christodoulides and Polina Mackay
Dante edited by Rachel Jacoff (second edition)
Daniel Defoe edited by John Richetti
Don DeLillo edited by John N. Duvall
Charles Dickens edited by John O. Jordan
Emily Dickinson edited by Wendy Martin
John Donne edited by Achsah Guibbory
Dostoevskii edited by W. J. Leatherbarrow
Theodore Dreiser edited by Leonard Cassuto and Claire Virginia Eby
John Dryden edited by Steven N. Zwicker
W. E. B. Du Bois edited by Shamoon Zamir
George Eliot edited by George Levine
T. S. Eliot edited by A. David Moody
Ralph Ellison edited by Ross Posnock
Ralph Waldo Emerson edited by Joel Porte and Saundra Morris
William Faulkner edited by Philip M. Weinstein
Henry Fielding edited by Claude Rawson
F. Scott Fitzgerald edited by Ruth Prigozy
Flaubert edited by Timothy Unwin
E. M. Forster edited by David Bradshaw
Benjamin Franklin edited by Carla Mulford
Brian Friel edited by Anthony Roche
Robert Frost edited by Robert Faggen
Gabriel García Márquez edited by Philip Swanson
Elizabeth Gaskell edited by Jill L. Matus
Goethe edited by Lesley Sharpe
Günter Grass edited by Stuart Taberner
Thomas Hardy edited by Dale Kramer
David Hare edited by Richard Boon
Nathaniel Hawthorne edited by Richard Millington
Seamus Heaney edited by Bernard O'Donoghue
Ernest Hemingway edited by Scott Donaldson
Homer edited by Robert Fowler
Horace edited by Stephen Harrison
Ted Hughes edited by Terry Gifford

Ibsen edited by James McFarlane
Henry James edited by Jonathan Freedman
Samuel Johnson edited by Greg Clingham
Ben Jonson edited by Richard Harp and Stanley Stewart
James Joyce edited by Derek Attridge (second edition)
Kafka edited by Julian Preece
Keats edited by Susan J. Wolfson
Rudyard Kipling edited by Howard J. Booth
Lacan edited by Jean-Michel Rabaté
D. H. Lawrence edited by Anne Fernihough
Primo Levi edited by Robert Gordon
Lucretius edited by Stuart Gillespie and Philip Hardie
Machiavelli edited by John M. Najemy
David Mamet edited by Christopher Bigsby
Nelson Mandela edited by Rita Barnard
Thomas Mann edited by Ritchie Robertson
Christopher Marlowe edited by Patrick Cheney
Andrew Marvell edited by Derek Hirst and Steven N. Zwicker
Herman Melville edited by Robert S. Levine
Arthur Miller edited by Christopher Bigsby (second edition)
Milton edited by Dennis Danielson (second edition)
Molière edited by David Bradby and Andrew Calder
Toni Morrison edited by Justine Tally
Nabokov edited by Julian W. Connolly
Eugene O'Neill edited by Michael Manheim
George Orwell edited by John Rodden
Ovid edited by Philip Hardie
Petrarch edited by Albert Russell Ascoli
Harold Pinter edited by Peter Raby (second edition)
Sylvia Plath edited by Jo Gill
Edgar Allan Poe edited by Kevin J. Hayes
Alexander Pope edited by Pat Rogers

Ezra Pound edited by Ira B. Nadel
Proust edited by Richard Bales
Pushkin edited by Andrew Kahn
Rabelais edited by John O'Brien
Rilke edited by Karen Leeder and Robert Vilain
Philip Roth edited by Timothy Parrish
Salman Rushdie edited by Abdulrazak Gurnah
John Ruskin edited by Francis O'Gorman
Seneca edited by Shadi Bartsch and Alessandro Schiesaro
Shakespeare edited by Margareta de Grazia and Stanley Wells (second edition)
Shakespeare and Contemporary Dramatists edited by Ton Hoenselaars
Shakespeare and Popular Culture edited by Robert Shaughnessy
Shakespearean Comedy edited by Alexander Leggatt
Shakespearean Tragedy edited by Claire McEachern (second edition)
Shakespeare on Film edited by Russell Jackson (second edition)
Shakespeare on Stage edited by Stanley Wells and Sarah Stanton
Shakespeare's History Plays edited by Michael Hattaway
Shakespeare's Last Plays edited by Catherine M. S. Alexander
Shakespeare's Poetry edited by Patrick Cheney
George Bernard Shaw edited by Christopher Innes
Shelley edited by Timothy Morton
Mary Shelley edited by Esther Schor
Sam Shepard edited by Matthew C. Roudané
Spenser edited by Andrew Hadfield
Laurence Sterne edited by Thomas Keymer
Wallace Stevens edited by John N. Serio
Tom Stoppard edited by Katherine E. Kelly
Harriet Beecher Stowe edited by Cindy Weinstein
August Strindberg edited by Michael Robinson

Jonathan Swift edited by
Christopher Fox
J. M. Synge edited by P. J. Mathews
Tacitus edited by A. J. Woodman
Henry David Thoreau edited by
Joel Myerson
Tolstoy edited by Donna Tussing
Orwin
Anthony Trollope edited by Carolyn
Dever and Lisa Niles
Mark Twain edited by Forrest G.
Robinson
John Updike edited by
Stacey Olster
Mario Vargas Llosa edited by Efrain
Kristal and John King
Virgil edited by Charles Martindale

Voltaire edited by Nicholas Cronk
Edith Wharton edited by Millicent Bell
Walt Whitman edited by Ezra Greenspan
Oscar Wilde edited by Peter Raby
Tennessee Williams edited by
Matthew C. Roudané
August Wilson edited by
Christopher Bigsby
Mary Wollstonecraft edited by Claudia
L. Johnson
Virginia Woolf edited by Susan Sellers
(second edition)
Wordsworth edited by Stephen Gill
Wyndham Lewis edited by Tyrus Miller
W. B. Yeats edited by Marjorie Howes
and John Kelly
Zola edited by Brian Nelson

TOPICS

The Actress edited by Maggie B.
Gale and John Stokes
The African American Novel edited by
Maryemma Graham
The African American Slave Narrative
edited by Audrey A. Fisch
African American Theatre
by Harvey Young
Allegory edited by Rita Copeland and
Peter Struck
American Crime Fiction edited by
Catherine Ross Nickerson
American Gay and Lesbian Literature
edited by Scott Herring
American Modernism edited by Walter
Kalaidjian
The American Modernist Novel
edited by Joshua Miller
American Poetry Since 1945
edited by Jennifer Ashton
American Poets edited by Mark
Richardson
American Realism and Naturalism
edited by Donald Pizer
American Science Fiction
edited by Gerry Canavan and
Eric Carl Link
American Travel Writing edited by
Alfred Bendixen and Judith Hamera

American Women Playwrights edited by
Brenda Murphy
Ancient Rhetoric edited by
Erik Gunderson
Arthurian Legend edited by Elizabeth
Archibald and Ad Putter
Asian American Literature
edited by Crystal Parikh and
Daniel Y. Kim
Australian Literature edited by
Elizabeth Webby
Autobiography edited by Maria
DiBattista and Emily Wittman
The Body in Literature edited by David
Hillman and Ulrika Maude
British Fiction since 1945
edited by David James
*British Literature of the French
Revolution* edited by Pamela Clemit
British Poetry, 1945–2010 edited by
Edward Larrissy
British Romanticism edited by Stuart
Curran (second edition)
British Romantic Poetry edited by James
Chandler and Maureen N. McLane
British Theatre, 1730–1830, edited by
Jane Moody and Daniel O'Quinn
Canadian Literature edited by
Eva-Marie Kröller

Children's Literature edited by
M. O. Grenby and Andrea Immel
The Classic Russian Novel edited
by Malcolm V. Jones and Robin
Feuer Miller
Contemporary Irish Poetry edited by
Matthew Campbell
Creative Writing edited by David
Morley and Philip Neilsen
Crime Fiction edited by Martin
Priestman
Early Modern Women's Writing edited
by Laura Lunger Knoppers
The Eighteenth-Century Novel
edited by John Richetti
Eighteenth-Century Poetry
edited by John Sitter
Emma edited by Peter Sabor
English Literature, 1500–1600
edited by Arthur F. Kinney
English Literature, 1650–1740
edited by Steven N. Zwicker
English Literature, 1740–1830 edited by
Thomas Keymer and Jon Mee
English Literature, 1830–1914 edited by
Joanne Shattock
English Novelists edited by Adrian Poole
English Poetry, Donne to Marvell edited
by Thomas N. Corns
English Poets edited by Claude Rawson
*English Renaissance Drama, second
edition* edited by A. R. Braunmuller and
Michael Hattaway
English Renaissance Tragedy edited by
Emma Smith and Garrett A. Sullivan, Jr.
English Restoration Theatre edited by
Deborah C. Payne Fisk
The Epic edited by Catherine Bates
European Modernism edited by
Pericles Lewis
European Novelists edited by
Michael Bell
Fairy Tales edited by Maria Tatar
Fantasy Literature edited by Edward
James and Farah Mendlesohn
Feminist Literary Theory edited by
Ellen Rooney
Fiction in the Romantic Period
edited by Richard Maxwell and Katie
Trumpener

The Fin de Siècle edited by
Gail Marshall
The French Enlightenment edited by
Daniel Brewer
French Literature edited by
John D. Lyons
*The French Novel: from 1800 to the
Present* edited by Timothy Unwin
Gay and Lesbian Writing edited by
Hugh Stevens
German Romanticism edited by
Nicholas Saul
Gothic Fiction edited by
Jerrold E. Hogle
The Greek and Roman Novel edited by
Tim Whitmarsh
Greek and Roman Theatre edited by
Marianne McDonald and
J. Michael Walton
Greek Comedy edited by Martin
Revermann
Greek Lyric edited by Felix Budelmann
Greek Mythology edited by
Roger D. Woodard
Greek Tragedy edited by P. E. Easterling
The Harlem Renaissance edited by
George Hutchinson
The History of the Book edited by
Leslie Howsam
The Irish Novel edited by
John Wilson Foster
The Italian Novel edited by Peter
Bondanella and Andrea Ciccarelli
The Italian Renaissance edited by
Michael Wyatt
Jewish American Literature edited
by Hana Wirth-Nesher and Michael
P. Kramer
The Latin American Novel edited by
Efraín Kristal
The Literature of the First World War
edited by Vincent Sherry
The Literature of London edited by
Lawrence Manley
The Literature of Los Angeles edited by
Kevin R. McNamara
The Literature of New York edited by
Cyrus Patell and Bryan Waterman
The Literature of Paris edited by
Anna-Louise Milne

The Literature of World War II edited by Marina MacKay
Literature on Screen edited by Deborah Cartmell and Imelda Whelehan
Medieval English Culture edited by Andrew Galloway
Medieval English Literature edited by Larry Scanlon
Medieval English Mysticism edited by Samuel Fanous and Vincent Gillespie
Medieval English Theatre edited by Richard Beadle and Alan J. Fletcher (second edition)
Medieval French Literature edited by Simon Gaunt and Sarah Kay
Medieval Romance edited by Roberta L. Krueger
Medieval Women's Writing edited by Carolyn Dinshaw and David Wallace
Modern American Culture edited by Christopher Bigsby
Modern American Poetry edited by Walter Kalaidjian
Modern British Women Playwrights edited by Elaine Aston and Janelle Reinelt
Modern French Culture edited by Nicholas Hewitt
Modern German Culture edited by Eva Kolinsky and Wilfried van der Will
The Modern German Novel edited by Graham Bartram
The Modern Gothic edited by Jerrold E. Hogle
Modern Irish Culture edited by Joe Cleary and Claire Connolly
Modern Italian Culture edited by Zygmunt G. Baranski and Rebecca J. West
Modern Latin American Culture edited by John King
Modern Russian Culture edited by Nicholas Rzhevsky
Modern Spanish Culture edited by David T. Gies
Modernism edited by Michael Levenson (second edition)
The Modernist Novel edited by Morag Shiach
Modernist Poetry edited by Alex Davis and Lee M. Jenkins
Modernist Women Writers edited by Maren Tova Linett
Narrative edited by David Herman
Native American Literature edited by Joy Porter and Kenneth M. Roemer
Nineteenth-Century American Women's Writing edited by Dale M. Bauer and Philip Gould
Old English Literature edited by Malcolm Godden and Michael Lapidge (second edition)
Paradise Lost edited by Louis Schwartz
Performance Studies edited by Tracy C. Davis
Piers Plowman by Andrew Cole and Andrew Galloway
The Poetry of the First World War edited by Santanu Das
Popular Fiction edited by David Glover and Scott McCracken
Postcolonial Literary Studies edited by Neil Lazarus
The Postcolonial Novel edited by Ato Quayson
Postmodernism edited by Steven Connor
The Pre-Raphaelites edited by Elizabeth Prettejohn
Pride and Prejudice edited by Janet Todd
Renaissance Humanism edited by Jill Kraye
The Roman Historians edited by Andrew Feldherr
Roman Satire edited by Kirk Freudenburg
Science Fiction edited by Edward James and Farah Mendlesohn
Scottish Literature edited by Gerald Carruthers and Liam McIlvanney
Sensation Fiction edited by Andrew Mangham
Slavery in American Literature edited by Ezra Tawil
The Sonnet edited by A. D. Cousins and Peter Howarth
The Spanish Novel: From 1600 to the Present edited by Harriet Turner and Adelaida López de Martínez

Textual Scholarship edited by Neil Fraistat and Julia Flanders
Theatre History edited by David Wiles and Christine Dymkowski
Travel Writing edited by Peter Hulme and Tim Youngs
Twentieth-Century British and Irish Women's Poetry edited by Jane Dowson
The Twentieth-Century English Novel edited by Robert L. Caserio
Twentieth-Century English Poetry edited by Neil Corcoran
Twentieth-Century Irish Drama edited by Shaun Richards
Twentieth-Century Russian Literature edited by Marina Balina and Evgeny Dobrenko
Utopian Literature edited by Gregory Claeys
Victorian and Edwardian Theatre edited by Kerry Powell
The Victorian Novel edited by Deirdre David (second edition)
Victorian Poetry edited by Joseph Bristow
Victorian Women's Writing edited by Linda H. Peterson
War Writing edited by Kate McLoughlin
The Waste Land edited by Gabrielle McIntire
Women's Writing in Britain, 1660–1789 edited by Catherine Ingrassia
Women's Writing in the Romantic Period edited by Devoney Looser
Writing of the English Revolution edited by N. H. Keeble

For EU product safety concerns, contact us at Calle de José Abascal, 56–1°, 28003 Madrid, Spain or eugpsr@cambridge.org.